Professional
Civility

This book is part of the Peter Lang Media and Communication list.
Every volume is peer reviewed and meets
the highest quality standards for content and production.

PETER LANG
New York • Washington, D.C./Baltimore • Bern
Frankfurt • Berlin • Brussels • Vienna • Oxford

JANIE M. HARDEN FRITZ

Professional Civility

COMMUNICATIVE VIRTUE AT WORK

PETER LANG
New York • Washington, D.C./Baltimore • Bern
Frankfurt • Berlin • Brussels • Vienna • Oxford

Library of Congress Cataloging-in-Publication Data

Fritz, Janie M. Harden.
Professional civility: communicative virtue at work / Janie M. Harden Fritz.
p. cm.
Includes bibliographical references and index.
1. Professional ethics. 2. Business ethics. I. Title.
BJ1725.F75   174—dc23   2012034869
ISBN 978-1-4331-1985-9 (hardcover)
ISBN 978-1-4331-1984-2 (paperback)
ISBN 978-1-4539-0947-8 (e-book)

Bibliographic information published by **Die Deutsche Nationalbibliothek.**
Die Deutsche Nationalbibliothek lists this publication in the "Deutsche
Nationalbibliografie"; detailed bibliographic data is available
on the Internet at http://dnb.d-nb.de/.

© 2013 Peter Lang Publishing, Inc., New York
29 Broadway, 18th floor, New York, NY 10006
www.peterlang.com

Contents

Preface   ix

Acknowledgments   XIII

INTRODUCTION: A FRAMEWORK FOR PROFESSIONAL CIVILITY   1
    A Call to Responsibility: Civility and the Professions   1
    Professional Civility: Communicative Virtue at Work   11
    Structure of the Book   15

CHAPTER 1: VIRTUE ETHICS AND THE PROFESSIONS   23
    Introduction   23
    A Foundation for Professional Civility as Communicative   24
      Virtue at Work
    MacIntyre's Virtue Ethics Applied to the Professions   30
    Conclusion   43

CHAPTER 2: THE TRADITION OF PROFESSION AS PRACTICE   45
    Introduction   45
    The True Professional Ideal   46
    Goods of Professions   58
    Conclusion   62

CHAPTER 3: THE COMMUNICATIVE VIRTUE OF CIVILITY   63
    Introduction   63
    Civility in Context   64
    Incivility as Communicative Vice   71
    Civility as Communicative Virtue   74
    Theoretical Coordinates of Civility as Communicative Virtue   78
    Conclusion   85

CHAPTER 4: PROFESSIONAL CIVILITY AS COMMUNICATIVE VIRTUE AT WORK   87
    Introduction   87
    Virtues, Professions, and Civility: Professional Civility as   89
        Communicative Virtue
    Professional Civility: Conceptual Coordinates   96
    Practices of Professional Civility: A First Look   107
    Conclusion   109

CHAPTER 5: A PRAGMATIC CASE FOR THE EFFECTS OF COMMUNICATION   111
        IN THE WORKPLACE
    Introduction   111
    Communication as Constitutive   112
    Communication and Work Environments   117
    The Organizational Socialization Process as Context for   119
        Communicative Shaping
    Effects of Incivility   128
    Conclusion   131

CHAPTER 6: PROTECTING AND PROMOTING PRODUCTIVITY   133
    Introduction   133
    Work and the Human Condition   134
    Productivity and Communicative Action   139
    Levels of Engagement   148
    Conclusion   153

CHAPTER 7: PROTECTING AND PROMOTING THE GOOD OF PLACE   154
    Introduction   154
    Care for the Local Home: The Metaphor of "Guest"   156
    Organizations as Public Narratives   160
    Unity of Contraries: Support and Dissent   164
    Enlarged Space   168
    Conclusion   171

CHAPTER 8: PROTECTING AND PROMOTING THE GOOD OF PERSONS   173
     Introduction   173
     Workplace Relationships   174
     Public and Private Life: Historical Shifts   177
     Interpersonal Practices of Professional Civility   187
     Conclusion   194

CONCLUSION: PROTECTING AND PROMOTING PROFESSIONS   195
     Introduction   195
     The Ongoing Story of the Professions   196
     Toward a Renewed Professionalism: Professional Civility   202
     Professions and Communicative Practices: Enactment and   206
       Construction
     Summary: Protecting and Promoting the Good(s) of Profession   208

References   209

Author Index   235

Subject Index   245

Preface

This work is an elaboration and extension of the organizing principle of a course Ronald C. Arnett and I taught together years ago. Since that time, Ron and I have conducted independent and collaborative scholarship on professional civility; those projects are referenced in these pages. I ended up pursuing the idea in book-length format because of my interest in civility and incivility in workplace relationships.

Connecting the terms "professional" and "civility" was a primary conceptual task for this project. Sandra Borden's application of Alasdair MacIntyre's virtue ethics to the profession of journalism in her award-winning work, *Journalism as Practice: MacIntyre, Virtue Ethics, and the Press,* provided insights relevant to the professions as practice more generally, a reading consistent with Bruce Kimball's history of the "true professional ideal" in America. The "professional" part of professional civility now had a connection to virtue ethics and to traditions of practice (or, put another way, to practices that constitute traditions), and the goods internal to profession(s) as practice could be seen through a reading of Kimball's documentation of the rhetoric of the professions from the early 1600s to the present.

Civility, which I reconceptualized as the communicative manifestation of civic virtue, and profession(s), understood as tradition(s) of practice, met in the work of William Sullivan on the crisis and promise of professionalism in America. Civility appeared to be part of the "professionalism" that Sullivan held up as the distinguishing attitudinal and behavioral mark of a professional, an enduring ideal despite the erosion over the last several decades of the public recognition of professional work as a calling with service obligations. However, the work of Andersson and Pearson suggested that incivility—the inverse of professionalism—was a serious problem in organizational settings, where professionals typically practice today.

MacIntyre's announcement of the metanarrative crisis of our era provided insights relevant to the incivility crisis—there is no public agreement on the "good" for human life and conduct; the self has become the primary guide for moral decision-making. At the organizational level, emotivism plays out in lack of shared understandings of appropriate interpersonal behavior; "common sense" becomes meaningless without shared standards. Incivility and other troublesome behaviors in the workplace are more likely when publicly agreed-upon guidelines for conduct are absent.

Following this reasoning, the crisis of professionalism and incivility in the workplace could be fruitfully connected. Professionals, once the standard bearers of an occupational ideal of responsible self-direction and service, were now working in bureaucratic, corporatized contexts. Bereft of a collegial environment for work and a sense of vocational engagement, professionals no longer modeled the communicative practices of professionalism as a distinctive element of professional identity in everyday work interactions.

Pulling these strands together suggested a question: What if the professions reclaimed, in association with the civic professionalism Sullivan urged, a civility tied distinctively to the tradition of professional practice—a tradition that now embraced contemporary organizations as a site for work? Organizations were the new "local home" for the professions, joining the historic goods internal to professional practice—productivity and persons—visible in Kimball's story. Professional civility could be, at the level of organizational interaction, what Sullivan's civic professionalism would be at the level of the larger society. Professional civility as communicative virtue at work could nourish internal organizational environments and lay the groundwork for civic professionalism as service to communities and society at large. Connections to Arnett and Arneson's dialogic civility, with its responsiveness to the historical moment, limits, and sense of hope, and to Organ's construct of organizational citizenship were natural next steps, and from that point, it was a matter of identifying representative work in conceptually related areas that could be understood through the lens of professional civility.

There is a natural connection between this book and the collections Becky Omdahl and I coedited for Peter Lang (*Problematic Relationships in the Workplace,*

2006; *Problematic Relationships in the Workplace, Volume 2*, in press). As a set, the three books address an array of workplace relationship difficulties, communicative remedies, and a philosophy of communication/communication ethic for the workplace. Several ideas from the *Problematic Work Relationships* volumes and this book are cross-referenced. For example, Ronald C. Arnett's chapter on professional civility and Becky Omdahl's chapter on effective work relationships from the 2006 volume provide conceptual touchstones here, and the chapter on protecting and promoting workplace relationships in the second volume can be read as an extension of Chapter 8 (protecting and promoting persons).

Acknowledgments

I have many persons and communities to thank for ongoing support in bringing this work to completion. Leeanne Bell McManus provided much-needed impetus to persuade me to undertake the final stages of this work. Jeanne Persuit was instrumental in moving the project forward. Annette Holba and Elesha Ruminski prompted my thinking on care for institutions through an invitation to write a chapter for their edited volume, *Communicative Understandings of Women's Leadership Development: From Ceilings of Glass to Labyrinth Paths* (2012, Lexington Books). I offer deep appreciation and thanks to Mary Savigar, Bernadette Shade, Phyllis Korper, and all the Peter Lang staff who brought this book to finished form through their outstanding professional work, and to Hannah Belmonte, who constructed the author index.

Students in multiple sections of the Communication Ethics and Professional Civility course listened to draft chapters of the first half of the book. Participants in the National Communication Association's 2011 Hope Conference offered constructive feedback, insights, and thoughtful responses. Robert H. Woods Jr. offered good counsel and enthusiastic encouragement. Becky Omdahl's friendship and care are precious gifts; she embodies the true professional ideal. My brother, Bobby, who began his own professional studies as I worked on this book, supported me with prayers and encouragement. My husband, Carl, patiently awaited the completion of this project and provided all manner of support.

Duquesne University is a wonderful academic home. Chancellor John Murray and President Charles Dougherty have provided years of outstanding leadership for this place. I honor in this work the memory of Michael P. Weber, who believed in me when the evidence was yet to emerge. He understood the difference between imagination and fantasy. James Swindal, dean of the McAnulty College and Graduate School of Liberal Arts, provides a model of scholarly leadership and productivity, as did his predecessors Christopher Duncan and Francesco Cesareo. My colleagues in the Department of Communication & Rhetorical Studies bring joy to the work; I will always be grateful to them, especially to Ronald C. Arnett, who taught me to love the work, care for institutions, and support people—Ron, you make places and persons flourish through productivity.

I offer this book to the Spiritans, the priests and brothers of the Congregation of the Holy Spirit, who remind us that there is always a heart propelling the best practices.

—Janie Harden Fritz, PhD

Introduction

A Framework for Professional Civility

A Call to Responsibility: Civility and the Professions

A growing body of research points to the presence of interpersonal communicative practices contributing to problematic relationships in the workplace (Fritz & Omdahl, 2006a, Omdahl & Fritz, in press). Problematic workplace behaviors such as social undermining, interpersonal harassment, and bullying, for example, continue to receive attention in the scholarly literature and the popular press (Fritz, 2009, 2012a; Keashly, in press). Identification and conceptualization of additional behaviors—for example, backstabbing (Malone & Hayes, 2012) and swearing in the workplace (Johnson, 2012)—join existing research on organizational misbehavior (Fritz, in press-a) as further refinement and clarification of the domain of problematic behaviors in the workplace ensues. This crisis of incivility (Fritz, 2012a) in workplaces in the United States carries significant implications for organizations and their members, resulting in outcomes such as employee turnover, lowered productivity, and stress (Fritz & Omdahl, 2006b; Davenport Sypher, 2004; see Pearson & Porath, 2009, for a book-length review of personal and institutional costs associated with incivility). We spend a large proportion of our lives in the company of other persons in the workplace; when interactions are marked by rudeness and incivility, the quality of work life is diminished, compromising the "good" of organizations as dwelling places for shared constructive activity (Arnett, Fritz, & Bell, 2009).

Several explanations for this increase in incivility have been advanced: a climate of informality in the workplace in the midst of diversity of cultural and generational backgrounds, prompting misunderstandings due to differences in implicit communication rules; proliferation of technology that removes face-to-face interaction, making impulsivity more likely; increased demands for productivity, generating stress and frayed tempers; and changing norms in society at large for standards of behavior (Andersson & Pearson, 1999; Davenport Sypher, 2004; Johnson & Indvik, 2001a, 2001b; Pearson, Andersson, & Porath, 2000; Pearson & Porath, 2009; Zemke, Raines, & Filipczak, 2000). This latter point prompts a key question: Why be civil at all? Why should we bother to engage others with a discourse of care, respect, and thoughtful attentiveness befitting their humanity? Work by authors such as Steven Carter (1998), M. Scott Peck (1994), and P. M. Forni (2002, 2008) suggests that being civil to others is no longer a "common sense" communicative practice in a world lacking a shared virtue structure (Arnett et al., 2009). In a moment of economic collapse, failing corporations, irresponsible institutional leadership, and rampant individualism (Putnam, 2000), civility no longer appears to be a taken-for-granted or normative interactive practice for either public life in general or organizational life in particular.

In academic circles, explicit disputes about the theoretical and practical status of civility ensue. Some scholars argue the case for civility and note its benefits, tying civil discourse practices to justice in the public sphere. Carter (1998), for instance, holds civility as the only hope for those in positions of low status and power, because civility as a normative practice calls those who have power into account. Kingwell (1995) offers civility as the foundation for "just talking" necessary for democratic societies to function. Bone, Griffin, and Scholz (2008) suggest that civility helps establish an invitational stance between and among citizens with deeply held differences on issues of importance in the public domain. Other scholars recognize civility's pragmatic functionality, proclaiming it a vital resource for business and professional life (Davenport Sypher, 2004; Gill & Davenport Sypher, 2009; Troester & Mester, 2007) and a necessary remedy for incivility and related problematic behavior in the academy (Hickson & Roebuck, 2009; Omdahl, in press; Twale & De Luca, 2008). P. M. Forni (2011b) connects civility to the "thinking life"—one that is marked by reflection, a holistic sense of meaning, and service to the larger human community. However, some scholars identify civility and its communicative restraint as a problematic concept linked to hegemonic formations of class and race (e.g., Ashcraft & Allen, 2003; Cheney & Ashcraft, 2007; Kisselburgh & Dutta, 2009; Lozano-Reich

& Cloud, 2009), a dangerous and superficial substitute for political critique (Mayo, 2002). The very idea of civility is contested terrain.

I propose that civil communicative practices fostering coordinated action in institutional settings establish a minimal common ground of the good (Arnett et al., 2009; Bok, 1995) for life together in organizations. The history of civility as an interactive norm reflects an ongoing concern for order and structure in public and private life that permits the accomplishment of personal, institutional, and community goals (Carter, 1998; Davetian, 2009; Elias, 1978, 1982; Forni, 2002, 2008, 2011a; Kingwell, 1995, 2000; Selznick, 1992/1994), contested though these goals may be at particular points in time. What Sypnowich (2000) referred to as "the accessibility of the modern idea of civility" (p. 110) suggests that behavior showing consideration toward others is a pragmatic practice adoptable by, and efficacious for, any group, class, or status level. The constraints of civility permit honesty in communicative action and the free exchange of ideas (p. 111), protecting and promoting public discourse necessary to accomplish shared goals in civil society (Arnett et al., 2009; Kingwell, 1995; Sellars, 2004). This framing of civility is consistent with Patton's (2004) distinction between a "civility that supports a common good for an inclusive collectivity" (p. 65) and a hegemonic civility that suppresses and silences opposition in support of an oppressive status quo.

The purpose of this project is to place civility within a theoretical framework of ethical interpersonal communicative action in organizations, with a specific focus on the role of the professions in embracing a communicative ethic of civility that remains an implicit element of the historic legacy of the professional ideal in the United States, as articulated by Kimball (1995). At the broadest level, I conceptualize civility in interpersonal interaction in public and private settings as a communicative virtue (Fritz, 2011). From a virtue ethics perspective, behaving with civility toward others is an integral part of a flourishing human existence that defines the good of, and for, human life; civility contributes to the well-being of others with whom one comes into contact in the course of daily life. Civility, within this general framework, is a communicative virtue that protects and promotes respect for human beings and supports the various social contexts within which human lives find meaning and significance (Laverty, 2009).

In the workplace, treating others with civility creates a constructive, humane environment that makes the context of work functional and even enjoyable (Fritz, 2011; Omdahl, 2006; Davenport Sypher, 2004). Workplaces that encourage civil interaction among employees reap the benefits of increased employee satisfaction and productivity and decreased personal and organizational harms associated with incivility (Pearson & Porath, 2009; Troester & Mester, 2007). The work of most occupations requires coordinated action carried out in some form of organizational setting, which civility can sustain and foster. This understanding of civility resonates with emerging work on positive organizing (Fredrickson & Dutton, 2008) that is being explored by organizational communication scholars (e.g., Lutgen-Sandvik, Riforgiate, & Fletcher, 2011), a perspective that highlights a generative, constructive approach to the workplace for the flourishing of institutions and persons.

Although all work done in organizational settings would appear to be helped along by a work environment marked by civil interaction, professional work—broadly conceived—seems particularly connected to an understanding of a civil workplace as a necessary condition for excellent practice. From the perspective of the professions, a civil work environment creates conditions for the accomplishment of a larger project that contributes something good and necessary to the world, one of the defining features of the professions (Kimball, 1995). Kimball's (1995) history of the professional ideal in America traces shifts in the way professions have been understood in the context of the larger society, highlights the increasingly broad scope of occupations considered to be professions, and notes changes in conditions of professional work that have brought a closer connection between occupations once considered to be autonomous and the contemporary organizational context within which civility as a professional interactive norm becomes relevant. Kimball's work, along with Sullivan's (1995, 2005) exploration of the crisis and promise of professionalism in America, provides a background for the relationship of the professions to the communicative virtue of civility.

The Professions: A Legacy of Civility

The professions hold a unique role in the public imagination of the United States as a social ideal (Sullivan, 2005, p. 4). The four original "learned" professions are traditionally identified as theology, law, medicine, and education (Kimball, 1995). Today, the professions represent a wide variety of occupations engaged in specialized and/or knowledge work in a service economy. In previous centuries, practitioners of professions were assumed to work, for the most part, with a high degree of autonomy (Kimball, 1995). In our contemporary moment, professionals are employed primarily in organizational settings (Kultgen, 1988; Noordegraaf, 2007; Sullivan, 2005; Wallace, 1993, 1995), where they work with members of other professions and support staff who make the conditions for their practice possible.

Professionals as a group have been characterized as having an esoteric knowledge base essential to fulfilling society's needs, as working with relative autonomy, as controlling access to those who practice a given profession, and as espousing an ethic of service (Barber, 1963; Brien, 1998; Friedson, 1991; Larson, 1977; Moore,

1970; Sullivan, 2005). As Sullivan (2005) noted, the professions are high-status occupations that bring power and privilege to their members. The scope of occupations claiming professional status has increased over time (Hatch, 1988; Oakley & Cocking, 2001); the category of "profession" now encompasses a wide range of job types, including architecture, engineering, forestry, journalism, management, scientific agriculture, and social work (Blackburn & McGhee, 2004; Borden, 2007; Gardner, Csikszentmihalyi, & Damon, 2001; Schein, 1968; Squires, 2005; Sullivan, 2005), to name a representative few.

Kimball (1995) examined rhetorical moments characterizing changes in societal images of, and expectations for, the set of occupations categorized as professions, including how persons who practice professions are expected to behave in personal and professional life and the place of the professions in the marketplace, community, and larger public sphere. Throughout these changes, at least two enduring features have continued to characterize both the "original" professions and the extended set of occupations that now claim professional status: an expectation of relative autonomy stemming from their specialized knowledge base, and an expectation of adherence to ethical norms, which professionals bring to the workplaces in which they practice. The ethical norms binding members of professions and guiding their practice define what it means to be a "good" member of a profession (Borden, 2007; Brien, 1998; Pritchard, 2006). These ethical norms provide a basis for self-evaluation of professions as communities of practice, defining the good that is protected and promoted by a given profession.

For professionals, who now conduct most of their work in organizational environments populated with other professionals and members of affiliated occupations, civility as an interactive norm should be relevant not only as a feature of the work environment that permits professional practice to take place with a minimum of disruption, but also as a salient communicative element of professional identity, given the educational background, vocational dignity, and service orientation historically associated with the professions (Kimball, 1995; Sullivan, 2005). It might be expected that professionals would consider civil communicative behavior toward others an indispensable part of a professional ethic, that professionals would comport themselves in interaction with others with a high degree of civility—courtesy, tact, and forbearance—befitting the identity of a member of what is still considered in the public imagination to be a respected and honored calling (Sullivan, 2005). Growing evidence, however, suggests that professional employees' interaction is marked by incivility to an alarming degree (e.g., Gonthier & Morrissey, 2002; Sutton, 2007; Twale & De Luca, 2008). Furthermore, professionals as a group have experienced a decline in attributed respect and status, stemming from what Sullivan identified as a public deconstruction of the professional ethos. The ideal of the "good professional" has been challenged as the landscape of the social milieu has changed over the last half century.

To some extent, this challenge stems from the uneasy relationship between the ideals of democracy and the assumed privilege embodied in the very idea of a profession. As Hatch (1988) noted, "Americans admire professionals for their dedication to public service and revile them for the extent to which such claims serve as masks for financial greed" (p. 2). Many scholars have articulated concerns related to the professions in the marketplace, noting increased cynicism and doubt on the part of the general public accompanying discovery and revelation of professionals' unethical behavior (Kultgen, 1988; Ohman, 2003; Sullivan, 2005). Professionals are characterized by critics as status- and power-hungry oppressors who hoard the deposit of indispensable knowledge—specially trained and valuable members of society who have abandoned professed accountability to the larger public and an ethic of service for pursuit of private gain (e.g., Kimball, 1995; Kultgen, 1988; Larson, 1977; Ohman, 2003, pp. 65–69; Pellegrino, Veatch, & Langan, 1991, p. vii). The larger picture within which these issues arise includes concerns about the nature of life in an "organization society" that threatens colonization by corporations (Deetz, 1992) and control of more and more of workers' lives in the service of profit and accumulation (MacIntyre, 2007).

Scholars have answered this critique in volumes written to rehabilitate the "good work" (e.g., Gardner et al., 2001) of the professions, noting the commitment to "responsibility at work" (Gardener, 2007) that many professionals exhibit and addressing "the crisis and promise of professionalism" in the United States (Sullivan, 2005). These writers typically examine the role of the professional with regard to service to the larger community—the call to envision responsibility beyond immediate profit and self-interest, a concern paralleled by a move toward social responsibility in the marketplace engaged by corporations in the last decades (e.g., Carroll, 2008). These volumes, however, do not typically address the crisis of incivility in interpersonal interaction in the workplace (Fritz, 2012a), a condition that affects the well-being of all employees as well as the health of organizations within which most professionals carry out their vocations and, hence, affects the amount and quality of personal and institutional resources available for both ordinary tasks of the workplace and civic participation.

Professionals are uniquely poised to address the crisis of incivility in the workplace, beginning with their own day-to-day practices in organizational settings. Professionals, marked historically by a tradition of service to the human community defined by their position as bearers of elements of the "good" in life necessary for human flourishing (Oakley & Cocking, 2001), develop incipient habits of service as a result of their conduct within the institutions that are the primary location for their work, as well as through professional socialization and training in educational settings. The narrative of the professions carries with it an implied ethic of civility as a marker of professional identity. The high standards of ethical conduct expected of professionals in their professional practice and interactions with others are evident in the evaluative terms "professionalism" (Maister, 1997; Sullivan, 2005) and "professional behavior" (Hall & Berardino, 2001), which are recognized in everyday parlance (Sullivan, 1995).

Expectations for exemplary behavior are tied to the coordinates of professional practice in distinctive ways: The professions embed the work of a particular vocation that has value both as a practice (MacIntyre, 2007) and as a contribution to the human community, and members of professions pursue their callings within communities of others both within and external to the boundaries of their specific professions. From the perspective of professions, civility can be understood to contribute to the good of work, to the organization within which that work is done, to others in the organizational environment, and to the communities of professional practice and traditions that embed them (MacIntyre, 2007). Civility makes its contribution through its operation as a communicative virtue in the work environment, a virtue that manifests the good of professional identity and contributes to the accomplishment of the goods of profession(s) (Fritz, 2011).

By enacting civility, practitioners of professions can reclaim a position of service, beginning with interpersonal interactions in the workplace that cultivate constructive communicative "habits of the heart" (Bellah, Madsen, Sullivan, Swidler, & Tipton, 1985) and nourish internal organizational environments, thus laying the groundwork for renewed contributions within and outside the boundaries of their organizational contexts, thereby restoring to the professions an ethic of organizational and civic responsibility described so well by the concept of organizational citizenship (Organ, 1988; Organ, Podsakoff, & MacKenzie, 2006). Cheney, Lair, Ritz, and Kendall (2010) pointed in this direction with their recognition that worthy professional work is more than "just a job," as did Davenport Sypher (2004), who noted that incivility in the workplace has the potential to ripple out to other spheres of life and urged us to reclaim civil discourse in the workplace. The coordination of internal communicative practices with external contributions of service to the community takes place within the context of a whole life that finds balance in multiple spheres of human engagement (Arnett, 2006). Rather than understanding public and private life as bifurcated, this perspective sees these two spheres coming together and finding connection within the unity of a (professional) life (MacIntyre, 2007).

The aim of the current project is to articulate a communicative ethic of civility associated with the tradition of the professions within the organizational context: professional civility as a communicative virtue in organizational life—communicative virtue "at work." Communication is a good of human life—conversation, the prototypical form of interpersonal communication (Oliver, 1961), is an essential element in the ontology or telos of human beings (MacIntyre, 2007, p. 210), hence a good for human life, a necessary element in enacting and achieving the human telos. Civil discourse in organizational settings does the conversational "work," in an Arendtian (1958) sense, of world-building—constructing institutional dwellings within which all may contribute to meaningful tasks.

If work itself, as Arendt (1958) and others suggest, is an integral part of a complete human life, then professional work, like any work, becomes a contributing good for human life extending beyond the labor that is consumed through biological necessity and the enduring artifice of Arendtian "work." The status of the professions as occupations responsible for complex and specialized undertakings on behalf of society's achievement of a good human community—Arendtian action—makes them architectonic occupations (Kimball, 1995): the prototype or ideal on which other occupations model their highest aspirations. In this sense, the professions are the standard bearers of occupations in today's historical moment because of their unique and indispensable contribution to the human endeavor and to flourishing human lives (Hatch, 1988; Kultgen, 1988). Indeed, some scholars argue that all occupations could benefit by adhering to particular distinguishing elements of the professions, such as codes of ethics and a sense of obligation to the larger society (Kultgen, 1988). Civility, long considered a civic virtue (Shils, 1997), is inherent to the professions, whose vocational calling directs them toward service in the public arena (Sullivan, 2005); civility's additive reconceptualization as a communicative virtue invites reflection on interactive practices that manifest this civic virtue in the workplace (Fritz, 2011).

Professional civility as a communicative virtue protects and promotes the good, or telos, of professions as practice (MacIntyre, 2007) and supports other goods of professions: productivity, the work that is done in organizations; place, the local organization within which professional activity is accomplished; and persons, people working in, or associated with, particular organizations. These goods of professions, which make possible, and support, goods of human life, are implicit within the history of the "true professional ideal" in the United States (Kimball, 1995) and emerge explicitly from conceptualizations and critiques of the professions that seek to recall their contributions to the larger community (Sullivan, 2005). An ethic of professional civility in the workplace can contribute to the rehabilitation of the professions by restoring their communicative integrity within the context of organizations that are host to many professions and professionals today, moving from the "inside out" (Groom, Fritz, & Arnett, 2007) to restore the identity of the professions as architectonic occupations in the eyes of the public in the twenty-first century. Professional civility as a philosophy of communication for work life provides a background framework for understanding the work of communicative practices in organizational settings (Arnett et al., 2009; Arnett & Holba, in press).

This project assumes that concerns about the future of professionals and concerns about civility in the workplace can be addressed in tandem, beginning with an identification of contributing factors common to each of these concerns in the attributes of contemporary culture. The roots of the crisis of incivility in the workplace are embedded deep within trends in the social world that have affected society at large and shaped the context of both professions and organizations. As attributes of society have changed over time, conditions for professions and organizations have also changed.

A study of larger societal trends and the contemporary milieu of the professions yields two observations salient to this project. First, competing virtue structures or understandings of "the good" mark our postmodern historical moment (Arnett et al., 2009; MacIntyre, 2007; Taylor, 1989, 2007). This lack of consensus on what constitutes the good for human life manifests itself in many ways, including the public recognition of varying conceptions of what is good for human beings to be and to do and disputes about what practices contribute to furthering a given good for human life (Arnett et al., 2009). These competing virtue structures emerge in many public contexts, including educational institutions (e.g., Alexander, Mundrake, & Brown, 2009) and other complex organizations (e.g., Primeaux, 1992) that support the bulk of contemporary professional work today (Sullivan, 2005).

Second, although the status and power of the professions have been challenged in the academy, and the reputation of professionals tarnished to some degree in the public eye, the idea of professions as important callings necessary for human flourishing remains fixed in the popular imagination (e.g., Cheney et al., 2010; Sullivan, 2005). Professional codes of ethics and understandings of professional ethics grounded in the virtues (Oakley & Cocking, 2001) offer alternative ways of considering how professions and those who practice them may contribute a renewed sense of hope to organizations that host their work and to larger communities to which their practices contribute. The professions can be understood again, explicitly, as necessary contributors to the good life for human beings. This understanding is part of the history of the professions in the United States (Kimball, 1995), part of the tradition that defines the professions as practice (Borden, 2007; MacIntyre, 2007), and part of a legacy unique to professionals that can be recalled, restored, and reenacted (Sullivan, 2005), beginning with professionals' treatment of one another and others in day-to-day communicative life within the organizations that support their activities and coordinate their contributions to the labor, work, and action that define the human condition (Arendt, 1958).

These coordinates—the lack of a shared virtue structure guiding interaction, and the history of the professions as practice embodying a tradition accompanied by virtues that enliven goods internal to that practice—locate a rationale for articulating professional civility as a communicative virtue that protects and promotes the good of professions and their associated contributing goods. Organizations can no longer assume commonality of virtue structures embedding their participants; organizations need a common center (Arnett, 1986) and mission to anchor public agreement among diverse members. Professions, guided by traditions of practice, secure agreement for internal ethical principles from their narrative history and offer the opportunity for an ethic of civility in the workplace to guide interaction directed toward task accomplishment, care for institutions, and support for persons in organizational contexts. The next section addresses these points.

A Moment of Virtue Contention: Incivility and Opportunity

As noted earlier, the increasing prevalence of incivility in the workplace is propelled by a number of factors, including a growing sense of informality in the workplace, mirroring similar expectations in the culture at large (Forni, 2011a), combined with little agreement on norms of conduct to guide public interpersonal interaction (Andersson & Pearson, 1999; Fritz, Arnett, & Conkel, 1999; Arnett & Fritz, 2003). Many scholars have noted the challenges facing organizations seeking to establish codes of ethical conduct (see Kaptein & Schwartz, 2008, for a review of studies of effectiveness of codes of ethical conduct in organizations). Organizational leaders can no longer assume shared understandings of right and wrong or proper and improper behavior. Because of this lack of consensus on the good, codes of conduct must be made explicit and direct in organizational contexts (Primeaux, 1992), lived out in action modeled by managers who serve as standard bearers of an organizational mission (Arnett & Fritz, 2003; Fritz, O'Neil, Popp, Williams, & Arnett, in press; Fritz et al., 1999).

As Carter (1998) pointed out, the 1960s witnessed a change in the way people thought about rules of social behavior, the role of authority structures, and the obligations of public life, with accompanying erosion of many taken-for-granted practices that once defined public common sense (Arnett et al., 2009). The interpersonal communication literature echoes this shift in its changing focus over the decades ranging from the 1940s to the 1980s. Whereas the study of interpersonal communication was once focused on how the individual fitted into the social group (social integration), the emphasis moved to individual integration—with communication serving the function of personal wholeness—and finally to goal enactment, with a focus on personal strategic action (Rawlins, 1985). The focus on personal wholeness emerged in the 1960s, reflecting shifts in American culture and society toward greater individual freedom from traditional norms and expectations and the importance of the expression of the authentic self; the move to strategic action focused attention on atomistic individual purposes and outcomes, a functional context stripped of any holistic human ontology and lacking a telos.

MacIntyre's (2007) work on the virtues offers an understanding of what he termed our moral crisis today, which has touched every sphere of life, including the professions. Adopting MacIntyre's framework of virtue ethics permits conceptualizing professions as practices that have as their purpose or end a "good" that partly defines human life. Borden's (2007) work on the profession of journalism as practice offers an example of this approach.

MacIntyre's (2007) work guides an understanding of professional life and its contribution to human flourishing in the context of the collapse of a common ground of the good by pointing to the authority of a tradition that might guide professional communicative conduct in workplaces, the usual site of professional practice in today's historical moment. Without a definition of the good for human beings, guidelines for behavior fail to secure agreement and consent. Professions are communities of practice grounded in a tradition that carries their contribution to human flourishing understood as goods internal to their practices. These goods provide guidelines for ethical behavior, pointing toward a common center (Arnett, 1986) for communicative life in organizations and defining an ethic of professional civility.

Professional Civility: Communicative Virtue at Work

MacIntyre's (2007) work provides grounding in ethical theory for professional civility as communicative virtue in the workplace through an understanding of profession(s) as practice. This framework addresses a number of dimensions of professional life. Professions today are engaged in embedded practice, which extends their goods beyond the particulars of a given occupation or technique to include a concern for the specific location of professional activity. Professional civility as communicative virtue at work becomes a foundation for productive, constructive action in organizations, action that protects and promotes human flourishing, defining the role of professions as part of a good human life. Arendt (1958) articulated labor, work, and action as characteristic activities of human beings, a conceptualization that provides a basis for the ontological value of work for human beings—the good of productivity. Labor meets necessity; work generates a constructed world for human beings; action defines participation in the public sphere—all of these elements are part of professional life as defined by its emergent tradition and history (Kimball, 1995).

Professional civility addresses the tension between professions as autonomous or semi-autonomous groups and the organizations within which they practice, which require adherence to their own purposes (Noordegraaf, 2007). Professional civility as a component of a philosophy of work life permits constructive management of the tension between "cosmopolitans" and "locals" (Gouldner, 1957, 1958; Krause, 1996), because by defining professional civility within a framework of profession as practice as a tradition that responds to the demands of the historical moment (Arnett & Arneson, 1999), the defining features of professions now include the notion of a local "home" (Arnett, 1992, p. 126) in which professionals typically practice—institutions as a context for professional practice—with morality as "tied to the socially local and the particular" (Krause, 1996, p. 126), or the good of place. This framing resonates with the work of Wallace (1993), who defined commitment to profession and place as two distinct dimensions rather than opposing ends of a continuum. Professionals can care for both the profession and the local organization within which professional practice is enacted.

Professional civility is needed to combat the corrosive effects of incivility in the workplace and attacks on the good of "persons," and to foster healthy, constructive human interaction with the potential to generate a number of outcomes associated with positive experiences in the workplace (Lutgen-Sandvik et al., 2011). This focus on the micro level of interaction within institutional homes where professionals work is a necessary first step for providing a foundation for service beyond the organization's boundaries. Enactment of professional civility will help diminish the increasing prevalence of incivility in the workplace (Andersson & Pearson, 1999; Troester & Mester, 2007), replacing it with constructive interactive routines and establishing a foundation for renewed efforts outward toward the community and public sphere (Sullivan, 2005).

By protecting the goods of productivity, place, and persons, professional civility promises to protect the good of professions. As Sokolowski (1991) noted, "Professionals must act to preserve the profession…[U]nprofessional conduct…damages [a] profession" (p. 36). Addressing micropractices at the level of the workplace forms the bedrock of a foundation supporting outward service—those macrolevel practices observed at the group or institutional level necessary to restore the integrity of professions in the public eye.

Thoughtful consideration of the meaning of professional life establishes a "why," or a compelling, propelling rationale (Arnett & Arneson, 1999), for ethical professional communication (Cheney et al., 2010). As practitioners of professions manifest constructive communicative action in organizations, professions will reclaim their status as dignified occupations focused on service to others. Professional civility may assist in two ways. First, ameliorating the crisis of uncivil interaction in the workplace (Fritz, 2012a) through professional civility provides resources for enhanced participation in civic culture. With distressed interaction in the workplace no longer a salient feature of the organizational environment, one's focus can be turned to constructive elements of work and other elements of a whole life—private life, recuperative leisure (Holba, 2007), and service to the larger community and civic sphere. Second, and just as important, professional civility works at the level of enacted practices, shaping proclivities of character through repeated meaningful action: "we become what we practice" (Arnett & Arneson, 1999, p. 54). The theorizing of Grant (2007) pointed in this direction as he considered how the "relational architecture" (p. 395) of job design, or the way structural properties of work shape opportunities for interaction with others, may contribute to employees' desire to make a prosocial difference, not only in their workplaces, but for entities outside the workplace, including their communities.

Professional civility works as a communicative virtue defining a professional communication ethic, a set of communicative practices protecting and promoting "goods" of productivity, place, persons, and profession(s) as a minimal common ground for constructive work in organizations. Professional civility guides communicative life in organizational settings. Communicative interaction in the form of conversation in the workplace can be enacted with a degree of excellence described as arête; communication competence in professional interaction can be understood as communicative *phronesis*, or practical wisdom (Aristotle, 1962).

Communication also results in definable outcomes. The power of communicative activity is significant; communication shapes us and the organizations in which we work. As Kimball (1995) stated regarding discourse about professionals and their place in society, "changing language can change behavior" (p. 15). Research within the field of communication is replete with findings documenting the power of communication to construct understandings of, indeed, the very substance of, our social worlds, our self-concepts, our relationships, and our workplaces (Ashcraft, Kuhn, & Cooren, 2009). Public evidence supports the connection of language, communicative practices, and discourse patterns and outcomes that define the context within which we must then continue to enact communities and relationships (Baxter & Montgomery, 1996). In a subsequent chapter, I present a pragmatic case for the effects of incivility on organizational and personal outcomes.

From a virtue ethics perspective, the effects or outcomes of civility are not relevant; this good for human beings holds intrinsic value, with positive outcomes as a happy byproduct of virtuous action (MacIntyre, 2007). In the workplace, professional civility honors human dignity, a good in itself. Professional civility also prevents the deleterious effects of the corresponding communicative vice of incivility on a number of other organizational goods, and promotes coordinated action, which could be considered a utilitarian outcome. Thus do virtue ethics and consequentialist ethics meet in the contemporary workplace. In both cases, professional civility protects and promotes "goods": the intrinsic good of the human being, both individually and collectively, and a number of "external" goods associated with the workplace, which could also be considered internal goods of professional practice (MacIntyre, 2007) because of the status of the workplace as a context for human flourishing in this historical moment.

An individualistic ethic of emotivism (MacIntyre, 2007), placing personal standards for ethical judgment ahead of publicly agreed-on standards, offers insight into the value of professional civility as an undertaking that defines goods emerging from, and manifested in, communicative praxis (Schrag, 1986) by human beings, as embedded agents, about phenomena relevant to the workplace, for the purpose of manifesting and achieving the human telos. When understood as a defining feature of professional identity, professional civility can define and manifest the "good" of professionalism as an element of profession as a community of practice, as opposed to private, individual, and often conflicting personal preferences. Professional civility provides a minimal common center (Arnett, 1986) or good (Arnett et al., 2009; Bok, 1995) that defines appropriate workplace behavior, in contrast to emotivism (MacIntyre, 2007)—decision-making by personal preference.

Professional civility works against the plague of incivility in the workplace. The presence of incivility in organizations where professionals practice affects the entire gestalt of professional life. Incivility compromises the nature of professional work through its damage to the overall organizational climate, harm to the work itself (as it drains energy and takes attention away from productivity), and hurt to others in the work environment (Pearson & Porath, 2009). Incivility distorts the way professionals relate to the external environment and degrades the image of professionals in the eyes of external constituencies. The argument of this project strikes at this internal problem of incivility in hopes of ameliorating its deleterious effects in the workplace and laying the groundwork for professionals' renewed contributions to society at large—the external picture of professional life. I will only be making occasional references to the latter concern in these pages, however, as the primary focus of the current project is the internal sphere of professional life in organizational settings.

I situate the professional civility framework within a virtue ethics perspective, drawing on the work of MacIntyre (2007) and Oakley and Cocking (2001) as applied to the story of professions (Kimball, 1995; Sullivan, 1995, 2005); upon the philosophically grounded interpersonal communication literature (Arnett, 2006; Arnett & Arneson, 1999; Arnett & Fritz, 2001, 2003; Fritz, 2009); and in relation to the work on organizational citizenship (Organ, 1988; Organ et al., 2006) to define an ethic of interpersonal interaction in organizational settings. With an echo of Arnett and Arneson's (1999) critique of a therapeutic communication style imported into public settings (see Arnett, 1997, for the original critique), an articulation of organizations as public contexts requiring a distinction between public and private discourse and relationships (Arnett, 2006; Arnett & Fritz, 2003), and a call for a focus on productivity and care for institutions (Fritz, 2012b) in the workplace, professional civility offers the possibility of temporal guidance in a moment rife with virtue disagreement, cynicism, and the potential collapse of organizations that have lost the ability to coordinate in constructive ways the labor, work, and action of the participants who contribute to their products and services. Professionalism's crisis (Sullivan, 2005) calls for the reclamation, rehabilitation, and restoration of the tradition of the professions (Kimball, 1995), extended to accommodate the contemporary conditions of professional work. Professional civility is a communicative start.

Structure of the Book

The first chapter addresses virtue ethics as a foundation for professional practice, as suggested by Oakley and Cocking (2001). I highlight the work of MacIntyre (2007) as the cornerstone of a treatment of profession(s) as practice with a tradition and history supporting goods internal to practices, contributing to the good of, and for, human community and flourishing. Here, I follow Borden (2007), who applied MacIntyre's work insightfully and creatively to the profession of journalism. The larger notion of "profession" can be understood as a metapractice in this sense.

In the second chapter, I introduce Kimball's (1995) history of "the true professional ideal in America" as support for this framing of professions as (meta)practice, along with the work of Sullivan, whose original (Sullivan, 1995), and more recent (Sullivan, 2005), treatment addressed the recent history and current status of professions. This examination of the history and current moment of professions points to goods protected and promoted by the tradition of the professions. Understanding profession(s) as practice establishes a foundation for professional civility as a communicative virtue: Through discourse, professional identities and communities emerge, and it is through discourse that the telos of professions is attained. Professions and their context of operation have changed over time, but those changes can be understood as extensions and elaborations of the tradition of profession(s) as it has developed over time. The legacy of the professions is a "resource for invention, not just continuity" (Borden, 2007, p. 76), particularly for broadening the "canon" of the professions (e.g., Kultgen, 1988). Here, the goods of profession(s) as goods internal to practice (MacIntyre, 2007) emerge within the understanding of what a profession can, and should, be, based on understanding "profession" as a metapractice with a history and tradition. The work of Gardner and colleagues (Gardner, 2007; Gardner et al., 2001) offers additional material assessing the current state of the professions and providing support for the existence of various goods of, and for, the professions. I provide a brief summary of the four goods of professions, offering a rationale for their place in the framework of professional civility as communicative virtue in the workplace.

The third chapter addresses civility as communicative virtue and, by way of contrast, incivility as communicative vice, drawing from a number of literatures, particularly those addressing civility as civic virtue. A brief review of the scholarship on civility in public life, including the foundational work of Elias (1978, 1982) and representative current work on the topic (e.g., Davetian, 2009; Kingwell, 1995), provides evidence for civility's indispensable role in functioning and flourishing human communities. In this chapter, I pay particular attention to work done on civility within the communication field, exploring elements of civility that can be properly understood as emerging from the conceptual resources of communication theory (e.g., politeness theory, message design logic, defensive and supportive communication, communicative dialectics, phatic communication, argumentativeness and verbal aggression). I foreground communicative practices and outcomes within a conceptual background constructed from these varied contributions to frame civility as the communicative embodiment of civic virtue.

Chapter 4 brings chapters 1 through 3 together to offer a treatment of professional civility as communicative virtue in the organizational setting, focusing on its role in protecting and promoting goods internal to professional practice in today's historical moment. Because civility as civic virtue operates in a broad public context, it must be situated and theorized within the history and tradition of profession(s) and within the scope of the organizational setting in order to function as a communication ethic specific to the professional workplace. The first chapter offers a treatment of virtue ethics within which the professions can be situated. The second chapter offers the background story of the history and tradition of the professions within which to situate civility as civic virtue. The third chapter offers an understanding of civility as the communicative manifestation of civic virtue. In the fourth chapter, these coordinates merge to manifest professional civility as communicative virtue at work. Professional civility protects and promotes the goods of productivity, place, and persons and, by extension, the good of the profession itself. Each good needs protection; these goods are jeopardized not only by incivility, but also by failure to attend to them and support them—by communicative sins of omission as well as commission. Each good needs promotion; through communicative action, these goods are supported, reinforced, and extended throughout the organizational setting in the course of everyday work life.

To build the professional civility framework on the foundation of profession(s) as tradition(s) of practice and civility as communicative virtue, I turn to the domains of philosophy of communication and organizational behavior. In particular, I focus on Arnett and Arneson's (1999) treatment of dialogic civility and the construct of organizational citizenship (Graham, 1991; Organ, 1988; Organ et al., 2006). I situate work from earlier chapters within the context of professional communicative interaction, and introduce relevant work on the communicative activities of professions as an integral part of professional practice (e.g., Barge & Little, 2008). I offer an initial integration of these conceptual areas and suggest forays into potential practices of professional civility.

The fifth chapter provides evidence for the power of communicative action to shape elements of organizational life and demonstrates the deleterious effects of incivility on the goods of professions. This material offers a complementary perspective to virtue ethics by adding a pragmatic or utilitarian rationale for enacting professional civility—professional civility matters because communication shapes our understanding of self, others, and our environment, and contributes actively to the construction of organizational cultures and climates (Ashcraft et al., 2009). This last section provides a transition to the next three chapters, which form the application section of the book.

Chapters 6 through 8 address, respectively, the three goods of productivity, place, and persons, exploring their philosophical and applied foundations and identifying communicative practices that embody the virtue of professional civility through their action of protecting and promoting these goods. Literatures from communication theory, organizational studies, social psychology, and other areas contribute synthetically to our understanding of the virtue of professional civility and figure prominently in these chapters. Works for a general audience by scholars such as Forni (2002, 2008) also inform these chapters.

Chapter 6 addresses the good of productivity; Arendt's (1958) work on labor, work, and action joins the history of profession(s) as practice to provide a conceptual foundation for the good of work. I point to the metaphor of the craftsman

(Arnett, in press-b; Sennett, 2008) as a corrective reminder of the importance of practices to the occupational category of the professional. Sennett's treatment of craftwork offers a new understanding of Gibb's (1961) defensive and supportive communication by pointing to a standard of judgment that can give legitimacy to what have traditionally been understood as problematic "defensiveness-provoking" communicative practices, such as evaluation. I explore levels of engagement of professional civility at the managerial level by drawing on Arnett and Fritz's (2003) discussion of professional civility as an approach to management that emphasizes organizational mission, relational communication appropriate to the workplace, and productivity. Arnett and Fritz noted that the focus of discourse in the workplace should be work. While other types of discourse are inevitable and natural, the key is to err in favor of the "task" side of the narrow ridge (Buber, 1948) of the person/task dialectic, inviting limited personal discourse to embellish the margins of work life and, in some cases, to embroider the interstices of task-related events. I answer the questions, "Which communicative practices help people work well?" and "How does context shape the nature of professional civility?" to consider how peers enact professional civility.

Chapter 7 addresses the good of "place," the organization within which much of professional work is accomplished. Professional civility recognizes the value of the organization as a site for enactment of practices of a given profession in a particular place. The organization is both a dwelling place and a community of memory (Arnett et al., 2009), whose mission is honored by professional civility. The organization works as a public narrative, inviting diverse participants to contribute productively to a common center (Arnett, 1986).

A local institutional home invites professionals to work within a mission and structure not of their making (Noordegraaf, 2007). Professionals may face difficulty in striking a balance between professional autonomy and organizational demands, a balance that requires reflective navigation of multiple goods. I address communicative practices that protect and promote the good of place—for instance, focusing conversation on what is good about one's place of work instead of habitual complaint, drawing particularly on the work of Arnett and Arneson (1999) on hope and cynicism. Arnett and Arneson's distinction between appropriate and routine cynicism contextualizes the "sportsmanship" dimension of the organizational citizenship construct, and offers a place for organizational dissent (e.g., Kassing, 1998, 2001) to reflect the "civic virtue" dimension of the organizational citizenship construct (Graham, 1991; Organ, 1988). Communicative processes of organizational hiring and mentoring protect an institutional home, as noted by Arnett and Fritz (2003); the organizational socialization process, as explored in detail by Kramer (2010), is a particularly important factor in protecting and promoting the good of organizations. I address the concept of "care for institutions" (Fritz, 2012b) as an element of professional civility that extends the theoretical framework of organizational citizenship.

Chapter 8 addresses the good of "persons" in the workplace. I explore the nature of public and private relationships in order to identify challenges facing what Bridge and Baxter (1992) called "blended relationships," private relationships engaged in the public context of work. Organizational relationships form and deteriorate in patterned ways, as suggested by Sias (2009a) in her volume on workplace relationships. Understanding organizational peer relationships from a perspective of professional civility offers insights into maintaining constructive public relationships that orient toward the "third party" of the organization as a locus of relationship accountability. Despite variations in organizational culture, which invite a range of expectations for interpersonal interaction, keeping public connections at the forefront is the key to professional civility as protection and promotion of persons. Peer relationships and superior/subordinate relationships engaged with professional civility form a foundation for constructive and productive organizational interaction, and are marked by communicative practices that organize the relationship's interactive routines around productivity.

Chapters 6 through 8 are of specific relevance to microprocesses of communicative action defining professional civility as enacted in the contemporary workplace. Productivity, place, and persons are goods salient to, and operative as part of, the organization and its activities. In this capacity, the theoretical contours of civility as communicative virtue, in their application to conversational routines and practices, receive treatment in each of these chapters within the horizon of the conceptual and theoretical framework laid out in Chapter 3's treatment. For example, utterances from coworkers representing particular types of face support in the context of the task, managerial messages that work within the parameters of an organization's mission, and conversation among peers in the workplace that offer tactful respect for professional boundaries emerge in these chapters.

In the concluding chapter, I explore the idea of respect for professions in this historical moment and examine the role of communities of discourse in providing guidelines for professional practice, inviting discipline and self-correction for ethical standards as constitutive of professions as an identity. Professions as integral parts of the marketplace and public sphere in the form of traditions that exhibit responsibility and a story of excellence are the focus of this chapter. I draw on Sullivan (2005), along with a number of other authors addressing professional ethics, to frame communicative interaction as an element of professional praxis that protects and promotes the good of profession(s). Professional civility as ethical communicative praxis counters the decline of professions, and the attacks against them, that I review at the beginning of the chapter. The chapter engages the topic of professional civility at the macro level rather than at the level of microprocesses. The assumption is that the work of professional civility, which takes place at the level of microprocesses relevant to productivity, place, and person, spills upward and outward to protect and promote profession(s) as practice.

Professional civility brings together several conceptual coordinates to define an approach to, and/or understanding of, the good for human life and action, communication, and work, and can be understood from several approaches. These various approaches, or capacities, suggest different facets of, or perspectives on, the lived experience and meaning of work, and of work's relationship to the integrity of a human life. These different understandings move in dynamic interplay, highlighting particular facets of communicative experience and its meaning in the workplace, and of the meaning of work itself. The final two sections of this introductory chapter offer ways of thinking about professional civility, as well as some cautionary statements related to its application.

Modalities of Professional Civility: Communicative Virtue, Professional Communication Ethic, Philosophy of Communication, Philosophy of Work Life

"Professional civility as communicative virtue" focuses on the role of a particular orientation to work and its associated discourse/communicative style and substance in protecting and promoting various goods emerging from the tradition of profession(s) and an understanding of civility as civic virtue. In its application and enactment of virtue, professional civility suggests that underlying the content of a particular message or discourse style is a particular good or goods. A communication ethic points to goods underlying discourse that are protected and promoted by communication (Arnett et al., 2009). Bringing these two elements together highlights professional civility as a virtue-based approach to communication ethics.

A philosophy of communication highlights the role of communication as a carrier of meaning (Arnett & Holba, in press)—an understanding of communicative action as orienting communicators within a particular epistemological, ontological, and axiological space. A communication ethic may emerge from, or interact with, a philosophy of communication. A philosophy of communication offers a "why" for the "doing" of communicative action (Arnett et al., 2009, p. 27), inviting meaning to emerge as connected to a human good expressed in communicative action.

A philosophy of work life points to a background understanding of work within the larger context of human existence and meaning; a philosophy of communication works within a philosophy of work life to highlight and bring forth messages and modalities of discourse reflective of that philosophy of work life, which in turn works within a broader philosophy of life in general, or a worldview. The scope of this treatment is limited to the action of communicative virtue as an element of a communicative ethic coordinated with a philosophy of communication connected to a philosophy of work life.

Intercultural communication provides a way of understanding the interrelationship of these various elements. Dimensions of culture, including power distance, individualism/collectivism, and uncertainty avoidance (Hofstede, 2001), are elements contributing to a culture's philosophy of life, understood as an existential standpoint from which to engage others and phenomena in the material, social, and spiritual world. A philosophy of life undergirds a philosophy of work life. Elements of a philosophy of communication might be derived from a culture's philosophy of life. For example, indirect communication and high-context communication represent elements of a philosophy of communication connected to dimensions of culture that orient members in particular ways toward the relationship of the individual to the collective (individualism/collectivism). A culture's communicative practices are tied to a culture's implicit philosophy of communication, contributing to cultural variability within and across workplaces (Gannon, 2008; Hofstede, 2001; Sanchez-Burks, Lee, Choi, Nisbett, Zhao, & Coo, 2003).

Cautions and Caveats

Professional civility is not a panacea; many situations in organizational life call for drastic action that moves beyond professional civility and into other paradigms of discourse and action. Fritz and Omdahl (2006a) and Omdahl and Fritz (in press) addressed problematic relationships in the workplace and ways to navigate them. The current book is designed to offer one way to prevent problematic relationships, or perhaps move them in a positive direction, but this approach is only one way to think about work life.

In the course of development of these ideas, the holistic, interactive nature of the various goods of profession in the context of professional civility becomes clear. Productivity, place, persons, and profession are integrally interwoven. In the context of treatment of a particular good, other goods necessarily come into play in some implicative location—as background, periphery, or antecedent or consequent factor. A focus on productivity necessarily implies a particular type of engagement of persons and points to the primacy of "place" as context for productive activity. A focus on place necessarily implies the importance of productivity and attention to the activity of persons within the purview of the organization. A focus on persons highlights the organizational context and productive purposes of interpersonal communicative interaction. The various theoretical strands that the professional civility framework is composed of interconnect differently from good to good and for goods as a whole.

The purpose of this treatment of professional civility is to develop its philosophical and theoretical framework. For this reason, the bulk of the material within these pages is conceptual. I integrate examples from time to time in order to provide touchstones for understanding and application, but I avoid a list of communicative techniques or formulas for communicative practices. I reference a number of excellent books as resources offering conversational exemplars for various contexts, which can serve as "primers" for professionally civil communicative engagement (e.g., Forni, 2002, 2008, 2011b; Troester & Mester, 2007; Fairhurst, 2011).

Professional civility, as I develop it here, is bound to culture, particularly to an occupational culture of the United States that is shaped by a particular set of historical and sociocultural circumstances. As Davetian (2007) and others have pointed out, practices of civility are rooted in cultures and given their form by circumstances particular to a given culture. As others have also pointed out, the minimal coordinates of cooperative human action appear to have manifestations in every culture (e.g., forms of politeness, as noted by Brown and Levinson, 1987/1978). A virtue ethics framework does not presuppose the universal status of the particular goods of given cultures, but it does permit an agreed-upon outcome or telos to serve as reference point and evaluative standard to assess human and institutional action toward goods that define that end. Professional civility as understood within a cultural structure embedding the tradition of the professions in the United States and enacted in the context of organizations in the United States is theorized here as particular to this context. Within different cultural systems, alternative particulars that nonetheless express protonorms of shared cultural virtues (Christians & Traber, 1997) may give rise to institutional communicative norms and ideals that look quite different from what I propose here.

1

Virtue Ethics
and the Professions

Introduction

A virtue ethics approach to professional roles offers a constructive framework for a communicative ethic of professional civility. Within this approach, civility in professional interaction takes the form of a communicative virtue supporting professional practice and its associated goods. Scholars addressing professional ethics from a virtue perspective argue that a virtue ethics approach provides a foundation for the good for professions that explains professional practices in terms of their contribution to the human telos, and in terms of the telos to which a particular profession tends (e.g., Oakley & Cocking, 2001). From this perspective, professions are communities that define goods for a particular occupation; professional virtues enacted by professional practitioners help support those goods, which, in turn, participate in and support the general good of human flourishing.

Scholars of professional virtue ethics build on the work of a number of theorists. One of these theorists is Alasdair MacIntyre (2007), who offered what some scholars consider the most successful contemporary articulation and reformulation of Aristotle's notion of virtue (Pellegrino, 1995). MacIntyre situated virtue ethics within a moment of widespread public disagreement about the nature of what is good for humans to be and to do (Arnett, Fritz, & Bell, 2009). Scholars such as Borden

(2007), Blackburn and McGhee (2004), and others (Brewer, 1997; Moore, 2002) have applied MacIntyre's work to particular occupational areas, including journalism, and the context of business and management. MacIntyre's work offers a framework for professions in a postmodern moment in need of a guiding ethic for public communicative practice—communicative interaction that protects and promotes the goods underlying professional practice within the matrix of task and interpersonal factors that constitute the organizational context and that are significant elements of professional life today. The next sections address the scholarship of virtue ethics in the professions and the work of MacIntyre to identify coordinates within ethical theory for professional civility as communicative virtue in organizational life.

A Foundation for Professional Civility as Communicative Virtue at Work

Virtue Ethics and the Professions

Virtue ethics has experienced a scholarly revival over the past decades (Oakley & Cocking, 2001). One of the most prominent understandings of virtue ethics is an Aristotelian approach, which assumes a telos or "good" of human life defined by the nature of human beings. Virtues are character traits that enable a person to pursue and embody a good human life, a life characterized by human flourishing (Oakley & Cocking, 2001). Because professions are understood to play an important role in the ends or purposes of human life, professions and the work of professionals can be understood as fitting within the broad scope of virtue ethics. Furthermore, professions have a teleological structure of their own that is agreed upon by those who practice the profession. For example, journalism is marked by particular goods and ends (see Borden, 2007), and the medical profession's purpose has been defined for millennia (Pellegrino & McElhinney, 1982), although controversy with regard to particular goods in bioethics marks the domain of moral decision-making in the medical profession in this historical moment (Englehardt, 2000). With shared agreement on a professional telos, the good that grounds virtue can be identified, making a virtue ethics perspective specific to professions viable (Pellegrino, 1995, p. 253).

Plato conceptualized virtue as arête, or "excellence in the knowledge of the good" (Pellegrino, 1995, p. 256), which leads to a good and happy life. One searches for one's own good within the framework of a knowledge of this universal good, which provides parameters for virtuous human action. One is good to the extent that one possesses virtue, which predisposes one to act in particular ways oriented toward accomplishing the good. Aristotle adds the idea of telos, or "the orientation of virtues to the ends and purposes of human activity" (Pellegrino, 1995, p. 256), with both the happiness of human beings in general and the good performance of one's work as orientations of virtue. The concept of an end, or purpose, of human activity speaks to the nature of human beings as having certain goals or aims that they characteristically tend towards (MacIntyre, 2007, p. 148), and this notion of a telos provides a standard against which to judge action as it assists or impedes achieving the end or purpose of human activity. Aristotle's inclusion of work as an orientation of virtue points in the direction of professions, which define particular vocational purposes and the practices that embody them as capable of being done more or less well, in ways that demonstrate, or fail to demonstrate, the good defined by excellent practice—or goods intrinsic to their performance (Barber, 1963).

Professions can be evaluated as to their contribution to the good of human flourishing, and they can be understood as a practice with a defined end, aim, or good against which particular instantiations of practices can be evaluated as meeting, or failing to meet, that end, aim, or good, as defining more or less well the particular good internal to that practice. Professional accrediting bodies for accounting, for example, define the skills and knowledge any accountant must know. Although public relations is not a formally licensed profession, there are acknowledged practices associated with the understanding of what a public relations professional is expected to know and do that make up the content of professional practice for public relations, despite continued struggles for formal definition of the area (e.g., Baker, 2002; Hutton, 1999). The Public Relations Society of America defines both the practice areas of a public relations practitioner and specific curricular requirements for colleges and universities that seek to conform their curricular offerings to those larger guidelines defined by that professional body (http://www.prsa.org/).

In his articulation of virtue ethics, Pellegrino (1995) recognized the need to identify a goal outside a system—an external standard—in order to define the good for human life or for any activity. Pellegrino argued that, despite lack of moral consensus on the good for society at large in today's historical moment, the good in professional ethics can be identified because its telos functions as just such a standard outside the system toward which the practice (of a profession) tends and by which it can be evaluated. In MacIntyre's (2007) terms, the tradition or history of a profession is the source of such a standard, defining its end, or the good to which it tends. MacIntyre's notion of a tradition as a context for practice provides a narrative framework within which one can define the scope of a practice as an activity or endeavor, the characteristic ends of that practice, and the goods that define those ends—goods that emerge through the practice itself and by which the particular telos is realized. A profession can be understood as a practice with a tradition that defines its good or goods both as an end of the practice itself and within the larger picture of the good of human life. As professions succeed in achieving their particular telos, they contribute to larger human goals and are thus understood to be integral contributors to the good of human life.

From the preceding material, the virtue of professional civility inclines toward excellence in knowledge and performance of communication in professional contexts. Excellence in this case would be defined as protecting and promoting goods identified as key elements of a profession that are internal to professional practice within an institutional or organizational context in today's historical moment. The good performance of one's profession as it promotes the ends and purposes of human activity is the hoped-for outcome; the end or telos of professional performance assists the end or telos of human activity or life, a framing consistent with the history of the professional ideal in the United States (Kimball, 1995).

Oakley and Cocking (2001) laid out a virtue framework for ethics in the professions, examining the profession of medicine as an exemplar. They argued that a virtue ethics framework permits better understanding of professional roles than other perspectives. I examine their treatment here as a general application of virtue ethics to the professions before turning to Alasdair MacIntyre's work on virtue ethics for specific conceptual grounding for the project at hand.

Virtue Ethics as a Framework for Professional Ethics

Oakley and Cocking (2001) noted that virtue ethics is founded on the understanding that acting virtuously is part of what defines a good human life. They note Aristotle's view that what humans need, or are, as human beings defines the content of virtuous character, and that virtues are part of an interconnected system of intrinsic goods necessary for human beings to flourish. Virtue ethics presupposes a human nature defined by an end toward which human beings characteristically tend—rationality, in an Aristotelian framework, and accompanying attributes that form a matrix of the good life for human beings. Friendship, a sense of community, and engagement in meaningful activity, for example, are some of those intrinsic goods. Human beings are social creatures; to be fully human, we need friends, groups of others with whom we can gather, and meaningful activity that engages our talents and abilities in worthwhile pursuits. Virtues permit enactment of practices that carry or define that good as it has been enacted by particular human communities in the form of a tradition that has developed over time. One such tradition, for example, is that of liberal democracy and the rule of law. Oakley and

Cocking (2001) drew on MacIntyre's conceptualization of goods internal to practices that support traditions within communities as a substantial part of their treatment of professional ethics.

Oakley and Cocking (2001) noted that roles define an important element of professional ethics. This focus on roles resonates with MacIntyre's (2007) discussion of the role-driven ethics of a Homeric heroic society, in which a good life is defined by excellent enactment of one's role. A role-driven approach to ethics can be applied to professions, writ large as "metaprofession," given the applicability of the role concept to all professions and to elements of the organizational context that provide the setting for professional practice today.

Understanding ethics from a role-based perspective does not preclude recognition of the personal "face" of others in the workplace, the essential humanity of role inhabitants, but permits a background understanding of work to guide a foreground focus on professional role identity as the primary locus of ethical action. Since professions find their purpose as contributors to the good of human existence, professions themselves, and the roles they engender, are subject to the larger goods of human existence, eschewing a "rogue" or disembedded role calcification characteristic of the bureaucrat who, accused of committing atrocities, claims only to have been following orders (Arnett, in press–a). From a standpoint of professional civility, we engage others through their roles and within our roles, while never reducing others or ourselves to mere roles. Roles identify guidelines for coordinated action and expectations for behavior within a given institutional setting, providing the formal distance (Forni, 2011a) necessary for engagement of tasks despite either deep personal differences or close personal connection.

A virtue ethics framework requires a focus on professional socialization (e.g., Gecas, 1981), because the regulative ideals, those standards that guide the behavior of professionals toward the enactment of the good (Borden, 2007), emerge in the process of taking on a professional role, of entering and becoming a full member of the profession. At the personal or individual level, phronesis, or practical wisdom, is a virtue that connects or coordinates the application of virtue with respect to the good, directing particular virtues toward given goods. Phronesis is a general regulative ideal, identifying guidelines for enactment of virtue in a particular setting, and is developed through continued practice and feedback from the task itself and from others—a process that begins in professional socialization. Professional civility as an element of professional socialization would operate similarly; as one learns professional occupational practices through professional mentoring, repeated enactment, and reflection on experience, one also develops communicative virtue through professional mentoring, enactment of communicative practices, and reflection on experience.

Professional socialization is not technique driven, but involves learning norms and expectations accompanying a particular professional practice, not all of which can be specified in advance (see Squires, 2005). Oakley and Cocking (2001) noted that "a virtue ethics criterion of rightness is perhaps less precisely specifiable and less easily applicable than that given by consequentialist theories" (p. 33). Socialization to a particular organization requires attentiveness to local norms in the development of embedded or localized professional competence. For example, what is the culture of this particular accounting firm, this investment brokerage, this animal rescue organization, this integrated marketing communication firm, this law office, or this university? One's professional training provides the basic vocabulary for a given profession, but a particular place of employment invites engagement of that profession in a distinctive way.

The particularity of professional enactment resonates with the gestalt nature of professional civility, the actions of which cannot be specified in advance, but which admit of a general sense or tendency with a horizon that accommodates a variety of modalities of communicative application. We cannot generate a fixed list that indicates exactly what to say in every possible circumstance, but we can identify general principles that are applicable and adaptable to different contexts and environments, as well as some potential communicative practices that serve as guidelines for generating unique and particular verbal and nonverbal messages that represent professionally civil discourse. Professional civility is also, therefore, a special type of communicative competence—a metaprofessional communicative competence that requires communicative phronesis, or practical wisdom, to be enacted well within the guidelines of a particular institutional setting.

Virtue ethics as a type of character-based ethics fits within a narrative framework appropriate to the history of professions as a tradition specifying a particular type of role-grounded interpersonal interaction among members as normative. A narrative- or tradition-grounded framework identifies friendship as a great human good (MacIntyre, 2007), which permits a focus on professional relationships within role boundaries as a case of public friendship, a relationship guided by a telos shaped by one's profession and local organizational home (Arnett, 1992) and oriented toward a common project or task. MacIntyre (2007) spoke of the virtue of friendship in civic life, a life that is oriented toward a common good and goals; civic friendship is consistent with public friendship, in which the partners recognize the relationship's embeddedness in the larger structure of an organization, a third party to which the relationship is accountable (Arnett et al., 2009). How I talk to a fellow employee who happens to be a good friend is a valid concern of our common employer. In virtue ethics, the "good" of, or for, persons is tied to a recognition of, and subsequent focus on, what is owed to a human being as a human being. Professions recognize humans as both role-constituted and persons in themselves—a human being in community must inhabit some role; elements of both Homeric and Aristotelian/Athenian virtue systems as described by MacIntyre (2007) apply to professional work and relationships, and hence to professional civility as I outline it here. A treatment of the work of MacIntyre later in this chapter will address this point.

Virtue ethics defines a telos-based approach to life and the professions, permitting a focus on the "moral significance of professional roles" (Oakley & Cocking, 2001, p. 74). Professions themselves articulate a telos for a thriving human life because of their self-understanding, and the understanding on the part of other relevant groups, such as communities and the larger institutional public, that the professions are valuable—indeed, necessary—for thriving human communities. In this sense, professions are partially constitutive of the human good. Professions make life better for the human community.

Oakley and Cocking (2001) noted that "good professional roles must be part of a good profession," and that "a good profession is one which involves a commitment to a key human good, a good which humans need to live flourishing lives" (p. 4). Oakley and Cocking connected enacting the good in a professional role to that role's place in serving the goals of the profession, observing, in turn, that those goals of the profession are connected to goods for human beings—to "characteristic human activities" (p. 74). Human communities need accountants, day-care providers, pharmacists, hairdressers, teachers, musicians, and engineers—their work makes life in contemporary society possible. Without healthcare practitioners of various sorts, we would not be able to secure human health at the current level; without scientists to investigate the material world, our knowledge of human disease, understanding of the physical properties of our environment, and much of what permits society to function would not be possible. Lawyers, journalists; occupational, physical, and speech therapists; nurses; persons working in the multitude of business and industry occupations; members of religious communities—all make a good human life as we know it possible.

Oakley and Cocking's (2001) perspective reflects Kimball's (1995), Sullivan's (2005), and others' discussions of professions throughout the history of the United States and in today's historical moment. Indeed, implicit in the notion of a "profession," according to Kimball (1995), Larson (1977), and Sullivan (2005), is the idea that "norms of the profession…must be shown to reflect a commitment to an important substantive human good that contributes to our living a flourishing human life" (Oakley & Cocking, 2001, p. 75). This discussion points the way to a philosophy of the professions that finds grounding in the work of Arendt (1958) on labor, work, and action mentioned in the book's introduction, and to be discussed later at greater length. For example, in his article pointing to a phenomenology of the professions, Squires (2005) argued that professions are defined in terms of action assisting the human community; "[professionals] do not leave the world as they found it" (p. 130). Professions are functional not in a reductionistic sense, but in a way that makes possible the recognition of their contribution to a characteristic or defining purpose (a telos) (p. 131) that contributes to the greater human good.

From this perspective, a virtue ethics approach to the professions opens up the broader discussion of what it means to live a flourishing human life by pointing to a "broader concept of 'well-being'" (Oakley & Cocking, 2001, p. 77), or eudaimonia, also noted by Nussbaum (2000) in her extension of Sen's (1985, 1993, 1999) work on human capabilities. In this framework, professional civility is intrinsically good, because in its communicative manifestation it honors others as they are in their roles and as human persons-in-roles—professional civility manifests the good and protects and promotes goods: the very action is valuable because of its achievement of valuing human persons.

MacIntyre's Virtue Ethics Applied to the Professions

MacIntyre's (2007) treatment of virtue ethics provides a specific focus and ground for "profession" as [a] practice. History and tradition, for MacIntyre, are keys to the foundation of ethics (Lutz, 2004/2009, p. 40), both of which are part of the professional ideal (Kimball, 1995). MacIntyre situated the telos of human life assumed by virtue ethics within a tradition that functions as a petite narrative (Lyotard, 1984), offering a particular understanding of the good for human life. The good for human beings and the ends to which human beings strive, the telos of human beings as a species, determines the human qualities that count as virtues (p. 184). Exercising the virtues is a vital element of what it means to live a good human life, and such exercise leads to achieving the good for human beings. The "virtuous character" of an agent is situated within a narrative framework grounded in the tradition of a practice that embodies a given good and provides parameters for the exercise of the virtues. MacIntyre's approach is fruitful for application to professions, and hence to the communicative virtue of professional civility, because of his focus on goods carried by a tradition of practice with a history embodied in enactment of those practices by a community. Professions are practices with a narrative history (Kimball, 1995), and the encompassing notion of "profession" itself can be understood as a practice, or a metapractice, embodying goods internal to practice. Pellegrino (1995) noted:

> MacIntyre has most successfully built on the Aristotelian notion of virtue and reformulated it in more contemporary terms, taking into account the erosion of the tradition and the moral consensus that gave the classical doctrine its normative strength. MacIntyre (1984) builds his definition on three elements; he regards virtues as dispositions or acquired qualities that are: (1) necessary to achieve the good internal to practices, (2) necessary to sustain communities in which individuals can seek a higher good as the good of their own lives, and (3) necessary to sustain traditions that provide necessary historical contexts for individual lives. Virtue, thus, is a character trait necessary to achievement of a good—a perfected excellence (MacIntyre 1988, p. 74). In this, MacIntyre adopts the teleological thrust of the Aristotelian definition of virtue and adds to it the sustaining force of a historical community of values. (p. 261)

MacIntyre's (2007) virtue ethics is consistent with that of Oakley and Cocking (2001) in its potential to frame the activity of profession as practice as part of what defines a good life for human beings. Here, the work of Arendt (1958) is helpful. Arendt's understanding of the human condition assumes the necessity of labor for the human community's enduring through time, the responsibility of work to create a world for human beings to inhabit, and the manifestation of the most characteristically human action in the public sphere of life in human community. These three elements constitute the good of productivity for professions. Professional civility supports the internal goods of professions as valued human activity and contributes to external goods relevant to organizational life, including prevention and amelioration of the deleterious effects of incivility (e.g., Fritz & Omdahl, 2006b).

MacIntyre's (2007) work provides a way to address a variety of concerns emerging in today's marketplace, particularly the phenomenon of fragmentation of expectations for the good for human life and practice, which has made its way into organizations (Fritz, Arnett, & Conkel, 1999). MacIntyre noted that understanding the notion of virtues requires an account of a practice, an account of the narrative order of a single human life, and an account of a moral tradition. These concepts emerge as he lays out the story of a tradition of the virtues that takes its most coherent form in Aristotelian virtue ethics and runs through the medieval era as it meets Christian thought, where it is extended and adapted.

The Tradition of Virtue Ethics: Implications for Professions

MacIntyre (2007) argued that virtues are understood contextually, within a framework of social and moral life that gives the virtues meaning. For MacIntyre, the virtues are defined primarily in terms of practices, reflected, for example, in both the Homeric and Aristotelian rendition of virtues. In the Homeric system of virtues, virtue is that which enables one to perform a social role. Virtues in the Aristotelian framework extend to the good for human beings in general and are not limited in relevance to a particular social role, although role-related work is included in this framework.

MacIntyre (2007) traced the history of virtue ethics as a tradition from classical times to the present historical moment. In each moment, particular virtues were prominent, in each case tied to a particular goal or end for human beings in terms of which particular practices were enacted. A Homeric ethic takes the virtues to be characteristics that permit role enactment. An Aristotelian approach understands virtues to support the good life for human beings as human beings rather than as inhabitants of a particular role. The virtues in the medieval context assist in achieving a quest for the good of human life from a story-centered perspective in the framework of a narrative now connected to Christian, as well as classical, virtues—introducing the notion of forgiveness. Each of these historical moments contributed substantially to the tradition of virtue ethics, of which the Aristotelian approach remains a foundational core (see also Pellegrino, 1995). The introduction of narrative, or story, connects to the framework of professions as tradition-grounded and guided, with professional civility as a communicative virtue supporting and enabling the continuation of that story.

A practice- and tradition-grounded understanding of the professions and professional ethics draws substance from each of these historical ethical frameworks. Professional civility, conceptualized here as emerging from this understanding of professions, requires a neighborly or civic concern for persons who inhabit roles and thereby contribute to the organizational community within which the narrative or story of a particular professional tradition is enacted and renewed. Today's emotivistic framework, where an understanding of the good is characteristically based on personal preference rather than on an understood or agreed-upon narrative (MacIntyre, 2007), provides a challenge to the notion of a shared or agreed-upon good that governs individual choice and action. A professional ethic provides narrative ground for virtuous professional practices within a defined framework, supplying resources for judgment and evaluation as well as parameters for identifying excellence. Professional civility as a communicative virtue works within this larger framework of professional ethics.

The account MacIntyre (2007) offered for an adequate understanding of virtue requires consideration of two other elements along with the notion of a practice: an account of a moral tradition and an account of the narrative order of a given human life. This contextual conceptual trio emerged as he laid out the story of a tradition of the virtues that takes its original form in Aristotelian virtue ethics and threads through the medieval era, where it is extended and adapted by Aquinas and other scholars of that era. As MacIntyre conceived it, virtues are necessary to achieve goods internal to practices, to support communities that provide a context for persons to seek the good, and to support traditions that provide a historical background or context for both persons and practices.

The concepts of a practice, a tradition, and the narrative unity of a life are of primary relevance for this project because professions, as I will show, manifest all three of these elements. The virtues are necessary to tie these three concepts together; virtues are goods that connect all three elements to human communities that work together on a common project of the good for human beings. Professions, in their "true professional ideal" (Kimball, 1995), participate in, and are constituted by, a tradition of practice; their members represent, carry, and instantiate the profession through their actions, and in so doing contribute to the narrative unity of their own lives, which are characterized by professional identity shaped by tradition and given substance through practices. I argue that profession is a metapractice that contributes to the greater human good through multiple constituent practices defined by particular professions. The story of the professions in America (Kimball, 1995) defines the history and tradition of a (meta)practice with underlying goods of productivity, place, and peersons, and the practice of profession itself. Professional civility as communicative virtue protects and promotes these goods.

Traditions of Virtues

MacIntyre (2007) identified several locations for virtues throughout Western history in his account of the virtues. One context is Homeric society, part of the tradition from which Aristotelian virtue ethics emerged, in which roles are the key locations for virtues. In this type of "heroic" society, persons know who they are by the roles they inhabit. Virtues are those characteristics that help one accomplish a role. Virtues in this sense are action-based (p. 122). They show up in actions required by the role, which fits within a larger structure of roles that define the community (p. 122). In Homeric times, "community" was kinship and household. Courage was a virtue necessary to sustain households and communities. A courageous person was a reliable person (p. 122), willing to come to the aid of someone in need.

In heroic societies, we find identity in our actions within communities (MacIntyre, 2007, p. 122). This identity is developed as we participate in practices that define traditions that shape our identities (pp. xv, 122). Here, there is a direct tie to professional identity. Identity comes from one's role, which demands account-ability (p. 126). A role occupant is answerable for fulfilling what anyone who occu-pies the role owes to others. The self becomes what it is through its role; it is a social, not an individual, creation (pp. 126, 129). This perspective applies to professions in general and to professions operating within organizational contexts through roles, although this perspective does not define professions reductively. From a framework of professional civility, both roles and the idea of a complete human life as articu-lated by the Aristotelian tradition are vital. Professions are enacted through social roles that form part of a complete human life.

The exercise of the virtues defines the good life lived by human beings; virtues are not connected to outcomes in a "means-ends" relation. The exercise of the virtues is *part of* the good life for human beings, not a means to that end (MacIntyre, 2007, pp. 148–149). Virtues are dispositions to act and feel in par-ticular ways (p. 149); they are qualities that move human beings toward the telos of "being well and doing well in being well," achieving "a complete human life lived at its best" (p. 149), which includes exercising the virtues. Borden (2007) described this state as "maxing out as a human being" (p. 16). MacIntyre (2007) suggested that given traditions help specify the content of the good life for human beings, the particulars of which are left largely open by Aristotle (MacIntyre, 2007, p. 148), permitting a broad horizon of potential elements to fulfill that content. Across human societies, some general sense of "the good life" for human beings can be identified, along with the virtues that enable support of the communities that embed their members through practices that sustain them. On this point, the work of Christians and Traber (1997) on protonorms is relevant, highlighting further evidence for some common understanding of the good for human beings that, although similar at its core, manifests itself some-what differently across cultures and time periods.

Application of Virtues

The application and exercise of the virtues moves beyond technique, or mere application of a rule, into a capacity for judgment. Exercising judgment is differ-ent from following rules. In a later chapter, this point will be explicated with ref-erence to particular communicative practices that take on different valences in different contexts. For example, an encouraging nod of affirmation might be sup-portive of the good of continued discussion in a context where more talk is called for, but in a context where someone is gossiping or complaining about a fellow coworker, such encouragement would not be constructive or helpful, and therefore not virtuous.

MacIntyre (2007) tied the notion of judgment to the issue of the particular. In the Aristotelian framework, virtues find their place in the life of the city, a particular location; the individual is intelligible only as a "political animal" (p. 150) in a particular polis—that of Athens. The communicative virtue of professional civility operates in the context of a public polis, defined as the organization, which requires coordinated action to accomplish various tasks. Coordinated action is an element of professional practice that takes into account the needs of the local home within which a professional person functions. Professional civility as a professional communicative virtue protects and promotes coordinated action in organizational life.

MacIntyre (2007) noted Aristotle's distinction between intellectual virtues and virtues of character (MacIntyre, 2007, p. 155). Phronesis is the intellectual virtue needed to exercise virtues of character in a particular circumstance, which permits practical intelligence to be applied in that instance. Intellectual virtues are learned through instruction; virtues of character are learned through their habitual exercise. To exercise practical intelligence requires the presence of virtues of character. Virtues of character keep practical wisdom from degenerating into simply a means to any end rather than to ends that are genuinely good. Character provides a framework to understand the good for human beings and guides practical intelligence, which then turns a natural disposition into a virtue. Borden's (2007) application of MacIntyre's work to the profession of journalism highlights several virtues enacted by journalists that are applied through phronesis and can be translated within the context of other professions. Courage, ingenuity, stewardship, justice, honesty, integrity, sense of legacy, accountability, and modesty sustain journalistic practice through defending against corruption by external goods, sustaining institutional bearers of the practice, maintaining relationships needed to achieve the goals of the practice through a discipline of verification, preserving the practice's link to the tradition of journalism, and supporting journalism's capabilities to regenerate a practice through a discipline of confirmation (see Borden, 2007, Table 5.1, p. 89).

As applied to professional civility, phronesis points to the connection of virtuous communicative habits, which are practiced enough to be carried out fluidly and skillfully (see Barge & Little, 2008), to communicative discernment, which operates to guide application of a given communicative habit in a particular situation. Professional civility contains elements of virtues of both intellect and character. A philosophical understanding, for instance, of why one might avoid excessive personal self-disclosure in a given setting might identify the intellectual element of the virtue of professional civility, and the tactful utterance of an appropriate comment marked by limited self-disclosure might stem from habitual practice of the communicative good.

In MacIntyre's (2007) framework, virtues are tied to a community—in the case of the professions, to a professional community that one is initiated into and contributes to as a member. Virtues, in their interrelated complexity, happen in a community whose shared aim is the realization of the human good, which "presupposes a wide range of agreement in that community on goods and virtues" that makes possible the bonds constituting a polis (p. 155). In the case of professions, the aim is the good as defined by the professional ideal. As discussed in this chapter's earlier treatment of Oakley and Cocking's (2001) framework, this connection or bond can take the form of a type of friendship and is necessary to any instantiation of community.

Friendship, in Aristotle's terms, is a public phenomenon that constitutes community; it is "the sharing of all in the common project of creating and sustaining the life of the city" (MacIntyre, 2007, p. 156), rather than a relationship based on mutual advantage. In this sense, friendship requires a moral unity emerging from a shared conception of the good. It is important to note here that "a common project" and "mutual advantage" are two very different concepts, and it is the former notion of a common project that binds friends together—not their separately conceived ends for which one receives support in exchange for support of the other's project. For professional civility, friendship is a type of professional relationship defined by, and supportive of, bonds connecting persons to the polis of the organization—a public friendship, as noted earlier in this chapter.

Practices

MacIntyre's (2007) notion of a practice forms the foundation of his treatment of the virtues. All practices aim at some good that helps define the nature of human beings, identified as that at which humans characteristically aim. For MacIntyre, a practice is defined thus:

> [A]ny coherent and complex form of socially established cooperative human activity through which goods internal to that form of activity are realized in the course of trying to achieve those standards of excellence which are appropriate to, and partially definitive of, that form of activity, with the result that human powers to achieve excellence, and human conceptions of the ends and goods involved, are systematically extended. (p. 187)

Many human activities count as practices, including architecture, football, chess, and some types of cooperative fishing—depending on how it is engaged (MacIntyre, 1994). Creating and sustaining human communities, including households, cities, and nations, are practices as MacIntyre defines the term.

MacIntyre (2007) identified two types of good associated with a practice: goods internal to the practice, and goods external to the practice. Goods internal to the practice are those that cannot be achieved other than through the practice. One can recognize those goods only by the experience of participating in the practice, and that is also the only way one can judge the achievement of an internal good. MacIntyre offered the game of chess as an example of a practice, which, when played with skill, manifests a good that defines excellence relevant to chess. The practices that define chess bear the good of excellent chess; they are goods in and of themselves and are, hence, internal to those practices. In the context of practices, virtues support the living out of the good(s) internal to practices. External goods are those goods derived as a result or cause of the practice, but are not internal to the practice. They are byproducts of the practice. In the case of chess playing, fame, fortune, and money gained from playing well and winning tournaments are external goods. MacIntyre further broke down internal goods into two types: the good as excellence of performance and of product, and the good of a certain kind of life—not necessarily the entire life, but that part of life lived out by a person as one who engages in that practice—in the framework proposed here, a professional (p. 190).

To enter into, and participate in, a practice means to be guided by standards of excellence of the practice and to obey the rules associated with that practice as established by its tradition, while engaging in achievement of goods associated with that practice. The standards of the practice as realized so far constitute an evaluative authority for those engaged in the practice (MacIntyre, 2007, p. 190). Professional training and socialization, in the context I propose here, supply initial participation in the practice—indeed, they supply the context within which goods of the profession take on the form specific to a given profession, and they are also the context within which professional civility as communicative virtue might first be instantiated as a virtue of professional character. Professional civility as communicative virtue touches standards of professional practice that are the best realized so far. It supports professional practice and systematically extends the excellence of that practice. Professional civility supports the good of professional life, and it is itself a good in its definitive existence as a communicative practice fitting for professional persons in communities.

Communities of Practice

A practice is a community effort oriented toward achievement of goods internal to the practice and guided by standards received from the tradition. The achievement of those internal goods benefits the entire community of practice

(MacIntyre, 2007, pp. 190–191). A virtue supports a practice as "an acquired human quality the possession and exercise of which are internal to practices and the lack of which effectively prevent us from achieving any such goods" (p. 191). We achieve the goods internal to a practice by "subordinating ourselves within the practice in our relationship to other practitioners" (p. 191). We accept virtues of justice, courage, and honesty as necessary components of practices. As will be illustrated in later chapters, professional civility is both substance and echo of the goods of professional practice carried through several contributing virtues: communicative justice, which provides what is due evaluatively in a particular communicative context, or renders appropriate credit; communicative courage, which speaks up in the face of problematic evidence or a direction that needs correction, even when others might not appreciate the suggestion; and communicative honesty, which speaks the truth in context, revealing role-appropriate information to the right person at the right time, guided by the tact necessary to preserve the face of others (Kingwell, 1995).

Practices are instantiated by communities. A community is more than a conglomerate or aggregate of individuals seeking support for pursuit of their own private goods. Here, Sullivan's original and updated (1995, 2005) critique of professions today is relevant: professionals are increasingly understood to have taken on the form of an aggregate of individuals pursuing their own purposes and ends, contrary to the underlying tradition of service that marks their history as a practice. Practices require relationships among those who participate in the practice (MacIntyre, 2007, p. 191). The relationships among professionals are a vital element of a profession, because these relationships define the profession, contributing to the continuity and integrity of a given profession. Entering a practice means entering into a relationship with others who engage that practice, and with whom one now shares purposes and standards that inform the practice. Entering a profession is stepping into a history of many others who have defined and extended that profession as a practice. Our practice-situated relationships are supported and given life by virtues that sustain the goods of the practice.

MacIntyre (2007) defined several of these virtues, noting that practices entail cooperation, recognition of authority and achievement, respect for standards, and risk taking. The exercise of these virtues demands fairness in judging self and other, truthfulness, and trust in authority. These virtues support the relationships of those engaged in practice through their inclination to support communities, others, and/or the practice itself. As is evidenced throughout the history of professions in the United States (Kimball, 1995), professions manifest these virtues, and professional civility serves as a communicative virtue that protects and promotes goods of professional practice through discourse forms fitting for a given task and organizational context, role relationship, and historical moment.

Practices, according to MacIntyre (2007), have histories, and relevant goods internal to those practices are transmitted by the history of the activity. The implication here is that practices have no definitive goal for all time, but respond to the historical moment and the practitioners who engage those practices within a given historical moment. When we enter a practice, we enter into a relationship with previous practitioners. In other words, we meet or enter into a relationship with a tradition. The history of the professional ideal in the United States (Kimball, 1995) highlights professions' responses to the historical moment and to communities that provide ascriptive support for those claiming professional status. As a profession adapts and develops over time, particular practitioners may discover or develop more excellent approaches to practice, which become part of the tradition. In this sense, a professional community may experience expanded and clarified conceptions of the good or telos for the profession over time. Professional civility's operation provides a communicative substrate that permits this development.

MacIntyre (2007) addressed the relationship of practices to institutions, noting that institutions bear or sustain practices and are necessary for their existence. Institutions, by virtue of their coordinating function for the activities of professionals, can provide a matrix within which practices are sustained and contribute to the good of communities. MacIntyre noted that "the ability of a practice to retain its integrity will depend on the way in which the virtues can be or are exercised in sustaining the initial forms which are the social bearers of the practice" (p. 195). Modern commercial society presents a real danger to practices and the virtues that realize their goods. MacIntyre pointed to Adam Ferguson as offering a sociology that examines the empirical connection between virtues, practices, and institutions (p. 195), along with potential dangers to virtues associated with commercial society. Ferguson's work on civil society is directly related to civility (Arnett, 2001), and hence to professional civility as I conceptualize it here, and the concerns raised by MacIntyre are relevant to the work of professionals in modern commercial society as it exists today, highlighting the need for ethical professional practice within institutions that support professionals' work.

MacIntyre (2007) noted that institutions are concerned with external goods, and that sustaining institutions is a type of practice (p. 194). Virtues help practices resist the corrupting power of institutions as institutions seek external goods. For example, Borden (2007) noted the struggle of journalists to assist news organizations in their resistance to pressure from advertisers and other constituencies to censor or shape reporting of news in ways favorable to those constituencies. In this way, internal goods are protected and promoted by counteracting excessive focus on external goods. External goods are necessary, and they are designed to provide a context for the achievement of internal goods, but these external goods must never threaten or supplant internal goods.

The Unity of a Human Life

MacIntyre (2007) located the point and function of virtues in terms of practices. He noted that Aristotle located practices in a whole "good" human life. Without the virtues, one cannot achieve human life at its best. The notion of a human life aiming toward a point, and lived out through engaging goods as a virtuous person, is needed to arrange and organize the virtues, because human beings are engaged in many practices that could be in conflict. MacIntyre offered the example of an artist caught between the goods of artistic practice and the goods of family life. He therefore moved in the same direction as Aristotle to offer a more complete account of the virtues by including the narrative of a single human life in his portrayal of ethics. This point resonates with Arendt's concern for a public/private distinction, later elaborated by Arnett (2006) as an important element of professional civility. A whole human life derives its unity from maintaining the integrity of different spheres of human existence. However, this "single human life" is not framed individualistically, but in terms of traditions, practices, and communities that embed a person. The whole human life is lived with others and in concert with others in various communities of experience and practice.

Arendt (1958) established work/professions as an important element of human life, addressing public and private domains as sites of potentially rival practices that are brought into order through the unity of a life—from the perspective of professional civility, within a particular tradition, that of the professions. This view of human life harks back to the framework of profession as vocation, which provides a unity of public and private spheres of life through the idea of a calling, but which also permits distinction between them for balance. Both spheres are important, but distinct, areas of human engagement. In this sense, the problematic realm of the social, the importing of the private domain into the public, is a failed ordering of potentially rival practices.

Each human life partakes in its good as defined within the larger scope of the good for human beings, and the virtues serve to foster a particular type of unity of a life. The context of a particular life shapes the content of various virtues. The specific content of a given virtue, such as patience, for example, is determined by the hierarchy of goods in our lives (MacIntyre, 2007, pp. 202–203). In fact, some virtues only make sense in the context of a whole human life—for instance, the virtue of integrity or constancy. This point highlights the possibility of communicative content for the virtues of patience, courage, fortitude, and the others. Many of these virtues, in their communicative form, are specific to professional civility. The most important one is probably prudence, or restraint; these points will be developed in a later chapter.

Contemporary life has been segmented and fragmented, so achieving unity in a life is difficult. The virtues cannot function in a fragmented life, because there is nothing to direct their action, nothing for them to support. The virtues need the unity of a whole life (MacIntyre, 2007, p. 205). In similar fashion, our lives only make sense as a type of narrative. The meaning-making significance of narrative seems to be fundamental to the human condition, a point noted by Arendt (1958). The treatment of professional civility offered here highlights the importance of multiple spheres of life that function together to create a whole life without collapsing into one another, narrating the story of a complete life with coherence and fidelity (Fisher, 1987).

In the communicative realm, virtuous practices emerge in particular forms in public and private life. Professional civility as a public communicative virtue has a private counterpart—Troup and Fulmer's (2007) treatment of domestic courtesy as communicative action within the family context. Holba's (2007) work on recuperative leisure fits into this framework through highlighting the importance of submitting to the discipline of a craft, artistic practice, or performance as a way of restoring one's engagement with practices tied to elements of life other than work. Professional civility fits within a gestalt framework, gaining its meaning from a whole life (Arnett, 2006).

Professional civility requires thinking about life in a particular way. Professional work is not just doing a job (Cheney, Lair, Ritz, & Kendall, 2010), but engaging a calling. Phenomenology focuses on how we "turn" toward those various spheres of life, and the nature of the turning makes a great deal of difference in the life of a professional (Squires, 2005). Likewise, the unity of professional life is made complete through an ethic of service. Professional engagement invites a whole human life composed of public and private domains, as well as a commitment to service to the human community. The communicative virtue of professional civility presupposes a life that has public, private, leisure, and service dimensions in various proportions appropriate to one's state of life.

Professional civility as virtue works out its application within the context of a given profession in its instantiation within a particular organizational setting. Professional civility functions in the area of public communicative social relations, but it is part of the gestalt of an entire professional life in its modality as a communicative ethic, in that a "good" professional life/role is part of a whole good life. This understanding fits with the history and tradition of professions as a type of life in a broader context—life as involving labor, work, and action as a good life. Professional civility provides the possibility of a restored unity of life through cultivation of an ethic of service, which becomes once again an integral part of "profession." Professional civility supports this possibility among professionals in their day-to-day activity as they live out virtuous communicative action in everyday life in organizations.

MacIntyre's (2007) work can be read as supporting the perspective articulated in the next section, which assists our understanding of professions as contributing to the good of human communities through marketplace and civic participation. The narrative of a single human life as a bearer of a tradition of practice gives shape to the type of life one lives out and helps to make a life of one sort rather than another. The traditions of practice and the communities that human beings inhabit, and to which they contribute, provide a context for the contribution of particular persons' gifts and capabilities that serve to build up the communities of which they are a part.

Practices, Traditions, and Persons

MacIntyre (2007) went on to say that our individual lives are embedded within larger communities and narrative traditions. We know what we are about when we know the stories in which we participate (p. 216): "The story of my life is always embedded in the story of those communities from which I derive my identity" (p. 221). We are characters in a narrative; this identity gives our lives unity and is part of that telic substance needed to order the goods in our lives. Part of the good for any individual human being is the good for human beings in general, which permits all of our goods to share in that larger good of which professions are a part. We learn the good as we move toward it and seek after it—always in a community context. The virtues, therefore, play a part in an individual life as part of a larger context. We are part of a history—a past that is in our present—we are part of a tradition, and we are "bearers of a tradition" (p. 221). This tradition is the history of a practice, and it consists of the movement of a practice through generations that have contributed to its meaning and shaped and reshaped it. Therefore, we have responsibilities to our professions: "Virtues sustain the relationships required for practices" (p. 221), including relationships to the past, future, and present.

Traditions are an important part of MacIntyre's (2007) virtue ethics framework, providing ground and historical context for both practices and individual lives. A tradition is "partially constituted by an argument about the goods the pursuit of which gives to that tradition its particular point and purpose" (p. 222). Professions are traditions in that sense. Vital traditions are marked by conflict (p. 222), because arguments about what the good is for a particular practice or tradition imply a sense of life and movement. Arnett et al. (2009) noted the challenges to particular communities of memory within organizational contexts by rival conceptions of an organization's narrative, and professions engage in dispute or conflict over what a profession is or what constitutes a profession, as noted by Kimball (1995). Persons are embedded in a number of traditions that make an individual life intelligible, highlighting the value of understanding an entire human life as a context for professional action and its accompanying professional civility.

Conclusion

Virtues, practices, traditions, and professional civility are related thus: Virtues sustain practices, traditions, and relationships that make goods internal to practices achievable. Practices and lives are given meaning by traditions. Practices have histories, are part of traditions, and help constitute traditions. Virtues, including the communicative virtue of professional civility, help persons within narratives accomplish practices that embody traditions.

Professions' goods are rooted in the "real and true" good for human beings that derives from their ontology as beings in the world who labor, work, and act (Arendt, 1958) in particular locations with particular others and within particular professional traditions. Professional civility recognizes the importance of participation through productivity with others in a larger whole, defining a common order in two senses: the institution or organization, and the profession. The framework of rules and precepts defining the role structure of a particular organization defines the expectations of a local place, and it is within this structure that purposes are formed that give intelligibility to life and action at the local level. This point resonates with the notion of "place" as a good of professional civility. Morality and ethics are tied to the socially local and particular—the local home, in Arnett's (1992) terms. At the level of the profession, MacIntyre (2007) noted, an important virtue is having a sense of the traditions to which one belongs, or with which one is confronted (p. 223). A sense of the history of a profession provides context and continuity for professional work; professional civility helps ensure the durability of a professional tradition. The others with whom one works join cooperatively with the productive purposes that give organizational life meaning, forming a community of co-laborers, workers, and actors in the organizational setting.

The next chapter traces Kimball's (1995) history of the professional ideal in the United States, identifying goods of productivity, place, and person in terms of MacIntyre's framework. Kimball's work is extended by Sullivan (2005), who issued an invitation to recall the original purposes of the tradition of professions, which has come into question over the last decades, offering the virtue of civic professionalism as a way to return to the lost ideal inherent in profession as practice. This story of the professions is one of the elements of the background against which professional civility takes shape, along with a conceptualization of civility as communicative virtue. The roots of the story of the profession still have life, and their connection to the virtue of civility rests partly in the notion of professionalism, an orientation to work and life that reflects, in popular summary form, the goods of traditional professional practice.

2

The Tradition of Profession as Practice

Introduction

This chapter grounds an understanding of professions in the scholarship of Kimball (1995), Sullivan (2005), and Arendt (1958), in a move toward a communicative phenomenology of work in which the tasks of professions are engaged as mean-ing-filled human action (Arnett & Holba, in press) relevant to human life and flourishing as a foundation for an ethic of professional civility. Kimball offered a history of the professional ideal in America, and Sullivan reminded us of the importance of service and civic engagement as elements of professional identity, focusing on "professionalism" as an implicit virtue associated with professions, in his treatment of the crisis and promise of professionalism in America. Their work provides evidence that professions define communities of practice with a tradition and history. Arendt offered an understanding of labor, work, and action as exis-tential realities shaping the human condition, to which professions as communi-ties of practice offer a response, guided by an understanding of the good life. In this context, professional life becomes an arena for the operation of the commu-nicative virtue of professional civility, which protects and promotes the goods of profession(s) through constructive interpersonal interaction.

An exploration of the literature on professions and professionals supports the idea that the professions constitute a practice with a history that defines a tradition in the MacIntyrean sense (Borden, 2007; MacIntyre, 2007). The professional tradition carries virtues that enable the achievement of goods defining the practice of professions; those who practice professions are embedded in, and interact in, communities that protect and promote the goods of practice (Arnett, Fritz, & Bell, 2009). Part of the tradition of professions is the understanding that professions contribute to the good of human flourishing, an assumption reflected in the work of many scholars of the professions and related areas. Members of the professions, or professionals, as the embodiment of professional ideals, carry the goods of professions through their engagement of professional practice and interaction. This engagement of goods typically takes place within an organizational setting in cooperation with others and within the economic constraints of contemporary capitalism (Noordegraaf, 2007), conditions that have shifted the context within which professions do their work, but which have not eradicated the tradition of professions.

To establish these claims, I examine the history of the term "profession" and the idea of a professional practitioner. Employing Kimball (1995) in particular, I trace the general contours of behaviors expected of a member of the professions as the "ideal" changed over time. Despite these changes, the concept retained important coordinates defining expectations for professional action; although the cultural ideal changed concurrently with shifts in the story, the behavioral expectations and essential ethic remained anchored in the idea of a dignified vocation or calling dedicated to civic service. The different "moments" of the meaning of "profession" have contributed to the ongoing tradition, enriching it and providing resources for ethical practice—shaping, as Barge and Little (2008) noted, "the Discourses that inform a tradition or a community of practice" (p. 513). The work of Arendt (1958) on different types of engagement of activity in the world—labor, work, and action—is relevant to definitions of the professions, and Sullivan (2005) provided a current treatment of professionalism, including contemporary concerns with the status of the professions and professionals, which intersects with the work of Kimball. Sullivan's original treatment was written in 1995, with an updated second edition published in 2005; a comparison of these observations provides a brief glimpse of a decade of continuity and change in the context of professional work and its ongoing ideal as it has moved into the twenty-first century. In this chapter, I focus on establishing the general category of "profession" as a practice as defined by MacIntyre (2007).

The True Professional Ideal

The "professional ideal" in America, identified as the culmination of profession as practice carried by a tradition, was articulated by Kimball (1995) in this manner: "Ideally, a 'profession' is a dignified occupation espousing an ethic of service, organized into an association, and practicing functional science" (p. 17). Sullivan's (2005) treatment included these three major attributes as enduring elements of professions. Larson (1977) cited Goode on the special community of professions (p. 55), who noted eight characteristics of professions, including a distinct identity; continuing membership in a community of practice; shared values; a role definition for members and nonmembers that is agreed upon and identical for all members of the profession; a common language; acknowledged community authority over members of the profession; clear definition of social, rather than physical or geographical, membership boundaries; and self-reproduction through the process of socialization of new members. Two important implications of membership in a profession that Larson highlighted are that "professions are characterized by a minimal equality among the members" with respect to definition of occupational role, and they operate according to an "ideology of participation among equals" (p. 55)—what Sullivan (2005) referred to as a collegial organization of work (pp. 11, 13).

The behaviors and communicative practices associated with professions and professionals emerge from the work of Kimball (1995) and other scholars of the professions (e.g., Gardner, 2007; Gardner, Csikszentmihalyi, & Damon, 2001; Larson, 1977; Selznick, 1992/1994; Sullivan, 2005), as well as scholars of professional ethics specifically (e.g., L. May, 1996; W. F. May, 2001). These norms are the interactive features of Kimball's "true professional ideal." This ideal points to both a telos, or a purpose or end, and a context within which that telos is realized for the professions in general, just as specific professions have a telos and associated contexts within which that telos is realized (e.g., Borden, 2007). Identifying the telos of professions as a general category permits defining goods internal to profession(s) as metapractice, within the context of which can be situated the idea of professional civility as communicative virtue in organizational life and as architectonic, or idealized formation (Kimball, 1995), of professional behavior. This foundation will provide a starting point for an enlarged analysis of conditions under which a tradition of professional practice can contribute to a flourishing human life in contexts of the private sphere, organizations, and communities. Elements in the larger scope of the term's domain include the practice of philosophical leisure (Holba, 2007) as part of a dignified style of life (Sullivan, 1995, p. 6) and a commitment to a rich private life (Arnett, 2006), which makes participation in the public realm of organizations distinctive and meaningful.

As reviewed in the previous chapter, a practice, in MacIntyre's (2007) terms, is defined as follows:

> [A]ny coherent and complex form of socially established cooperative human activity through which goods internal to that form of activity are realized in the course of trying to achieve those standards of excellence which are appropriate to, and partially definitive of, that form of activity, with the result that human powers to achieve excellence, and human conceptions of the ends and goods involved, are systematically extended. (p. 187)

A profession, generally considered, is a socially established and cooperative human activity embedded within a tradition and aimed at some good end (see W. F. May, 2001). A tradition is a "historically situated, ongoing argument about what constitutes the good life" (MacIntyre, p. 13). This sense of a tradition of the professions permits a definition of what the goods and telos of a profession are (Pellegrino, 1995) and what is required to be a good professional, understood as a good practitioner of a profession. Following MacIntyre, virtues are needed to realize and extend the internal goods of profession(s) as practice (see Borden, 2007).

Borden (2007) added extra elements to the definition of practice from a close reading of MacIntyre: technical skills, a distinct overriding purpose, a moral community that can maintain a level of relationships needed to achieve the practice's internal goods, partial definition of members' way of life, operation within an institutional context, and formal social organization to push back institutional corruption. The story of the professions, as told by Kimball (1995), Sullivan (2005), and other scholars of the professions, shows professions to include these elements. A profession—that is, the general category of "profession," or "metaprofession"—is a practice with a history (Kimball, 1995; MacIntyre, 2007) exhibiting all the hallmarks of a tradition: it has endured through time and has developed through successive stages, with each stage maintaining and contributing elements to the successive ones. Professions have a telos, or end, and internal goods that help realize that telos—goods that can be realized only through professional practice.

The overarching goods internal to this practice of professions that are protected and promoted by professional civility as a communicative virtue are fourfold: productivity, or the work that is accomplished through the "craft" skill (Sennett, 2008; Sullivan, 2005, p. 11) of professions; place, or the local institutional home (Arnett, 1992) within which professional work is engaged; persons, or the human beings with whom one works (as well as the clients whom one serves, the original focus of concern and care; see, for example, Charleton, 1996); and the profession itself, the larger occupational community that provides identity and guidelines for practice for the professional practitioner. Professional civility is the communicative enactment of the professional ideal—communicative virtue at work. The next sections explore profession(s) as a MacIntyrean (2007) practice.

Profession(s) as Tradition(s) of Practice

A profession, as Kimball (1995) stated, historically pointed to particular cultural ideals and values (p. 9) that defined expectations for behavior for those claiming identity as a practitioner. These expectations can be understood to define a professional ethic guiding professions as a practice with a tradition. This professional ethic had its origin in goods defined, protected, and promoted through the practices of the original professions, became part of the tradition of professions more broadly conceived, and now lives on in a wider scope of shared public expectations for what a professional is and does—the virtue of professionalism (Sullivan, 2005, p. 37).

Several bodies of literature inform the contours of profession as tradition of practice recognized by practitioners of professions and by society at large. This understanding is implicit in the extensive and multi-disciplinary scholarly work in the area of professions in the twentieth century (Kimball, 1995, pp. 309–310) and onward, which ranges from critical treatments of professions as ideological formations (e.g., Ashcraft & Allen, 2003; Larson, 1977) to histories of various professions in the United States, such as higher education, law, medicine, the clergy, the military, science, engineering, journalism, government service, psychology and counseling, and management (e.g., Hatch, 1988). Disciplines hosting research on professions and professionals include communication studies, discourse studies, history, occupational psychology, and sociology.

Scholars of the professions have not come to a consensus on a definition of the term "profession" or of the defining attributes of a profession (Barber, 1963; Kimball, 1995; see also Becker 1962, Cogan, 1953, and Greenwood, 1957, as cited in Kimball, 1995). Many scholars assume that occupations known as professions came to be called professions "'by common consent'" (Carr-Saunders & Wilson, as cited in Kimball, p. 1), or that professions were developed by the middle class during the industrialization and urbanization of the late nineteenth and early twentieth centuries (a view that Kimball challenges; see p. 199). Larson (1977) stated that professionals are those who have esoteric knowledge that is important for the good of society and that "professions were and are means of earning an income on the basis of transacted services" (p. 9). Sullivan (2005) offered the commonly accepted depiction of a profession:

> [A]n occupation characterized by three features: specialized training in a field of codified knowledge usually acquired by formal education and apprenticeship, public recognition of a certain autonomy on the part of the community of practitioners to regulate their own standards of practice, and a commitment to provide service to the public that goes beyond the economic welfare of the practitioner. (p. 36)

These attributes, as mentioned earlier, define the three elements of the professional ideal articulated by Kimball (1995). Barber (1963) included the criterion of work done as an end in itself as one of the elements of a profession.

Theology, law, medicine, and education have historically been identified as "the four great traditional professions" (Kimball, 1995, p. 6; Larson, 1977, pp. 4–5). These four professions were understood as encompassing sets of expected virtuous practices derived from underlying philosophies of vocation or work as a religious calling. Kimball's (1995) history of the "true professional ideal" in the United States ties this history to a rhetoric of the term "profession," demonstrating how, in particular historical moments, a leading profession drew its strength from the ideals connected with that term and, in turn, shaped the term in reflexive fashion. In this sense, the "true professional ideal" identified by Kimball reveals a practice with a tradition, in MacIntyre's (2007) framework.

The English term "profession" comes from a Latin verb meaning to declare or avow publicly. The word "professed" was employed only in its reference to religious matters throughout the Middle Ages (Kimball, 1995, p. 19). By the sixteenth century, it referred to making any vow, including declaring oneself proficient in a craft or art. The noun "profession" meant a promise or vow made on entering a religious order. It gradually came to refer not to the vow itself but to the act of joining, and then was used to refer to the group of persons who made a particular vow (Kimball, 1995, p. 19). The meaning of the term also extended, in popular understanding, beyond a religious group to encompass any occupation.

These shifts in meaning are part of what Kimball (1995) identified as six moments in the rhetoric of profession that identify changes in the term "professional," the term's usage, and its cognates. These moments mark the narrative tradition of "profession" as practice in the United States. Kimball's history identified features of the professions and their practitioners that denote goods of a profession to be protected and promoted by the communicative virtue of professional civility.

The Term "Profession": Continuity and Change in the Tradition

The meanings of the term "profession" and its cognates, professor, professed, and professional, have changed over the course of the last four centuries in America (Kimball, 1995). First, the term "profession" was extended from referring to a religious vow to the action of joining and belonging to a group, and then to the group making the vow. Kimball's treatment stressed the reflexive nature of rhetoric, language, and discourse in relation to understanding, articulation, and practice of professions. As cultural ideals, associated dominant forms of knowledge, and the status of the preeminent vocation that upheld the ideal changed, "changes occurred in the way people thought and spoke about 'profession'" (Kimball, 1995, p. 198).

This first moment in the rhetoric of professions is important because it begins the shift to valuing ordinary life (Taylor, 1989) that characterized a new ideology of espoused equality of secular and religious occupations. Next, the sense of a general calling and particular calling that were joined in the occupation of clergy moved apart again, with the term "profession" carrying with it the sense of dignity it had gained from being associated with vocations affiliated with theology. The term once more pointed to an occupation—but now it pointed to any dignified, non-religious occupation. All occupations became dignified as the fulfillment of a Christian's spiritual calling (Kimball, 1995). That dignifying shift elevated the vocational sense of the term profession—the sense of being called or chosen to engage in a particular occupation or endeavor—and that sense of calling to a particular occupation became paramount while the reference to religious vows declined. That was the second moment in the rhetoric of professions. Here, the emphasis on ordinary life continued, and the understanding of "profession" and "professional" expanded. The application of the term "profession" to many vocations, both dignified and ostensibly less so, was still occurring, although theology's link with law and education led to the term's particular application to these two occupations.

The third moment was marked by the introduction of the terms "learned professions" and "liberal professions," signifying both education and a breadth and generosity of thought and character, as well as access to financial resources, which led to an increased narrowing of the term's scope and a connection to status and class. An ethic of selfless service associated with the term "profession" was attributed to theology's preeminence as an occupation—its status as "architectonic," or leading, guiding, and defining, profession (Kimball, 1995, p. 10)—during the seventeenth and eighteenth centuries. Around the end of the nineteenth century, the legal profession rose to prominence, accompanied by a shift in the understanding of the interconnection of members of society as contractual rather than covenantal, a change accompanying an increasing focus on commerce and the marketplace as a foundational metaphor for social relations. This shift reflected a change in the cultural ideal from "religion" to "polity" noted by Kimball (1995).

The fourth moment was defined by the new prominence of the term "professional," rather than the term "professed," as the adjective denoting "occupational" or "vocational." This shift was initiated by legal practitioners, who continued to invoke an ethic of selfless service, following the respected tradition of theology. The fourth moment describes the rise of politics and the law as the ideal professions as the sense of constructing and nurturing a political society or public sphere took precedence over an emphasis on theology and religious framings of social life. Law became the architectonic profession (Kimball, 1995, p. 302). During this time, our contemporary understanding of "professional" as "vocational" emerged. The legal profession shifted the usage from "professed" to "professional," but continued to embrace the sense of dignity and ethic of service of those working in the realm of theology.

This transferred meaning worked reflexively; law practitioners, who inherited this sense of the term "profession," acted into that meaning and adopted the original sense of the term (Kimball, 1995). In turn, the term itself picked up additional meaning from the vocational ethos of lawyers. The most noted shift was that "profession" and "professional service" now signified a contractual commitment to a client to provide services, for which the professional practitioner received a fee (Kimball, 1995). Accompanying this change was the emergence of the professional association or society, which provided an institutional identity for members of particular professions (Kimball, 1995). The theological ethic of service and selflessness remained, so the shift was an additive one. In this fashion, the term "profession" became disembedded from one story, that of the larger society and its structure and needs, and became embedded within a distinctive, developing story of a professional polity. The connection to the larger community remained, however, at the same time that "profession" came to denote this more narrow sense, because the connotation of service to the larger society remained. Likewise, the roots of the expectations for what I define as professional civility as proper behavior befitting someone dedicated to service to others stayed secure through the shift.

The fifth moment, occurring between the 1860s and 1910s, was marked by the ascendance of education beyond the legal profession as the preeminent profession, with the term "professor" now referring to someone in an educational occupation (Kimball, 1995). This shift occurred "as 'science' became the architectonic and the fundament of cultural legitimacy.…[and] the field of education emerged for a brief period as the most attractive among the 'learned professions'" (Kimball, 1995, pp. 302–303). The sixth moment, taking place in the early twentieth century, notes the return of the term "professional" to refer to many occupations, as it had done before in eighteenth-century English nomenclature, with subsequent decline in usage of the terms "learned" and "liberal" as descriptors of professions (Kimball, 1995). By this time, the profession of medicine, based on the sciences, had risen in ascendency (Kimball, 1995). As an example of the power of this shift, Mary Parker Follett, writing in the 1920s, adopted the nomenclature of "profession" for management, noting its foundation in science and service (Follett, 1941).

The Contemporary Moment of the Professions

Sullivan's (2005) narrative intersects with Kimball's (1995) in the twentieth-century world of the professions and continues the story, turning attention to the contemporary moment of the professions in the United States. Sullivan continued the focus on professional ethics, the telos of a profession, and the possibility of what I am proposing as the communicative virtue of professional civility as he sought to recall professionals to a lost ideal. Sullivan's focus on the crisis of professionalism will emerge in greater detail in the final chapter, which treats the good of profession. The concerns expressed in Sullivan's 1995 volume remain largely the same in his 2005 treatment, which covers additional developments in the intervening decade.

Sullivan (2005) addressed the continuing question of which occupations are considered professions, a question appearing in his 1995 work. In 1995, Sullivan noted that twenty percent of the workforce was classified as professional or managerial (p. xiv), stating, as did Kimball (1995), that "[p]rofessional is a very loosely defined term[,]" originally referring "to the classic honorific occupations of medicine, the bar, and the clergy" (Sullivan, 1995, p. 2). The same statement indicating loose definition held true in 2005, with government, health care, and education still identified as major homes of professional work, echoing Kimball's (1995) discussion of the learned professions of church and university as distinguished from the trades and artisans by a liberal education. Sullivan (1995) stated that the ideal of professionalism articulated by reformers in Great Britain and the U.S. portrayed highly skilled workers with a sense of calling to significant social responsibility, bringing to occupations an almost religious dedication combined with civic ideals "respecting diverse viewpoints, while aiming at a consensus about common purposes" (p. xvi). In 2005, as in 1995, Sullivan highlighted the professions' contribution to human flourishing: "An authentic profession…is a way of life with public value" (Sullivan, 2005, p. 39).

Professional status is a sought-after achievement for both individual persons and occupational groups (Sullivan, 2005, p. 38)—as Noordegraaf (2007) noted, "Nowadays, indeed, almost everyone wants to become professional" (p. 761), with the attractiveness of occupations assumed to be enhanced by professionalization. As Larson (1977) wrote, "The quest for professional status spread as a typical concern of educated middle class occupations, promising individual advancement through collective efforts" (p. 155). The power and prestige associated with professionalism come from a profession's value to society, but the ideal professional, as noted by Kimball (1995), serves with a sense of commitment to the common good that goes beyond contractual obligations, understanding professional work as a calling to serve the larger public good. The true professional is devoted to public service beyond monetary gain. Therefore, professional status carries with it a strong sense of social obligation. As Sullivan (2005) stated,

> Becoming professional is a key dimension of success for occupational groups as well as for individuals. The very dispute over just which occupations deserve to be called professions indicates the symbolic power of the designation 'professional.'…Professional work…requires the practitioner to adhere to demanding standards of competence and public service. (p. 38)

Sullivan (2005) noted, as did Kultgen (1988), that the ideal of professionalism came to be seen as an aspiration for every occupation, redeeming the single-minded, narrow focus of technical expertise by resituating it within a moral framework supporting the good of society and tending toward service rather than purely self-serving ends. Competence, dedication, and service, the values of traditional professionalism, could enrich and rejuvenate the meaning and significance of all work. Sullivan recommended that "positive features of professionalism must be extended to all work in the modern economy" (p. 160). The variety of occupations and activities seeking professional status continues to increase; "[f]inancial planners, information technology workers, biotechnologists, architects, journalists, designers, translators—even cartoonists, body piercers, and pet sitters portray and organize themselves as professionals" (Noordegraaf, 2007, p. 762).

Professional Identity and Professionalism

Approaches to the professions as centers for identities and communicative expectations include the work of Barge and Little (2008), which focuses on discourses of the professions and examines communicative elements, such as skilled practice, that define professional interaction. Friedson (1991) noted particular rules of etiquette defining "professionalism," pointing to a protonorm (Christians & Traber, 1997) of professional civility as an ethical ideal for professions (Sullivan, 2005) guiding communicative interaction. Professionalism as an ethical orientation is specifically identified within professional groups as an expected standard for conduct and rests at the level of public understanding as a desirable and valued approach to work and others (e.g., Anderson & Bolt, 2011; Maister, 1997).

Professional identity, in its enactment as professionalism, is not limited to workplace behavior, however. Professionalism emerges from an underlying philosophy of life connecting one's occupational calling with the totality of a life, extending beyond the workplace into other existential spheres of a responsible and responsive human being. For example, Anderson and Bolt (2011) discussed professionalism as "appropriate workplace behavior" (p. xiii), but they included elements of private life, as well, as part of what being a professional—embodying profession-alism as a way of life—entails. Personal financial management, etiquette, proper attire (see also Leoussi, 1996), how to communicate appropriately and "deal with conflict, teamwork, and accountability in a fair and ethical manner" (p. xiii)—all work together to form professionalism, which Anderson and Bolt referred to as "soft but vital skills" (p. xiii). Professionalism encompasses a number of workplace con-cerns, ranging from productivity (Anderson & Bolt, 2011, p. 91) to avoiding foul language (Anderson & Bolt, 2011, p. 134). Professional behavior is contrasted with incivility in a section on bullying, including a definition of "unprofessional" and "rude" behavior (Anderson & Bolt, 2011, p. 176).

Professions relate to the larger community through a model of trust unique among occupations; "[t]he professions depend upon a kind of social compact of reciprocal trust and good faith between the practitioners and the publics they serve" (Sullivan, 2005, p. 37). Professions are distinctively devoted to the commu-nity and are distinguished by a "special dedication and clear accountability" that differentiates the professions from the trades and business (Sullivan, 2005, p. 5). As Sullivan (2005) put it, "A profession is 'in business' for the common good as well as for the good of its members, or it is not a profession" (p. 5).

One example of the expectation that professionals will serve the public good is work done *pro bono publico*. This giving to contribute to the public good is "the eth-ical spirit of civic life manifested and given specific direction in professional life: the spirit of profession as a calling" (Sullivan, 1995, p. 10). From Sullivan, we see that the "good" embraced by professions includes the "goods" of useful labor in service to others and the resulting common good to the community that these goods entail.

Kimball (1995) used the term "architectonic" to refer to a "dominant science or discipline" that provides "systematic formalization to the highest values and ideals of the culture" (p. 12) and a "coherent, rationalized order" among philoso-phies or ideologies, explaining how a belief system comes to have "intellectual sov-ereignty" (p. 13). The architectonic is one belief system among many that comes to serve as the reference point for all other systems, ordering them within its framework. Using "architectonic" to refer to "profession" as an idealized occupation permits rec-ognizing ultimate ends and values promoted by the idea of professionalism at a given point in time in relation to the culture that sustains it. Profession as the architec-tonic occupation describes a set of ideas and understandings that function to define "ultimate ends and highest values" (p. 13), or a telos, associated with the idea of occu-pations, of which "profession" is the ideal (see Kultgen, 1998). The attributes of "pro-fession" as architectonic vocation form the professional ideal that has emerged, however generally, in the attributes marking professions mentioned here: specialized training, contribution to human ends and flourishing, an ethical code or set of guidelines, and a history and tradition of practice.

Today, there remains ambiguity about which occupations are to be considered professional (Sullivan, 2005, pp. 37–38), and to the extent that they manifest what could be considered the minimal defining characteristics of specialized knowledge and training, relative autonomy and self-regulation, and a commitment to public service, occupations can be said to be "professional," whether or not they are licensed (Sullivan, 2005). As Kimball (1995) stated, "professional" eventually began to refer to many occupations, just as it had in eighteenth-century English. However, the designation "professional" still invokes high status and carries with it expectations for competence and public service (Sullivan, 2005).

Over the course of the development of the professional ideal in the United States, several sets of terms—professions, the trades, and business; learned professions and mechanic professions—served to differentiate various occupations (Kimball, 1995), with learned and liberal professions serving as interchangeable terms. The general occupation of business was eventually recognized as a profession (Kimball, 1995). Although at first relegated to the trades rather than the "professions" (Kimball, 1995, p. 9), business-related occupations gained status and came to be referred to by many scholars as emerging or marginal professions (Kimball, 1995). Parsons (cited in Kimball, 1995), from a functionalist perspective, at first excluded business from the professions, but eventually included it because it was "functionally and rationally organized" (Kimball, 1995, p. 9). Brandeis argued that business should be (indeed, already was) one of the professions, in order to curb its acquisitiveness and call it to altruism (Tawney, 1920, as cited in Kimball, 1995). Durkheim also made such a recommendation (Barber, 1963). Flexner (1915/2001) noted the defining feature of profession as "professional spirit" (p. 165) and indicated that all activities have the potential to be approached with this "genuine" (p. 165) attitude of unselfishness and of striving to make the world a better place. Trades "rise toward the professional level" (p. 165) to the extent that they are carried on with this sense of obligation to the greater good.

Because of these shifts in understanding of the nature of professions and the development of the tradition of professions such that their associated attributes took on a socially recognized form, the tradition has expanded to accommodate many occupations. Krause (1996), for example, highlighted the professionalization of baseball and social work (p. 31), which took place after the Civil War, as an indicator of the expanding realm of professions during the nineteenth century. However, the ideal remains consistent, as Sullivan (2005) noted. Kultgen (1998) observed that there is much to be admired in the professional ideal, and that more occupations should take on the attributes of a profession. Just as professionalism in a religious sense "reflected the highest ends and values…of colonial culture" (Kimball, 1995, p. 22), the professions today represent the architectonic occupation.

Arendt (1958) offered a perspective on occupations and their potential classification as she traced the distinction between, and conflation of, manual and intellectual labor, between labor of the hand and labor of the head. The question of productivity—is any "thing" produced by the work?—marks the identifying feature of labor and work as distinct from action. Much of the work we term today as done by "professionals" was once done by scribes, servants of the court, elevated in time to positions of rank within a bureaucratic system (see Elias, 1982). These "unproductive" professional positions, as Adam Smith would label them (Arendt, 1958, pp. 85–86, 93), generate "work" that perishes visibly at the moment of production. Arendt (1958) described this type of work as "the products of action and speech" (p. 95).

This type of "nonproductive" work depends for its existence upon others who will see, hear, remember, and transform it. Because of its transitory nature, this type of professional work is, by definition, cooperative. Professions themselves, and the institutions that provide a context for their work, are cooperative endeavors generated by the transitory work defined by the thought and action of many of today's professionals. Much professional work resembles action, too, in its manifestation as performative activity and speech. It is not accomplished alone (Arendt, 1958). (The work of health care professionals, to the extent that their work involves the physical, corporeal being of others, could be considered as generating a type of "action," in that the "product" is activity corresponding to part of another human being. Although the product of such work is visible or discernible, it is not so much "world building" as providing the means by which persons may continue to participate in the public sphere, and much of the work of consulting with others about health takes place purely in the sphere of "action," with no visible product resulting.)

For the purposes of this project, when an occupation is engaged with dignity and with the recognition that it has significance for human existence (Flexner, 1915/2001), it can be experienced as reflecting the architectonic "profession" to some degree and could be supported by the communicative virtue of professional civility, although the primary domain of the concept as I develop it here is the currently expanded notion of "profession" as directed primarily toward service-oriented, white- or pink- or even gray-collar occupations, including business and management, engaging task activities that resemble Arendt's notion of action, or that translate directly or indirectly into production of some intellective product or service. The move to professionalize multiple occupations (Noordegraaf, 2007) and the efforts on the part of some firms, such as construction companies, to elevate expectations for professional communicative behavior in the presence of customers (e.g., Galanti, 1986), suggests that the interactional attributes of professions are adoptable by any vocation (Kultgen, 1998), with the understanding that dignified work is defined by how one engages the work and others with whom one works (Noordegraaf, 2007). The notion of "profession," then, is connected with its embodiment in its practitioners, or professionals, its intimately affiliated term, which has necessarily shared a history with the term "profession," but now carries a connotation of its own still closely associated with "profession" but occupying a broader domain. Noordegraaf's (2007) discussion of pure, situated, and hybridized professionalism captures this sense well; he argued that professional work is experiential and inferential, less about occupational and organizational control than about enacting professionalism through "meaningful and legitimate work practices" (p. 778).

Goods of Professions

From this history, we gather important components of what a profession is, what members of society at large consider a profession to be, expectations for professional communicative behavior, how professional identities are constructed, and how professions relate to the larger society and to particular institutions in which their work is carried out. Members of the professions "know how to behave and also appear professionally. They know how to act, speak, and dress; they know how to act as professional[s]," even when they are not engaged in the specific tasks of the profession (Noordegraaf, 2007, p. 766). These elements provide a definition of the tradition of profession, its status as a practice, and the conferral of legitimacy of profession as social formation by external audiences. The professional ideal that eventually emerged from the changing moments in the rhetoric of "profession" forms the telos or set of goods guiding the virtue structure of professions that professional civility as communicative virtue protects and promotes: the goods of productivity, place, persons, and profession.

Productivity

Productivity is both a good in itself and a good that fits within the larger web of goods in professional civility, including place and persons. Productivity permits the organization to thrive and contributes to the realization of the good of persons as contributing beings. The good of productivity is seen in the purpose of the professions and emerges as part of the tradition of professions as an element of the human good assumed by that tradition and addressed by Arendt (1958) and as discussed by contemporary authors (e.g., Gardner et al., 2001). Work is the central element of professional identity; in Sullivan's (2005) words, "[p]rofessionalism seeks freedom in and through significant work, not by escaping from it" (p. 15). Work is a manifestation of an urge or impulse endemic to the human creature; the concentrated effort required by work is visible very early in human development (Gardner et al., 2001, p. 15); professional work invites reflection on the practices engaged in accomplishing the tasks of a worthwhile occupation (Schöen, 1983).

The work or action each profession contributes to the public sphere is a practice with internal goods. Each profession is also a good for the human community, defining some factor that enhances and guarantees human flourishing (Noordegraaf, 2007). In the case of theology, a connection to the divine is understood as a necessary part of human being (Kimball, 1995). The human being and human community need health as a good (Arnett et al., 2009), and the medical profession guards that good. Coordinating human interaction to guarantee a minimum of procedural justice is a foundational element of human being, which the law profession and its practitioners guard (Kimball, 1995). Education guards the way of life of a people, ensuring minimum literacy and historical knowledge to preserve a community's continuity throughout time and over the generations (e.g., Brubacher & Rudy, 1997; Kimball, 1986). These four professions are prototypical for the current set of professions and other occupations functioning as professions, a group much larger in scope but with aims and ideals resonant with those of the traditional professions.

Place

Productivity is typically enacted within a place, as is noted by contemporary scholars of the professions (e.g., Noordegraaf, 2007). Work is done within the confines of an organization, which needs to be protected and promoted by those working within it. As Sullivan noted, "Professionals in their organizational lives must be active citizens, committed to working out a common good as new problems and possibilities arise" (Sullivan, 2005, p. 279). Without these institutional complexes that now define our social landscape, professional productivity would not take place. Therefore, the organization as a place is a good; Arnett et al. (2009) noted the importance of an organization's mission and identity as explicit components of an organizational communication ethic. Arnett and Arneson (1999) noted the risk of cynicism from unmet high expectations that may arise from inadequate or misplaced conceptualizations of the purposes of organizations. An organization is a particular place of work with a specific mission, and that particular place and mission need support. When we inhabit organizations, we are guests in that local home (Arnett, 1992) in order to do our professional work; we may become more closely connected to it if we are committed to it for the long haul, which may lead to our assuming an additional metaphorical role as stewards. We leave it better than we found it.

Today, as Noordegraaf (2007) noted, professionals are embedded within organizational systems. He reviewed a number of theorists who noted the rise of professional occupations termed program professionals, occupational professionals, quasi-managerial practitioners, and managing professionals. He drew on the work of Brint, who expanded the idea of professionalism from "traditional, elite professionalism toward expert professionalism" (Noordegraaf, 2007, p. 773), a professionalism characterized not only by academic standards, elitism, disciplinary training, and political progressivism, but also by training and skills valued in the market for services (Brint, 1994, cited in Noordegraaf, 2007, p. 773). The "managed professional business" that is home to the situated professional is essentially a business that works from a culture marked by collegiality, consensual decision-making, and professional autonomy characteristic of the traditional professions (Noordegraaf, 2007, p. 773).

Persons

The work of professions is done for persons, members of the human community. To the recipients of professional practice is now added the corollary audience of coworkers—other professionals and those who work with and for professionals in varying capacities. Our work lives are accomplished with others and in relation to others (Sias, 2009a); organization is enacted within an institutional matrix of "getting things done efficiently while constructing and maintaining collegial relationships" (Holmes & Stubbe, 2003, p. 53). We carry civic and social responsibility for a variety of others in workplaces and beyond (Nakamura, 2007). One might also include clients in this category, but I will leave this point for another treatment. For now, the focus is on members of given institutions or organizational settings.

People or persons as participants in organizational communities are a good, and particular elements of people's lives need protection in organizations—specifically, their status as creative, producing persons and as contributors to the common good. Persons are ends in themselves, and therefore, their larger lives must be protected, as well—their ability to have a life outside of work and to maintain privacy and professional boundaries. However, that good may conflict with the goods of the organization and with productivity, as personal elements of one's life inevitably enter and influence the public sphere. The good of persons must be protected and promoted, held in creative, dynamic tension with these other goods. Hodson (2001) noted the role of coworkers in the quest for working with dignity (pp. 200–233); through affective and instrumental functions, the people with whom we work can provide assistance in getting work done and preventing abuse from management, for instance.

The goods of productivity, place, and persons are closely interconnected and can be separated only analytically. As an example of the interweaving of these areas of good, consider Sennett's (2008) description of the work of making the mobile phone—a type of productivity as I portray it here. He notes that the key to this new device lay in combining the technologies of the radio and the telephone, a challenging task that involved transforming the switching technology of the landline phone. The key to progress on this switching technology problem lay with the collaborative, cooperative teamwork at the companies that succeeded in this endeavor. Companies that were delayed in the breakthrough were characterized by internal competition in which information was hoarded (Sennett, 2008, pp. 32–33).

In this example, the good of productivity was intimately connected with the nature of the relationships among persons within teams in each organizational "place," shaped by the climate and culture of these institutions. Sharing information openly and freely worked, in this case, as a broad-based communicative virtue appropriately operative in a task context for groups that required creativity (Larson & Lafasto, 1989), manifesting as an element of professional civility in its work on behalf of these various goods. We see in this example that the various goods of profession work in conjunction with professional civility at various levels of engagement—and at differing levels of relative ordering or prominence for a particular context.

Profession

A profession exists as a type of good, as well; professions themselves sui generis constitute a good for human flourishing, as defined by the work they do (Gardner et al., 2001). Shön (1983) noted that our society's functioning is dependent on "professionals specially trained to carry out [society's business], whether it be making war and defending the nation, educating our children, diagnosing and curing disease, judging and punishing those who violate the law, settling disputes, managing industry and business, designing and constructing buildings, [and] helping those who for one reason or another are unable to fend for themselves" (p. 3). However, the very practice of a profession as an element of human phenomenological consciousness that demands allegiance, discipline, and adherence to something larger than the self is also a good, and the community of professionals that defines "profession" can be considered a good because it is something that emerges from, and identifies itself as something generated by, human productivity—this activity by human beings is a good. From a Christian perspective, those "made" or constructed things, whether ideational or material, are "goods" to the extent that such "work" or "action" mirrors the act of the Creator (Harrison, 2004; Naughton & Laczniak, 1993; Volf, 1991). The tradition of a profession thrives as it finds new soil to take root in with each new historical moment. Entering the story of a profession makes one a steward of a story with a duty to contribute to its flourishing.

Professional civility, through protection and promotion of the first three goods, protects and promotes the profession itself. As Sullivan (2005) noted, the professions have come under attack, often from within their own ranks: "It is now a commonplace that the prestige of the traditional professions is under siege....Lawyers now routinely expect denigration for their professional affiliation (even from other attorneys)" (pp. 42–43). Sullivan suggested a renewed sense of civic professionalism as a source of inspiration for professions, which are called to account by the public at large.

Sullivan's call is echoed in the work of many scholars of the professions today, who ask for a rethinking of the accountability of professionals both internally and externally (Gardner, 2007; Cheney, Lair, Ritz, & Kendall, 2010). The hope offered in the current project is that internal practices of professional civility will make attention to external audiences (e.g., communities) through service involvement possible. The "work" of professional civility is to restore and renew members of the professions through fostering a climate in the organizational setting within which the "good work" (Gardner et al., 2001) of the professions can take place.

Conclusion

This brief treatment of the goods of professions will be expanded in later chapters. Chapter 4, which develops the idea of professional civility, offers additional elaboration of how the components of civility as a communicative virtue meet these goods and become, through the framework of the professions within an organizational setting, professional civility. The theoretical foundations of conceptualizing each good of professions, and associated implications for the theoretical treatment of civility as communicative virtue in its move to professional civility as communicative virtue at work, find elaboration in Chapters 6, 7, and 8; the concluding chapter returns to the ongoing story of the professions, identifying implications suggested by the preceding chapters.

The next chapter explores civility through an examination of the development and elaboration of the concept of civility over time, with a particular focus on civility as civic virtue. I draw on work from several disciplines, primarily the communication field, to offer a conceptualization of civility as communicative virtue. Civility as communicative virtue joins the current treatment of professions as practice to form a background against which dialogic civility and organizational citizenship will be held up to reveal professional civility as communicative virtue at work.

3

The Communicative Virtue of Civility

Introduction

The topic of civility has held a prominent place in the cultural imagination of the West since medieval times. Civility has been associated with politeness, manners, and etiquette. Furthermore, it has been associated with the behavior found in royal courts (hence the etymology of the word "courtesy"), with morality, and with a particular class-based understanding of appropriate behavior (Carter, 1998; Davetian, 2007; Forni, 2002, 2008; Kingwell, 1995). In our contemporary moment, civility continues to hold the interest of the general public and scholars alike, and is addressed from multiple disciplinary perspectives. From humanities scholar P. M. Forni (2002, 2008), psychiatrist M. Scott Peck (1994), and legal scholar Steven Carter (1998), who are responsible for renewing popular interest in the topic of civility in the late twentieth and early twenty-first centuries, to Giovinella Gonthier and Kevin Morrisey (2002) and Rod L. Troester and Cathy Sargent Mester (2007), who address civility in the world of business, to communication theorists Ronald C. Arnett and Pat Arneson (1999), sociologists Edward Shils (1997) and Benet Davetian (2007), and philosopher Mark Kingwell (1995, 2000), who offer scholarly approaches to the topic, civility remains very much a part of our collective social imagination, a term signifying the interactive ideal for personal conduct in the public sphere.

In this chapter, I offer a selective treatment of civility as it has been understood in popular and scholarly work in order to conceptualize civility as a communicative virtue—the communicative manifestation of civic virtue in its protection and promotion of human social and pubic generativity through citizenship, understood as (rhetorical) action in the public sphere (Arendt, 1958); place, or the public sphere itself and its institutions; and persons, or social/political actors identified as both individual citizens and members of groups with interests in the public sphere (Habermas, 1984, 1987)—members of communities adhering to petite narratives (Lyotard, 1984), who must live and work together in an age of diversity and difference (Arnett, Fritz, & Bell, 2009). This broad conceptualization of civility as communicative virtue is the foundation for the more specific conceptualization of professional civility as communicative virtue in the workplace. Of particular interest is Kingwell's (1995) treatment of civility in relation to the sociolinguistic theory of politeness as an approach to "just talking" in the public deliberative sphere, and Davetian's (2007) understanding of civility practices across cultures, which highlights civility's fluid and situated nature.

Civility in Context

Civility and Civilization

Civility is a marker of civilization as civilized society, a state of human organization characterized by institutions such as a legal system, commerce, and education, and by citizens participating in matters concerning the good of the larger whole, including protection from outside forces (Ferguson, 1767/2004). Scottish Enlightenment author Adam Ferguson argued that it is the natural state of human beings to live in association with one another in civilized or "civil" society, contrary to Rousseau's claim of some pre-civilized "state of nature" imagined to be more characteristic of essential human existence (Davetian, 2007). Civility, for Ferguson, is connected with being a citizen—a social actor responsible for the welfare of the larger society. Civility is a moral call connected to action in the public sphere. The health of the public sphere depends upon the quality of interaction among members of society, which serves as a marker of the extent to which social actors are committed to the cooperative project of civic life and defines the discursive climate within which decisions affecting the larger community are made.

The French and English concept of civilization, according to Elias (1978), refers to people's attitudes and behaviors (p. 4), mirroring the German notion of kultivert (cultivated), which refers to "the highest form of being civilized" and "refers primarily to the form of people's conduct or behavior" (p. 5)—"a social quality of people," including "housing, their manners, their speech, [and] their clothing" (p. 5). The form of manners characteristic of civilized society, or of civility, shifts with time and with what Elias (1978) referred to as the civilizing process, but the concept of manners and culturally prescribed practices of civility endures, taking different forms in different cultures (Davetian, 2007). Practices of civility, despite real variations, manifest a common set of social concerns related to the dialectical tension between solidarity and independence among members of social groups (Brown & Levinson, 1978/1987; Kingwell, 1995).

The figure most associated with the notion of civility is the renaissance scholar Erasmus, whose book *On Civility in Children* was widely read and circulated in the sixteenth century; a number of books of the same name emerged after that point, each addressing behaviors deemed appropriate for the public presentation of self in the company of others (Elias, 1978). This original volume addressed "the behavior of people in society and was directed toward children" (p. 54). Elias cited Erasmus at length, stating that civilité eventually became the word "civilization" (p. 54). The way people dressed, walked, and carried their bodies—all were outward expressions of inward realities of character, or learned habits expressing virtues necessary for living a full and complete human life.

Erasmus's concept of civilité is often translated as politeness, but the term captures more than what we typically understand as formally prescribed conduct expected in social interaction: "it suggests an approach to life, a way of carrying one's self and of relating to others—in short, living in a way that is civilized" (Carter, 1998, p. 15). Civility encompasses the existential phenomenology of public conduct as an ontological facet of the human condition. If human beings find their telos as part of communities, then civility is a necessary element of human flourishing required for fostering public decision-making under contingency, for sustaining the very institutions that make such decision-making possible, and for offering support for human persons and their contributions to this larger process, even in the face of serious disagreement (Tracy, 2008). Civility is not reducible to politeness or "niceness," although in many contexts of interaction it may take such forms (Fritz, 2011), and in some contexts, what appears to be incivility (Lozano-Reich & Cloud, 2009), but is actually an alternative form of communicative work for the public good or civic sphere, may do the work of "civility" as protection and promotion of the civic or public sphere. As Peck (2004) noted, the hallmark of civility is not conflict-avoidance, but a commitment to deal with the issues of life together (p. 142), and civility might, in appropriate circumstances, involve hurting someone's feelings (p. 5). An examination of literature on various approaches to civility shows its necessity for goods characterizing human existence.

Civility as Civic Virtue

Shils (1997) addressed civility as a civic virtue, noting that civility enables persons to live and work together by fostering the cooperative action that makes civilized life possible. Sellars (2004) referred to civility as "standards of behavior that should govern public discourse" (p. 15), designed to achieve the common good. Civility protects and promotes the social order and institutions that permit communities to function. Civility as civic virtue builds up communities and the bonds between people, working to bring communities and the persons in them to their telos, or naturally flourishing state. Kingwell (1995, 2000) developed this point in his treatment of civility in a public square marked by plurality and difference, and Davetian (2007) explored the functions of civility in human interaction across three different cultures, highlighting points of commonality defining norms of conduct in the social sphere in different locales.

Kingwell (1995) offered a treatment of civility grounded in a commitment to discerning the ways in which people with differing conceptions of the good can live together. He argued that "most citizens…want…the sort of public debate that will address the hard questions of political life" (p. vii). Contemporary models of dialogic justice were developed to respond to the failure of the citizen as "rational chooser" posited by theory-generated principles of justice, principles that were not capable of modeling real human commitments (pp. vii–viii). Dialogic models, instead of defending abstract principles of justice, point to the possibility of conversational spaces in which these principles of justice can be addressed by real citizens through conversation. The question is now "What is just talking?" rather than "What are principles of justice?" Kingwell's answer takes a corresponding communicative form: "the conversational virtue of civility" (p. viii).

In his justification for the turn to dialogic models of justice, Kingwell (1995) identified a shift in political philosophy away from a context of rational choice as the foundation for rules governing social organization, and toward the character of citizens and the discussion through which citizens struggle to understand other citizens, with an emphasis on phronesis, or practical wisdom (p. 6). The citizen emerges as a talker, a dialogic citizen, rather than a rational chooser (p. 6). Kingwell's model of "just talking" (p. 8), or "civil dialogue" (p. 15), explored "justice as a problem of social interaction in a pluralistic society" governing how citizens committed to different visions of the good life will live together in ways that are justifiable to all of them through practices of interpersonal talk (p. 8).

Kingwell (1995) argued that principles of justice are needed to support a well-ordered society consisting of institutions oriented to citizens' needs and interests, marked by a justifiable, legitimate basis on which to distribute goods, material and otherwise; that concern, at its heart, is Kingwell's framing of justice. Dialogic theories of justice examine "the conversational spaces in which [these norms and principles] are generated and justified" (p. 8). This shift to a dialogic model opens up space for civility as civic virtue to take a conversational embodiment.

The tradition of civility as civic virtue reaches back at least to Cicero (Kingwell, 1995), and it is within this tradition that Kingwell (1995) situated his understanding of civility. His conceptualization of civility assumes that social institutions are imperfect but must still be engaged, rather than abandoned for an impossible ideal of perfection. Civility implies corrective action that also seeks to preserve the ordering function of social structures: "Civility is the virtue of citizens that allows the state to have authority, while at the same time allowing us to exercise our faculties of critical judgment about state institutions" (p. 26). Corrective engagement is undertaken in ways that preserve the greater good, and is therefore composed of "a set of conversational practices...governed by a commitment to self-restraint and sensitivity" (p. 26).

More specifically, Kingwell (1995) articulated civility as a type of "sensitivity and acumen necessary for the daily discernment and toleration of varying moral conceptions" of the good for human life (p. 42). Civility's goal is social coexistence of citizens with varied private conceptions of the good. Kingwell admitted variations in the form of civility that emerge across cultures, as Davetian (2007) articulated, so civility must be understood and engaged within the scope of the citizenry of a given society "who, because they share pragmatic goals of living together, may also aspire to share the deeper goals of living together well—that is, justly" (Kingwell, 1995, p. 43). Davetian's work provides an insight into how civility varies by culture.

Davetian (2007) noted that American, English, and French cultural expressions of civility vary, given the different styles of conversation fostered by each nation. For example, French and American people are more comfortable with directness than are the English, who seek to avoid embarrassment and direct engagement of conflict in typical daily interactions (e.g., shopping at a store and dealing with customer-service personnel). For the English, the use of understatement "softens the process of blame and avowal" (p. 512), and humor often assists in defusing the tension resulting from embarrassment. Criticism is offered with great tact and is usually avoided (p. 512). The French, on the other hand, have worked out a system in which periodic outbursts of irritation and anger are enacted as a duel of words, marked by quick, competent responses to what could be considered insult or anger, which keeps violence at bay. Americans have been trained to express their sentiments—the right to individual expression is one of the guiding tenets of American culture (Carbaugh, 1988). However, Americans also are "unsettled by strong emotions" (p. 513); the low-context, direct style of Americans does not typically host the nuance needed to offer insults that are buffered enough to avoid abrasiveness. Given these differences, civility as a civic virtue may take different forms but still accomplish the goals Kingwell (1995) hoped to achieve through his model of dialogic citizenship.

Kingwell (1995) turned to communicative pragmatics for its provision of utterances that work within the context of identifiable social tasks that are, by their nature, cooperative. Goals are associated with these different routine contexts, and these goals provide parameters for saying certain things and refraining from saying others—hence, Kingwell's notion of civility employs a type of restraint oriented to a particular end or good of cooperative social action: "In society we always operate under voluntary restraints, restraints associated with social role-taking, sensitivity to context, and the perceptions of the pragmatic goals particular to a given situation" (p. 43). This restraint is associated with Gadamerian interpretive "tact," understood as "the ability to assess claims other than my own with sensitivity and openness" (Kingwell, 1995, p. 43). Such tact decenters the self, taking one beyond one's own interests and orienting one toward those of other citizens, traditions, or texts. Tact is phronesis, or practical wisdom (Kingwell, 1995, p. 43). Civil discourse involves not saying all one could say, as well as interpretive sensitivity to the legitimacy of others' claims (Kingwell, 1995, p. 44). In Gadamer's terms, tact involves passing over something, leaving it unsaid—it creates distance, such that one sees that thing but slips by it rather than knocking against it (Kingwell, 1995, p. 44).

Kingwell (1995) was aware of civility's critics and sought a conceptualization of civility that allays fears of repression and hegemony (pp. 40–41) expressed by those who consider civility to be "constructed by privileged voices in privileged institutions or societies" in which "what constitutes civil communication is fundamentally tied to the goals and objectives of dominant social actors"—in other words, "a white, middle class, *corporatized* notion" (italics in the original) (Kisselburgh & Dutta, 2009). Civility is not to be abandoned because of claims that it represses those with less power—to be civil, as Kingwell explains,

> does not imply [being] quiet, obedient, or even necessarily well-mannered. It means open and restrained—not in the interests of the ruling claims or the dominant power-holders, but rather in the interests of pragmatic social goals we all share and the vibrant social debate necessary to keep them in play. (p. 48)

Civility recognizes the need to work together to achieve ends that are dedicated to continued co-existence in the public sphere while permitting commitments to a variety of disparate and incommensurate conceptions of the good. Kingwell's (1995) conceptualization of civility corresponds generally to other conceptualizations of civility as civic virtue, but his recognition of the communicative nature of civility is particularly fruitful.

In sum, civility functions to provide a pattern for behavior that people living together can follow, and can rely on others to follow, in order to coordinate their activities (Kasson, 1990). More than coordinating activities, however, civility permits individuality and social connection to co-exist. Carter (1998) recognized this tension between the individual and society: "Civility…is the sum of the many sacrifices we are called to make for the sake of living together" (p. 11). In order to live together, we need standards of conduct that limit our freedom and enable the larger group to carry out its tasks on behalf of all its individual members. Carter cited Cuddihy's statement that civility permits us to "live with unknown others without transforming them into either brothers or enemies" (Cuddihy, 1974, p. 12, cited in Carter, 1998, p. 58). Richard Sennett (1974) concurred that civility is "the activity which protects people from each other and yet allows them to enjoy each other's company" (p. 264).

The shared norms of proper conduct highlighted by Erasmus, as Carter (1998) pointed out, carry a sense of the good for human interaction in the public sphere. Civility involves disciplining personal desires for the good of the whole. Civility is self-discipline that generates space for others to move about freely in the public sphere—to participate together in common life. On a day-to-day level, civility permits public communicative interaction between and among persons of private differences to carry on smoothly (Arnett & Arneson, 1999); as Tracy and Tracy (1998) described it, politeness, one of civility's particular forms, functions as a traffic signal for human interaction—and incivility (or rudeness) is tantamount to running a red light.

Civility, Manners, Politeness, and Courtesy: Interpersonal Ritual

Civility, manners, politeness, and courtesy are different but interconnected terms, as Forni (2002, 2008) observed in his popular treatment of the topic. What it means to be "civilized" involves manners, as Elias (1978) pointed out—ritualized behavior oriented toward others' well-being and comfort. Caldwell (1999) tied these four terms closely together in his treatment of their opposite—rudeness. Kasson's (1990) work likewise associated the terms rudeness, civility, and manners. Manners are a manifestation of civility at the level of interpersonal ritual—through manners, the virtues of public life meet the interactive routines of communicative agents. Troester and Mester (2007) suggested an everyday understanding of civility as involving etiquette, manners, decorum, and politeness, "a set of basic behaviors that show respect for others sharing our space and provide for smooth accomplishment of whatever goals are applicable in that space" (p. 3). Peck (1994) added choice and intentionality to the equation.

Forni (2011a) highlighted the role of distance that characterizes formality in interpersonal interaction. Formal rituals provide a sense of certainty for persons and groups, the protection of a public "known" in the face of the private "unknown" of strangers. Ritual permits unknown others to interact without undue stress, functioning as an implicit guide for interaction.

The increased informality of public interaction that Forni (2011a) discussed encourages individualized understandings of communicative routines. At the level of a personal relationship with a known other, ritual is also recognized and enacted, and in the context of a small number of familiar persons, enactment of private rituals becomes a type of provincial or stylized routine. When these expectations are exported into the public domain, however, the result is often misunderstanding. What one person considers harmless teasing may be understood as an insult or, worse, harassment, due to lack of shared meaning for behaviors that, in the private context, constitute accepted interpersonal ritual.

When public ritual is lost, a heightened concern for shared ground emerges. During periods of social change, a search for common ground among groups that also differentiates groups from one another ensues. Elias (1982) noted the role of within-group solidarity and distinctiveness from out-groups that manifests in communicative practices of civility. Adoption by one group of the practices of another group (say, middle-class adoption of upper-class speech styles) creates similarity and commonality rather than distinctiveness (Giles & Powesland, 1975; Giles & Smith, 1979). In a democratic public sphere, the commonality of public participation calls for a set of public practices that unites groups who seek to participate in public discourse. That is the role and expectation of Kingwell's (1995) "just talking" (p. 8) and Paolo Freiere's attempt to bring disenfranchised groups into the public sphere through education (Arnett & Arneson, 1999).

An understanding of civility as civic virtue, joined with an understanding of the function of interpersonal communicative ritual, highlights the role of communication in civility and brings the recognition that civility is the communicative manifestation of civic virtue. It is through communicative interaction that civility operates to protect and promote various goods, from the work of the public sphere to its institutions and groups. Civility functions at the level of interpersonal interaction in multiple contexts: from conversation and connection among strangers to interaction with known others in various venues of public participation; from the citizen's group to service and professional organizations—exemplars of the various self-organized associations de Tocqueville (2000) noted as the strength of a new nation. Civility's enemy is incivility, the destructive force that erodes action, institutions, and the dignity of persons through its deconstruction of both the ties that bind us and the distance necessary for freedom of engagement. In the next section, I offer a brief treatment of incivility as communicative vice to provide contrast and context for a conceptualization of civility as communicative virtue.

Incivility as Communicative Vice

A vice is a disposition tending toward actions that compromise or prevent accomplishment of the good for human life (or that prevent "internal goods," those goods internal to practices that define excellence; Borden, 2007, p. 23). Incivility is a communicative phenomenon manifested in human interaction through destructive verbal and nonverbal messages (Fritz, 2009). Incivility is unthinking or deliberate rudeness, failure to respond, cutting remarks, lack of attentiveness, and violation of expectations for interpersonal interaction (Andersson & Pearson, 1999). Incivility, because of its manifestation as the antithesis of the communicative good, and its tendency to reproduce itself in a vicious disposition, is a communicative vice. Pragmatically, incivility results in deleterious effects on personal and communal outcomes, so from a utilitarian perspective as well as a virtue ethics perspective, incivility is an undesirable practice.

Whereas civility coordinates action toward the end of human flourishing, incivility as a communicative vice is characterized by lack of restraint and/or appropriate initiative and moves away from the good for human beings as manifested in a flourishing community. Incivility rends the social fabric that weaves our lives together. It destroys the interspaces (Arnett, in press-b) between persons and the connective tissue that synthesizes the structure of human interactive potential. Incivility threatens productive action in the public sphere through damage to those institutions and persons that are necessary to sustain productive action. Incivility is a less-than-fitting response to the human being as human being in community. Incivility reduces the human to the less-than-human through inattentive or deliberate communicative inaction or action. Incivility denies the honor and dignity due the human, and, in its enactment, reflexively degrades the person enacting incivility.

Incivility and rudeness are shaped by the historical moment. Caldwell (1999) traced the idea of rudeness and incivility, focusing on processes by which particular behaviors come to be seen as rude or uncivil. From his treatment, we see a juxtaposition of civility and incivility in their effects on action in the public square, the public environment and institutions, and people. Kasson (1990) explored how our contemporary understanding of rudeness and incivility has roots in the nineteenth century. Rudeness in bourgeois culture during that era, noted Kasson,

> violated codes of civility in such a way as to make public that which should remain private, to single out for special attention that which should remain inconspicuous, or else to cast public actions, conduct, and individual actors in an unworthy or degrading light. (p. 115)

Forni (2008) defined rudeness as disregard for others, a withdrawal of respect and consideration. Forni identified two types of rudeness, unfocused rudeness and focused rudeness. Unfocused rudeness occurs when someone slights another with behavior of benefit to the self that inconveniences or disregards the feelings and/or plans of the other person. Unfocused rudeness might involve, for example, breaking a lunch date with someone in order to go to lunch with a different person who might be of more professional benefit—in other words, changing pre-existing plans when a "better offer" comes along. Forgetting to return phone calls and speaking loudly on a cell phone in public are also types of unfocused rudeness. This type of incivility functions as disregard for others that emerges as an indirect effect or a byproduct of self-regard. Focused rudeness, on the other hand, involves actions directed at a particular target—for example, asking embarrassing questions in front of others, gossiping or spreading rumors, and related behaviors (Forni, 2008, pp. 7–10).

The focus of much work on incivility has been the contemporary workplace, where incivility takes the form of low-level insults, nonverbal affect displays such as disparaging looks, snippy retorts, ignoring others' remarks, screaming, and related communicative behaviors that send messages of contempt and disregard to others (Andersson & Pearson, 1999; Fritz, 2009). Incivility creates unfavorable conditions for productivity, damages organizational climates and cultures, and hurts persons in the workplace who either receive or witness uncivil behavior (Pearson & Porath, 2009). Incivility strikes at the goods of productivity, place, and persons. It takes attention away from work and shifts energy and focus away from the task and toward self-protection or defense. Work by Sutton (2007) and Pearson and Porath (2009) documents the damaging effects of civility on the work environment. Incivility is particularly problematic in contexts in which those engaging professional occupations practice, because it compromises the many goods associated with professional action.

Troester and Mester (2007), who framed civility as a communication construct, offered a continuum of behaviors ranging from civility to incivility. Actions such as self-sacrifice for the common good, selflessness in everyday encounters, addressing others with respect, listening to others, and acknowledging others are arrayed on the civility side of the continuum. Incivility begins with ignoring others and proceeds to gossip, arrogance, and condescension, then on to yelling, harassment, intimidation, damage of others' goods or reputation, and violence (p. 9). These problematic practices are consistent with behavioral dimensions of troublesome bosses, peers, and subordinates in the workplace—for example, backstabbing, making excessive demands, being controlling or bossy, lording power over others, professional incivility, and unprofessional focus of attention (Fritz, 2002, 2006). Such behaviors cluster to form gestalt impressions of others in the workplace. Although in some cases, "troublesome others" in the workplace are perceived as simply "different from me" (Fritz, 2006, p. 40), other behaviors representing incivility and related problematic behaviors lead to unhelpful constructions of others and exert a measurable impact on outcomes important to persons and organizations (Fritz & Omdahl, 2006b; Omdahl & Fritz, 2006).

Davenport Sypher (2004) took a communicative perspective in her review of workplace incivility. She urged a broad-based understanding of uncivil behavior in the workplace and offered a typology of uncivil behavior varying along dimensions of intensity and intentionality based on the work of Geddes and Baron (1997). Workplace violence lies at the extreme of the continuum of activity, intentionality, and aggression, and ignoring lies at the other extreme (low intensity, indirect, and not aggressive). Verbal abuse, bullying, rudeness, and interrupting range along the multidimensional space in decreasing intensity, directness, and aggressiveness (Davenport Sypher, 2004, p. 261). Davenport Sypher further elaborated the nature of incivility as controlling, assessing how it functions to "clarify, document, refuse, subvert, assert, and reassert authority and control" (p. 262). The clarification function, which seems counterintuitive, works to limit inappropriately what one is allowed to know, what is possible, and what is expected.

Civility combats the communicative vice of incivility, strengthening the twin bonds of solidarity and respectful distance, permitting both the strength of unified action and the necessary freedom of movement in the public domain that makes such solidarity possible. From this perspective, civility becomes a communicative virtue that protects and promotes goods associated with the public sphere. Civility's identity as communicative virtue is tied to the ideal of protection and promotion of the public sphere, and its various groups, through interactive practices that make space for all at the table. That is the world we want in our civic spaces (Kingwell, 2000) and in our workplaces (Davenport Sypher, 2004). I turn now to address civility as communicative virtue.

Civility as Communicative Virtue

The earlier review of virtue ethics (see Chapter 1) suggests that virtues are directed toward the good of human flourishing. As civic virtue, civility is directed toward the flourishing of human communities. Civility as the communicative manifestation of civic virtue points to a conceptualization of civility established on the principle of discursive initiative and restraint oriented to life together in the public sphere. Civility as communicative virtue emerges as a fitting response to the existential necessity of the human condition for interaction with others. Civility involves communicative initiative with, and toward, others, and in response to others, marked by some degree of formality (Forni, 2011a) and restraint. In this sense, civility encompasses assertiveness and responsiveness as modalities of communicative engagement with others (Richmond & McCroskey, 1992).

Civility as the communicative manifestation of civic virtue resonates with Habermas's (1984, 1987) focus on the role of discourse as the unique human resource for accomplishing work in the public sphere (see Kingwell, 1995, for a discussion of Habermas's ideal speech situation in relation to civility). In the history of human society, civility marks a change from external, physical restraint to internal self-restraint of words and actions, a shift traced by Elias (1978, 1982) in his history of the civilizing process and outlined by Davetian (2007) in his cultural history of civility. As the communicative manifestation of civic virtue, civility protects and promotes coordinated action, institutions, and persons in the space of the public sphere. Civility as communicative virtue emerges in human interaction through verbal and nonverbal messages; it is the constructive counterpart to the destructive communicative vice of incivility (Fritz 2009, 2011). The works of Laverty (2009), Barrett (1991), and Kingwell (1995) offer an explicit treatment of civility as communicative virtue.

Laverty (2009) highlighted communicative elements of civility in relation to virtue ethics, drawing on Hume, Kant, Dewey, and Aristotle. Laverty argued for civility as an aesthetic-ethical good, regardless of its function in establishing character or its role in a just democracy. Hume noted the inarticulate joy and satisfaction emerging from the pleasure of communicating, a perspective given context with Kant's aesthetic philosophy. From Kant, Laverty inferred that communication can be beautiful when manifested as harmonious interaction between and among persons, and sublime when we recognize connection with others, a connection that lifts us out of our contingent situatedness and brings us to a realization of a shared humanity.

Laverty argued that civility provides a context within which to navigate multiple contextual elements of the social sphere, such as hierarchy and identity politics (p. 299). From Dewey, she highlighted the importance of manners as "minor morals," exercises in consideration for others and in mutual accommodation that open possibilities for contact and communication. Laverty noted that manners, an element of civility, create in us a disposition to be agreeable, which results in an intentionality to craft behavioral responses that are likely to be well-received by others, and involves attentiveness to the unique other with whom one is interacting. To enact civility in this way is to think carefully about choice of words, tone, and gestures, which become a kind of dress "in order to honor the occasion and the company" (p. 230). Even criticism can be delivered with civility; constructive criticism can serve as an acknowledgment of others' efforts and the worthiness of one's work as a focus of commentary.

Laverty identified three "communicative virtues" in Aristotle's *Nicomachean Ethics*: tact or tastefulness; a virtue that defines the mean between obsequiousness (pleasing one's conversational partner by flattery and indulgence) and churlishness (disregarding another person's sensitivities, resources, or interests); and a virtue that defines the mean between boastfulness and mock-modesty. The first two virtues relate to concern for the other; the latter relates to how one talks about oneself. These three virtues are unified, such that one possesses all three or none at all. Laverty identifies the unity of these virtues as expressed in varying modes of civility. The civil person is concerned for the feelings of others but is also willing to speak the truth to another for that other's good. To act with civility involves evaluating one's own accomplishments and successes rightly and knowing when to mention them; one's appropriate appreciation expressed for other persons, and concern for their interests, as well as the virtue of tact, have conceptual kinship with positive and negative face in politeness theory (Brown & Levinson, 1978/1987).

Barrett (1991), in his treatment of rhetoric and civility, identified four cardinal virtues required to adhere to civility: courage, temperance, justice, and wisdom (p. 146). Barrett cited Zwieback's understanding of civility, which requires "'traditions of restraint, forbearance, grace, tolerance, [and] compassion'" (Zwieback, cited in Barrett, 1991, p. 147). Each of these virtues or attributes can be connected to communication constructs or practices. Barrett noted that rhetorical process is a function of civility, which ties civility to human interaction. Barrett drew on the work of Eulau, who noted that civil behavior involves communicative actions such as "'persuading, soliciting, consulting, advising, bargaining, [and] compromising" and identified uncivil behaviors as consisting of "'coercing, confronting, deceiving, [and] manipulating'" (p. 147). Civility is expressed in our symbolic behavior with one another—"it is effected rhetorically" (p. 147). Barrett noted the role of the "good audience" in ensuring civility in the human community—we call each other into account when failures of civility occur. This point resonates with Laverty's discussion of the virtue falling between the mean of obsequiousness and churlishness. We offer honest responses to others' behavior as a good audience, just as they do for us. In this way, communities become self-correcting, with expected standards serving as a public benchmark or guideline for evaluation.

Kingwell's (1995) account of civility as the civic virtue of just talking, addressed earlier, draws on Brown and Levinson's (1978/1987) treatment of politeness, with which he understands civility to have much in common. In Kingwell's framework, politeness captures "conversational strategies of indirection, self-restraint, and face-saving" (p. 196), elements that correspond to Brown and Levinson's conceptualization of negative face needs, the need to be unimpeded in one's actions, as well as an orientation toward understanding others (p. 227), an orientation grounded loosely in positive face needs, the need to have a desirable self-image. Kingwell's goal is to suggest a theory of communicative competence with politeness as a central component.

Kingwell (1995), following Leech (Leech, 1983, cited in Kingwell), suggested that there may be a cooperative principle urging politeness that is not a deviation from the maxims of quantity (say only as much as needs to be said), quality (speak the truth), relation (say things relevant to the topic at hand), and manner (be clear) proposed by Grice (1975) and elaborated by Brown and Levinson (1978/1987) as governing rational, efficient language use, but is potentially in conflict with them. Polite speech is motivated by other-regarding interests, interests that rest in the interpersonal or social domain. Kingwell believed that politeness forms part of our background principles of communication—it is one of our "rational" commitments in conversation that rests not with informational clarity, but with concern for the relationship with the other. The notion of "perfectly rational speech" (p. 198) that is tied to clarity and efficiency of discourse—reminiscent of the utilitarian discourse system articulated by Scollon and Scollon (2001)—and to saying all that can be said is not an adequate description of how people actually communicate with one another in lived experience. Principles of politeness show us that in conversation with others, we manifest concern for both autonomy and solidarity, concerns that emerge in verbal discourse in the form of our utterances.

Civility, for Kingwell (1995), primarily involves restraint in discourse; civility and its associated politeness turn on that principle as well as on a principle of attentiveness to others. Kingwell's understanding of civility rests within a recognition of the content and relationship dimensions of language that communication theorists have studied for decades (e.g., Watzlawick & Beavin, 1967; Watzlawick, Beavin, & Jackson, 1967)—that human beings engaged in communicative interaction with one another are never concerned only with the content of utterances, or only with rational and efficient information exchange, but also with the feelings of others, social harmony, and other goods operative in the situation, also understood as goals guiding influence strategies (Dillard, 1990; Dillard, Segrin, & Harden, 1989) that are manifest, and often emergent, in interaction, and relevant to persuasion in the interpersonal context. Kingwell recognized what communication scholars have noted for decades—"communication is not simply about phrasing interests and arguments in the maximally efficient transfer of information; it is also about not hurting people's feelings, not having [ours] hurt, not saying all we could say, oiling the wheels of mundane social interaction, and strengthening the ties that bind us together" (Kingwell, 1995, p. 211).

True politeness, or civility, as Kingwell (1995) articulated it, is the effect of "socialization, insight, and intuition, not of slavish obedience to a code" (p. 217). It is instinctive, the result of practical judgment, not conformity to rules. In the language of communication theory, civility involves specific domains of communicative competence: interpretive competence—knowing what the context calls for; role competence—understanding one's role in a given context; goal competence—setting achievable and appropriate goals given one's role and the context; and message competence—generating messages to achieve those goals within the operative constraints of the setting (Trenholm & Jensen, 2004). Civility respects persons by permitting distance through tactful discourse.

In these perspectives that point toward civility as communicative virtue, we see that our discourse with others has the potential to support our shared community and social world through protecting and promoting the good of action together in the public sphere, our shared public environment and its institutions, and others' face and dignity. Civility as communicative virtue becomes part of sound civic moral character. The next section, by means of a review of points covered thus far, points the way to communicative coordinates of civility as communicative virtue, which can then be applied to the professional context as professional civility at work. These theoretical suggestions do not exhaust an understanding of the communicative virtue of civility, but they suggest scholarship from the communication field that touches some concerns relevant to civility as it has been discussed to this point, and they open the way for identifying specific practices of communicative virtue. Civility as the communicative manifestation of civic virtue protects and promotes multiple goods in interaction with others.

Theoretical Coordinates of Civility as Communicative Virtue

Civility's enactment emerges in human communicative interaction, in the context of a defining feature of the human condition—conversation—which has been neglected in philosophical treatments, as MacIntyre (2007) and Kingwell (1995) noted. Oliver (1961) identified the prevalence of conversation, the interpersonal speech process, as an integral part of the humanities tradition, tracing principles of conversation over the centuries, pointing to the rhetorical importance of this distinctively human attribute. The implicit norms carried by a style or mode of discourse oriented to a common purpose—enhancing the public image or face of each participant (Brown & Levinson, 1978/1987)—protect and promote a concern for social harmony characteristic of a high-context style of communication. In this orientation, the background of participants permits shared meaning to emerge without a great deal of explicit verbal encoding, and the quasi-ritualized nature characteristic of this form of communication permits interaction to proceed along predictable lines, as Goffman (1967) noted in his treatment of rituals of human interaction, the foundation for current and ongoing conceptualizations of politeness theory (Brown & Levinson, 1978/1987) and related work on violations of interaction rituals, such as rudeness (e.g., Tracy & Tracy, 1998).

The quality of conversation affects interactants in a context of discourse but also reaches beyond them. The proximal effects of incivility as communicative vice—that is, incivility's effect on persons to whom it is directed—are immediate and localized (e.g. Porath & Erez, 2007), but its distal effects emerge at the larger social level, beginning with those who witness uncivil behavior (Porath & Erez, 2009) and extending to the level of the organization—and even to the larger public sphere, through the social imaginary (Taylor, 2004, 2007), which fosters or inhibits practices on the basis of the salience of cultural expectations for interactive behavior. Giddens's (1984) structuration theory provides a mechanism for connecting individual action to the larger social unit through rules and resources by which social actors accomplish tasks of daily living. To conceptualize civility as communicative virtue requires a focus on the extent to which properties of discursive elements of interpersonal interaction permit ideas to emerge in ways that invite and encourage participants in discourse to remain part of the conversation, and on processes by which civility spreads to other elements of a system through processes such as structuration or collective minding (Cooren, 2004). Civility as communicative virtue operates at both content and relational levels, although the relational elements emerge as primary, permitting the content dimension to receive studied attention within a space of attentive distance (Forni, 2011a; Laverty, 2009; Mayo, 2001).

The next sections highlight elements of communication theory with particular relevance for civility as communicative virtue. These theoretical domains are not the only relevant ones, but they are salient in their direct links to civility (e.g., Davenport Sypher, 2004) and can be connected to the goods suggested here that define civic virtue.

Civility and the Face of the Other

Civility as communicative virtue protects the face of others as full participants in the social sphere and contributors to decision-making in the public realm. Human actors across cultures seek both solidarity with and independence from others; these potentially competing needs result in what Goffman (1967) described as face and facework and Brown and Levinson (1978/1987) conceptualized as face needs in their proposal of politeness theory. Politeness theory has received significant theoretical elaboration over the last decades (Watts, 2003). As originally laid out, politeness theory assumes that people have a need to have their wants and desires validated by others and to be seen as worthy and valuable participants in the human community. This need is referred to as the positive face need. Likewise, people do not want to be imposed upon; people need to be free in their actions and to make significant choices regarding their outcomes—the need for autonomy. This need is referred to as the negative face need.

One elaboration of politeness theory emerges from the work of Lim and Bowers (1991), who proposed a reconceptualization of the positive and negative face dimensions as fellowship face, autonomy face, and competence face, with fellowship face corresponding generally to positive face and autonomy face to negative face. Competence face provides a unique way of integrating the autonomy and fellowship needs, which were assumed to be in dialectical tension with each other. Fellowship face recognizes the uniqueness of a given person in that person's contribution to the larger group, essentially meeting the fellowship face need by means of a feature of autonomy face characteristics. In other words, the unique gifts and capabilities of a given person are brought to bear on the needs of the community, providing benefit to the larger whole and appreciation to the person.

Politeness theory receives treatment in communication scholarship from a sociolinguistic perspective in studies of request forms—when we ask someone to do something, we threaten the negative, or autonomy, face need. The work of politeness is to offer "redress" to those needs through the form of the request, such that the force of the request is mitigated. The politeness framework offered by Lim and Bowers (1991) provides a conceptual entrance into an important element of civility as the communicative manifestation of civic virtue. The need for autonomy and self-determination emerges in the democratic process through the potential for individual contributions that promise at least a chance of making a difference in outcomes about which one cares, while the need for solidarity and fellowship emerges in the recognition that social life is not lived alone, that human beings flourish in the context of others—decisions emerge with others. Competence face brings together individual recognition and group benefit as the gestalt of life in the public square. Kingwell (1995), whose work was reviewed earlier, addressed discursive elements of civility in conditions of public plurality. The notion of "a civil tongue" highlights the role of civil communication in establishing agreed-upon plans for action in the public sphere.

Gill and Davenport Sypher (2009) offered a review of research that ventured entrance into communicative coordinates of civility by way of Brown and Levinson (1978/1987). Gill and Davenport Sypher addressed the work of McGlone and Batchelor (2003), who offered indirect or euphemistic ways of dealing with uncomfortable topics (such as excretory behavior) as methods of avoiding positive face threat and suggested request forms that minimize imposition as ways of avoiding negative face threat. These strategies are direct applications of politeness theory. Gill and Davenport Sypher recommended the use of inclusive pronouns and "micro-affirmations," such as saying "thank you" (p. 68), as further applications of politeness theory with respect to positive face. Cooperative interruptions indicate solidarity and enthusiasm for others' contributions (Zhao & Gantz, 2003, cited in Gill & Davenport Sypher, 2004); effective listening promotes civility by reaffirming others and is also tied to positive face for the listener and the one listened to (Gill & Davenport Sypher, p. 69). Protecting the positive face of others is a manifestation of supportive communication.

In Defense of Supportive (and Defensive) Communication: Civility in a New Key

Through protecting the face of others, we show support and reduce the likelihood of defensive responses. Initially proposed by Jack Gibb (1961) and referenced in basic interpersonal communication textbooks to the present day, the concept of defensive and supportive communication climates is foundational for conceptualizing civility. Defensive climates are generated by statements oriented toward certainty, superiority, evaluation, neutrality, strategy, and control, while supportive communication climates are characterized by provisionalism, equality, description, empathy, spontaneity, and problem-solving. The types of utterances characterizing supportive communication typically offer face support, or support for the identity of the person being addressed.

In general, supportive communication could be classified as a manifestation of civility, while defensive communication (either in initial utterance or response) might be considered an uncivil response—a response oriented toward communicative vice. However, these categorizations are not unequivocal and are closely bound to context. On the one hand, when one is gathering information and seeking alternatives, certainty would not be a virtuous communicative act; it would close off discussion and prevent alternatives from emerging. On the other hand, in a different context, a certainty orientation might be an appropriate behavior, and would qualify as a virtuous communicative response. Furthermore, given that civility is a communicative virtue that protects and promotes the good of a social unit, society, or group, then acting within one's role to provide a sense of clarity and direction when one has been asked to take on a leadership role would be a virtuous communicative action, although it might appear as "certainty" in a content-coding scheme looking at the purely formal properties of the utterance.

As another example of the potentially civil nature of formally defensiveness-provoking communicative utterances, using certainty again, if one functions as an ally (DeTurk, 2011) by taking a stand on behalf of a person who is a member of a group of little social privilege and who is being subjected to injustice or belittlement by stating directly and definitively—with certainty—that the person being belittled is a person worthy of respect, and that the person's group is worthy of respect, or that an utterance someone has made is unacceptable in its downgrading of a group of people, certainty is serving the cause of justice, protecting and promoting the good of persons and, by implication, the larger social unit as a context for human flourishing. However, it is possible to confront or address potentially challenging topics through discourse that is both supportive in nature (through tactful utterances) and corrective (see, for instance, DeTurk, 2011, p. 580). Each of the defensive/supportive behaviors in Gibb's (1961) treatment could be engaged in a civil or uncivil way, depending on the context, which provides support for the argument that civility as communicative virtue requires phronesis, or practical wisdom, for its enactment.

The defensive/supportive communication framework is conceptually similar to active listening (Gordon, 1970), often contrasted with "bad" listening. As in the case of defensive/supportive communication, there are times when messages that appear to be indicative of poor or unresponsive listening may serve the purposes of civility or a higher good connected to the common narrative ground of each participant (see Fritz, 2010, for this perspective). Sensitivity to context and awareness of one's goals in discourse guide choice of utterance to manifest civility in a given case, which emerges in a particular type of message design.

Civility by Design: Message Design Logic

The enactment of civility as communicative virtue requires skilled communicative practice and an awareness of one's goals in discourse. Message design logic (e.g., Hullman, 2004; O'Keefe, 1988, 1991; O'Keefe & McCornack, 1987; O'Keefe & Shepherd, 1987) posits that people carry differing implicit definitions of communication that underlie the way they construct and interpret messages. Different understandings of language give rise to different styles of communicating, with the style and content of messages reflecting an orientation to communication's function. Three different design logics can be engaged: expressive, conventional, and rhetorical.

Expressive design logic describes a style in which emotions are given full rein, there is no apparent goal of the speaker or the listener taken into account, and the purpose of the utterance is simply to express feelings. "I am so angry at you right now! How could you forget to pick me up!" is an example of a message designed from the expressive standpoint. In contexts requiring negotiation or solving problems, expressive design logic provides little traction.

Conventional design logic reflects the goal-driven nature of discourse and results in messages that take into account the rule-governed nature of human communicative interaction in particular contexts. Conventional design logic makes the goal of the speaker clear and notes the action the speaker hopes to take. The focus is on communicating "by the rules," and the utterances take the form of standard, expected structure. The patterned, typical nature of conventional design logic is helpful for everyday interaction when rules are agreed on, but less helpful when working out differences in positions, claims, or distribution of resources, and when addressing potentially conflict-ridden contexts.

Rhetorical design logic is a way of organizing messages that seeks to align the goals of self and other in a creative reconfiguring of a communicative context. Persons working from a rhetorical approach to message design manifest a constructive approach to solving problems, addressing concerns, or resolving conflict in ways that honor self and others. Rhetorical design logic requires identifying a new "hermeneutic entrance" into a conversation or context and may take more time than other logics. For simple tasks or routine interactions, rhetorical design logic may provide more than is required or desired.

Each of these design logics may manifest civility as communicative virtue in an appropriate context. An expressive message of delight or appreciation may serve the cause of civility—for example, a spontaneous "That's great news! Good for you!" can do wonders for group solidarity and individual support. A conventionally designed message that emphasizes role responsibilities and obligations may direct discourse in very public ways to connect persons experiencing animosity or dislike, requiring only carrying out of tasks and necessary communicative activity. Conventionally designed messages create room for interaction between people for smooth public interaction that transcends personal liking or dislike. Forni (2011a), for example, highlighted the importance of formality, a conventional style with agreed-upon rules that permits interaction to take place with a sense of healthy distance and respect, and Hess (2006) noted the importance of distance when dealing with disliked others. Rhetorically designed messages help negotiate new approaches to seemingly intransigent obstacles, interpret uncertainty, and redefine reality (e.g., Fairhurst, 2011). For example, in addressing an employee who regularly comes back late from lunch, a supervisor employing rhetorical design logic might highlight the person's value to the organization, express an assumption of the employee's good intentions, and explain that others look to that employee for leadership in order to encourage prompt returns in the future, thereby supporting the employee's positive face (Brown & Levinson, 1987/1978) and showing a pathway to enhanced contributions.

Dialects of Discourse: Civility as Communicative Dialectics

Civility as communicative virtue works within the dynamics of the complexities of human relationships. Much as politeness theory notes, we have multiple needs that co-exist in tension with each other; we need to be with others, and we need to be separate from others. A relational dialectics perspective (Baxter & Montgomery, 1996), particularly in its treatment of revelation and concealment, disclosure and reticence, helps us understand the way civility as communicative virtue protects distance between people and permits constructive connection. As Forni (2011a) pointed out, formality in discourse creates respectful distance that gives people space for self-protection.

Relational dialectics provides another way of conceptualizing the linguistic form of civility as communicative virtue. Two of the dialectics are of particular interest here: the revelation/concealment dialectic focuses attention on the goods associated with self-disclosure—both restraint and revelation; the integration/separation dialectic focuses attention on goods associated with two concerns emerging from politeness theory: fellowship and autonomy. Each dialectic emerges in the form of discourse—conversational utterances—responsive to particular contexts.

Civility as communicative virtue, drawing from its original identity as civic virtue and from its theoretical coordinates as discussed to this point, leans toward restraint, or the concealment end of the self-disclosure dialectic, and toward the autonomy end of the integration/separation dialectic. The distance associated with civility that makes us neither siblings nor enemies provides opportunity for closer relationships to emerge if opportunity arises. Communication privacy management theory (Petronio, 2002) also applies in this case; the dialectics of integration and separation operate according to one's sense of the boundaries that are desirable and necessary in various public and private settings. If privacy management theory is applied to microcontexts, one may see a move toward restraint in an intimate conversation in which choices are made to refrain from uttering all that could be uttered, or in public contexts in which tact (Kingwell, 1995) guides an interlocutor to refrain from pointing out verbally that which should pass unremarked.

Civility and the Ties That Bind: Phatic Communication

The communicative virtue of civility manifests itself in discourse that maintains a social connection among persons in a way that respects boundaries between public and private space. Phatic communication (Malinowski, 1923/1972; Placencia, 2004), small talk (Coupland, 2003), or rapport talk (Tannen, 1991)—such as greetings, talk about the weather, and discourse about mundane, obvious things—which engages connection that rests on the level of common humanity and citizenship without feigning an intimacy that does not exist, protects the interspaces among people (Arnett, in press-b) and permits the common task of getting on in the world to continue (Holba, 2008). Phatic communication as public relational communication protects the face of interactants by permitting smooth social interaction to take place without embarrassment. Phatic communication illustrates conventional design logic in its adherence to the rules and regulations of social life, and it rests in the ritual of everyday interaction. Communicative commonplaces (e.g., "Nice weather today, isn't it?" "It sure is. Maybe spring is finally here!") strengthen the public ties connecting human beings to each other. Phatic communication honors the communicative routines of daily life that form the interactive matrix of the human condition.

A Civil Argument: Civility and Argumentativeness

The constructs of argumentativeness and verbal aggression (e.g., DeWine, Nicotera, & Parry, 1991; Infante & Rancer, 1996) offer important insights into the understanding of civility as communicative virtue. Argumentativeness refers to the tendency to engage in discussions and disputes about ideas; verbal aggression involves attacking one's interlocutor by means of discourse and manifests very clearly one dimension of incivility. Infante (1987) considered interpersonal behavior to be aggressive if it applied physical or symbolic force to "dominate and perhaps damage or…defeat and perhaps destroy the locus of attack, [which] can be a person's body, material possessions, self-concept, position on topics of communication, or behavior" (p. 158). Aggression can be symbolic or physical, constructive or destructive.

Verbal aggression is a subset of hostility, which is defined as destructive symbolic aggression (Infante, 1987). Verbal aggression is an attack on others' self-concepts as well as, or instead of, others' positions on issues. Argumentativeness, a subset of constructive symbolic aggression (which is considered assertiveness, in Infante's terms), is, in Infante and Rancer's (1982) conceptualization, a predisposition to mount a verbal defense of a position and a verbal attack on others' positions. Tannen's (1998, 2002) work suggests that we inhabit an "argument culture" that may blur the lines between these apparently different conceptual forms. Scholarship on academic discourse (Tracy, 1997; Tracy & Baratz, 1993) identifies discourse forms, such as challenging questions, that appear to reflect an orientation to argumentativeness that is understood in that context as an appropriate, necessary, and desirable style of communication, but which may reflect a culture of critical discourse characteristic of an orientation to life tied to progress and technical rationality (Lasch, 1991). Discourse taking a form consistent with an argumentative orientation may count as civil communication in contexts where direct communication and strong assertion guide norms of interaction (e.g., Woolley, 2008).

Conclusion

Civility, when seen through the lens of communication scholarship, is the communicative manifestation of civic virtue. Civility as communicative virtue protects and promotes persons and institutions in the task of living together in the public sphere. Communication research offers a plethora of resources for identifying theoretical and applied manifestations of civility as communicative virtue. These communicative coordinates lay an initial foundation for thinking about civility as virtuous discourse in everyday life in its manifestation as messages that offer support for human interconnection and personal autonomy. Civility as communicative virtue becomes professional civility as communicative virtue at work when it appears within the walls of particular organizations where professionals carry out their vocations, adding goods of the workplace and goods of professional identity to the more general goods underlying civility. In the next chapter, I lay out the professional civility framework.

Professional Civility as Communicative Virtue at Work

Introduction

The last three chapters addressed virtue ethics, the history of the professions as practice, and a conceptualization of civility as communicative virtue. This chapter situates civility as communicative virtue in the context of the organization, organizes and integrates material addressed in earlier chapters (primarily Chapters 2 and 3), and introduces the remaining conceptual coordinates of dialogic civility and organizational citizenship to the professional civility framework. I begin with a brief conceptual overview.

Professional civility encompasses civil communication in the workplace emerging from a constructive orientation to tasks, the host organization or institution, and others in the workplace as positive goods integral to the existence and identity of profession(s) in our contemporary historical moment. Professional civility is a communicative virtue protecting and promoting goods of productivity, place, persons, and profession that are integral to, and emerge from, the tradition of profession as practice. Professional civility is practiced as a professional communication ethic as practitioners carry these goods of profession into everyday interaction in the workplace. In this sense, professional civility is a philosophy of communication integral to a constructive philosophy of work life. A culture of professional civility emerges when professional civility becomes the norm for an organization's interactive routines.

The historic understanding of "profession" has undergone many shifts over the centuries, yielding an expanded scope of occupations categorized as "professions," or seeking at least the spirit of such categorization (Kimball, 1995; Sullivan, 2005). Any occupation can be engaged as a profession when framed as a practice that is part of a tradition as articulated here. Some treatments of professionalism point to the signal feature of care about one's work as the defining element of professions (e.g., Maister, 1997), a position consistent with this assumption. However, professional civility as communicative virtue is most relevant to service and intellective occupations, many, if not most, of which have attained at least informal status as professions or quasi-professions as the term is understood today (Noordegraaf, 2007; Sullivan, 2005). The expectations for interaction of members of a profession fitting the "true professional ideal" (Kimball, 1995) are consistent with an ethic of professional civility.

Each occupation has a set of practices that invests it with an ethic that defines good performance (MacIntyre, 2007), but occupations face varied interactive contexts. The culture of some occupational traditions may call for a very different sort of discourse ethic marked by different constraints and possibilities and different interactive norms from that of professional civility as articulated here. For example, the occupational culture of debt collectors includes norms of discourse marked by insistence, urgency, and harshness with selected targets of collection calls (Rafaeli & Sutton, 1991; Sutton, 1991). The risk of the routine nature of such communicative practices lies in potential spillover into the larger organizational culture that shapes interaction among organizational members, where norms may develop from habituation in the context of interaction with clients. Sometimes, norms emerging in a professional context appear to push the limits of civil discourse in their encouragement of assertive argument (e.g., Tannen, 2002; Tracy, 1997), but the contextualization of such apparent violations and the presence of identifiable boundaries in these contexts make it possible to recognize violations of norms of civility in such contexts, as highlighted by Twale and DeLuca (2008) and Hickson and Roebuck (2009) for the case of incivility in higher education.

I articulate professional civility here as relevant primarily to the set of professions explicit and implicit in Kimball's (1995) and Sullivan's (2005) treatment of the history, legacy, and current status of the professions in America. Representative professions include education, the legal profession, management, public affairs and other communication-related occupations, the various health and human services occupations and helping professions, government positions, engineering, architecture, and any other occupation that requires education and training to engage and that carries a distinctive identity defined by a professional association and/or is recognized by relevant others as having such a distinctive identity. Professional civility takes the form of a virtue at the level of communicative practices, an ethic and philosophy of communication at the level of a particular professional life, and a culture when supported at the level of the organization.

Enacting professional civility in the workplace as a communicative ethic is part of the larger scope of professional responsibility that includes obligations to communities and the larger public sphere. The restoration and rehabilitation of professions in the public eye starts in the local "microcommunity" of others, where professionals give appropriate communicative attention to a number of goods—to work, to the organization, and to people in the workplace. This localization becomes a defining element of professions and extends professional civility beyond norms of politeness or forms of courteous discourse; the three-dimensional soul of professional civility makes a phenomenological turn toward the work of the profession, the local home (Arnett, 1992) or organizational context, and other human beings in the work environment. Attention to these elements of professional life prepares the way for outreach to the external community through engagement beyond the confines of the organization; in this sense, professional civility is the foundation for professional service to the larger public sphere and contributes to the strengthening of the profession itself. Finally, professional civility is protected, nourished, and cultivated by attention to private life through leisure (Holba, 2007, 2011). In this manner, the identity of a "professional" contributes to a whole and flourishing human life. Here, I address professional civility's protection and promotion of four of these goods—productivity, place, persons, and, as a byproduct of attention to those three, the profession itself.

Virtues, Professions, and Civility: Professional Civility as Communicative Virtue

Virtues are needed to realize and extend the internal goods of professions and to tend to the telos of the human end toward which professions are historically oriented. Goods internal to professions as embedded practice—productivity, place, persons, and the profession itself—are achieved in part through the communicative virtue of professional civility, which finds its origin in the tradition of professions understood as practice, its discursive shape in an understanding of civility as communicative virtue, and its context in the workplace. Civility takes a particular form as it supports the goods of profession in the organizational setting. This responsiveness to the workplace context gives the communicative virtue of civility the form of professional civility as communicative virtue at work.

In the workplace, professional civility as communicative virtue protects and promotes the multidimensional set of goods characteristic of professions. Professional civility as communicative virtue at work is grounded in a particular understanding of the nature of the goods of the professions today—productivity, place, and persons—emerging from the history of the professions that formed the tradition of the professional ideal in America (Kimball, 1995). Professional civility protects and promotes an interconnected web of goods emerging from professions as architectonic occupations contributing to the common human good in the context of professional practice in today's historical moment.

MacIntyre (2007) discussed three frameworks for virtue: the Homeric, the Aristotelian/Athenian, and the utilitarian. In the Homeric framework, a virtue is tied to a role or position, enabling someone to enact the requirements of that role or position (p. 184). In the Aristotelian sense, virtue is tied to what is good for human beings as human beings (p. 184)—the telos for humans as a species determines qualities that count as virtues. In the utilitarian tradition, a virtue is a means to an end, where the "good" is external to the practice. Professional civility is consistent with each of these frameworks.

A professional role requires professional civility as a condition of its existence and enactment—professional civility is an interactive communicative virtue manifested by anyone filling the role of a member of a profession, a role with expected behaviors defined by the developing tradition of a given profession. Enacting professional civility is part of what being a member of a profession entails. Professional civility as communicative virtue at work is tied to the role of a professional within the tradition of profession as practice (Kimball, 1995).

Professions themselves, as defined and described by Kimball (1995) and Sullivan (2005), are part of the "good" for human life today. A profession provides valuable and necessary services to the human community (Larson, 1977); such services define an element of a good life or telos for human beings. Professional civility as a communicative virtue at work is tied to the good for human beings.

As a byproduct of its existence and enactment as communicative virtue, professional civility plays a constructive role in organizations. Professional civility prevents the destructive effects of incivility on organizational communities and brings about positive outcomes of its own, and is, therefore, useful to that end. In this sense, these outcomes of professional civility are external goods that exist along with the internal goods defined as part of the practice itself (MacIntyre, 2007, p. 188). Internal and external goods are not incompatible; Moore (2002), for example, argued that business is a practice that balances internal and external goods.

Professional civility is a communicative virtue that protects and promotes, supports and enables, and brings life to the goods that define the practice of a profession as it is carried out within the public context of an organizational setting. The conceptual contours of professional civility emerge from the professional ideal tied to the history of professions in America (Kimball, 1995) as they meet a new contextual moment of engagement with the contemporary marketplace, where the conceptual framework of organizational citizenship (Organ, 1988; Organ, Podsakoff, & McKenzie, 2006) offers theoretical ground for a citizenship model (Graham, 1991) of professional participation in organizations. Virtue ethics provides a foundation in ethical theory tied to the history of professions as practice (Borden, 2007; MacIntyre, 2007) and to their contemporary situatedness within organizations, to which they must respond in this historical moment (Arnett & Arneson, 1999).

The enacted, communicative form of professional civility finds its theoretical coordinates in communication theory—specifically, a conceptualization of civility as communicative virtue (Fritz, 2011) and dialogic civility as a philosophy of communication that expresses a constructive understanding of responsiveness to what meets human beings in existence (Arnett & Arneson, 1999). A conceptualization of civility as communicative virtue defines a connecting point between virtue ethics and the communicative enactment of a professional community as a tradition of practice; the nexus of dialogic civility and organizational citizenship provides coordinates for recognizing the various goods of professional civility within the context of philosophy of interpersonal communication and organizational theory as these frameworks correspond to, and resonate with, the history and tradition of professions in response to the questions of this historical moment, and as they inform each other's constructive articulation of the potential for productive, meaningful life in organizations.

Professional civility is a "hypervirtue" or "gestalt virtue" that is theoretically textured, shaped, and enlarged by elements from several disciplinary domains, all of which work together in the service of those goods that define excellent enactment of professions within local institutional homes. Professional civility exhibits a "sensibility" (Barge & Little, 2008, pp. 513–514) for responsiveness to contexts of practice. Through the responsive, constructive communicative action of professional civility, professions and professional identities are constituted and reconstituted as human discourse shapes the nature of work, the organization, people, and the continually reforming profession.

The theoretical framework of professional civility could be summarized in this manner: The foundational background of professional civility consists of two components; one component is the history of professions as describing a tradition of practice from a virtue ethics and perspective, and the other is an understanding of civility as the communicative manifestation of civic virtue. When these background elements are brought together, a meeting of the horizons of dialogic civility and organizational citizenship against this background of profession(s) as practice and civility as communicative virtue reveals a conceptual space for professional civility as communicative virtue at work; the fusion of horizons of dialogic civility and organizational citizenship resolves as the communicative virtue of professional civility, revealing the goods of productivity, place, and persons.

Dialogic civility and organizational citizenship find a place of contribution within the professional civility framework as they bring into view several elements of the background components of profession as tradition of practice and civility as communicative virtue. Dialogic civility contributes responsiveness to the historical moment as a way of seeing professions as operating primarily within organizations, of which they are now citizens, a conceptualization consistent with their history as noble and worthy occupations. One of the conceptual articulations of organizational citizenship has pointed in the direction of civic virtue (Graham, 1991; Organ, 1988), which frames the organization as a civic space (see also Fritz & Arnett, 2007) in which discourse plays a key role. These two concepts bridge the tradition of profession(s) as practice and civility as communicative virtue and situate the organization as a contemporary home for professions, which is now added to professions' original goods of productivity and persons. In this manner, we understand professional civility as a communicative virtue that protects and promotes what are now revealed as the goods of profession(s) in this historical moment, which could be considered an extension of the tradition of profession(s) as practice that now engages work within organizations. The local home is an emergent good in this moment and becomes part of the tradition of professional practice.

In addition to these major conceptual contributors, the work of Arendt (1958) on labor, work, and action as part of the human condition, as well as a perspective on care for institutions (Fritz, 2012b) as an orientation of professional civility, the importance of public roles in protecting and promoting persons in organizations (Fritz, 2012a), and the importance of differentiation of public and private spheres (Arnett, 2006), offer theoretical texture here, or in subsequent chapters, addressing each of the different goods protected and promoted by professional civility. Other conceptual domains will also be brought to bear as they have relevance to the theory and practice of professional civility as communicative virtue at work. The framework of professional civility exists as a conceptual network that emerges in minimal form with the basic coordinates of profession as practice within a virtue ethics perspective and civility as the communicative manifestation of civic virtue. These elements are sufficient to highlight the idea in a very general form as a distinct contribution to our understanding of work life. The additional components of dialogic civility and organizational citizenship provide important content that permits the scope of the perspective to take a more definitive form. The additional conceptual contributions add detail connecting the foundational ideas to the lived experience of communicative action in organizational settings, bringing the theoretical formation into the pragmatic manifestation of communicative praxis.

Professional civility is presented here with fuzzy clarity (Arnett, 2001) as an understanding of the communicative elements of work life within the horizon of a constructive approach to institutions and organizing. Professional civility thus theorized serves as a public road map (Arnett, Fritz, & Bell, 2009) to provide shared common sense for a productive, engaged workplace. Professional civility works as a metaphor for the organizational domain (Arnett, 2001), offering an understanding of ethical interpersonal action for the workplace. This metaphorical vision begins with large scope and general strokes, finds definition as new conceptual content finds its place within the framework, and locates mobility and traction with the finer-grained minutiae of conversational utterances or speech acts. The vision moves to action in the communicative experience of professional life at work.

Because civility is grounded in conversational communicative practice, a defining feature of the human condition (MacIntyre, 2007), it is an essential attribute of what is good for a human being to be and to do—it is a constitutive element of the human telos. Professional civility encompasses conversations of various types undertaken in the course of carrying out a professional role, typically within the confines of an organizational setting. The conversation characteristic of professionally civil discourse shapes and defines professional practice (Barge & Little, 2008). Professional civility is the height of skillful communicative practice defining professional conduct and task accomplishment in organizational settings, shaping the culture and climate of the workplace and expressing the distinctive identity of the professional practitioner.

Barge and Little (2008) offered an analysis of micropractices of professionally skillful discourse—communicative interactions that focus on the tasks or work practices of professionals that define the actual "product" of the service professions they examined. Andersson and Pearson (1999) and Pearson, Andersson, and Porath (2000) addressed the importance of civility as a norm of interaction in organizational settings. Norms of interpersonal interaction defining professional work practices and guiding participation in organizations as contexts for work give rise to professional civility as communicative virtue at work and sustain productivity— the generativity of professional practice—as a defining feature and outcome of organizational action. Productivity is a key element in the history of the professions, demarcating the domain of professional action and training and the professions' contributions to the human community (Kimball, 1995; Sullivan, 2005).

The practice of profession(s) as moral metacommunity takes place within a local home constituting a community of memory and dwelling place (Arnett et al., 2009). The contextual nature of professional civility distinguishes professional civility as communicative virtue in organizations from civility as communicative virtue. Both civility and professional civility are communicative virtues. Professional civility has as its protected and promoted end a particular set of goods derived from the history of professions and the contemporary circumstances facing professionals today that run parallel to the more general end of civility as civic virtue, which protects and promotes the goods of cooperative public life. The "virtuous" discourse of professional practitioners is particularly attentive to just those goods, one of which is the local institutional home within which a profession is practiced. The unfolding tradition of the professions finds shape today within organizations that provide contexts for professional work. Professions as practice include host organizations as sites of professional labor, work, and action.

Civility as communicative virtue is the constructive counterpart of incivility as communicative vice (Fritz, 2011, 2012a, 2012b) and attains its status by its support of persons, communities, groups, and entire societies through development of normative communicative practices that define and enable cooperative public ways of life (Kingwell, 1995, 2000). Our discourse with others supports the good of others' personhood and their capabilities as manifested in their contributions to shared projects of enduring significance (Arendt, 1958). Professional civility as communicative virtue becomes part of sound moral character, an inclination or attitude toward other human beings who share the workplace that moves us to treat them as equal and valued members of the human community who inhabit roles that may be different from our own, and who contribute in unique ways to human flourishing and wholeness. Professional civility protects and promotes the good of persons in the organizational context.

The history of professional practice in the United States reveals the professions as dignified occupations espousing a tradition of service and concern for others. This concern for persons emerges in communicative action as professionals carry out their productive tasks in organizations. Bies (2001) and Bies and Moag (1986) pointed in this direction with the concept of interactional justice, which highlights the importance of communicating with others in a form that conveys dignity and respect in organizational contexts, as did Lutgen-Sandvik, Riforgiate, and Fletcher

(2011), who offered specific insights for professional civility in their study of positive experience in organizations, specifically, "discourses, or historical systems of meaning that inform positive assessments" (p. 3).

From Kimball's (1995) and Sullivan's (2005) treatment of the ongoing story of the professions, a framework for professional practice becomes clear, providing a backdrop against which other theoretical and applied work on the professions emerges to contribute to our thinking about the work and purpose of professional activity in a dynamic and changing world. Professions generate the conditions of their existence through the practices of their members. Professional civility gives birth to a constructive enactment of profession and avowal of professional identity, inviting enhanced ascription of worth and excellence on the part of external audiences as professional practitioners partake in concerted efforts of service made possible by renewed energies fostered by a supportive organizational climate and enriched by all the resources of communicative practices contributing to excellence. Professional civility draws on the historic tradition of professions as valued and honored occupations, putting this legacy into communicative practice as the story of the professions meets the communicative virtue of civility in this historical moment.

These coordinates of professional existence emerge through, and can be identified within, the various manifestations of civility in the workplace found in the various domains of concern for the face of the other as manifested in politeness theory, appropriate application of defensive and supportive communication, message design logic, communicative dialectics, verbal aggression and argumentativeness, phatic communication, and related areas of communicative action, which become professional civility by virtue of their enactment in organizations within the larger narrative of profession as practice and as they are given substance by the theoretical elements relevant to professional civility found in dialogic civility and the organizational citizenship literature. The placement of civility within the professional context gives character and shape to professional civility's particular communicative manifestation. These specific applications will be sketched in outline form at the end of this chapter and addressed more fully in Chapters 6, 7, and 8, which treat the goods of productivity, place, and persons. The practice or "craft" (Sennett, 2008) of profession(s) as a good in itself and as a contribution to the larger human good, the institution within which professionals practice, and the many others with whom work is done define coordinates of engagement for professional excellence and are protected and promoted through domains of discourse that manifest as professional civility.

Professional Civility: Conceptual Coordinates

Philosophy of Communication: Dialogic Civility

Arnett and Arneson (1999) pointed to the importance of limits, hope and cynicism, and the historical moment in their treatment of dialogic civility. Their work connects the constructive role of limits in organizational life to the dialectic of hope and cynicism in human engagement with institutional structures and responsiveness of persons and institutions to questions arising in a particular historical moment. Dialogic civility offers an interpretive engagement of and response to the uncertainties of life in a changing world of diversity and difference (Arnett et al., 2009).

Professional civility's conceptualization of meaning in human life and interaction as it draws on Arnett and Arneson's (1999) theorizing suggests that human wholeness emerges from multiple engagements with the world—public and private spheres of life provide balance and nourishment for each other (Arnett, 2006). Limits are necessary in each sphere to prevent "overrunning reality" (Arnett et al., 2009, p. 110) stemming from inappropriate expectations for either sphere. The course of work life offers both joy and disappointment; acknowledging the multiplicity of life's experiences provides the possibility of response and resilience in the face of the unwanted (Arnett et al., 2009; Hammoud & Buzzanell, in press). The confluence of a given historical moment, context, and relationship calls for discernment of what is required and possible as a fitting response (Schrag, 1986) in a given organizational event. Limits, hope and cynicism, and responsiveness to the historical moment work together in multiple domains of organizational experience relevant to the goods of professions: productivity, place, persons, and profession. Responsiveness to the historical moment is perhaps the architectonic key for the professions, one that orders and textures the other metaphors of conceptual engagement within the dialogic civility framework.

For the professions, this historical moment invites a commitment to home institutions within which professional work is done and to communities within which these institutions are situated. The model of situated professionalism addressed by Noordegraaf (2007) notes the movement of professions to new contexts of engagement, requiring greater attentiveness to limits defined by organizations within which professionals work. This historical moment asks professionals to attend to others in the work environment as valued co-laborers in meaningful tasks that make a difference for the human community, and to be of service to persons and projects outside the bounds of the organization. The historical moment asks the professions for a fitting response (Schrag, 1986) appropriate to the context within which professional work is accomplished today.

The fitting response in this instance, a response that serves and preserves the tradition (Schrag, 1986, p. 207) of professions, is one that protects and promotes the good of professions themselves through attentiveness to goods of productivity, place, and persons. As professionals respond creatively to their new situatedness, an approach closer to a hybridized professionalism than to a pure professionalism grounded in restricted categories of professions based on traditional criteria (Noordegraaf, 2007) offers a way to think differently about occupational and institutional loyalties. In hybridized professionalism, professionals become reflective practitioners with links to outside worlds as part of professional identity, a reconceptualization that harks back to the "age-old meanings of professionalism" (Noordegraaf, 2007, p. 774) as relational, involving interconnections among professionals and others in the social world and a concept of practice as intuitively constructive. This conceptualization of hybridized professionalism responds to an enlarged set of vocations moving toward professional status, reflecting an understanding of professionalism as an orientation to work rather than membership in static occupational categories. Although the current moment appears to reflect a situated professionalism (Noordegraaf, 2007), in which professional work is located within bureaucratic organizations, a shift in understanding of professions as reflective engagement with work, no matter the occupation, appears to be at hand. For the moment, the salience of a local home as location for professional practice is clear.

Arnett and Arneson (1999) addressed the role of narrative in human life in a historical moment of virtue contention and disagreement. Narrative provides continuity of meaning and opportunities for engagement as participants in a meaningful rendering of human existence. Narrative functions in an organization to secure public support for and participation in a corporate story or mission that guides an organizational "project" seeking contributions from persons committed to a variety of private or personal standpoints. An organization's narrative supplies argumentative parameters within which all participants find potential within publicly understood limits for conduct (Arnett & Fritz, 2003). Organizational leaders find traction within these limits. When managerial word and deed align with an organization's expectations, reduced cynicism and enhanced organizational commitment emerge from this behavioral modeling (Fritz, Arnett, & Conkel, 1999; Fritz, O'Neil, Popp, Williams, & Arnett, in press). Practices consistent with the mission generate trust and confidence in the organization, enhancing the organization's viability and offering hope to its participants (Arnett & Arneson, 1999).

Arnett and Arneson's (1999) discussion of the necessity of organizational limits urges institutional leaders to keep in mind the importance of productivity, of the mission and purpose of an organization, and of the capabilities of organizational participants who contribute to the organization's project. Organizational limits encourage leaders never to promise more than can be delivered, an injunction resonating with Arnett's (2006) emphasis on the importance of different domains of human engagement—the public sphere and the private sphere, each supporting the other. The organization cannot be a genuine family to all, but it can provide realistic limits and expectations for work done within its premises, identifying public parameters for decision-making and action at each institutional level. In this way, hope, rather than cynicism, emerges as a genuine alternative. Hope becomes grounded in what is possible and achievable, yielding concrete outcomes manifesting success and efficacy in one's endeavors directed toward the common good, and given acknowledgment by one's community of others (Lim & Bowers, 1991).

When organizations promise more than they can deliver, or when organizational participants expect more than is reasonably possible from work life, employees experience cynicism from unmet high expectations and fall prey to trivialization of crisis (Arnett, 2006, pp. 233, 235). Trivialization of crisis happens when one's focus of attention rests so much in one domain (e.g., the workplace) that every disappointing event (for example, an argument with a work colleague) assumes gargantuan proportions—it takes on the appearance of a crisis but does not deserve such a label. Under such conditions, one can no longer recognize a true crisis that deserves attention. Expectations for an organization to deliver more than it can—e.g., to be a "family" to organizational members—prompts this unrealistic focus on the domain of work and the subsequent distortion of events (Arnett, 2006). Such distortion compromises the goods of profession—productivity, place, and persons—and narrows the possibilities of professionals' contributions to organizations and communities. Respecting organizational limits provides realistic hope for organizations to play a role in human life and experience that attains significance and meaning in its proper place. Such is the substance of the existential question of this historical moment for professions.

Colleagues acknowledge limits by respecting boundaries of coworkers who seek to separate private and public life. By offering support to the autonomy needs of others, work associates inspire hope and reduce cynicism as they help each other focus attention on what is possible and attainable in organizational life within mission limits and role boundaries. Colleagues help each other discern the parameters of a particular historical moment facing an institution and its members. In moments of change, particularly, when ambiguity characterizes the organizational environment and it is not clear what to do, messages that construct an environment of possibility and hope rather than despair and distress respond to the inevitable with constructive framings, fostering resilience in self and others (Buzzanell, Shenoy, Remke, & Lucas, 2009; Hammoud & Buzzanell, in press).

A dialogic civility approach to organizations acknowledges differentiation of public and private spheres, a marker of professional civility as a reclamation of organizational limits (Arnett, 2006). Limits emerge from various facets of human life and provide protection from overextension (e.g., Wieland, Bauer, & Deetz, 2009). As organizational members find possibilities for transcendence and joy in work, limits may shift within a horizon of possibilities, opening the way for development of constructive work relationships that enrich life in many ways while still working within guidelines of organizational policies and expectations. Our behaviors build who we are (Arnett & Arneson, 1999, p. 54), and through our collective becoming, an organizational environment takes shape.

Professional civility becomes a type of public "common sense" in an era of virtue and narrative contention when instituted at the organizational level (Arnett et al., 2009). Professional civility provides space to live and communicate, as well as connection to guide meaningful action together; in the organizational setting, creative contributions to the workplace emerge through the interspaces of distance (Arnett & Arneson, p. 286); through attentiveness to others, professional civility provides the solidarity needed for concerted effort around a common center (Arnett, 1986). A dialogic understanding of professional civility points toward the responsibilities of organizational citizenship as a metaphor for engagement in institutional life.

Organizational Behavior: Organizational Citizenship

Organizational citizenship provides an important conceptual touchstone for the manifestation of professional civility as communicative virtue through specification of elements of behavior that assist others, enhance one's own and others' productivity, and support the organization and its purposes. Organizational citizenship (Bateman & Organ, 1983; Organ, 1988; Smith, Organ, & Near, 1983) describes behavior helpful to others and to the organization that is not part of the formal job description and is done without coercion or expectation of immediate reward. Organizational citizenship is formally defined as "individual behavior that is discretionary, not directly or explicitly recognized by the formal reward system, and in the aggregate promotes the efficient and effective functioning of the organization" (Organ, Podsakoff, & MacKenzie, 2006, p. 3).

Organizational citizenship extends beyond the realm of the professions as traditionally understood (Kimball, 1995) and is applicable to a variety of occupations and workplace configurations, a flexibility that connects it to a situated and hybridized professionalism emergent today, characterized by a vastly expanded set of professionalizing occupations (as Noordegraaf, 2007, described it, the "professionalization of everyone," p. 771). To date, limited research exists on organizational citizenship in relation to the professions. One study involving nurses noted that organizational citizenship appears to have a complex relationship to professionalism as measured by a modified version of Hall's professionalism scale (representative items include "I read professional journals," "Nursing is accounted indispensable," "I will work as a nurse even with a low income," "I have a sense of calling for work in nursing," "Idealism maintained in nursing," Cohen & Kol, 2004, p. 395), which suggests that the link between professionalism and organizational citizenship behavior (OCB) may be stronger for professions requiring extensive education, a characteristic of the traditional professions (Kimball, 1995).

Multiple approaches to conceptualizing and operationalizing the organizational citizenship construct have emerged over the last decades, making systematic assessment of its status difficult. According to Podsakoff, MacKenzie, Paine, and Bachrach (2000), close to 30 potentially different forms of OCB can be identified in the literature (cited in Organ et al., 2006, p. 297). As noted by Organ et al. (2006), "A major unresolved issue is whether important additional forms of OCB that have not been recognized in the literature exist and whether those forms that have already been identified are really distinct from each other" (p. 236). For assessing the organizational citizenship construct's relevance to professional civility, I rely primarily on Organ et al. (2006), who reviewed the literature on organizational citizenship behavior and related constructs (e.g., contextual work behavior) and organized the extensive set of conceptualizations and operationalizations of this construct.

The emerging conceptualization of professional civility and current conceptualizations of organizational citizenship share several underlying assumptions, although the disciplinary and philosophical lineage of each construct is distinct, making organizational citizenship a fitting contributor to the professional civility framework. Organizational citizenship taps a voluntary contribution to the organization as community that can be understood within the framework of *hesed*—that which must be done for the good of the community but cannot be demanded. It is an ethical response grounded in concern for the Other (Arnett et al., 2009, p. 128). Smith et al. (1983), for example, developed their scale by asking managers about employee behavior that they "appreciated but could not demand, enforce, or directly reward" (Organ et al., 2006, p. 247). Professional civility, likewise, has at its heart this *hesed* commitment to the good of the whole (Arnett et al., 2009), reflective of an orientation of care for institutions (Fritz, 2012b). It is a gestalt engagement of work, rather than a piecemeal accounting for specified units of labor in exchange for precise remuneration.

The axiological foundation of professional civility is a trust in the potential of human beings to work together cooperatively for the good of the whole on a proximal common task, as part of a narrative or story of the professions (Kimball, 1995; Sullivan, 2005). The ongoing history of the professions becomes a larger project or distal common task engaged and generated through actions in the proximal sphere. A similar impulse, although more diffuse, underlies organizational citizenship as it was originally conceptualized and throughout its continued refinement and development. Organ et al. (2006, p. 247) highlighted the work of Smith et al. (1983), who focused on the notion of cooperation, a concept that ties into theoretical material by W. F. May (2001) that focused on cooperative endeavors as an element of professionalism. Smith et al. distinguished cooperation from productivity, but from a professional civility standpoint, these items form a gestalt, a larger picture given coherence by a background structure of meaning derived from the narrative of profession(s) as practice.

May (2001) warned against too much focus on process, of which he considers cooperation a specific instance, and emphasized the need for a substantive good as central to any group or organization: "Subjectively acting in concert with others summarizes the virtues of process. Objectively, the common good defines the goal which the leaders of the enterprise must pursue" (p. 133). Hence, the common project or task toward which, or for which, cooperation is engaged remains the focus of attention for professional civility. The common task provides a focal point for energy and cooperative effort, reducing the relative importance of other concerns, which, while still present, shift into either supportive elements aligned with the goal of accomplishment of a given task, or into peripheral matters that can be attended to when time and energy permit. The task becomes the primary criterion by which effort is evaluated. However, the accompanying goods of place and persons are also present in dynamic tension with the good of the task—a conceptual configuration anticipated by, and theorized within, the organizational citizenship construct, which addresses the good of the organization and the good of others within the larger organizational community. Although productivity is primary, it is not the only good to take into account, as is also the case for professional civility as conceptualized thus far.

One conceptualization of the organizational citizenship construct situated its foundation within the political science literature (Graham, 1986, 1991), which prompted inclusion of civic virtue as an element of organizational citizenship in Organ's (1988) theorizing. Citizenship from a political perspective "describes the status of belonging somewhere, and it implies both rights and responsibilities" (Graham, 1991, p. 251) and a commitment to cooperation, negotiation, and compromise when conflict arises, along with a willingness to raise objections and advocate change when needed. Graham focused on the covenantal nature of the connection of employees to organizations, following Buber (1958), emphasizing the moral dimension of this type of belonging (see also Kimball, 1995, p. 123) that results in generosity toward the collective manifesting in extra effort expended toward its flourishing.

Graham's (1991) "civic" formulation of organizational citizenship has the strongest conceptual kinship with professional civility, and it highlights the civic virtue connection between "civility" and "citizenship" as a link between the constructs, emphasizing a commitment to the common good and a responsibility for personal contributions to a shared project through communicative action. Professionals become citizens in their participation within the context of the organization; their "civic virtue" becomes professional civility, manifested in particular types of constructive discourse protecting and promoting productivity, place, persons, and the profession. This dimension appears in several conceptualizations and operationalizations of organizational citizenship—for example, in Podsakoff et al.'s (1990) work, which revealed five categories of organizational citizenship behavior (Organ et al., 2006).

Podsakoff et al.'s (1990) five categories of OCB each have relevance to professional civility. The five categories refer to employee discretionary behavior consisting of altruism, conscientiousness, sportsmanship, courtesy, and civic virtue. Altruism refers to helping another person with an organizationally relevant problem, and hence is related to protecting and promoting the good of others, of productivity, and of the organization. Conscientiousness describes an employee who goes well beyond what is required by the organization in terms of attendance, following rules and regulations, taking breaks, and similar elements. Conscientiousness is behavior focused on the good of the organization, and marks the identity of a professional in its protection and promotion of the organization. Each of these dimensions holds implications for communicative practices tapping significant areas of organizational life.

The dimension of sportsmanship addresses communication specifically. Sportsmanship refers to communicative behaviors that protect and promote goods of productivity and the organization; good sportsmanship involves avoiding complaining when one doesn't get one's own way—in other words, avoiding trivialization of crisis (Arnett, 2006)—and resists behaviors such as starting arguments with others and talking about wanting to quit the job. Other items include making positive statements about one's supervisor and making constructive statements about one's department. Connections to dialogic civility (Arnett & Arneson, 1999) emerge here as avoiding routine cynicism and promoting realistic hope within limits.

Courtesy can be understood as taking a communicative form in its conceptualization as preventing work-related problems with others from occurring by, for instance, alerting others to impending actions that might affect their work, thereby protecting and promoting the goods of productivity and persons. Civic virtue refers to responsible participation in, and concern for, the life of the company, protecting and promoting the good of place, or the organization. The dimensions of courtesy and civic virtue reflect the verbal action necessary to carry on public life in institutional settings. Courtesy's meaningful action works rhetorically to shape organizational climate and culture in constructive directions. Civic virtue, which refers to sharing ideas for the good of the whole, including dissent (Graham, 1991; see also Kassing, 1998), protects and promotes the good of place. Civic virtue, with its emphasis on suggestions and contributions, tempers organizational dissent in its constructive engagement of and turning toward the common center (Arnett, 1986) or good of the whole, and resonates with a conceptualization of civility as the communicative manifestation of civic virtue practiced in the local home of contemporary professions. When suggestions work within the limits of an organization's mission, they function as a type of Kantian imagination (Arnett, forthcoming-b), pointing to the possible rather than wishing for the unworkable in a given local home.

The categories of altruism and courtesy may not be empirically distinct, according to the results of some studies (Organ et al., p. 255). Conceptually, a connection between these two categories resulting in low discrimination between them would be expected, since courtesy is, by definition, concern for the sensibilities of others—an altruistic orientation (Forni, 2002, 2008). This dimension may be particularly relevant to the good of persons in the professional civility formulation.

An approach to organizational citizenship taken by Williams and Anderson (1991, cited in Organ et al., 2006) identifies behaviors that benefit the organization and behaviors that benefit a specific person, with the latter assisting the organization indirectly. Several of these items have a communicative manifestation. One of the individually focused items measures the extent to which an employee "takes time to listen to co-workers' problems and worries" (Organ et al., 2006, p. 256). For professional civility, this item could be contextualized as a temporally appropriate active listening (Gordon, 1970) focused on work-related concerns for which one might offer some type of assistance or corrective action, rather than supporting a "soap opera star" (Fritz, 2002, 2006) who dwells obsessively on personal problems and worries to the detriment of the task, taking others' time and energy away from work.

Another communicative item in the Williams and Anderson (1991) conceptualization is "passes along information to co-workers" (Organ et al., 2006, p. 256). Some examples of organizational citizenship behavior focused on the organization (OCBO) include "gives advance notice when unable to come to work," the reverse-scored "great deal of time spent with personal phone conversations," and the reverse-scored "complains about insignificant things at work" (Organ et al., pp. 256–257). These items are discursive or conversational in nature and tap the conceptual domain of professional civility in its protection and promotion of productivity. Time spent in personal phone conversations takes time away from work; complaining about issues of minor significance takes the focus of attention away from the task and can lead to trivialization of crisis in the workplace (Arnett, 2006), further hampering productivity.

The scale used by Smith et al. (1983) likewise includes items related to making good use of time or not wasting it—for example, not spending time in non-work-related conversation (Organ et al., 2006, p. 248). Examples from Smith et al.'s scale include avoiding taking unnecessary breaks and refraining from idle conversation—compliance with constraints needed to make a cooperative system. Specifically, Organ et al. (2006) noted that the dimension of generalized compliance or conscientiousness involves adhering to the spirit of rules/norms of the cooperative system (p. 19). Organ et al. (2006) highlighted explicitly how more productivity results from less time spent on excessive breaks, personal phone calls, and idle chatter—"more productive labor can be expended in doing the job" (p. 20). The relationship of the nature of communication to productivity is salient in this rendering.

The items defining generalized compliance "seem to reflect compliance with internalized norms defining what a good employee ought to do" (Organ et al., 2006, p. 248). The value of these items for professional civility lies in their resonance with supporting productivity, the organization, and other persons in the workplace. These items define important elements corresponding to the underlying components of professional civility and resonate with Sullivan's (2005) treatment of the virtue of professionalism (e.g., punctuality, avoiding undeserved breaks, does not "coast" toward the end of the day, does not take unnecessary time off work). This particular element is relevant to productivity and, when juxtaposed with the altruism items (e.g., volunteers for things that are not required, makes innovative suggestions to improve department; helps others who have heavy workloads), reflects the joy of the doing of the craft, a "laboring together in harmony" (Sennett, 2008, p. 161) that marks the professional practitioner (Sullivan, 2005).

Many of these measures are relevant to each domain of professional civility—productivity, place, and persons. For example, in terms of people (or relationships), organizational citizenship offers the professional civility framework a willingness to go the extra mile and to exhibit communicative behaviors that help and support the work of others. In that way, it also protects productivity—or work—and the place—or local home—through civic virtue (as a counterpart or parallel term to organizational dissent). Likewise, the profession grows or becomes bigger and more expansive through the constructive actions of its members, because the profession itself is shaped by its members and expands its capacities through its members—the tradition of practice extends and develops (MacIntyre, 2007).

Just as organizational citizenship may resonate with the conceptual foundations of professional civility, so may professional civility's conceptualization provide insights into organizational citizenship. For example, Organ et al. (2006, p. 246) had a question related to the operationalization of Bateman and Organ's (1983) original scale. They wondered why "seeking others' help when needed" would be related to OCB (e.g., helping others). The philosophical foundations of professional civility offer a good reason—from a perspective of cooperative action around a common task, one avoids the "lone wolf" syndrome, recognizing the interconnectedness of coworkers engaged in a common task.

Another insight relates to the connection of talking about wanting to quit one's job and job satisfaction. In Bateman and Organ's (1983) original study, a correlation was found between talking about wanting to quit the job (as assessed by employees' supervisors, reverse-scored) and job satisfaction (as reported by employees); Organ (1988) wondered about the connection, and suggested that the former item, and many related to it, might be assessing the supervisor's perception of an employee's job satisfaction, resulting in an artificially high correlation. Another explanation emerges when the connection is examined from the perspective of professional civility: Talk about wanting to quit the job focuses attention on private distress and is not constructive for the unit as a whole. It is better kept quiet or discussed with a limited number of others—select persons or mentors who can help contextualize concerns and make plans for a constructive response. This conceptual underpinning explains why refraining from talk about wanting to quit one's job would reflect organizational citizenship. Understanding organizational citizenship within the broader construct of professional civility may also add to an explanation of why satisfaction leads to productivity in the long run (Organ, Podsakoff, & MacKenzie, 2006, pp. 66–69) rather than in the short run.

Integration

Dialogic civility (Arnett & Arneson, 1999) and organizational citizenship (Bateman & Organ, 1983; Organ, 1988) inform one another, from the perspective of professional civility, in a number of ways. It is my goal here to illustrate how these coordinates and the background framework of the tradition of professions and civility as communicative virtue interact. I see this framework as something akin to a conceptual kaleidoscope in which the various pieces or fragments of these perspectives, in all their multiplicity of color and shape, come together in novel and interesting ways when the object case, the part of the tube that contains the conceptual fragments, is turned. The position of the object case at any given point defines a context of organizational life; the pieces form and reform each time as the context changes, with the pieces reconfiguring responsively in each case. Another way to consider this framework is as a phenomenological encounter with an object that manifests sides, aspects, and profiles (Sokolowski, 2000). Different parts can come into view at different times as a focus of attention, with the other parts at that time appearing as background when one is working with, or observing, the object; it has a reality to it that is perceived differently, depending on the position, but there are definite attributes that form its parts. It has a horizon (Gadamer, 1986) with conceptual integrity.

One locus of interconnection between dialogic civility and organizational citizenship lies with Kingwell's (1995) understanding of civility as civic virtue through "just talking" (p. 8)—civility as communicative virtue manifested in the organizational context through attentiveness to the "positive face" of the organization (Brown & Levinson, 1978/1987). For example, Arnett and Arneson's (1999) distinction between appropriate and routine cynicism contextualizes the "sportsmanship" dimension of the organizational citizenship construct, and offers a place for organizational dissent (Kassing, 1998, 2001) to reflect the "civic virtue" dimension of the organizational citizenship construct (see also Graham, 1991). This connection ties to Kingwell's model of civility in public discourse, which was designed to help citizens engage political compromise stemming from competing visions of "the good" for human life. In that sense, it may reflect a concern for recognizing and advocating what is possible in organizational contexts—that is, within the context of organizational limits. Professional civility involves active support and constructive dissent within the argumentative parameters of an organization's mission limits to protect and promote the organization.

An organization's limits, in the context of Kingwell's (1995) work, can be understood as publicly defined goods that function as a priori commitments to organizational "citizens." The function of Kingwell's (1995) "just talking" in the context of organizations could rest with working out, through deliberative discourse, how best to achieve or support the organization's narrative or mission in a given circumstance—to identify the best way to realize that good. When a violation of the mission is perceived, a sense of injustice emerges, resulting in dissent (Graham, 1991, p. 266–267; Kassing, 1998) as a result of appropriate cynicism stemming from a mismatch between organizational words and deeds (Arnett & Arneson, 1999, p. 17). "Just talking" might then take the form of dissent to offer correction to practices that do not reflect the organization's mission. When dissent works to encourage action to assist or restore an organization that has lost its way, it works constructively as a reminder of the importance of direction, even in the midst of change, calling for "responsiveness to a reflective tradition" (Arnett et al., 2009, p. 177) as well as to new circumstances.

"Just talking" in organizations may also work to reinterpret or change some element of the publicly articulated good of an organization, or to offer an alternative narrative or understanding of the good that calls into question current communicative practices (Arnett et al., 2009, p. 146). Such changes may reflect shifted commitments taken on as the "change" part of the dialectic of direction and change in response to a new historical moment, while still being attentive to a reflective tradition (Arnett et al., 2009, p. 176). In each case, "just talking" is an element of professional civility that works to protect and promote the organization. Protecting and promoting the organization reflects responsible action on the part of the tradition of the professions responding to this historical moment from the perspective of situated professionalism (Nordegraaf, 2007).

Practices of Professional Civility: A First Look

In everyday conversational practice in organizations, discourse emerges as professional civility from an orientation to the meaning of work within the larger context of the unity of a life (MacIntyre, 2007). Professional civility as communicative virtue at work joins civility as communicative virtue to the tradition of profession(s) as practice with the philosophical framework of dialogic civility and organizational citizenship. Here, I bring into the field of vision civility as communicative virtue and point to its intersection with the other conceptual coordinates contributing to professional civility as communicative virtue at work. Skilled professional discourse embraces varied lines of action to accomplish the enactment of professions in the workplace.

Politeness theory's framing of negative/autonomy face, positive/fellowship face, and competence face (Lim & Bowers, 1991) suggests an orientation to communicative distance and space, connection and appreciation, and respect for others' contributions that builds communities through coordinated action within organizational limits. Positive politeness, through protecting competence face, expresses appreciation for others' work, making the likelihood of continued focus on the task as an element of pride in one's work greater. When I tell Pat, "I couldn't have done this project without you. Your suggestion made all the difference," I make explicit and clear the value of her contribution to our work together. "We are such a good team!"

marks her affirming and affirmative response as supportive of the work we do together as organizational citizens, professionals contributing work of value to the human community through our participation in this institution's purpose.

The indirectness of tact buffers feelings and permits attention to remain on the task at hand, protecting persons and productivity, and also protects the organization through influence on communication climate (Guzley, 1992). "Perhaps another day would be better to work on that advertisement," Erik says to Randy, who has clearly come unprepared for a meeting. Erik does not draw attention to Randy's failure, but provides space for a recovery. Such tact does not prevent directness and accuracy of communication about problems, but permits such discourse to take place in a time and place that permits remedy and repair in private, out of the scrutiny of the public eye. Such contextual care avoids the appearance of incivility and rudeness as interpreted by third parties that may contribute to decreased task performance (Porath & Erez, 2009). The discourse of politeness protects relationships through navigating comfortable levels of relational closeness, as we see when coworkers negotiate relational processes of escalation control (preventing a relationship from growing closer) and decline intervention (preventing a relationship from growing more distant) through tactics such as indirect conversational refocus—limiting conversation to work-related topics, for example (Sias, Gallagher, Kopeneva, & Pederson, 2012). Such communicative action respects dialogic limits of organizational relationships and keeps attention on the task, redirecting energy toward productivity.

Negative politeness (Brown & Levinson, 1978/1987), or protection of autonomy face (Lim & Bowers, 1991), protects and promotes the good of others at work by permitting coworkers the professional distance necessary to operate with a degree of independence supportive of professional identity. Such protection of independence permits the possibility of joint work that emerges as a result of appropriate attention and attentiveness available only through distance in relationships (Arnett et al., 2009; Fritz, in press-c). Distance permits one to see the other in perspective and enables a return to connection through task interdependence (Kiggundu, 1983; Tagger & Haines, 2006). In the case of disliked coworkers, limits of ritualized communication based in conventional design logic provide space for cooperative action without the tyranny of intimacy (Sennett, 1974).

In the case of each type of politeness, context needs to guide. Stating, "Let me know if I can help out with those folders" rather than simply taking over the project protects the other's independence, and may be the needed contribution in some cases. However, joining in the task without a word might be called for at another time. In that case, the co-construction of coordinated activity without the verbal declaration of "I will help you" (and without the need for the other to ask directly for help) is a smoothly instantiated execution of "direct indirectness" that keeps attention on the task engaged together rather than the need (and implied lack of ability, however understandable) of the other. The organization as a whole takes on an expansive nature when the dialectic of autonomy and interdependence (Baxter & Montgomery, 1996) finds room for free play. Further, the acknowledgment of need for another's help provides assurance that each person's efforts are vital for the success of the work. Such reinforcement returns as support for competence face (Lim & Bowers, 1991) with its recognition of one's contributions to the community.

Message design logic's various modalities of communicative engagement suggest contextually bound lines of action for accomplishing goals in discourse. Spontaneous outbursts of appreciation and recognition punctuate the workday when an accomplishment defies the formality of structured accolades. Tactful engagement in public conversation leaves opportunity for private correction and redirection through attentiveness to the negative face and autonomy needs of coworkers. Communicative ritual and formalities of the everyday provide moments of respite and routine engaged through conventional design logic and phatic communication, resulting in stability and certainty during moments of change. Similarly, adherence to conversational ritual in moments of stress protects future projects; such displays, in their external affirmation of connection amidst differences, provide hope for future action to bring about change as ideas vie for adherence in the public sphere of work. Through attentiveness to one's own goals and those of others, creative framing of possibilities in response to mistakes employs the richness of rhetorical design logic to open up spaces for engagement in unexpected ways. When conflicting aims emerge, rhetorical design logic enables coworkers and supervisors to negotiate creative solutions to problems through learning and responsiveness to the "rhetorical interruptions" (Arnett et al., 2009, p. 129) inevitable in institutional and personal life. Fairhurst's (2011) work offers examples of the use of rhetorical design logic in leadership discourse that illustrate these principles' application in organizational contexts.

Conclusion

Two problems have emerged in today's organizational milieu. The problem of incivility in organizations is serious and severe, and professionals, who now do most of their work in organizations rather than as autonomous or semi-autonomous practitioners, are facing challenges to their integrity. These two phenomena are related. If we examine the history of professions through the lens of MacIntyre's virtue ethics, we see the professions as a tradition of practice marked by goods internal to practice. If we examine civility as the communicative manifestation of civic virtue, understand the professions as extending their tradition in response to the historical moment as suggested by the framework of dialogic civility, and consider the "civic" of civic virtue to be the organizational setting as suggested by the organizational citizenship literature, then we see the virtue of professional civility emerging as a potential answer to both the crisis of incivility in the workplace and the crisis of profession(al)s today.

The next chapter provides a pragmatic perspective on professional civility by offering a case for the shaping influence of communication on organizational and interpersonal outcomes. A perspective on communication as constitutive (Ashcraft, Kuhn, & Cooren, 2009) provides a part of the conceptual framework for considering the role of communication in the process of organizational socialization through the perspective of representative theories of sociolinguistics as a context to exemplify the power of communication in the workplace. In the last part of the next chapter, I review literature on the effects of incivility on workplace processes and outcomes and offer some concluding thoughts on the implications of a professional civility perspective for professional and organizational socialization.

A Pragmatic Case for the Effects of Communication in the Workplace

Introduction

Professional civility matters because of its work on behalf of environments in which people encounter one another while accomplishing tasks. The social spaces we inhabit draw their nourishment from the treatment we accord one another, as Carter (1998), Forni (2002, 2008), Kingwell (1995), Peck (1994), and others have illustrated. The work of professional civility is accomplished through communicative interaction in the workplace, as is the deconstructive work of incivility and rudeness (Fritz, 2009, 2011, 2012a; Pearson & Erez, 2007; Pearson & Erez, 2009; Pearson & Porath, 2009). Professional civility matters because of its communicative power for constructive influence on environments; professional civility combats incivility's deleterious effects and creates a supportive ambience conducive to accomplishing work (Fritz, 2011, 2012b).

This chapter gathers evidence to answer the "so what" question—why does professional civility matter pragmatically in organizational environments? I begin with a general discussion of the shaping force of communication, drawing on representative findings from scholarship on the effects of communication on persons, relationships, and institutions, focusing primarily on the organizational context. I then explore the specific case of effects of communication on employee values during the organizational socialization process. If professional civility is to do its work on behalf of organizations and their members, one of the most important moments for this virtue to be cultivated is during the initial stages of the socialization process; as Kramer (2010) noted, socialization occurs "through communication between organizational members" (p. 4), and it is through these communication processes that members make sense of, and adopt, practices that both define and construct organizational culture.

Although professional civility as a professional communication ethic ideally would be embraced and inculcated during professional socialization, the instantiation of professional civility's application in a particular local organizational home makes the organizational socialization process an important context for learning professional civility as it may be practiced in a particular organization. To that end, I offer some commentary on professional civility as it fits within conceptual frameworks discussed in the section addressing organizational socialization. To conclude the chapter, I draw on evidence from research on incivility and related negative communication behaviors in the workplace to highlight the growing body of research documenting the effects of incivility in the workplace in terms of human and material costs (e.g., Pearson & Porath, 2009), which professional civility aims to combat.

Communication as Constitutive

Communication theorists taking one of many social approaches to communication (e.g., Leeds-Hurwitz, 1995; Pearce, 1994) follow the symbolic interactionist tradition (e.g., McCall & Simmons, 1978; Mead, 1936) in maintaining that our social worlds are structured through interaction with others. Definitions of self and of the surrounding environment created and enacted during communicative interaction guide further interpretations of action, creating ever broader patterns of meaning that form the web of interpretive schemes guiding meaningful human activity (Giddens, 1984). Kimball (1995) took a rhetorical perspective in his examination of the tradition of professions in his recognition that language shapes understandings of reality and phenomena in the social world: "Expressing the thoughts and feelings of an individual, rhetoric is itself shaped by the exchange with others' expressions, and that shaping inevitably reforms the individual's thoughts and feelings and influences their future expression" (p. 15).

Work by organizational communication scholars during the last decades highlighted the importance of microprocesses of interaction and language, which carry the power of communication in work environments (Ashcraft, Kuhn, & Cooren,

2009; Collins, Gill, & Mease, in press; Fairhurst 2011). Communication creates our social worlds (Holmes & Stubbe, 2003; Pearce, 1994, 2007); it is constitutive of organizational processes and structures that constrain and enable organizational actors (Miller, 2006)—some say communication *is* organizing (e.g., Cooren, 2000; Taylor & Van Every, 2000). Communication is structured, exhibiting regular, recognizable patterns in relationships (Rogers & Farace, 1975; Seibold & Myers, 2006; Stech, 1976; Watzlawick, Beavin, & Jackson, 1967). The importance of this structure to relational outcomes is evident in the literature on interpersonal interaction (e.g., Albrecht & Cooley, 1980; Cappella, 1984; Myers, 2010; Ward, 1968). Communicative patterns exert influence on expectations for key aspects of social life in larger group contexts through socialization practices in both the family (Hunter, 1984; McLeod & Chaffee, 1972; Tims, 1986) and the workplace (Jablin, 1984; Katz, 1980; Leitko, Greil, & Peterson, 1985).

Ashcraft et al. (2009) reviewed the constitutive view of communication, which assumes that communication is "a central organizing process that manages the intersection of symbolic and material worlds"—that "communication generates, not merely expresses, key organizational realities" (p. 2). This perspective captures the power of communication processes in organizational contexts, reflecting social theory's linguistic turn, which identified language as a producer rather than a reflector of realities in the social world (Rorty, 1967, as cited in Ashcraft et al., 2009). Language is an ontological condition of human experience, inherently tied to human being, and communication is the constitutive vehicle of the work of language—communication creates social realities (Searle, 1995, as cited in Ashcraft et al., 2009). Communication puts abstract structures in organizational settings "into live motion" (p. 4), manifesting the joint production, among and between organizational members, of the organization itself, from role relationships and organizational structures to organizational culture and climate. Communication creates the realities of organizational life (p. 4).

Communication also creates realities of interpersonal life. Communication interaction structure is an important property of a dyadic system (Albrecht & Cooley, 1980; Ward, 1968), yielding predictable relational outcomes (Gottman, 1994). Patterns of messages define a system through the form of communication and by means of what the act of communication itself implies: for example, patterns of mutual self-disclosure at an intimate level may define a close friendship and shape a sense of trust between two parties. In this sense, the meaning carried by an utterance in the context of the relationship conveys information crucial to interactants' roles in relation to each other beyond the actual content of the message (Bateson, 1972; Watson, 1982), although the content itself also carries meaning that is likewise influenced by the context of the relationship in which it is uttered. For example, if Eliza, who is Ralph's workplace mentor, typically provides corrective feedback to Ralph, but one day gives him a compliment, that compliment may mean something quite different and carry more weight than a compliment from Jerry, who is Ralph's long-time personal friend and offers positive comments on a regular basis. Each relationship takes on meaning through the utterances contributed by each relational participant (Pearce & Pearce, 2004). Sias's (2009a) treatment of workplace relationships offers multiple instances of research on the communicative constitution of workplace relationships from a social constructionist perspective.

The influence of relational messages begins in the initial stages of relationship development where the nature of the dyadic entity first takes on potential definition; as communicative practices develop regularity, the relationship's meaning gradually takes form, following the trajectory of the initial pattern. This initial influence is typically broad in scope, serving to shape the general contours of an evolving relational form marked by role-limited interaction (Rawlins, 1981). Fairhurst, Rogers, and Sarr (1987) suggested that the nature of the relationship that emerges through message patterns influences participants' abilities to process messages and serves to mediate judgments of each other's appropriateness and competence that add to the context of the relationship and shape the nature of further communicative contributions to its developing trajectory. Furthermore, message attributes, such as level of politeness, serve to influence judgments of the power and status of the recipient of such messages made by third parties (Bauman & Harden, 1990). Duck, Foley, and Kirkpatrick (2006) made a related point in their theorizing about the influence of organizational roles on perceptions of "difficult" coworkers. They focused on the structural requirements of work roles as contributing factors to perceptions of others as "difficult," but their treatment of the rhetorical construction of others in the workplace through verbal utterances serves to illustrate this process well.

The effect of language on relationships and relational participants through communication is closely related to the power of communication to constitute organizations through linguistic action. Persons and larger social contexts do not exist in isolation from each other, but are mutually constitutive. The mutual shaping of interactants holds implications for the larger context in which a relationship is embedded. As communicative interaction with others contributes to each person's self-definition and to others' definition of that particular person as part of a larger unit (a relationship, team, department, or other unit), the cumulative effect of many such interactions on the resulting relational forms contributes to the constitution of an entire collective (such as an organization; e.g., Cooren, Thompson, Canestraro, & Bodor,

2006; Myers, 2010; Schneider, 1987; Giddens, 1984; Seibold & Myers, 2006). The gradual shaping of an organization's culture and climate takes place over time as communicative practices form and reform the patterned structure of interaction, shaping expectations for behavior and sedimenting those increasingly regular patterns. As Fairhurst (2004) noted, "Systems emerge over repeated actions that evolve into multi-leveled orders of pattern" (p. 342).

In this way, we see how social structure may be defined as communication patterning (Ritchie, 1987). A specific property of the communication between two individuals may, if repeated over time, take on structural characteristics, understood as more or less reliable patterns of behavior that work functionally to carry particular levels of certainty or uncertainty about another's behavior, or about two persons' behavior together (Berger & Calabrese, 1975; Berger & Luckmann, 1967). For example, status differences in a dyad compose one such "system" variable influencing the pattern of interaction (Ward, 1968). Regularities in interactional patterning become implemented as norms, or those aspects of structure perceived as "how things ought to be" (or "how we do things around here"; see Kramer, 2010, p. 3). This aspect of structure implies that repeated interaction leads to expectations for, or increased predictability of, each dyad member's behavior (although such behavior is not determined, but merely more or less likely or probable), with implications for the larger social unit by virtue of particular relationships' participation in, and contributions to, the larger system.

In this manner, roles that develop across several dyads or groupings of people carry both normative force for the larger unit, as their patterns of interaction become part of the continually developing system, and continued identity information for self and others (Myers, 2010). The normative force of these roles and the expectations they create are especially powerful, considering the tendency of human action to become scripted, or mindless (Langer & Newman, 1979). In other words, our everyday behavior takes the form of unreflective practices that are ordinarily unrecognized in everyday living, brought to mind only when violations of expectations for behavior occur (e.g., Johnson, 2012) or when conditions change and taken-for-granted practices no longer work (e.g., Arnett, Fritz, & Bell, 2009). Unreflective practices are functional "common sense" that work to guide behavior, not only in cultures (Arnett et al., 2009), but in relationships, as well.

Defining features of relationships and social systems, then, begin with utterances exchanged between persons—through communication during "routine and mundane" patterns of organizational conversational behavior (Cooren, 2004, p. 518). The nature of these utterances is shaped by the interactants and other contextual characteristics, which were themselves shaped by previous actions; once a pattern takes form, its continued structuring action not only shapes the immediate definition of the relationship, but also constrains future possibilities for interaction. Communication gives rise to expectations for interaction in relationships and larger social systems which, when acted upon and reinstantiated over time through repeated practice, become structural properties of a system (Giddens, 1984) at the dyadic and larger level. Through *praxis*, actors create subsequent conditions into which they act (Baxter & Montgomery, 1996; Holmes & Stubbe, 2003); as Fairhurst (2004) noted of communication in workplace settings, "The context of any individual action is the sequence of behaviors that preceded it, with that action destined to itself become part of the context as it unfolds" (p. 341). In this manner, communication constitutes both relationships and social system environments. Relationships shape the larger social system environment, which then feeds back to the relational level through continued and dynamic communicative processes that define organizing (Weick, 1976, 1995).

The power of communication to bring about effects on, and to constitute, a social system environment is particularly noticeable in organizational settings because of the frequency of interaction taking place there (or, put another way, because of the interaction emerging there constitutively as organizing) and the relatively demarcated environment characterizing its context that is subject to influence, structuring, or being constituted through processes described by Weick (1995) and Giddens (1984) and reviewed by Ashcraft et al. (2009). An important application of the constitutive power of communication in organizational settings that makes the point well is available in Fairhurst's work (2011) on framing as a meaning-making task of leadership. Communicative framing by organizational leaders has the potential to shape multiple arenas of organizational life; such framing carries ethical implications emerging from the responsibility of organizational leaders, whether in formal positions of power or in less visible contexts, to protect and promote institutions (Fritz, 2011).

Since the focus of the current work is professional civility as communicative virtue in work settings, in which the communicative virtue of civility is tied directly to the virtue structure of profession as practice enacted within the communicative spaces—whether local or virtual/remote (Fay, in press; Fay & Kline, 2011, 2012)—of organizational structures, this treatment of the influence of discourse on organizational and personal outcomes is fitting as a complementary examination of the pragmatic effects of professional civility as it is enacted in organizational life. Evidence for the effects of communication on organizational environments and persons provides a context for the claim that professional civility shapes communication's effects in a constructive direction and buffers organizational environments and people in them from the destructive effects of incivility and related problematic interpersonal behaviors in the workplace (Fritz, in press-d; Fritz & Omdahl, 2006b; Omdahl & Fritz, 2006, in press). In the section that follows, I offer a brief summary of evidence for the influence of communicative interaction on persons and on organizational structures and processes before turning to the context of organizational socialization.

In the interests of disclosure of theoretical/methodological standpoint, I state here that I value and embrace diverse approaches to communicative inquiry. I recognize the "common ground" (Corman & Poole, 2000) that exists among the "multiple perspectives" (May & Mumby, 2005) characterizing the work of organizational communication scholars. I draw upon work from multiple standpoints, including variable analytic (or post-positivistic), social constructionist, critical, and constitutive approaches to communication and organizational communication (e.g., Miller, 2000; Sias, 2009a; Deetz, 2005; Ashcraft et al., 2009). For fluidity of presentation, I will often use the term "influence" as a convenient summary for the work of communication in organizational settings, recognizing the limitations of such usage and the ongoing interplay of multiple understandings of the role of communication in human existence and in organizational settings, specifically. I elect to exchange conceptual and theoretical unicity for a heuristic and elastic creativity that plays within the horizon of accepted conventions of scholarly work.

Communication and Work Environments

In organizational settings, communication with others is a powerful contributor to the symbolic environment, affecting workers' perceptions of their jobs, the organization, themselves, and what is important to them (e.g., Ashcraft, 2007; Albrecht, 1979, 1984; Crozier, 1964; Crozier & Friedberg, 1980; Fairhurst, 2011; Fritz, O'Neil, Popp, Williams, & Arnett, in press; Leitko et al., 1985). Communicative processes in the work environment extend beyond the organizational setting in their impact, shaping multiple spheres of persons' lives. For example, Kohn and colleagues (Kohn, 1977; Kohn, Naoi, Schoenbach, Schooler, & Slomczynski, 1990; Kohn & Schooler, 1983) suggested that different structures of labor, characterized traditionally as "blue collar" and "white collar," are linked, independently from social class variables, to the values workers hold as important for their children. This claim is admittedly functionalist in its portrayal of the significant influence of communication directly—through superior-subordinate communication or peer-to-peer communication—or indirectly, through the types of messages fostered by organizational culture and structure, either imposed or supported by management. Such a functionalist interpretation, however, does not preclude other readings or renderings of these processes, but suggests one way of understanding the role of communication in human organizational experience.

Critical theorists are concerned with emancipation of individuals from "repressive social and ideological conditions…that place socially unnecessary restrictions upon the development and articulation of human consciousness" (Alvesson & Willmott, 1992, p. 232; see Alvesson & Deetz, 1996, for a review). Alvesson and Deetz (1996) urged critical work in the organizational setting as "the mindpower and subjectivities of employees" (p. 192) become increasingly an object for management control. Incivility and associated problematic communicative behaviors at the interpersonal level, such as bullying (e.g., Keashly & Jagatic, 2011; Lutgen-Sandvik, Namie, & Namie, 2009; Kinney, in press), ostracism (Sias, 2009b, in press), interpersonal mistreatment (Lim & Cortina, 2005), interpersonal workplace harassment (Meglich, 2007, 2008), and other processes (see Fritz, 2009, in press-b, and in press-d for reviews) are equally a cause for concern. Incivility creates oppressive conditions through its operation in the spaces of day-to-day life in organizations; it compromises not just the productivity of organizations, but the capacity for employees' contributions to worthwhile labor and the opportunity for meaningful interaction with others around shared tasks. As ongoing studies of microlevel conversational practices indicate (e.g., Cooren et al., 2006), the day-to-day discourse of organizational participants is a site of organizing that makes a difference, constituting conditions of organizational life for better or for worse in its ongoing emergence.

Communicative processes, because of their profound and demonstrable influence on organizational structures and processes and thus on the human lives working within them, hold ethical implications for organizations: the forces of organizational life are not neutral, and the discourse taking place in organizations works for good or ill on an organization's participants, both directly, through communicative interaction among persons, and indirectly, through discursive effects on the climate and culture of the organization (Guzley, 1992; Pearson & Porath, 2009; Fritz & Omdahl, 2006b; Omdahl & Fritz, 2006). Evidence for the influence of communication within organizational structures on human outcomes, including personal values and quality of life, and on organizational outcomes and environments, makes explicit the need for a continued focus on the ethics of organizational communication—in particular, support for civil discourse in organizational settings (Davenport Sypher, 2004; Davenport Sypher & Gill, in press). Awareness of the power of the communicative environment in and on the lives of organizational members can promote ethical reflection for potential change and emancipation, or at least make public the nature of processes taking place in organizations for more informed participation on the part of organizational participants.

The architectonic discourse structure of professional civility as communicative virtue constructs an organizational environment conducive to productivity, to the success of the organization within which professionals and other employees carry out activities, to the flourishing of organizational members, and to the viability and dignity of the professions. Professional civility is a fitting and desirable organizational communication ethic because of its power to shape the goods in organizational life that professional civility as communicative virtue protects and promotes (Arnett et al., 2009): productivity (the task or work), the place in which work is done (the organization), persons (coworkers), and, more distally—through these proximal factors—the profession itself. The next section explores organizational socialization as a context for the effects of communication on organizational members and for encouraging and developing professional civility within a local organizational setting.

The Organizational Socialization Process as Context for Communicative Shaping

The organizational socialization experience, the process by which members enter and become part of organizational communities (Kramer, 2010; Van Maanen, 1975; Van Maanen & Schein, 1979), is a salient context for the development of the communicative virtue of professional civility; it is in this environment that participants in organizations are influenced by language and interaction most prominently, and where habits of professional civility can be instilled. Therefore, my discussion about the shaping power of language will be oriented to the context of organizational socialization, although the power of language is assumed to carry across organizational contexts and can be inferred, from what is presented here, to be operative throughout both the life of an individual organizational participant and the duration of an organization, institution, or corporate entity. Furthermore, since new members enter organizations regularly, the operation of the discourse practices of professional civility in the socialization process will always be relevant. I argue for both a virtue ethics and a utilitarian or consequentialist approach to understanding professional civility; this section focuses on the consequences of communication to build a case for the pragmatic importance of professional civility.

The context of the socialization experience is illustrative of the power of spoken language as it is host to significant symbolic processes shaping participants, processes that are implicated and continue in practices of professional discourse (Barge & Little,

2008; Blyler & Thralls, 1993). Because of initiates' need to make sense of an unfamiliar environment (Louis, 1980), new organizational members are susceptible to the version of the organizational world presented to them upon entry. In turn, as novices learn the ropes, they may gain opportunity to contribute to, and thereby shape, the symbolic environment, reconstituting it (e.g., Crozier, 1964). As employees enact environments constitutive of a culture of professional civility, their communicative interactions contribute to an organizational climate that invites productivity and constructive organizational relationships. Communication between the new organization member and incumbents (and other new members) provides the ground for enactment processes (Weick, 1995), including constraints and enablements, such as power, which define each of the participants in the interaction in relation to others and to the organization, helping to build the local home (Arnett, 1992) or community of memory (Arnett et al., 2009) that defines the organization.

The Influence of Communication on Perceptions of Self and Others

Communication functions to define the self and the social world. This influence on organizational participants is demonstrated convincingly by Albrecht (1984), who investigated the influence of communication behavior on managers' views of their self-concepts and jobs. Although managers were the focus, these principles may well apply to other organizational participants. Albrecht proposed that work-related interaction with organizational others shapes one's self-concept and perceptions of success on the job and that communication mediates these effects. Her results indicated that identification with work is tied to position in the organization's communication network. Interestingly, over time, managers' concepts of self and job tended to converge, indicating that persons may become what they do.

Albrecht (1984) suggested that subordinates' communication with superiors is likely to have an effect on subordinates' perceptions as well, but she did not address that question directly. Fairhurst, Green, and Snavely (1984) investigated the influence of superior-subordinate interaction on subordinates' identity negotiation and relational control, finding that autonomy was associated with length of time between problem recurrence. This result suggests that greater self-direction contributes to perceptions of oneself as able to solve problems independently, which leads to subsequent action and interaction based on that perception. The recognition of one's ability to solve problems, along with taking action on that knowledge, becomes a strong contributor to the self, especially if that attribute is expected—and rewarded—by others.

Humphrey's (1984) investigation of organizational structure and cognitive processes provides further evidence for the influence of interaction on organizational identity. His simulated office investigation revealed that perceptions of others in the work environment were influenced by attribution biases. For example, persons made judgments of others' actual personal characteristics (e.g., skills and leadership qualities) based on enacted role behaviors (see also Duck et al., 2006). Although communication variables were not investigated in this study, Humphrey suggested that communication may serve to indicate structurally derived status and power, which in turn channels these attribution effects. For example, superiors can interrupt subordinates, a "control" move indicating to these "lower status" parties that they are less important (Eakins & Eakins, 1976). These findings, along with those preceding, provide evidence for the influence of communication on organizational participants' self and role perceptions.

That messages from others constitute a significant causal factor in the development of the self and self-perception does not imply that human actors are passive or that their lives are determined by their surroundings. Persons do enact, or "manage," their performances with others. However, these enactments work progressively, emerging as a product of previous interaction and constrained by past performances (Fairhurst, 2004; Giddens, 1984; Baxter & Montgomery, 1996). Likewise, circumstances vary in creative potential.

Language and Values

Moch and Fields (1985) offered insight into language and values in their treatise on language analysis in organizations. Language is a key to theories-in-use, or assumptions embedded within schemata that organizational members draw upon to interpret their experiences. These assumption-based schemata operate as values because they frame reality in particular ways. Language is one means by which these schemata are generated, transmitted, maintained, and changed (p. 83). Communication contributes to the construction of these schemata through the operation of spoken language forms, such as metaphors, that establish a particular framing of organizational experience, and then these schemata, as functional values, contribute to further shaping of meaning and communicative action based on those meanings. As Moch and Field stated, "The schemata evoked by speech create the meanings to which the speaker refers" (p. 85). This process resonates with Giddens's (1984) notion of structuration, which has been usefully theorized and applied to organizational settings to explicate communicative processes and their shaping power (e.g., Kirby & Krone, 2002; McPhee, 1989, 2004; Scott, Corman,

& Cheney, 1998; Sherblom, Keranen, & Withers, 2002) and provides a specific linguistic mechanism by which these processes may take place (but see Cooren, 2006, and Cooren et al., 2006, for an alternative perspective).

Organizational participants give meaning to what happens in day-to-day organizational life through communicative action, which both emerges from and (re)constructs these value-laden schemata (Moch & Fields, 1985). These schemata then condition the meaning of future organizational experiences and subsequent communicative utterances (Moch & Fields, 1985). In this manner, communication is connected to values—communication both reveals and conditions values through language. The very act of communicating is linked to values through articulation of frameworks that carry particular "goods" in discursive action. Through this process, communication contributes both to identities of organizational participants and to the climate and culture of the organization—"the performance of speech create(s) the world to which it refers" (Moch & Fields, 1985, p. 85).

Values become schemata for appropriate (communicative) action (Moch & Fields, 1985). Imagine that one of my assumptions serving as part of a schema for organizational life is that my office colleagues, as a group, are interested in making the work unit better and typically take action in support of the purposes and tasks of that unit. This assumption reflects a value for the worth of the contributions of others and trust in their good will and ethical intentions—a constructive schema for organizational life. I draw upon this value schema to interpret my experience—it is a way to understand my colleagues' actions, a theory about life in organizations (or in this particular organization). This value schema functions for me (and others) in the workplace as it opens up possibilities for interpretations of my colleagues in a constructive, positive light, which energizes and propels my own work and gives rise to particular forms of language in the workplace through my communicative action. For example, when Frieda, one of my team members, edits some documents that I wrote and asked her to review, I may say, "Thanks for these suggestions—they're helpful." This language of appreciation rooted in my schema for what life is like at work emerges in the message I communicate to her, which contributes to the larger communicative climate and thereby to the organizational environment. If multiple colleagues contribute messages like this one, the climate gradually takes on a constructive atmosphere, permeating the entire organization. The assumption, of course, is that Frieda also interprets my comment as one of appreciation, and not one of irony, which carries a different meaning entirely (Moch & Fields, 1985, p. 104).

Speech acts both evoke and adjust schemata through the medium of context (Moch & Fields, 1985). Context, intention, and institutions are three aspects of verbal interaction (Moch & Fields, 1985). Context provides a general stock of schemata that guides the selection and interpretation of verbal messages (Moch & Fields, 1985). For example, salient features of a relationship may dictate interpretation of an utterance as a command or a request; a task episode such as making a decision in a group will guide criteria for generation of an appropriate message (that is, utterances should exhibit work-related content). Intention, the individual level, is more difficult to identify, but is interpreted or assigned through context (Moch & Fields, 1985). Culture resides at, or constitutes, the institutional level. The particular configurations of schemata are determined by culture and kept in place by power (Moch & Fields, 1985). Content includes rules for, as an example, allocation of scarce resources (Moch & Fields, 1985). Schemata that allocate scarce resources among competitors for these resources function as ideologies (Moch & Fields, 1985). Ideology in this context represents a system of values that consistently dictates a preference or set of preferences among alternatives (Moch & Fields, 1985).

Hodge and Kress's (1988) social semiotics perspective can also be applied to communication of organizational values, because these theorists recognize that language serves as a text and derives meaning only in a given context. Any set of linguistic forms must take into account the contextual elements of power relations manifested in a group, the history of that group and its use of a linguistic form, and how the audience for any message comprehends that message (Hodge & Kress, 1988). In the organizational context, these considerations are bound up in the structure and history of an organization, the deposit of that organization's values or "community of memory" (Arnett et al., 2009, p. 139).

Language reflects what Hodge and Kress (1988) referred to as ideological complexes and logonomic systems. An ideological complex is "a functionally related set of contradictory versions of the world" offered by dominant and subordinate classes that exists to sustain relationships of power and solidarity (p. 2), similar to the "ideology" of Moch and Fields (1985). A logonomic system specifies rules prescribing conditions for production and reception of meanings (Hodge & Kress, 1988). Logonomic systems are visible in, for example, politeness conventions, etiquette, and legislation (Hodge & Kress, 1988). Logonomic rules rest on a set of classifications of people, topics, and circumstances that derive ultimately from ideas of the dominant group (Hodge & Kress, 1988). Hence, from this perspective, professional civility can be considered a type of logonomic system in its derivation from an identifiable group recognized as having some degree of power and influence in society at large and in organizational settings. "Dominant" can be understood in this context as those with role-based authority for organizational operations and outcomes, whose responsibility it is to protect and promote an organization's mission and identity (Arnett et al., 2009).

In the organizational context, interaction manifests these systems and rules to organizational entrants and incumbents (Hodge & Kress, 1988), a process by which rules become embedded and automatic (Hodge & Kress, 1988). Value is placed on certain acts, on specific manifestations of relations, through enactments of power and meaning; "a pattern of social relationships can be the motor for definitions of reality and truth" (Hodge & Kress, 1988, p. 144). A useful framework for examining communication of values in organizations derived from the work of Hodge and Kress (1988) includes several elements: (a) producers and production regimes: what meanings are produced, how, and for whom; (b) receivers and reception regimes, which constrain the semiosic potential of receivers; (c) texts, or genre regimes, which permit possibilities of meaning as well as production and reception relationships; and (d) referents, or regimes of knowledge, which articulate specific versions of reality and define social constraints on what can be articulated, as well as who can claim properly to know or understand reality.

The "texts" of the organization are constituted in interaction episodes "read" by organizational participants. Referents consist of sets of values of the organizational culture; they constitute a specific version of what is and what ought to be; constraints are the boundaries of acceptable norms (or organizational limits; Arnett & Arneson, 1999). In the socialization context, producers are the organizational incumbents: they generate meanings to be received by organizational initiates. Reception regimes constrain interpretation of messages sent in that recipients have their own histories constraining how the meanings will be interpreted. For example, what a newcomer perceives as being "helpful" may be understood as "interfering" by those who have been with the organization for some time. Since the semiosic potential of receivers is constrained by their unique histories, organizations are compelled to socialize beginning employees: new members must be a good semiotic fit with the "regime" they constitute so that the institution continues to function smoothly. Newcomers need to learn "how we do things around here" (Kramer, 2010, p. 3). From this framework, the contours of professional civility as it is enacted locally will be instantiated within the horizon of a particular organization's reception regime.

Other types of messages are not expected to lead to values directly, but it is reasonable to assume that the very existence of certain types of communication (for example, members asking each other how they are doing and expecting more than perfunctory answers) can communicate distinct interpersonal values. Professionally civil discourse, for instance, as a professional communicative practice in the organizational setting, manifests a distinct value for a particular style of communicative interaction within this framework. There are, then, several levels of analysis involved in any classification scheme. On one level is the actual utterance, which can be classified as to the content of the specific value being represented, if there is an explicit value evidenced. This content must then be classified as to its importance, which is the primary dimension on which values lie. The next level is the implication of an utterance if its form is not directly that of a value. Once the implicit value is identified (through an understanding of its context), its importance may also be classified.

An example of research partially based on language as a cultural indicator is Hebden's (1986) study of the changing perceptions of organizational members during their first year of membership. Hebden used Harrison's (1972) five-part organizational culture scheme to classify perceptions of culture in two organizations, based on participants' experience as new entrants. Interviews with participants revealed the influence of statements that organizational participants heard over the course of their socialization on their understanding of the nature of the organization, its values, and behavior expected of organizational members. For example, the "power culture" was exemplified by statements on the part of new members indicating the discovery of decision outcomes other than what was originally promised, which signified both the power of a supervisor to make decisions and the inability of subordinates to enforce the "contract": "That's contrary to what they told us they would do. We weren't very pleased about it, but what could we do? We're at their mercy" (Hebden, 1986, p. 66). Such statements put into discursive form the recognition of this new member's position; the behavior on the part of the supervisor was enacted verbally in the statement by the employee as a manifestation of a broken contract (broken promises or unfulfilled expectations), which signified both the power of the supervisor to make decisions and the inability of subordinates to enforce the contract.

Language functions to create and maintain socially constructed facts and to attribute characteristics and relationships to these facts (Moch & Fields, 1985). One function of language in the organizational context is evoking or indicating friendship by use of abbreviations and directness, or even insults (indicating intimacy within the context of a close relationship, perhaps on the level of the "special peer" relationship; see Kram & Isabella, 1985). These messages shape expectations for behavior of each participant in a relationship and for the relationship as a whole; they are the ontological substance of "organizing relationships" (Sias, 2009a) in the workplace context.

Another function of language is establishing, maintaining, and changing social identity. Speech styles express values toward others (Giles & Powesland, 1975; Giles & Smith, 1979); relationships within and between social classes are indicated by various linguistic markers that differentiate these classes. In the organizational context, "class" could be understood as "occupation" or professional specialty. Kolb and Bartunek (1992) presented several instances of conflict between and among occupations, manifested in differences in language forms. For instance, Dubinskas (1992) explored differences in language use among employees from different functional specialties—research biologists and management—in a biotechnology company, variations that illustrated larger cultural discrepancies in orientations to work and professional identity.

Language creates and maintains power relations: deference is indicated by pronoun alterations, forms of address, tone of voice, vocabulary, and grammatical form. The redress to negative face offered by particular forms of politeness (Brown & Levinson, 1978/1987) serves as an example of a type of deference that may emerge as a linguistic practice within the framework of professional civility in particular contexts. The work of Holmes and Stubbe (2003) offers multiple examples of the manifestation of the language of power and politeness in the workplace.

Finally, language serves to attribute desirable and undesirable characteristics to self and others (Moch & Fields, 1985). How we talk about others in the workplace shapes their professional identities (e.g., Duck et al., 2006) and also reflects (on) our own identities. Professional civility as communicative virtue at work crafts an image of others, but it also expresses valuing of work, upholds appropriate role relationships to others, and is answerable to the context of the organizational home and the larger profession that defines professional identity. Professional civility is rhetorical *praxis* relevant to multiple spheres of organizational life.

The role of language is crucial in the inculcation of values in the organizational setting. Speech acts make manifest the values held in high regard by an organizational community. These speech acts may include organizational stories (Brown, 1985), memorable messages (Stohl, 1986), or any utterance that takes on illocutionary force, such as a greeting, statement, warning, or command (Searle, 2000, p. 377), and other ambient information that individuals read as indicating a prescribed course of thought or action. Speech acts emerge in every context of organizational interaction and carry relevance for different types of organizational work (e.g., project management; see Alin, Taylor, & Smeds, 2011). Speech acts have relevance for relationships, as well (e.g., supervisor-subordinate communication; see Mayfield, Mayfield, & Kopf, 1995, and Sullivan, 1988). In each context, a speech act carries force in shaping organizational and interpersonal values for persons, relationships, and contexts.

Brown (1985) studied organizational stories as an indicator of new employees' progression through the socialization process. A story's potential to integrate values and characteristics of the organization increased as newcomers became more embedded in the organization during the entry process. These stories have socializing potential, as well. A story's function is similar to that of a briefer demonstration (such as a proverb or a maxim) of a value. There are two ways such presentations may function. On the one hand, propositions representing the values embedded in a narrative or a shorter linguistic form may be abstracted in the narrative form of the story. On the other hand, values in a narrative may bypass propositional form and work through identification (Burke, 1950). For example, a narrative is a paradigm case, putting the unknown into terms of the known. Especially when there is no alternative presentation of what ought to be, the narrative, or example, serves a persuasive function in that it invites imitation (Harden, 1984), establishing normative expectations that can be remembered and made present again (Cooren, 2004, p. 519) to guide future action.

Memorable messages (Stohl, 1986) are verbal statements made to an organizational member that are easily recalled because they signify something important about the way the organization works. A series of such messages could serve as a type of nomological network (e.g., Nunnally, 1978) built up over time that serves to categorize the various types of values (pivotal, relevant, peripheral) in an organization (Schein, 1971). Through stories and memorable messages, organizational novices and incumbents receive and structure the organizational environment, making it, and their places in it, meaningful. Another way to conceptualize this network is as a narrative that structures an organizational home, dwelling, or community of memory within which members find meaning as they contribute to its ongoing existence, or, from another perspective, as a "sacred canopy" (Berger, 1967) that serves as a value structure or externalization of the way things are—and should be—in the world.

Summary

Throughout the various stages of the organizational socialization process, the communication environment creates a structure for the initial setting in which organizational newcomers find themselves and by which they interpret their actions. Over time, as employees progress through career tracks with an organization, the pattern of communication with their coparticipants will either remain constant or change. This communication pattern will exert an influence on the self-perceptions and role expectations of workers and, along with, and through, these role expectations, values for particular forms of communication and values in general. In other words, the form of role relationships represented by the type of relational acts taking place between and among organizational members influences organizational members' understandings of themselves and their surroundings.

Just as important is the effect of communication interaction between an employee and others on supervisors' and peers' attributions, since the reflected images of the worker derived from these attributions feed back into the worker's constructed self. The cumulative effects of all one's communication relationships serve to generate cycles of perception, attribution, and enactment, which, unless interrupted and changed, can result in ever-stronger patterns that will, over time, prove ever more difficult to alter. A durable pattern of incivility and problematic behavior is likely to be dysfunctional for the person and for the organization. This model of communication processes at work is one explanation of the "social and communicative processes though which conditions of hegemony arise" (Mumby, 2000, p. 70). In this case, the hegemony of an uncivil organizational culture emerging from repeated problematic patterns at the interpersonal level is of great concern. Replacing a culture of incivility with one of professional civility takes thought, consideration, and decisive action on the part of organizational leaders (Sutton, 2007; Pearson & Porath, 2009) and the participation of the entire membership of the organization (Schneider, 1987). The results of such efforts will contribute to renewed institutional and personal flourishing (Davenport Sypher & Gill, in press; Omdahl, 2006, in press), which can extend outward to communities and the larger public sphere within which human existence finds meaning.

Effects of Incivility

The previous material focused on the power of communication through an examination of language and interaction during the organizational socialization process as a context for communication's shaping force, with an eye to the place of professional civility within some of the theoretical frameworks relevant to these processes. The implications of these findings for professional civility in the workplace rest in the power of language to shape organizational conditions within which human labor, work, and action take place as part of professional contributions to the human experience. This final section addresses, in brief, the effects of the communicative vice of incivility in the workplace, particularly on the goods of profession: productivity, place, and persons. These results are consistent with research, reviewed previously, related to the effects of communication patterning on various relational outcomes, and target more specifically the particular domain relevant to the "work" of professional civility. Along with this research, I present evidence from studies of communication phenomena relevant to the conceptualization of professional civility described here. Findings from both of these areas provide specific content for the frameworks of theories-in-use, value schemata, and logonomic systems presented earlier that offer particular pathways of influence for language in the organizational socialization context.

A number of studies document the negative effects of incivility, demonstrating its destructive influence on the goods of task outcomes of productivity, organizations as a place for coordinated action, and others in the workplace, both in their roles and as human persons. Problematic workplace behaviors related to incivility, such as verbal abuse and harassment, have negative effects on job satisfaction, satisfaction with work, supervision, and coworkers, organizational citizenship behaviors, organizational commitment, work effort, absenteeism, and turnover intentions, to name a few (Cortina, Magley, Williams, & Langhout, 2001; Sakurai & Jax, 2011). For example, in an early study of incivility's influence on workplace outcomes, following close on the heels of Andersson and Pearson's (1999) landmark conceptualization of workplace incivility, Cortina et al. (2001) found negative effects on job satisfaction and job withdrawal, along with effects on career salience and psychological distress. Sakurai and Jax (2011) found incivility to be associated with lower reported work effort, although this effect was moderated by level of perceived supervisor social support. Since that time, evidence demonstrating the deleterious effects of incivility and associated problematic behavior on personal and organizational outcomes has continued to accumulate (e.g., Fritz & Omdahl, 2006b; Omdahl & Fritz, 2006; Omdahl & Fritz, in press).

Pearson and Porath (2009) offered a comprehensive review of what is now an extensive literature on the deleterious effects of incivility and problematic organizational behavior on organizational environments. They explored the costs of incivility associated with a number of outcomes, including a shift in focus of attention away from work, time spent worrying about perpetrators of incivility, time lost avoiding the instigator, weakened commitment, reduced effort, reduced time spent at work, and leaving the job (p. 31). The equivalent of seven weeks of managerial time is spent dealing with the aftermath of incivility (pp. 61–62); such distraction is a drain on energy and a detriment to productivity.

Two studies in particular are worth noting for the specificity of their focus on outcomes relevant to personal and workplace goods. Porath and Erez (2007) found that rudeness decreased performance on routine and creative tasks and decreased helpfulness. In a subsequent study, Porath and Erez (2009) found that simply witnessing rudeness decreased performance on routine and creative tasks, decreased organizational citizenship behavior (i.e., staying to help someone with a task), and increased the likelihood of thinking in aggressive terms. These findings suggest that incivility has effects on organizational environments directly—on those who experience incivility—and indirectly, on those who witness it. These results also hold implications for the theoretical frameworks previously discussed on the construction of organizational schemata for interpreting experience in organizations (Moch & Fields, 1985), and they suggest one way in which these problematic behaviors do their destructive work. These findings speak specifically to negative effects on productivity and on others in the workplace—and on the organization itself, the place of work.

Madlock and Kennedy-Lightsey (2010) found negative supervisory communication in the form of verbal aggressiveness to be negatively associated with job satisfaction and commitment. In fact, negative supervisory communication was more strongly associated with job satisfaction and commitment than was mentoring (which had a positive association with these outcomes). These findings show both the proportionally greater influence of supervisory incivility than positive supervisory communication and the effect of supervisory communication, generally, on personal and organizational outcomes, which is consistent with the work of Fritz, Arnett, and Conkel (1999), who found a positive correlation between managers' "walking the talk" and lower-level employee commitment, and the work of Fritz, O'Neil, Popp, Williams, and Arnett, who confirmed the findings of Fritz et al. (1999) and revealed the partial mediating effect of cynicism between supervisory modeling of organizational values in word and deed—a type of supervisory behavioral integrity (Simons, 2002)—and employee organizational commitment.

The extensive documentation of the effects of hostile work relationships, particularly bullying relationships, suggests multiple negative outcomes for persons and organizations manifesting in many types of hurt and harm (Kinney, in press), including direct and indirect effects on victims' psychological state, emotions, self-esteem, health and well-being, job satisfaction, effort expended at work, and productivity, (e.g., Kinney, in press; Hoel, Sheehan, Cooper, & Einarsen, 2011; Hogh, Mikkelsen, & Hansen, 2011; Lutgen-Sandvik, Namie, & Namie, 2009). The potential for incivility to escalate (e.g., Andersson & Pearson, 1999) into these intense and damaging relational forms suggests high long-term, incremental costs of incivility. Such costs are borne not only by particular persons and organizations, but by much larger systems, of which persons and organizations are a part.

Emerging work in the area of organizational communication scholarship associated with positive organizing (Cameron, 2008; Fredrickson & Dutton, 2008) and constructive ways of organizing (Lutgen-Sandvik & Davenport Sypher, 2009) offers insights into the role of positive orientations and associated communication in organizational settings. Work in this area on discourses of positive assessment by Lutgen-Sandvik, Riforgiate, and Fletcher (2011) illustrates how constructions of reality focused on positive understandings and interpretations of experience in organizational life, which are, in turn, derived from cultural and historical systems of meaning, have the potential to improve a number of personal and organizational outcomes. In particular, Lutgen-Sandvik et al.'s work points to the role of interactions with others in positive assessment; relationships were the second most frequent category mentioned as a source of positive emotion in the workplace (Lutgen-Sandvik, et al., p. 16).

Lutgen-Sandvik et al. (2011) reviewed work on outcomes of positive affective states, noting that creativity, problem solving, decision-making, cooperativeness, graciousness, and trust, among other things, are associated with positive emotional experiences. They noted, as well, that outcomes of positive emotion are not always helpful in the organizational context. For instance, people who feel good want to continue in that positive state and may avoid tasks or situations that threaten that feeling. The relationships among the communicative virtue of professional civility, positive affect, and personal and organizational outcomes will need further investigation, but at first glance, it appears as though professional civility may provide a background framework with a sense of limits and responsibility (Arnett & Arneson, 1999) within which positive affect may operate constructively. This line of research holds much promise for scholars and practitioners who seek greater understanding of a constructive approach to work life.

Conclusion

Professional civility has the potential to reduce the effects of incivility and tap the positive outcomes associated with constructive communication patterns. Fostering a culture of professional civility requires a change in orientation to the workplace and a commitment to new patterns of interaction or encouragement of current practices that reflect professionally civil behavior in the workplace. Change, however, is not an easy undertaking.

Change is necessary and occurs in organizations in response to shifts in management and leadership styles, as is evident in the history of organizational theory and approaches to organizational communication as manifested in textbooks and trade books in circulation at the level of business and corporate culture. The current popularity of books addressing concerns about incivility and offering encouragement to pursue civility at the corporate/organizational level (e.g., Forni, 2002, 2008; Gonthier & Morrissey, 2002; Sutton, 2007; Pearson & Porath, 2009) provides evidence that organizations would welcome professional civility as an embedded practice, and the appearance of volumes dedicated to professionalism for students and practitioners (e.g., Anderson & Bolt, 2011; Maister, 1997) suggests a recognition of the importance of professional norms for interaction in today's marketplace, as well as the likelihood that professional schools may also elevate the importance of workplace civility as a professional ethic. As professional socialization increases attention to interactive norms, adaptation to those of employing organizations will be a matter of learning particular practices in a given location. A new awareness on the part of employees and managers of the power of communicative action, implemented by more far-sighted socialization practices, may begin the changes necessary for a more ethical and functional working environment for both organizations and the human beings who enact them, an environment supportive of professional civility as a professional communication ethic.

The next three chapters offer a philosophical and pragmatic approach to professional civility in relation to the goods of profession: productivity, place, and persons, followed by a final chapter on the good to which these other goods tend: the profession. In each of the next three chapters, I offer the professional civility framework as a hermeneutic entrance into the context of each of the goods addressed. These treatments are not offered as comprehensive engagements of these topics; they offer suggestions for how professional civility may manifest itself in a phenomenological turning toward the various goods, an orientation that ushers in particular communicative practices likely to lead to the positive outcomes and limit the negative outcomes reviewed here. In each case, professional civility is offered not as a panacea, but as a beginning orientation to focus attention on constructive engagement of a given good. Organizational life is complex, unpredictable, and shot through with human frailty, but the evidence we see for the constructive effects of particular communicative practices that emerge from constructive ways of seeing the world suggests the wisdom of a realistic view of hope (Arnett & Arneson, 1999) that can guide us through the challenges of day-to-day life in the workplace.

6

Protecting and Promoting Productivity

Introduction

From Kimball's (1995) history of the professional ideal in America, we understand the good work of professions as connected to the good life for human beings. Sullivan (2005), Gardner, Csikszentmihalyi, and Damon (2001), and others articulate the continued vital role of the professions in their essential contributions to society's flourishing. Professional practice is its own defined good as an expression of the tradition of practice; in the manifestation of that practice as enacted by professionals in a particular place, the tradition's good emerges as a form of productivity. The productivity of professional practice as the finished or ongoing outcome of professional activity in relation to others—clients and the larger society—contributes to the well-being of the larger human community; productivity is the primary focus of the professional ideal, and hence the primary element to be protected and promoted through the communicative virtue of professional civility. Sullivan noted, "In genuine professional work, the craft itself is a focus of attention" (p. 21). The tradition of profession as practice responds to the historical moment in its recognition of the limits of the human condition, in which labor, work, and action are required as existential activities, and through its embrace of hope rooted in an understanding of profession as craft, marked by love of the work carried out through reflective, thoughtful organizational citizenship.

Work and the Human Condition

The ongoing story of the professions in a context of virtue ethics supports the recognition of professional practice as a good for human flourishing. In Arendtian terms, work is part of the human condition. Arendt (1958) distinguished labor, work, and action; for ease of reference, I will use "work" to refer to the tasks of the professions, although in a later section I distinguish work and action as Arendt distinguished them.

Work, in our everyday lives, is that which is before us (Buber, 1958). Our coworkers are not chosen (Hess, 2006); they are there, over against us (Buber, 1958), and the work is before us, an existential part of our human condition (Arendt, 1958). We are aware of our coworkers' rightful place in our world, as inescapable inhabitants of our shared institutional space, the place of joint effort in support of a larger project—and the work is before us, that which presents itself for engagement and response. The professional understanding of work as vocation (Sullivan, 2005) provides an auditory understanding of work in relation to practitioners: work calls the professional to active engagement of excellence in practice. The work that is phenomenologically before us calls us as it faces us; the work brings before us a confrontation with the expectation for ongoing contribution. The work is never finished; we become part of the tradition of professional work in taking on the responsibility to participate in productivity as the craft of good work.

Labor, Work, and Action

Hannah Arendt's (1958) treatment of labor, work, and action provides insight into the multiple goods of productivity residing in professions and those occupations that carry a professional ethos in their orientation to work as a calling. Now that many vocations engaging different occupational endeavors are part of the scope of professions, an expanded view of labor, work, and action—all of which are involved or invoked to varying degrees and which rest in differing proportions in the carrying out of professional activity—is possible. Professional practice today engages elements of all three of these components of the *vita activa,* but the professions' participation in these three elements has emerged through their historical development, as noted by Kimball (1995).

Professions were historically considered to constitute a unique category of human activity, with endeavors distinct from other occupations such as manual labor, the trades, and business concerns (Kimball, 1995; Sullivan, 1995). Labor, as Arendt (1958) theorized it, is tied directly to the necessities of human life; its products do not endure, because they are consumed in the process of living. The resistance to admitting merchants pursuing business interests into the professional class of occupations (Kimball, 1995) reflects the concern of the professions to avoid that taint of necessity. The shift in the "true professional ideal" (Kimball, 1995) from service rendered without compensation, or not primarily for compensation (see Hall & Schneider, 2008), to work done for a fee moved professions closer to the notion of labor. Professional activity today, in its provision of sustenance for professional practitioners, participates in elements of labor as soon as wages are received.

Work, which produces a world of durable things within which human beings live, is also reflected in the professions as we know them today. Engineers and architects, insomuch as they produce things reflective of an ideal or image, approach the role of artist (Sullivan, 2005), but they escape this category of pure action by the telos of their product, which is meant for human use and appears in the world of things. The production of an environment within which to carry on human life is part of the professional contribution of productivity to the larger human community. The architect and engineer mirror the craftsman (Sennett, 2008) in their connection to the world of durable goods.

It is in the realm of action that professions find their spirit of distinctiveness and meaning in a way faithful to their historical ideal. The charge of W. F. May (2001), Sullivan (2005), and others to rehabilitate the professions reflects this concern as they remind us of the call to professional service—action in the public sphere directed toward the good of the community. The essential being of the human is defined by action (Arendt, 1958), so any apparent use resulting from professional activity as action is a byproduct of that activity rather than a deliberately sought instrumentality. The natural telos or end of action is ephemeral, intangible, and "useless" (Arendt, 1958). The "action" of professional practice is also "craft" in its fidelity to excellent practice, although the product may be something not touchable or durable in the material world.

The professions offer to their members a space or location for distinctiveness in the public realm based on contributions to the larger community, a way to distinguish the self with the great deeds (Arendt, 1958, p. 206) that are both part of everyday life and beyond it. The potential for equality of status and distinctiveness of function ties to the world of action and honors human plurality. Since it is through speech and action that human beings distinguish themselves (Arendt, 1958, p. 176), these qualities of the professions form the substrate of the communicative virtue of professional civility. The "who are you" (p. 178) answered by action in professional contribution discloses professional identity; through professional civility, the solidarity and kinship of professions emerge, and such solidarity and kinship extend beyond the "guild" of professions into the larger community of human existence. Professional productivity is the foundation of professional good in the world and the entrance of professionals into the world of service to the community.

Productivity is a manifestation of human fecundity. The labor element of work may vanish into our being through consumption (Arendt, 1958), but the trace of our labor in the memory of our hands and the legacy of our action in the world (Arendt, 1958), and within the storied experience of a group, becomes part of the success of our organization and of the professional life. Our productivity is part of our own professional identity and narrative history, and it is part of an institution's success and accomplishment. Here we see the various goods in their interconnectedness and relatedness—productivity, place, persons, and the encompassing profession, which is formed and given life by these goods.

Profession as Craft

Good work is the hallmark of the professional (Gardner et al., 2001). Good work is work done well, honoring a standard for excellence made public and embodied in the practitioner as craftsman (Sennett, 2008). The value of the practice is recognized and honored by the professional. The metaphor of craftsman (Arnett, in press-b; Sennett, 2008) situates the professional as a kindred spirit with those who work at a craft as an artisan. Professional practice has much in common with a craft; in an increasingly mechanized and electronic age, craftwork may be the architectonic vocation in its reminder of the worth of a visible and viable outcome, an iconic reminder of contributions of time, energy, and skill poured forth into a project, of the solidity of practice that images the creative work unseen as action in the public sphere.

Crawford (2009), in *Shop Class as Soul Craft*, reminded us of the necessity of skilled contributions to the human community offered by the mechanic, the carpenter, the plumber—by all the trades. Arendt (1958) termed the action of those contributing to the public sphere as unseen and "useless," yet action is a necessary and defining element of human existence. The work of professions and of craft can be engaged as action even as they take the form of work and the function of labor—as human activity, they can be understood as both instrumental and as meaningful human performance (Markell, 2011, p. 19). The craftsman reminds the professional of the visible value of good work manifested through its practice. For this reason, the metaphor of professional as craftsman is important in this historical moment. As professions seek to restore their historic legacy to the human community, the idea of craft is significant.

Hodson (2001) identified similarities between professions and the skilled crafts; he noted that both require high levels of skill and training, involve hands-on experience, and are marked by a high degree of autonomy (pp. 144–145). The key similarity from a perspective reflective of Flexner's (1915/2001) sense of a profession is pride taken in the work (Hodson, 2001, p. 145). The profession of teaching has been referred to as a craft (Hoban, 2002; Kervin & Turbill, 2003), but it has also been referred to as an art, as a contrast to science (Ardalan, 2006).

Art as a guide for the professions taps a different significance, foregrounding the tacit knowledge necessary for practice (Squires, 2005) that rests with "one dominant or guiding agent"; craft, in contrast, "has a collective agent" and proceeds along the model of the workshop, in which work rituals bind persons functioning together (Sennett, 2008, p. 73). The difference between the art and craft of medicine, the art and craft of teaching, and the art and craft of writing may not be sufficiently drawn for utility in this context. "Craft" captures the spirit of practice on the ground with others, part of the lived experience of the collective in everyday life. The metaphor of craft is needed in this historical moment to call professionals back to the importance of practices in concert with others guided by professional civility.

Those who take pride in their work done well are, functionally and existentially speaking, craftsmen as well as professionals. Dignity at work (Hodson, 2001) is the birthright of all participants in the human condition; although the professions continue as standard bearers of vocations in their exemplification of engaging work with dedication and civic spirit (Sullivan, 2005), the craftsman stands as a figure calling the professional to recognition of the importance of productivity. The spirit of the craftsman infuses the tradition of the professions even as the image of the professional continues in the public eye as the architectonic vocational practitioner. Throughout this discussion of the good of productivity and professional civility's work to protect and promote productivity, the metaphors of "craft" and "craftsman" will emerge from time to time, with pride of place in this temporal moment given to the spirit of the craftsman, who holds before the professional the good of the craft as practice, calling the professional community back to its tradition. The call is especially relevant for professions now overrun by administrative roles that have lost their moorings and are no longer tethered to practices for which those professions are known (e.g., higher education; see Ginsberg, 2011).

The professions as architectonic occupations have lent their aura of autonomy, dignity, and service to a vast array of positions that take on aspects of the "true professional ideal" (Kimball, 1995) as part of their occupational description. The shift over time from glorifying specifically defined work set apart as holy or consecrated, such as the contributions of those taking religious vows, to valuing the everyday contributions of the ordinary person (Taylor, 1989, 2007) is reflected in the opening of the scope of the professions, broadly conceived, to multiple occupations. A professional orientation to work as a vocation manifests itself in many roles, including that of the office manager and associated personnel who support the tasks of the professions more formally defined (Noordegraaf, 2007). Such supportive roles are necessary for the work of professional practice as craft.

Love of the Work

During the professional socialization process, professionals learn both the practice of the craft and love of the work. The history of the professional ideal in America points to the love of the craft evidenced throughout the various rhetorical moments in the story of the professions (Kimball,1995). In every case, the practice itself is a good, as is its outcome. This mark of the worth of professional practice endures into today's contemporary story of the professions (Sullivan, 2005).

Sullivan (2005) told the story of Jane Addams and Hull House and the foundational roots of professional social work. The professional vision of Addams extended outward to the larger community; Addams saw the potential of immigrants and invited them to participate in the civic spaces of education and public contribution, much like Paulo Freire would do later in Brazil (Arnett & Arneson, 1999) in literacy campaigns for the disenfranchised poor. The practices Addams initiated are exemplary of professional productivity as meaningful engagement, the basis of social work understood as moral citizenship (Manning, 1997).

The work of Addams is echoed in that of architect Daniel Burnham, whom Sullivan (2005) described as contributing to the larger society as an exemplar of Arendt's (1958) understanding of art as a contribution to the human community (Sullivan, 2005, pp. 126–127). The love of the craft, again, is foundational for this professional work, which finds meaning in its contribution to human existence. The social and civic purposes for which Addams and Burnham, with the support of writers such as Lewis Mumford and other members of the Regional Planning Association of America (Sullivan, 2005, p. 124–127), engaged their craft defined the goods brought forth from their contributions as civic goods, and the practices themselves stand to this day as goods defined by a tradition. In the case of Addams's social work, she, as initiator of this incipient profession, became the founder of the tradition of social work as a practice (Sullivan, 2005); she articulated the goods themselves and the scope of their practice through her pioneering work.

Threats to love of the work abound. In today's historical moment, a shift from the professional organization to the organizational professional (Sullivan, 2005) places professional practitioners in contexts where their professional autonomy may be constrained. Not always is the context of work what was hoped for upon embarking on a professional journey; high expectations may end in cynicism from disappointment (Arnett & Arneson, 1999). Sullivan (2005) noted the lack of satisfaction of lawyers with their careers (p. 6; see Chapter 2, this volume). The academic life faces challenges with increasing bureaucratization and administrative density, which are gradually crowding out what many professors consider the true task of higher education (Ginsberg, 2011). Professionals in various occupations, particularly in the human services, such as physicians, teachers, and social workers, experience increased demands for services and are at risk for burnout, and changes in the status of professions in general from "callings" to "modern occupations" have threatened the eclipse of recognized significance of work (Schaufeli, Leiter, & Maslach, 2008, p. 207). Problematic supervisors (Fritz, 2002, 2006) and other threats to the work environment compromise conditions for productivity.

Under less than ideal conditions, in which the context of organizational life is not conducive to pleasant or enjoyable experience of work, the work itself can become—indeed, must become—reason enough for engagement. For the professional, the craft is worth doing and becomes the "why" for the "how" of sustained engagement (Arnett & Arneson, 1999). The practice itself offers redemption of the experience of work, transforming it from the mundane to the meaningful. A professional valuing of the work itself is a foundation for productivity even in the face of compromised working conditions.

The conditions of work will not always be enjoyable. Economic downturns, the intrusion of the unexpected and unwanted into familiar routines, and demands of the historical moment itself offer rhetorical interruptions (Arnett, Fritz, & Bell, 2009) that disrupt our comfort, but these unwelcome events invite learning and adaptation. The unexpected offers a chance to reconsider work and its meaning and to find restoration in other spheres of life (Arnett, 2006) in order to preserve love of the work. The communicative virtue of professional civility seeks to enlarge space in the organizational setting to permit professionals' love of the work to find its stride, expanding its minimal scope to broader horizons. The range of professional potential expands as professional civility does its work of protecting and promoting productivity through constructive communicative practices.

Productivity and Communicative Action

Human engagement with one another in private and public settings is accomplished through interpersonal communication in the modality of conversation. "Conversation...is the form of human transactions in general," and the deeds we do speak for us because they are the deeds of those who have words (MacIntyre, 2007, p. 210). Action in the public sphere is intimately tied to the communicative activity of conversation, and the organizations within which we work present themselves to us through these interactive events—"[t]he reality of [organizations] that we experience occurs in conversation" (Ford & Ford, 2003, p. 142). Professional identities emerge in discourse and are tied to the productive, skillful work professionals do (Barge & Little, 2008); the work is supported by the discourse ethic of professional civility. In the organizational setting in which professional work takes place, the conversation of professional civility protects and promotes productivity. In each sphere of organizational activity, professionals in their various roles are accountable for communicative action that moves toward productivity. In its modality of protecting and promoting productivity, professional civility takes the form of "committed conversation"—conversation that is "for" something rather than "about" something (Ford & Ford, 2003, p. 147). (As will be evident later, conversation "about" something is likewise important and has implications for productivity—for instance, conversation about other people in the workplace, which can be constructive or destructive.)

Professional civility's grounding in organizational citizenship and dialogic civility points to elements in these conceptual frameworks relevant to productivity. The organizational citizen's action is directed toward the productivity of self and others through attentive discernment of opportunities to assist (Organ, 1988). Contributions to the work of others through encouragement and instrumental support move energy toward the focus of a shared project. Conversation directed toward tasks and away from extraneous matters permits attention toward creative engagement of work through limits derived from the organization's purpose. At the same time, such discourse creates patterns that reduce a focus on relational configurations that cannot be sustained within the matrix of role requirements and demands (e.g., Bridge & Baxter, 1992; Sias, Heath, Perry, Silva, & Fix, 2004) or on an understanding of the organization as anything other than a context within which the promise of work can be fulfilled.

Tending to the Task: Communicative Coordinates

Arnett and Fritz (2003) noted that the focus of discourse in the workplace should be work and those phenomena that support and surround work. While other types of discourse are inevitable and natural, such as casual conversation among colleagues or more intense and intimate talk characteristic of friendships that develop at work (Sias, 2009a), the key for professional civility is to favor the task, permitting natural, healthy, and pleasant personal discourse as appropriate for the nature of the relationship to emerge in the margins of work life. Not everyone is interested in disclosing—or hearing—elaborate details of a personal life. The Soap Opera Star (Fritz, 2002, 2006), for instance, describes a troublesome peer type whose primary attributes are an unprofessional focus of attention, characterized by talking about non-work-related problems in the workplace, and being distracting. Engaging in active listening with such a person would be likely to encourage more of the same behavior; professional civility in this case might involve refocusing conversational attention on the task at hand or offering to continue personal conversation on a break.

The difference between vociferous complaint in the form of an accusation of failure on the part of an office worker when a copy machine has ceased to function ("You knew that machine was on its last legs! Why didn't you have those repairs attended to earlier?! What is wrong with you?") and functional, deliberate inquiry as to what action needs to be done to rectify a mechanical malfunction ("We need to call the service person right away. The copy machine is broken. I know you've had a lot to do lately—let's do this now and get it taken care of. And while we're at it, let's document this recurring problem for the home office. Can you help me remember the last time it broke down? ") lies in focus of attention and the meanings invoked by the discourse in each case. In the first, an accusatory outburst of expressive design logic creates a relationship of antagonism and distress, severing the connection of cooperation. In the second, rhetorical design logic forms an utterance taking both parties' goals into account, as well as the primary concern of getting work done. As Willihnganz, Hart, and Willard (2003) observed, leaders who enact rhetorically designed messages work to facilitate goal accomplishment (p. 113).

Despite our best intentions, we will fail to keep focus on the task at all times; we will forget to exercise courtesy toward others; we will say things we wish we could take back. In such cases, we offer apology and seek forgiveness (Metts, Cupach, & Lippert, 2006; Waldron & Kelly, 2008; Waldron & Kloeber, in press). Productivity is served when attention moves away from the transgression and back to the task. A sincere apology is the best path to forgiveness (Metts et al., 2006), decreasing relational damage. Forgiveness is a constructive alternative strategy to revenge, which halts communication and may lead to a spiral of reciprocal negative acts (Waldron & Kassing, 2011), similar to the spiraling effects of incivility (Andersson & Pearson, 1999). Professionally civil discourse is marked by apology and forgiveness in their varied forms; these means of relational repair assist productivity in refocusing attention on work, the craft of the professional.

Professional civility takes as its domain the tradition of professions and the goods connected with that tradition—productivity, place, and persons. Productivity is listed first because of the primary definition of a profession as focused on good work and the supporting elements of the context within which work is done. Therefore, professional civility is not a therapeutic approach to discourse (Arnett, 1997). However, professional civility does recognize and take into account the multiple dimensions of communicative action that define human experience—that professionals in their public work roles, and because of their work roles, given the tradition of profession as practice, are colleagues who are whole selves (Sias et al., 2012) and whose professional identity is part of a calling (Sullivan, 2005). Therefore, much of the interpersonal communication literature derived from a psychological as well as a dialogic or phenomenological orientation (Arnett, 1981) has a place, appropriately textured, in the professional civility framework, as well as in an approach to civility as communicative virtue (see Chapter 3). Placing this material within the purview of professional civility permits it to be made useful within the workplace without the potential pitfalls of therapeutic discourse imported into the public domain (Arnett, 1997, 2001).

In particular, the craftwork model described by Sennett (2008) has much to offer professional civility as protection and promotion of productivity, particularly with regard to one of the communicative coordinates of civility as communicative virtue translated into the workplace as professional civility: Gibb's (1961) configuration of defensive and supportive messages. Sennett's work provides coordinates for evaluation and judgment that reconfigure the defensive/supportive framework, opening up a constructive understanding of productivity in organizations in relation to communicative practices. Sennett's treatment reminds us of the importance of practices and of evaluative standards for practices, and resonates with MacIntyre's (2007) framework, which forms part of the background of professional civility as communicative virtue at work.

Defensive and Supportive Communication: Craft Reconfiguration

Gibb's (1961) framework of defensive and supportive communication assumes no fixed standard against which judgments are to be made. It does not preclude them, but the work itself emerged from data gathered in contexts of group decision-making (specifically, "human relations training sessions in industrial, educational, and community settings," p. 141) in which there appeared to be no assumption of a fixed standard of judgment for a particular decision-making task. Gibb admitted the necessity of judgment in social life and recognized evaluation as a frequent occurrence in human interaction, but in his discussion of the defensive/supportive framework, Gibb tied judgment and evaluation to the values of the individual person (p. 144), not to an external standard.

Gibb's (1961) concern was the communicative form in which expressions of evaluation or judgment were to be carried out. Gibb hoped to learn how to reduce defensive reactions that blocked or distorted message reception, particularly in the context of decision-making in small groups. His focus was on the psychological reactions of listeners—defensive reactions—engendered by particular types of messages positioning the speaker as distant from, or superior to, the listener in significant ways, or engaged in strategic manipulation for a desired outcome. The historical moment in which Gibb's work was carried out coincides generally with the rise of third-force psychology (Arnett & Arneson, 1999, p. 87), with a focus on the dignity of the human person as central.

At the time of the article's publication, there appeared still to be some general underlying background framework of a shared understanding of the good, at least as expressed in public life and the media. However, that apparent consensus was already in the process of being replaced by the recognition of multiplicity that had always been present, but not acknowledged, and increasing challenges to institutions and social conventions (e.g., Carter, 1998, p. 43). Suspicion of persuasive messages from prominent institutions, such as "politics, education, special causes, advertising, religion, medicine, industrial relations, and guidance" (Gibb, 1961, p. 144), and concerns aroused by works such as Packard's (1957) *The Hidden Persuaders* (Gibb, 1961, p. 145) created a general climate of cynicism and suspicion of messages from socially authoritative sources.

In particular, Gibb noted a reaction against the human relations movement in organizational theory (pp. 145–146) as another source of suspicion of institutional messages, an approach identified as pseudo human relations (Argyris, 1957, p. 231), in which a façade of concern for employees and their contributions masked a paternalistic implementation of techniques on the part of organizational managers to increase productivity without recognition of the cognitive and creative potential of workers. For example, some managers began to ask for employees' suggestions with no intention of considering them, because "feeling included" was purported to motivate workers to greater productivity. This advocacy of "pseudo-participation" (Miller, 2011, p. 47) was part of the legacy of the much discussed, disputed, and reinterpreted Hawthorne studies (e.g., Sonnenfeld, 1985) that heralded the turn from classical organizational approaches to management to more person-centered approaches (Miller, 2011).

With regard to interpersonal interaction, the work of Goffman (1959), which articulated the presentation of self in everyday life as strategic attempts to shape others' perceptions, framed communicative activity in the social world as a series of role-playing activities taking place between, and among, selves devoid of any meaningful content (MacIntyre, 2007, p. 32). Such selves were necessarily unconnected to any transcendent moral framework. The implications of this understanding of human interaction, with its marked absence of any objective standards for evaluation (MacIntyre, 2007, p. 115), were that individual persons engaged in persuasive activity could only be carrying out strategic activity designed to manipulate others toward their own arbitrarily defined and personally valued ends, and any attempts at evaluation could carry no authority. Evaluative or judgmental messages were ammunition as the imperial self waged war against other imperial selves.

The way Gibb's (1961) work is used today is emotivistic (MacIntyre, 2007) at worst and rhetorical at best. The assumption is that there are no objective standards of judgment, merely one's own private or personal preferences. A skilled communicator might persuade others to adopt a personal viewpoint, wherever it is grounded, with sufficient skill in argument or other methods of persuasion, and thereby gain community consensus, but there are no agreed-upon external standards by which to judge the worth of an idea or proposed action—a reflection of a moment of narrative and virtue contention (Arnett et al., 2009), in which standards of achievement are established in and through interaction itself (MacIntyre, 2007, p. 115).

Gibb's (1961) work may serve as a marker of a new moment in an understanding of practical discourse that takes into account a lack of shared standards for evaluation in the public realm accompanied by a need to get things done together despite this lack. In such moments, we still recognize the deep commitments of human beings, commitments given the narrative texture of tradition in MacIntyre's (2007) teleological framework and a moral vocabulary in Taylor's (1989) analysis of the contemporary Western understanding of the self: human beings strive toward an end and recognize purpose and significance in life. We live in moral space as surely as we dwell in physical space, and we strive for meaning that is bestowed on the human purpose by our participation in moral frameworks that are not arbitrary, but rest within transcendent understandings of human life and existence. These frameworks may be incommensurable and beyond easy reconciliation (MacIntyre, 1988), but they have the functional authority of truth. Virtue ethics is consistent with such a framework.

Sennett's (2008) work on the practice of craftwork, although not framed within a tradition of virtue ethics, is set in the context of a recognition of the authority of craft practice. Within that understanding of craft activity, it is possible to understand the poles of the defensive/supportive dimensions differently. One can now contrast "sociable expertise" with "antisocial expertise" (Sennett, 2008, pp. 247, 249) as the new dimensions of defensive and supportive communication within a paradigm that has a defined, public standard set by the task or craft itself. The "well-crafted organization," noted Sennett, demands "standards framed in language that any person in the organization might understand" (Sennett, 2008, p. 249). The standards do not rest in a static code, but in the person of the master craftsman—not in the person as individual, but in the person as embodying the tradition of craft. In this sense, Sennett's work offers a way to anchor discourse within a framework tied to productivity.

In Gibb's (1961) framework, description and evaluation are placed at odds, with description moving away from judgment and evaluation to place emphasis and focus on facts and perceptions rather than holding an action or person up to a standard, which, in Gibb's conceptualization, emerges from the value standards of the person doing the speaking. In a craftwork understanding of defensive and supportive communication, evaluation is now an appropriate stance for an expert or master craftsman to take, with the "defensive" or problematic pole of the continuum defined as "humiliation." Evaluation is an expert's rendering of judgment that is received as important guiding information by the apprentice; humiliation is the bitter residue of the antisocial expert who anchors excellence in the self rather than in the standards of the craft. In an odd turning, the emotivist error is now shown up for what it is—in craftwork, the standards do not rest within the self, independently and autonomously, but with the group—within the craft itself, which was given definition through the tradition of craft, or, in the professional civility framework, by the profession itself. The expert embodies the standards and enacts them, thereby becoming the personification of craft guidelines.

The rest of the defensiveness/supportiveness framework follows suit. Problem orientation defines a supportive orientation of working together to figure out a challenge or difficulty, with control on the defensive pole as imposition of a solution (Gibb, 1961). In the craftwork framework, the expert craftsman appropriately owns "control," but a better term is now "authority." The authority stemming from well-practiced skill and experience rests with the expert in terms of the craft; the defensive end of the pole is now "colonization," in which an imposition of authority beyond the craftsman's area of expertise takes place in a hubristic effort to exert will over processes and people beyond the horizon of knowledge, skill, or responsibility of the expert. One is reminded of Ginsberg's (2011) critique of the all-administrative university, where many in positions of authority no longer practice the craft of teaching or research, if they ever did, effectively relinquishing their expertise and authority in those areas, and are now professional administrative "guardians" (Jacobs, 1992/1994, p. 24), definers and defenders of processes that slow productivity and direct energy into ever-increasing process tasks that justify their own existence and their increasing pseudo-authority over more and more areas legitimately belonging to professional "craft" educators.

Spontaneity is the supportive end of the spontaneity/strategy dimension; strategy refers to hidden intentions and stratagems masked by feigned genuineness (Gibb, 1961). In the craftwork paradigm, strategy is appropriate and conceived as having an end in view and a goal path by which to proceed—it is a telic approach operating under expertise that envisions a completed product and knows the way to get there—and knows the way to assist the apprentice in the journey to expertise. Strategy in the craftwork paradigm is a supportive orientation, with the defensive orientation now "ideology," which suggests a closedness and lack of responsiveness to new conditions that might shape the goals of the craftsman (or professional) in adapting to the unexpected.

In the empathy/neutrality domain, empathy is expressed concern for the feelings of one's interlocutor, whereas neutrality consists of ignoring the feelings of one's interlocutor (Gibb, 1961). Empathy is particularized, individualized, and localized at the level of the person. In the craftwork orientation, the task is the focus of attention, not the person; neutrality becomes disinterest—that is, the demographic background of the apprentice does not matter, nor the color of the eyes (Arnett, 2012), but only the willingness to learn the craft and participate under the discipline and authority of the expert (Sennett, 2008, p. 54). The defensive pole is now exclusion, in which any factor other than a desire to participate becomes the basis for refusal to let someone learn the craft, and hence demonstrates little concern for the future of the craft or profession.

Imagine a situation in which a male electrical engineer charged with educating a female intern has a strong bias against women entering the electrical engineering field. He states, "Women just weren't cut out to be engineers. I'm not sure you can make it in this field." This "exclusivist" statement might be countered by Corinna, the intern, who states, "My greatest desire in the world is to become an engineer, and I am sure you can help me become a good one." The subsequent response from the biased engineer might be, "Well, okay, then. I'll do my best to help you." This incident was adapted from a story told to me by a member of an underrepresented group about her successful navigation through the ranks of a profession in which she faced an educator with a bias against members of her group who believed she could not possibly learn the practices of her chosen profession. When asked for help, however, this educator was willing to extend mentoring—and became this aspiring professional's advocate.

In this example, a professionally civil and supportive response from the person in a position of lower power touched a professional heart and moved it in a constructive direction—toward the "disinterest" of a professional concern to protect and promote a tradition of practice. Also, in this instance, we see support for

Carter's (1998) claim that civility calls those with power into account (pp. 72, 181), and a reflection of Flexner's statement (1915/2001) that the professions are "thoroughly democratic in essence," with membership and practice predicated not "on birth or wealth or some other accident" (p. 156), but on qualifications related to the work itself. Research in the history of various professions as their boundaries expanded to include the previously excluded reflects the struggles and successes of underrepresented groups in their quest for participation in an endeavor to which they felt a call (e.g., McCarther, 2010, p. 299).

Equality and superiority define the supportive and defensive ends of another dimension in Gibb's (1961) formulation. From a craftwork orientation, "superiority" becomes "mastery." The expert has superior skill that is public and demonstrable. Variations in ability, as Gibb noted, are part of the human condition. The craftsman has real expertise that can be shared with others. The opposite pole of "mastery" is "hegemony," in which knowledge is hoarded and power from such knowledge is "lorded" (Ashforth, 1994) over others, a salient critique of the professions today (Sullivan, 2005). The mastery of sociable expertise, which consists "simply of good practices" (Sennett, 2008, p. 249), flourishes within an organization that "will focus on whole human beings in time [and] encourage mentoring" (Sennett, 2008, p. 249).

The mastery/hegemony dimension is closely related to that of disinterest/exclusion; the difference lies in the focus of attention of these dimensions. In the case of mastery and hegemony, the focus is on the skill itself and a contrast between wanting to share the skill with others and an inward turning that does not reach out in invitation to welcome others' learning of the practice. In the case of disinterest/exclusion, the focus of attention is on the craft itself as a tradition or practice that endures through time as an inclusive practice. Disinterest invites all who would come; exclusivity limits the potential bearers of the tradition on the basis of craft-irrelevant factors. As mastery and disinterest come together, we see that the accessibility of the language of expertise, as mentioned earlier, points to the role of public standards of practice and judgment in passing along craft (or professional) knowledge to the apprentice—who may be anyone who wishes to learn. The sociable expert's willingness to mentor (Sennett, 2008, p. 248) protects the practice as the craft lives on through time.

The last dimensional pair consists of provisionalism and certainty. Certainty, the "defensive" end of the pole, marks a definitive confidence in knowing, and provisionalism offers the humble uncertainty of openness (Gibb, 1961). Provisionalism and certainty have their craftwork counterparts in certainty (now anchored in expertise and resting with public standards) and its defensive partner, "totality," with totality describing a finalizing closure against the possibility of change or creative inno-vation through the "intuitive leaps" described by Sennett (2008, pp. 209–213). The expert, who has internalized the standards and moved them into daily practice, has practical wisdom, phronesis, which provides confidence that might be perceived as arrogance by the uninitiated.

In an apt introduction to their chapter on proposing new ideas as a type of risk in communication encounters, Waldron and Kassing (2011) described a head chef seeking new menu ideas who rejected suggestion after suggestion offered by staff, apparently interested only in importing ideas from a previous restaurant. The disap-pointed staff met later to continue brainstorming and developed a number of cre-ative ideas offering unique alternatives to menu items currently available at area restaurants. One of the brainstorming staff members, an assistant chef, eventually took those creative ideas to a competing restaurant after securing employment with this competitor. The idea-rejecting head chef, an expert who exhibited the closedness of totality, decreased creative productivity—at least, for the original establishment.

Levels of Engagement

Each domain of the workplace offers opportunity for members of the professions to enact professional civility to protect and promote productivity. Members of the professions who find themselves in various role capacities can enact professional civility in contexts of everyday work life. Managers protect and promote produc-tivity by their method of coaching and mentoring employees—for example, through relationally responsive interaction as an "author manager" (Shotter & Cunliffe, 2003, p. 20)—and by ensuring a work environment conducive to focus-ing on the task. Managers "can restore a flow of action, giving shape and direction to the actions of other participants in the [organization] when they are either dis-oriented or stuck" (Shotter & Cunliffe, 2003, p. 20). Through "committed con-versations" (Ford & Ford, 2003, p. 148), managers work to initiate change, create shared contexts for understanding, address and direct action, and bring closure to events, creating opportunities for future action.

The Professionally Civil Manager: Hope and Possibility

Employers who develop strong relationships, or in-group relationships (Graen, 1976; Graen, Dansereau, & Minami, 1972; Graen, Orris, & Johnson, 1973; Graen & Uhl-Bien, 1995) with their employees promote productivity. In-group relationships are constructed through communicative exchanges (Fairhurst, 1993).

Messages of trust and confidence that set employees free to reach their potential within mission limits permit creativity in task accomplishment, which creates the conditions for productivity to take unique and fruitful forms. In these relationships, communicative interactions involve joint meaning construction in the responsive interplay of interaction (Shotter & Cunliffe, 2003).

Professional employees, through the process of professional education and training, have been initiated into the practice of the profession, but are still in the process of learning both the craft itself in the lived experience of application and the particular instantiation of their domain of work in a local professional home (Arnett, 1992). Managers are often in a position of supervising or coordinating the work of a number of professionals who have expert knowledge different from that of the particular manager (Maister, 1997). The manager may have general knowledge of the organization's broad purposes and mission, and may understand the outcomes necessary from a particular professional employee whose work is an integral part of the organization's activities, but may not have the specific craft knowledge of that professional employee.

Managers who do not belong to the particular occupational group they are supervising face the task of stewardship of valuable professional skills and practice with which they are generally familiar, and their role involves guiding those skills toward a larger purpose within which they see professionals' contributions finding significance. This task of coordinated integration is one of translating, or "acknowledging and respecting many different agendas while translating them into a single objective" (Cooren & Fairhurst, 2003, p. 85). Such integration requires a sensitivity to a larger metaprofessional narrative that both transcends and encompasses multiple professional categories. The hospital administrator who coordinates the work of many different health care professionals, the academic dean who works with multiple units in different disciplinary domains, the director of a nonprofit agency, an army captain in charge of a company, the chief of staff of a head of state—all of these roles require respect for the larger sense of professional work as a contribution to society and the larger human community, and a general sense of appreciation for the work itself, even for work that is not within the area of expertise of the director, manager, or supervisor. For this reason, professional managers who engage professional employees must work carefully within the domain of content and relationship dimensions of messages, employing a message design logic oriented primarily toward the rhetorical and conventional (Willihnganz et al., 2003), depending on the relative expertise of the manager in relation to employees.

Supervisors and leaders protect and promote productivity by the way they communicate performance evaluations, offer encouragement, advance constructive criticism, and demonstrate behavior that matches their words (Fairhurst, 2011; Fairhurst, Green, & Snavely, 1984, Simons, 2002). All of these communicative actions are part of professional civility's work to protect and promote productivity. We know that specific feedback provides concrete means for improvement and produces constructive hope for an employee (Omdahl, 2006). Talk that belittles another person drains energy and provides no path to improvement.

Managers encourage productivity by targeting specific elements of work that need improvement while protecting the face of employees (Fairhurst et al., 1984); by highlighting employees' contributions to a common task through attention to their particular competencies (Lim & Bowers, 1991), managers help employees see how their unique gifts make a difference to the community, a significant element of professional identity (Sullivan, 2005). By offering strategies for improvement when appropriate, particularly if the manager is a member of the same specific profession as the employee, managers provide employees with traction for forward motion. For professionals in a specific occupational area outside the manager's expertise, peer mentors in the same profession can provide support (Comer, 1991; Kram & Isabella, 1985).

Omdahl (2006) offered examples of messages that reduce the likelihood of shame and increase the likelihood of hope for improved performance. Phrases such as "[as is the case for everyone else who is new], certain errors have been occurring in your work"; "now that you have a sense of what the work is like, it's a good time to try some strategies to target the types of errors you're making"; and "most people find that by devoting strategic effort, they can get the error rate down significantly" (p. 288) illustrate various components of professionally civil messages that assist productivity. By highlighting the fact that all new employees take time to get up to speed, supervisors create a sense of solidarity (Wagoner & Waldron, 1999)—in that I, the worker, am like others—and self-efficacy—others have improved, so I can, too. When information about specific actions an employee can take in order to improve is accompanied by reinforcing appreciation for the person, supervisors provide support for employees' positive face needs (Fairhurst et al., 1984).

Professionally Civil Peers: Talk Matters

Peers can help each other experience work constructively. How we talk about work shapes our engagement of it. Our experience of work is rooted in our consciousness of it, how work presents itself to us, and work's presentation to us emerges from our conversation about it. How we talk about work indicates our "turning" toward it in particular ways with a particular attitude or approach (e.g.,

Squires, 2005). The memorable messages others tell us (Stohl, 1986) and the stories we hear (Brown, 1985) tell us a great deal about others' understanding of elements of the workplace and shape our own engagement of work.

Because the way we talk about work to others shapes our experience of our tasks and their significance, complaint about work constructs it as problematic and closes down possibilities of creative engagement of a new task that emerges from alternative understandings of the work itself. The types of discourse that make our work joyous are comments and utterances that focus our attention on the meaning of the work within the larger scope of the organization itself, on the excellence of the way the task was carried out as craft, on the sheer facticity of its accomplishment and fruition. The key here is focus of attention (Gardner, Dunham, Cummings, & Pearce, 1987). Discourse that does not draw attention to itself but moves attention to the doing, and/or the meaning, of the task harnesses energy and effort of self and others toward productivity. The workshop of craft performance is a model of such productive communicative engagement, where "learning becomes local" and discussing back and forth assists working through a difficult procedure (Sennett, 2008, p. 179).

Utterances that focus attention on the faults and slights of others, on discomfort, or even on pleasant things that move attention away from the work at the wrong time are not fitting responses (Schrag, 1986) in the workplace context and are therefore not enactments of professional civility. However, the lull of momentary redirected attention may promote productivity. The role of small talk at work, which provides opportunity for collegiality (Holmes & Stubbe, 2003, p. 100), creates interspaces in the workday; the flow of intense focus (Csikszentmihalyi, 1990) takes breaks from time to time. At just the right instant, in just the right place, nonwork-related talk is professionally civil discourse; it protects and promotes productivity through pauses that refresh and renew participants against a backdrop of shared participation in the "busyness" (Holmes & Stubbe, 2003, p. 97) of a productive workplace. As one respondent in Lutgen-Sandvik, Riforgiate, and Fletcher's (2011) study of work as a source of positive emotional experiences noted, "Our 'fun time' at work, even if it is only a quick comment that makes us all laugh, is absolutely wonderful" (p. 10).

Thus may patterns of productive talk and occasional moments of discursive respite develop their own rhythm and create connections around shared work. The interweaving of discourse and work shapes public friendship in constructive ways, generating a relational culture with responsive routines that fall naturally to productive practices and can build outward toward greater breadth and depth as both parties have time to commit. There is no necessity tied to it (Arendt, 1958); protecting and promoting productivity provides spaces on the periphery for work friendships to develop as a byproduct of task engagement—relationships marked with a collegiality defined by a sense of compatibility, in which parties to the relationship are partners in the creation of value (Gersick, Bartunek, & Dutton, 2000, p. 1031). Productivity is the relational engine that constructs places of energy and creativity.

Articulated speculation about others' opportunities, failures, or intentions move the focus of attention away from work and open the door to envy and jealousy (Arnett, 2006), which also affects the organizational environment (see Chapter 7). Sias's (1996) study of coworker equity discourse, for instance, illustrates the construction of judgments about other people's opportunities, work habits, or effort, and other elements that draw attention away from the task. Such conversation, if it turns to routine cynicism (Arnett & Arneson, 1999) that reproduces itself as an unreflective practice and makes no move against real organizational injustice, substitutes talk for action and builds an organizational reality that does not privilege productivity.

One recent study explored the "tall poppy" phenomenon in the workplace (Mancl & Penington, 2011). The term "tall poppy" comes from the Australian phrase for someone demonstrating excellent qualities and outstanding ability (Peeters, 2003, cited in Mancl & Penington, 2011). Mancl and Penington (2011) explored verbal and nonverbal communicative strategies employed by "poppy clippers" (p. 81) to attack the reputations and accomplishments of high-performing women and "cut them down" to the common level.

Some of these nonverbal behaviors were described as passive-aggressive (e.g., pretending not to pay attention when the person is engaging other listeners; obstructing work by not doing a fair share; "losing" important information that the person needed). Nonverbal behavior included the "eye roll" or long stares and showing up late for meetings that the person was running. Verbal behaviors included gossip and backbiting, or offering contrary negative information in a context in which positive information was being shared about the person.

Mancl and Penington's (2011) findings are relevant to each good in the professional civility framework—the goods of productivity, place, and persons—and serve as a helpful illustration of the interconnectedness of these goods. In this chapter, the focus is on the damage to the good of productivity, which occurred in this study through concerted attacks on high-performing—highly productive—women. Such behaviors also compromise the good of the organization; as Mancl and Penington put it, not only do persons suffer, but the organization itself is held to a level of mediocrity (p. 80). These uncivil behaviors put a ceiling on how good an organization can become through their work against productivity tied to personal excellence. Professionally civil comments would, instead, celebrate the accomplishments of others, highlighting the value of their productive contributions—thereby protecting and promoting productivity and persons. For example, in Lutgen-Sandvik et al.'s (2011) study, one participant noted, "My best workplace experience was when I landed a huge deal for our company. For the following few weeks, people would mention my prior success" (p. 10). Professional civility works to focus attention on good work, and in response to mistakes or failure, professional civility provides a discourse of hope and resilience for creative ways to improve (Hammoud & Buzzanell, in press).

Conclusion

Productivity is the first good of the profession(s) as tradition(s) of practice; it manifests as labor, work, and action in the activity of professionals. Professional civility protects and promotes productivity through discourse that keeps the focus of attention on work rather than on the failings and faults of others; profession as craft connects love of the work to appreciation of excellence wherever it is found. At all levels of the organization, professional civility emerges in discourse that declares the work worth doing.

The next chapter turns attention to the place within which productivity emerges. The organization is the local home for professionals in this historical moment. Professionals do their good work within the place of a particular institution, which they care for with professionally civil discourse that works within organizational limits, acknowledges the organization as a public place of engagement for all who gather around its common center, offers constructive support and dissent, and thereby enlarges the space for excellence.

7

Protecting and Promoting the Good of Place

Introduction

The organizational setting within which much of professional work takes place today has become a salient feature of contemporary profession(s) as practice. The collegial model of professional work (Sullivan, 2005) finds its defined routines within the demarcated physical, virtual, and phenomenological space of the contemporary organization. Professional civility encompasses the good of the local organizational home (Arnett, 1992) as a site for public enactment of professional practice. Caring for a local home is a constructive response to the historical moment within the tradition of profession(s) as practice; such care recognizes limits and offers the possibility of hope for continued contributions from the professions to the human community through the constructive institutional participation of professionals who engage the local home as organizational citizens.

Sullivan (2005) noted the responsibility of professionals today to attend to the good of place: "Someone, or some group, must somehow act out of conviction to make any institution function....This is the disposition named by the traditional notions of vocation and profession" (p. 260). Organizational leaders and those who enact daily work as part of a particular place—a local home—become institutional stewards of an organizational dwelling, a community of memory responsive to ongoing direction and change (Arnett, Fritz, & Bell, 2009). Organizations today need the support of professionals to ensure their survival, just as professionals need organizations as a site for their "good work" (Gardner, Csikszentmihalyi, & Damon, 2001).

Professional civility protects and promotes the good of place by tending to the vulnerable internal environment of an institution through attentive communicative practices. As professionals engage the productive work of organizational citizens within the limits of a particular organization, joining with others who are likewise engaged, constructive elements of the internal environment work their way out, enriching and strengthening the organization's external reputation, purpose, and goals, and enriching the professions themselves. A perspective of care for institutions (Fritz, 2012b) encourages organizational leaders to pay careful attention to daily routines of discourse, remaining alert to opportunities for framing constructive understandings of the organization's mission and identity (Fairhurst, 2011; Fairhurst, Jordan, & Neuwirth, 1997) for both newcomers and those who have been part of the place for some time. Organizations are public narratives that gather private difference around a common center (Arnett, 1986); articulating organizational limits provides guidelines for participation on the part of everyone, inviting constructive support and dissent to enlarge the "space" of the organizational environment as a public place within which, and to which, all organizational members are invited to contribute. Professional civility's virtuous action works to enlarge organizational space through thoughtful discourse about everyday events and charitable responses to the unexpected by focusing attention in helpful directions.

Professional civility works at multiple organizational levels in each of these areas. Care for the local home requires concerted effort by members of the professions who carry out their activities under its auspices, initially as guests, but sustaining the possibility of long-term participation as indwellers (Arnett et al., 2009). Organizations as public narratives offer accessible and recognized expectations for participation and inclusion, providing parameters for support and dissent that sustain institutional direction and change (Arnett et al., 2009) supportive of an organization's mission and narrative. Through mission-sensitive hiring, organizational socialization, mentoring, and demonstrating an organization's mission and values in word and deed in daily life at work (Fritz, O'Neil, Popp, Williams, & Arnett, in press), organizational leaders sustain an institutional mission (Arnett & Fritz, 2003) and encourage confidence in an organization's publicly stated principles, thereby checking routine cynicism and its corrosive effects.

Participation by organizational members in positions other than formal leadership is equally vital in the work of organizational socialization (Comer, 1991) and mentoring (Kram & Isabella, 1985). Through communication with peers, organizational incumbents fulfill the role of the "good audience" (Barrett, 1991) by encouraging professionally civil discourse in word and deed in daily work life through their own embodiment of professional civility, as well as by offering corrective feedback in response to inevitable lapses. Through reflective organizational citizenship, professionals working within a particular local home balance hope and cynicism by offering both support for the institution and constructive dissent (Hegstrom, 1995; Kassing, 1998, 2001) as contributions to the common good. Constructive participation through professionally civil discourse in multiple contexts of organizational life creates enlarged spaces for productivity and participation.

Care for the Local Home: The Metaphor of "Guest"

Professional civility embraces an ethic of care for institutions that recognizes the fragility of human structures, despite their apparent durability, and that acknowledges the indispensability of these structures for human flourishing. A conceptualization of communicative leadership as care for institutions (Fritz, 2012b), originally articulated as a perspective on women's communicative leadership (see Ruminski & Holba, 2012), transcends gender-identity categories and calls all persons in leadership to account; caring is everyone's business (Baker-Ohler & Holba, 2009). Institutions perish for lack of attention from those whose "watch" it is at a given time (Arnett et al., 2009). An ethic of care approach to leadership illustrates professional civility in its recognition of the need for stewards to tend and nurture a professional local home for many, a place for the goods of professional practice to take root and flourish within a particular organizational community. The professions take on "corporate social responsibility" for their organizational environments, making a place sustainable through the "theory" of mission and the "practice" of professional discursive activity—the communicative praxis of professional civility.

Arnett et al. (2009) articulated the importance of protecting and promoting a "dwelling place" (p. 141) or "community of memory" (p. 139), an organizational narrative that invites diversity of occupational and private loyalties and commitments to contribute to a common center of productivity and accomplishment. Contemporary organizations are fraught with fault lines that make them vulnerable to internal and external forces. Professionals, in whatever position they serve, are responsible to the local home as stewards who encourage its flourishing. Professionals shape the setting within which productive work is accomplished through communicative interaction, which structures the organization's environment (Seibold & Myers, 2006). Routine communicative interaction becomes internalized; shared practices become "common sense" (Arnett & Arneson, 2006, p. 54), those tacit understandings of appropriate behavior enacted effortlessly by cultural indwellers (Arnett et al., 2009) within a given location. For this reason, ordinary, unremarkable contexts of institutional life become generators of organizational environments through communicative habits that create the organization's character (Harrison, 1972).

Those who would care for a local home face many challenges; it is no simple matter to protect and promote an organization as a good in the professional civility framework. One issue is the profession/local home tension. Professionals import the background of a professional ethos as a primary source of identification into a particular place, which functions as a convenient location to carry out professional practice but does not necessarily command loyalty. The professional is, in this sense, a "cosmopolitan," a citizen of no particular place, as opposed to a "local," someone whose primary attachment is to the organization and its mission (e.g., Blau & Scott, 1962; Gouldner, 1957, 1958; Krause, 1996). The professional vocational trajectory includes socialization to an occupational narrative that defines a relatively autonomous and disembedded identity; professional civility asks for attentiveness to the local and the particular, an appreciation for embeddedness within the local home. Despite shifts in conditions of professional work, with reduced opportunities for autonomy and increased bureaucratization of conditions of employment (e.g., Noordegraaf, 2007), professional socialization is still a primary source of occupational meaning for employees in many fields today (Sullivan, 2005).

The professoriate provides an example of this professional/local home tension. Academics trained in research universities may not necessarily land a position in a research-intensive school, and may instead find themselves teaching in one (or more) of a variety of educational institutions with a different focus. There are many varieties of the "academic home" (Arnett, 1992, p. 11), some public, some private, some claiming a religious affiliation, and others without a particular faith tradition. Different types of institutions protect and promote different goods (Arnett et al., 2009; Fritz & Sawicki, 2006)—for example, teaching institutions place a different emphasis on instruction than do research institutions. The academic professional educated in a research-intensive department who finds employment in a teaching-intensive institution faces a different ranking of "goods" in that local home than in the location of professional formation.

Academics trained within a research model, therefore, may not share the goals encompassing the goods of the educational institution within which they find employment because of their professional socialization experience (Twale & DeLuca, 2008, p. 65). Professional socialization to a research model focuses attention on publication in "tier one" journals, university or academic presses, securing prestigious grants, and a relatively low teaching load; a teaching-intensive institution expects faculty availability to students and a high class load. A research agenda is most likely replaced with an emphasis on professional self-development, which may include conference attendance and perhaps conference presentations, but publication may be the exception rather than the rule. Complicating the picture are student expectations, which may vary by institutional type. For example, students enrolled at Christian colleges and universities appear to have distinctive expectations for the "ideal professor" (Woods, Badzinski, Fritz, & Yeates, 2012).

This issue of tension between a cosmopolitan and local orientation has been addressed from different perspectives. Some suggest that the professional/local tension may not be as stark as originally imagined—loyalty to a profession and to an organization may constitute two different dimensions rather than two poles of a single dimension (Wallace, 1993). From either understanding, a metaphor to guide professional work in local homes from a perspective of professional civility as care for institutions is that of a guest in the home. Just as someone new to a culture inhabits the role of guest, taking a stance of learning to the task of cultural entry (Arnett et al., 2009), so may professionals with a primary loyalty to an occupational group find a place of contribution in an organization with which they do not see themselves identifying strongly. Incorporating care for institutions into identity expectations for professionals in both professional and organizational socialization develops and expands the professional ethic in a manner suited for a historical moment marked by lack of agreement on virtue structures (Arnett et al., 2009; MacIntyre, 2007) and in need of minimal common ground from which to engage shared work within particular places.

A Levinasian care for institutions could be appropriately termed "disinterested care" (Arnett, 2012), a care that lives out responsibility for a place without concern for reciprocity. The history of the professions as devoted to service through work on behalf of the community regardless of remuneration has some kinship with disinterested care. Disinterested care of professionals for their clients and the community may be accompanied by a covenantal understanding (Graham, 1991) of one's relationship to one's profession; a sense of connection marked by loyalty and a willingness to endure difficulties to remain part of the tradition may hold for professionals and professional institutions that define traditions of practice.

In organizations within which professionals practice today, the typical understanding of professional participation may be contractual or economic exchange (Graham, 1991). From an organizational citizenship perspective, a covenantal association with one's organization is likely, and may be embraced by professional participants, but such an orientation depends on perceived justice; frequent and serious violations may result in the shift of a covenantal orientation to an exchange orientation marked by reduced commitment and the possibility of seeking other employment (Graham, 1991; Organ, 1988). Such a shift in orientation may result from cynicism generated by lack of alignment of supervisory words and deeds with stated organizational expectations (Fritz et al., in press).

The most salient type of violated expectations may be those related to organizational proclamations of the value placed on its members. If organizational leadership declares an organization to be a family and then proceeds to fire "family" members (Arnett & Arneson, 1999, p. 18), appropriate cynicism is the likely outcome. Care for the local home involves careful choice of framing language (Fairhurst, 2011) to prevent rhetorical overreach (Arnett & Fritz, 2003)—promising more than can be delivered—on the part of organizational leadership.

In the case of professional/local home tension, the metaphor of "guest," which is less intimate in implication, paints a realistic and constructive picture for professional engagement. Guests may become long-term participants in an organization as they move their status from stranger to potential indweller (Arnett et al., 2009); a temporary home may become a permanent dwelling under the right conditions. The metaphor of guest moves into a paradigm that is neither merely contractual nor purely covenantal, but that offers opportunity and invitation for long-term commitment to a worthwhile endeavor that makes a difference in the world, a purpose that reflects the historical "good" of professional practice: the task. Through protecting and promoting the organization, the professional has the potential to protect and promote the important work of the profession.

Our understanding of who we are in relation to an organization, and our expectations for how organizations work with us, are defined by the metaphors we employ, which emerge from the stocks of knowledge and production regimes governing language use in organizations (e.g., Hodge & Kress, 1988; Moch & Fields, 1985; see Chapter 5, this volume). Metaphors function to shape our understanding of the world and carry a great deal of power in their ability to direct thought and action (Lakoff & Johnson, 1980). Morgan (1986) recognized the power of metaphorical thinking in his seminal work on metaphors of organizing. For example, the metaphor of an organization as an "iron cage" or "psychic prison," so prominent in critical theory, suggests an oppressive relationship in which organizational participants are prisoners or slaves. Fairhurst (2011) also noted the importance of metaphor (e.g., pp. 94–99) for communication practices of organizational leadership.

Metaphors are themselves relationally driven and often function in pairs; for example, the metaphor of "host" is not determined and eludes fixed meaning transfer. The metaphor of professional as "guest" moves the relationship of professional to organization away from an understanding of the organization as an entity with which the professional functions as a parasite in a symbiotic or destructive relationship, placing it instead within an understanding of the organization as a "home" into which the professional as guest and potential indweller is welcomed and offered a chance for meaningful contribution. These different metaphors work with alternative understandings of the term "host." The element to which this metaphorical term is connected and in relation to which the metaphorical relationship emerges shapes the understanding of the notion of host.

Similar principles are at work in our discourse about the organization for which we work. Our language constructs metaphorical understandings of "place," both directly, through how we talk about the organization, and indirectly, in how we imply an organization's orientation to its inhabitants. If we ask for volunteers to be "guinea pigs" in a test of a new software package rather than "pioneers," we reflect a very different understanding of an organization's approach to its employees and processes. Metaphorical environments matter.

A professional civility perspective offers an understanding of organizations as public narratives that accompanies care for the local home. The sense of "public" frames organizational space as a location within which many voices participate (Arnett et al., 2009); the notion of "narrative" indicates a defined trajectory that works as argumentative parameters (Arnett, 2006; Arnett & Fritz, 2003) for judgment and decision on the part of organizational leaders. Those who share a commitment to an organization's narrative may feel more comfortable within its confines than those who do not; in that sense, the "public" part of "public narrative" may risk eclipse, threatened by insularity and cliquishness that violates inclusive participation, forcing those who do not quite fit in into parvenu status. The parvenu, according to Arendt (1978), is the person who seeks acceptance but never quite makes it; the parvenu is on the outside and is denied entrance into places of collegiality and participation (Arnett et al., 2009). Keeping the metaphor of "public narrative" at the forefront permits invitation and welcome, belonging and connection, and distance and autonomy operative and in dynamic tension to emerge in practices of professionally civil discourse that enact these themes in varied ways.

Organizations as Public Narratives

In this historical moment of diversity and difference (Arnett et al., 2009), an understanding of organizations as public narratives (Arnett & Fritz, 2003) permits a focus on a minimalist understanding of shared common ground as a source of unity and purpose. In a workforce characterized by disagreement on narrative structures guiding private lives (Fritz, Arnett, & Conkel, 1999; MacIntyre, 2007; Primeaux, 1992), functional integration in public contexts must be achieved by means other than personal relationships based on shared worldviews or private orientations (Arnett & Arneson, 1999). The potential of narrative to connect diverse audiences (Bakhtin, 1981, cited in Barry & Elmes, 1997) receives support from Boyce's (1995) research, which illustrates how particular stories support a larger, corporately agreed-upon story by creating and recreating a common vision. Similarly, a publicly shared narrative creates a recognized common background despite diversity of private background orientations situating individuals in moral space (Taylor, 1989).

Although Boje (1991, 1995) considered the idea of a single mission to be the equivalent of a monologue that silences other voices, what Boje was talking about was an ideology rather than a narrative or a story. An ideology tolerates no opposition, but a narrative invites participation in unique ways that are bounded by the guidelines or horizon of a larger story. Public narratives provide parameters within which diversity can flourish through contributions to a common center.

Critical theorists' concerns with totalizing narratives, or metanarratives, are well founded. The past offers many lessons in the dangers arising from such totalizing ideologies (Arendt, 1951/1976), and the present moment does not lack for examples. Critical theorists thoughtfully question totalizing forces, and organizational scholars following their lead have raised important questions about societal and individual implications of a technocratic managerial ideology (Alvesson & Willmott, 1992). There is, however, an alternative perspective. Bellah, Madsen, Sullivan, Swidler, and Tipton (1985) offered the metaphor of a broken covenant: no narrative is perfect. Organizational stories are put into place by flawed persons operating within flawed systems who, despite imperfections, offer a public narrative that calls all into accountability and provides an argumentative standard by which organizational initiatives and personal practices can be evaluated. An agreed-upon public narrative, socially constructed and temporal (Pearce, 1994), provides criteria for participation. Every community will have limits; some will be more restrictive than others. The key is to make the narrative public, permitting the informed participation of all organizational members.

A perspective on organizations as public narratives recognizes the concerns of critical theorists and echoes the concern of postmodernists for particularity. This approach invites a perspective that grounds an organization in a publicly stated "petite narrative" (Lyotard, 1984) that gathers efforts around a common project defined by the organization's mission limits. A shared background narrative made visible in a publicly articulated mission or "saga" (Clark, 1972) provides definitional agreement for professionals' public positions in an organization. A background narrative offers role clarity, establishing guidelines for responsibility, accountability, status, and power, issues that routinely become contested terrain when there are no public guidelines. This perspective assumes the value of a common story or common center (Arnett, 1986) that unites and provides clear direction for all organizational participants, permitting stories that may contradict, challenge, or offer contradictory perspectives on "official" stories (e.g., Arnett et al., 2009; Boje, 1991) to exist in creative tension with the formally sanctioned story. This perspective does not deny the existence or value of individual stories or of counter stories, but suggests that to the extent that the larger organizational story or mission is clear and public, there will be an opportunity for public accountability for organizational participants at all levels, and competing stories can serve as checks and balances to the primary story.

Arnett and Fritz (2003) offered an approach to management that introduced a focus on mission, appropriate relational communication in the workplace, and concern for productivity that can inform professional civility as communicative virtue at work and as an ethic for professional practice. This approach focuses attention on the requirements of managers who work in a moment of virtue contention to protect and promote the mission of a local organizational home. Processes of hiring, organizational socialization, performance appraisals, and other communicative tasks are framed as mission-sensitive activities answerable to the larger organizational narrative. This attentiveness to the good of place directs managerial action toward behaviors marked by professional civility. Such an approach to management demonstrates care for institutions that protects and promotes institutional mission and values through careful attention to these important elements of organizational life. Such accountability to the local has its counterpart in institutional accountability to the community.

The first level of accountability rests with the hiring process. Managerial messages are particularly powerful and are manifested in both word and deed, a measure of behavioral integrity (Simons, 2002). Through practices of hiring, managers proclaim the extent to which they honor the commitments and values of the organization.

Hiring for mission is recognized by many institutions as a key factor in employment decisions. The organizational behavior literature speaks of "person-organization fit" (e.g., Bretz & Judge, 1994; Judge & Ferris, 1992; Kristof, 1996; O'Reilly, Chatman, & Caldwell, 1991; Van Vianen, 2000). For nonprofit organizations, mission fit has often been a criterion for self-selection (e.g., Lee & Wilkins, 2011), and the literature on person-organization fit suggests benefits of such hiring criteria. In the case of educational institutions with a faith-grounded mission, concern for mission is often a driving force that may come into conflict with other goods at hand that are also related to institutional identity. Faith-based colleges and universities have a dual commitment, one being to the religious narrative/tradition upon which they rest and within the ground of which their roots find nourishment, and the other being to the common purposes that define educational institutions in general (Fritz & Sawicki, 2006). Person-organization fit is key for faith-based institutions, therefore, but is also vital for any institution hoping to protect and promote its mission.

Attentiveness to mission is also an important part of a realistic job preview (Wanous, 1992), an important element of creating reasonable and realistic expectations for requirements of the position, coworkers, and the organization's culture, without which unmet high expectations about the job are likely to lead to newcomer dissatisfaction and turnover (Wanous, Poland, Premack & Davis, 1991, cited in Kramer, 2010). Professional civility involves skill in articulating an organization's mission commitments and practices tied to that mission. Professional civility also requires skill in listening and discernment, looking beyond the "artificial light" (Arnett, 2005) of credentials to find the genuine light of mission fit. Given a horizon of minimal qualifications, the temporary darkness of a missing skill set can be managed more readily than the enduring darkness that creeps into an institution when mission is ignored.

The organizational socialization process (Kramer, 2010) moves the new professional organizational member into the specific practices of a local home. As noted in the chapter on the power of messages during the socialization process, the various stages, or states (Harden, 1993), of socialization are shaping forces. During this time, new employees can learn practices of professional civility if such practices are modeled by supervisors (Fritz et al., in press). The mentoring process is a vital step in inviting the gifts and contributions of new hires into the practices of the local home. Mentoring requires sensitivity to the reality of the unsaid of an organizational culture (Arnett et al., 2009), accompanied by the wisdom to cultivate the interpretive schemata of new employees into routines and opportunities that provide not just the explicit rules, but the application of "common sense" in a particular place. This common sense requires patience to learn. Professional civility in the mentoring process exhibits concern for the organization and for the professional's contribution to its successful functioning.

Mentoring takes many forms, ranging from informal peer relationships (e.g., Kram & Isabella, 1985) to formal mentoring programs (Chao, Walz, & Gardner, 1992). Informal mentoring often emerges naturally within the context of work life and depends on the personal inclinations of both parties. Because of the likelihood of persons to gravitate toward persons who are similar (Byrne, 1961), leaving mentoring to the chance of informal connections may result in lack of mentoring opportunities for members of underrepresented groups. The advantage of a formal mentoring program is its role-governed nature; personal liking is secondary to a shared commitment to the organization (Arnett & Fritz, 2003).

A mentor can shape the expectations for what is possible in a given organizational setting, making the new employee aware of limits within which freedom is found (Arnett, 1986). The value of a publicly stated mission rests in its starting point as "ground" for an employee who does not yet have the experiential horizon to grasp the nuance of interpretive application garnered from years of experience. The challenge of mentoring the professional rests in the background of professional training and experience that is highly salient as a referential basis for judgment in various circumstances but needs the real referent of an organizational context for pragmatic engagement. Professional education gains its worth as theory meets the press of the world—through rubbing shoulders with others, encountering real clients, projects, tasks, and difficulties, and discovering the flaws and weaknesses of institutions, other human beings, and the self.

Peers play a key role as information providers (Comer, 1991) for new employees. The nature of the information they provide assists the socialization process. Barrett (1991) noted the role a "good audience" plays in cultivating civility in those who offer "performances" during the course of everyday life. As employees respond to each other with confirmation or correction, practices of professional civility are given support and reinforcement, becoming part of the routine of organizational behavior and shaping expectations for future behavior.

Embracing professional civility does not imply mechanical or automatic compliance, however, but increases the likelihood of dissent articulated in response to perceptions of mission violation or injustice (Graham, 1991). When organizational guidelines are clear, failure to meet those guidelines is more easily discernible. In such cases, professionals give voice to concern as organizational citizens.

Unity of Contraries: Support and Dissent

Professional civility manifests communicative practices that protect and promote the good of place. To flourish, organizations need support for ongoing activity expressed in the communicative practices of their members, constructive suggestions for change when needed, and correction within the parameters of an organization's purpose and mission, which serve as a public standard against which to measure organizational action. Organizational narratives remain open to alteration through the unity of direction and change with responsiveness to an ongoing tradition (Arnett et al., 2009); such change is reflective and thoughtful rather than reactive. Suggestions for change and constructive dissent work within the guidelines of an organization's publicly stated mission and within reasonable expectations for organizational involvement as a place of meaning in life. Constructive dissent steers away from habitual complaint and avoids trivialization of crisis. Constructive dissent is also different from complaint rooted in personal disagreement with organizational practices or disappointment with organizational life that has failed to meet one's expectations.

Support for organizational structures and suggestions for change work within the spirit of supportive communication (Gibb, 1961). If it is the case, as some organizational scholars suggest, that organizations are "drawn—almost cultlike—to embrace constant change" (Lewis, Schmisseur, Stephens, & Weir, 2006, p. 114), then protecting and promoting an organization involves assisting change in ways that preserve the integrity of the institution's aims and goals. Supportive communicative practices reflecting provisionalism and problem solving, in which ideas are engaged dialogically, offer constructive approaches to current practices that move organizational action in new directions, drawing on the support of all involved. Rather than a linear transmission of information about change, which may reflect strategy or control (Gibb, 1961), change efforts "wherein various stakeholders engage one another in clarification, negotiation of meaning, and perspective taking" (Lewis, 2006, p. 39) are likely to be successful. Organizational leaders work with professional civility as they invite appropriate participation, include and value employee contributions, and frame change in ways supportive of an institution's mission (Fairhurst, 2011; Lewis, 2006).

Support for organizational structures in times of stability and change manifests in both expressed communication and the restraint that marks professionally civil discourse—for example, refraining from habitual complaint about one's place of work. Constant complaint focuses attention only on what is problematic. One danger of confusing habitual complaint and legitimate dissent is the risk of trivialization of crisis (Arnett, 2006). Trivialization of crisis has the potential to jeopardize the well-being of an organization. If every organizational event is a crisis, nothing is. If all organizational attributes and every daily event are perceived as problematic at all times, then a real problem facing the organization will have no power to draw the sustained attention necessary for resolution. The ability to discern the difference between relatively minor issues that will work themselves out and those that deserve attention and must be addressed in order to be remedied is a type of practical wisdom operative at the observational level that translates into messages at the verbal level. The expressive reaction of "That's awful! What are we going to do?" becomes "Yes, that's unfortunate, but we can deal with it. Let's make a list of the affected units" in the form of conventional design logic. When the response becomes "You know, I think what's happened may actually work out better than we expected. We can learn from this one," then the work of rhetorical design logic has begun its creative process.

Expressing dissent in a professionally civil manner requires directing attention to elements of the situation relevant to mission, keeping the primary purpose of the organization in mind—a type of principled dissent (Waldron & Kassing, 2011, pp. 169–170). For example, if a proposed reorganization of a unit is likely to result in consequences that will jeopardize the organization's mission by shifting its focus onto short-term gains, someone who recognizes that possibility might express dissent by articulating the mission as a background metaphor and identifying how the proposed changes may compromise its viability. The form of this utterance might be a statement expressed as an idea for consideration and offered as a potentially helpful comment. In this manner, dissent works to assist the larger unit and, by extension, the entire organization.

Constructive expression of concern in the organizational dissent literature intersects with the research on civic virtue of organizational citizenship. In a turn of phrase, it is sometimes necessary to "protect and provoke" as a way to protect and promote (the good of an organization), with dissent functioning as corrective feedback (Hegstrom, 1995; see Waldron & Kassing, 2011). Arnett (1999) offered the metaphor of educational administration as building and renovation as a way of working constructively in an institutional setting; most of the time, we are called to work within a structure that is in place to implement changes responsive to existing parameters. Rarely does the house need to be torn down completely.

Selznick (1992/1994) warned that institutions are vulnerable to a degradation of values reflecting their "distinctive character and mission" (p. 333), so caution is necessary when offering insights for correction, redirection, and/or improvement. When institutions undergo inevitable and necessary change in their established structures and rules, revision should occur "in a principled way, that is, while holding fast to values and purposes" (Selznick, 1992/1994, p. 338). By identifying the organization's enduring mission principles as limits for change, new initiatives capitalize on existing strengths and expand the organization's capacity rather than constricting it.

Professional civility resting in organizational citizenship is marked by a tolerance for the minor inconveniences inevitable in everyday work life, as well as by avoiding complaint about matters of little consequence (e.g., Konovsky & Organ, 1996), reflecting the sportsmanship dimension of organizational citizenship (Organ, 1990). Sportsmanship is a broad construct that includes not only lack of complaint, but a number of positive attributes, as well. Good sports, in Organ, Podsakoff, and MacKenzie's (2006) words,

> are people who not only do not complain when they are inconvenienced by others but also who maintain a positive attitude even when things do not go their way, are not offended when others do not follow their suggestions, are willing to sacrifice their personal interest for the good of the work group, and do not take the rejection of their ideas personally. (p. 308)

Habitual complaint not only risks trivialization of crisis, but may degenerate into routine cynicism, where all organizational action is received unreflectively as contrary to stated purposes (Arnett & Arneson, 1999). Appropriate cynicism, however, is not inconsistent with the sportsmanship dimension of the organizational citizenship construct, and offers a place for different types of organizational dissent messages (Garner, 2009) directed to specific areas of concern to work on behalf of the organization, reflecting the civic virtue dimension of organizational citizenship. Such messages are a type of constructive criticism at the organizational level, leading to improvements and greater flourishing for the organization and those connected to it.

Organizational dissent is legitimate when stated words and deeds do not match (Arnett & Arneson, 1999). Disagreement with organizational actions and disappointment stemming from one's own self-generated expectations are not the basis of genuine dissent. Organizations cannot satisfy all needs; each place offers many opportunities for criticism, and distinguishing dissent based on legitimate concerns from generalized criticism resulting from personal disagreement with organizational actions (Arnett & Arneson, 1999) is important for a constructive understanding of dissent from a professional civility perspective. Dissent, in this context, takes the form of "just talking" (Kingwell, 1995), contributions that move the organization's actions back into alignment with a stated mission or identify ways that change can occur in a manner that maintains institutional integrity, or "fidelity to self-guiding principles" (Selznick, 1992/1994, p. 322).

One source of complaint may rest with high expectations arising from personal wishes taken to the organizational setting. Such expectations may rest with the anticipation of a particular type of work, satisfying relationships, and opportunities for creative growth in an organizational setting. Such expectations are part of the professional tradition of meaning and are not unreasonable as a possible outcome in professional employment within an organization. However, if the organization becomes the sole location for personal fulfillment, disappointment is inevitable (Arnett, 2006), and trivialization of crisis may happen in another way.

Expecting an organization to provide all one's needs for meaning, including companionship and loyalty, is likely to focus attention in one location—the organizational setting. When one expects an organization to bear more of the weight of a life than is possible, rhetorical interruptions (Arnett, Fritz, & Bell, 2009) in one's routine or in one's experience of work become magnified, occluding one's view of other elements by engulfing the field of vision. There is nowhere to turn for relief, and the event becomes a crisis. If, for example, a workplace relationship experiences a negative turning point (Hess, Omdahl, & Fritz, 2006), and one's relational life is invested primarily in the workplace, then this relational problem will become a phenomenological "crisis." In similar fashion, not everything that one disagrees with in an organization deserves the same level of comment or energy. The adage of choosing one's battles comes to mind.

In any context, there is always choice involved regarding where to place attention as a focus of energy and efforts. The literature on focus of attention at work (Gardner, Dunham, Cummings, & Pierce, 1987) offers some insights into this phenomenon, as does the scholarship on the phenomenology of work (e.g., Brewer, 2001). Avoiding routine cynicism stemming from a conviction that nothing is going right and nothing ever will involves thoughtful, deliberate framing—first to oneself, internally, as the first "conversation partner" (Arnett, in press-b), in constructive terms, and then outwardly to others in the discourse of conversation at the utterance level. The how and the why of dissent requires careful discernment. With one's focus of attention appropriately tuned, practicing professional civility has the potential to enlarge the organizational space available for creative and productive work. Whether highlighting organizational events in casual conversation with a peer or carrying out evaluative responsibilities as a supervisor, we affect organizational space through our utterances.

Enlarged Space

The task of professionals in organizations is to make the place bigger. Professionals encourage and support the work of others in ways that expand the organization's roominess by opening opportunities unforeseen, but falling within the bounds or horizon of what is possible in a given place. What is possible corresponds to the imagination rather than fantasy (Arnett, in press-b) and is brought into being by a focus of attention directed toward constructive action. Thoughtful attention begins in conversation with oneself through framing processes assisted by what was learned during organizational socialization, information that has now become implicit or tacit knowledge. The tacit becomes explicit once again through reflective, deliberate consideration and thought. An enlarged understanding makes space for one's own creativity and the creativity of others. One's words to oneself and then to others open up or close down possibilities.

Our focus of attention directs our words, which then direct our actions and the actions of others, effectively enlarging or shrinking organizational phenomenological space. Sias's (1996) work on equity discourse warns us to be careful in how we draw attention to organizational events with what we speak into the public environment of workplace conversation. Her findings suggest that people vary in their choice of messages in reaction to someone else's perceived advantage. For example, the utterances "Did you know Mike was leaving on Tuesdays at two to go to class?" and "David doesn't work as much as the rest of us" (p. 176) draw attention to the action of others in a way that has the potential to focus attention on inequities. Although such instances may need attention, highlighting these events sets them loose with announced attention as a type of "news," essentially enacting an environment (Weick, 1976) by defining an event as differential treatment (Sias, 1996, p. 179). Professionally civil discourse may involve restraint in expressing observations to coworkers, saving comments for private conversation with supervisors who can make a difference.

The concern with such utterances rests with their effects on the organizational symbolic environment. Messages such as those uncovered in Sias's (1996) study, similar to the messages critical of productive others, or "tall poppies," discussed in the previous chapter (i.e., Mancl & Penington, 2011), foster unhealthy climates of jealousy and envy (Arnett, 2006). Such climates shrink organizational space, limiting room for the creativity that can emerge when attention is focused on getting work done in a cooperative fashion. In a metaphor different from Mancl and Penington's, but consistent with the general sense, "poppy clippers," and those like them, become architects of institutional atrophy, lowering the ceiling and contracting the walls of the organization.

Professional civility works against this type of narrowing of boundaries, offering support and encouragement for the good work of others to enhance the organizational environment and create a climate of productivity. A climate of productivity is devoid of the neurotic guilt (Arnett & Arneson, 1999) that is bound to happen when people begin to look over their shoulders to see who may be noticing—and finding fault with—their good work. Professional civility expands and enriches the affective atmosphere of the organization, opening conditions for continued cooperative work, enhanced trust, and greater solidarity around the common center.

The application of Gibb's (1961) work on defensive and supportive messages to a craftwork model based on Sennett's (2008) discussion of sociable and antisocial expertise (see Chapter 6, this volume) offers a way to counteract the power of envy and jealousy in the workplace. Sennett described a condition of "invidious comparison," the result of emphasizing the superior expertise one has over another.

Expertise carries with it an inherent inequality, with the potential for arousing humiliation and shame in others (Sennett, 2008, p. 249, 251). It is possible to work as an expert in a way that de-emphasizes difference but does not eradicate it, and that also invites others' potential to come forth to achieve excellence—the potential for equality rests with task-mastery possible through achievement of public standards. "Sociable expertise addresses other people in their unfolding prospects . . . one's guiding standards are transparent, that is, comprehensible to nonexperts" (Sennett, 2008, p. 251).

Engaging expertise in this nondefensive way exhibits professional civility by inviting others to develop abilities through mentoring, encouragement, and modeling. When the less-skilled are open to learning from the more-skilled, organizational space expands. The language each employs in communicative practices of shared expertise and attentive learning continues to widen the space, which offers expanded opportunities. Professional civility protects and promotes learning (Arnett et al., 2009) as a contributing element to the good of organizations, creating joy in the work engaged together (Sennett, 2008).

Likewise, in everyday discourse about organizational routines and processes and in response to inevitable rhetorical interruptions in work life, our choice of words affects the affective atmosphere of the workplace. For example, Omdahl (2006) highlighted the difference between focusing attention on a failure in an expressivist rant, which accomplishes little positive good, and working functionally to solve a problem (p. 280). When the last cup of coffee is gone and no one has put more on to brew, it is probably more helpful to offer to bring water for the next pot than to launch a strident, shaming tirade at the administrative assistant.

In similar fashion, constructive criticism moves concerns away from persons and toward task and interpersonal processes and events. Critique is necessary for improvement, but how it is articulated matters. Peers offer valuable feedback to others through face-saving comments; rhetorical design logic opens up alternatives with creative insights. When addressing an action someone has taken that has been hurtful, damaging, or neglectful, choice of place for conversation about the issue and the way the conversation is engaged matter. Consider the following comment, which shows concern for the goals and face of both self and other:

> When you cut me off in the meeting this morning, I felt like you didn't want to hear what I had to say. I know time was short and you probably didn't think about it, but I need to let you know my concern. I so appreciate you as a colleague and don't want anything to get in the way of our working relationship.

Likewise, supervisors assist their direct reports with comments that support face while offering ways to improve performance (Fairhurst, Green, & Snavely, 1984).

Enlarged spaces may emerge from a manner of discourse that is suggestive rather than definitive. The hedges and qualifications so often highlighted as attributes of speech lacking power and authority (e.g., O'Barr, 1983; Hosman, 1989) work well as limits on proffered claims. The personalized language of "I think," "to me," and "from my perspective" offer conversational interspaces between oneself and one's ideas and between one's certainties and the reality to be constructed in concert with others. Literature on decision-making in groups warns of failing to examine ideas carefully for their positive and negative consequences (Hirokawa & Pace, 1983; Hirokawa & Scheerhorn, 1986), moving quickly to make a decision rather than spending time in careful discernment. Nonpersonalized language gives the impression of completeness, closure, and finality and may work to short-circuit exploratory processes necessary for accurate decisions. "That won't work. Nobody will want to put in the extra time." "That's the best we can do. Let's just have Mary change offices with Bob." If such utterances come at the conclusion of decision-making, they shift deliberation to action and may be helpful in moving forward. Coming at the beginning of discussion, however, they limit options and constrict space.

Conclusion

Professionals in this historical moment protect and promote the organization as local home through enacting the discourse of professional civility. Professional civility begins with a phenomenological turning toward the place of work as a guest if one's own values and those of the organization are not congruent. Understanding the organization as a public narrative permits guidelines for participation that reduce the likelihood of cynicism from unmet high expectations and encourage contributions from all organizational members to shape meaningful outcomes, whether products, services, or ideas. Professional civility's virtuous work includes support for an organization's mission, identifying creative options for change, and constructive dissent in the face of mismatched words and deeds.

The themes addressed here are exemplary rather than comprehensive, offering a hermeneutic entrance into further exploration of the form and content of professional civility as it works to protect and promote an organization. In the case of organizations that have lost a guiding mission and are in danger of failure, the question may be whether the institution should survive or pass from existence. In the case of Enron, decline resulted after corruption had eviscerated the institution's integrity, and the most constructive action on the part of professionals in such situations may be to leave if expressed concerns have no effect. Whistle-blowing, an option often of last resort (Johannesen, Valde, & Whedbee, 2008; Seeger, 1997), is a communicative act that brings to public light perceived wrongdoing on the part of an organization. The consequences to the organization and to the whistle-blower are far reaching; such action requires careful thought and consideration.

The next chapter's focus is on professional civility as it protects and promotes persons as a good of professions. Acknowledging differences between public and private domains and recognizing the value of roles and boundaries form the basis for professionally civil communication with others in the workplace. Relationships in the workplace are accountable to the organization and find their strength in collegial engagement of tasks. Professional civility calls us to engage others in the workplace with communicative practices that do honor to the work within the organizational setting.

Protecting and Promoting the Good of Persons

Introduction

The history of professions laid out by Kimball (1995) and explored by Sullivan (2005) reveals a tradition within which work is part of a good and meaningful life for human beings. The good of others who are served by professionals endures within the tradition of profession(s), and if we understand professions to function along the lines of the craft model discussed by Sennett (2008), the good of others with whom professionals conduct their work is also an integral part of the professional ethos. For the professions in this historical moment, work is usually accomplished with, or in the presence of, other persons in an organizational setting who may occupy different roles or specialties, all of which come together to accomplish the work of the organization. The set of others relevant to professional work includes a range of persons sharing the physical or virtual interactive space within or under the auspices of a particular place.

From a perspective of professional civility, we engage others at work in ways that honor the institution as the party to whom work relationships are accountable (Arnett, Fritz, & Bell, 2009; Fritz, in press-c), and we protect the dignity of persons by differentiating public and private spheres of life (Arnett, 2006). What this differentiation means will vary from person to person and from relationship to relationship. As will be evident, the good of persons and the good of relationship are closely connected in this treatment. The communicative interaction defining and structuring particular relational forms (Sias, 2009a) also defines relational participants, and the quality of a relationship may foster or impede the professional and personal flourishing of its members.

Professional civility protects and promotes persons in the workplace through communicative practices that permit the closeness and distance necessary to function within organizational roles on behalf of productivity. As conversation in organizations ebbs and flows around work routines, professional civility enacts a rich collegiality that turns together toward tasks (e.g., Gersick, Bartunek, & Dutton, 2000), balancing the personal and professional realms of engagement by negotiating the development and maintenance of work relationships (Sias, Gallagher, Kopeneva, & Pederson, 2012) and discovering ways to navigate differences and difficulties when they arise.

Workplace Relationships

The good of relationship (Arnett et al., 2009) takes different forms in different settings. Private relationships are different in nature than public relationships; each type of relationship requires a different type of communicative nourishment (Fritz, in press-c). Public relationships—those organized and sustained within a context oriented toward roles and joint action for a purpose other than the relationship itself—require different types of attention and invite different types of discourse than private relationships (Arnett et al., 2009). Relationships in the workplace are sites of personal and professional challenge, requiring negotiation of multiple dialectical tensions (Bridge & Baxter, 1992) in order to attend to multiple, often competing, goods. While it is inevitable that relationships of some type will form in the workplace (Sias, 2009a), the characteristics of these relationships (such as closeness) are often the result of reflective choice (Sias et al., 2012). From a framework of professional civility, relationships in the workplace can be pleasant, nourishing, and enjoyable as they focus attention on protecting and promoting the good of the organization and the task at hand, accomplishing good work done well.

Several relational types have been identified in organizational settings, including information, collegial, and special peer relationships (Kram & Isabella, 1985); friendships (Bridge & Baxter, 1992; Fine, 1986); mentorships (Chao, 1997; Kram, 1985, 1983); romances (Dillard & Witteman, 1985; Horan & Chory, 2009; Pierce, Byrne, & Aguinis, 1997; Quinn, 1977); and supervisory relationships

(Dansereau, Graen, & Haga, 1975). These relationship terms describe varying levels of relational intensity or quality. For example, Kram and Isabella (1985) found that information, collegial, and special peer relationships differ in levels of intimacy and in their functions for relationship partners. Leader-member exchange (LMX) theory (e.g., Liden & Graen, 1980) suggests that subordinates and their supervisors develop relationships that range from the in-group relationship, characterized by high trust and support, to the out-group relationship, characterized by low trust and support (Fairhurst & Chandler, 1989). Research on LMX theory (see Graen & Uhl-Bien, 1995) reveals that organizational relationships span the scope of relational forms, often blending public and private dimensions due to close proximity and daily interaction (e.g., Bridge & Baxter, 1992; Sias, 2009a).

Not all organizational relationships reach a high level of connectedness. Some relationships remain politely collegial, at the level of Kurth's (1970) friendly relations or Kram and Isabella's (1985) information or collegial peer relationship, which are primarily agentic relationships (Rawlins, 1992), formed for the purpose of a particular function, such as completing a task. Other relationships, however, transcend the task-related association of work colleagues and attain the intimacy of close friendship, acquiring features of a private relationship in addition to those of a public relationship (Bridge & Baxter, 1992). Marks (1994) reported that about half the persons who hold jobs in organizations have close friends at work, persons with whom they socialize outside of the organizational context. From a perspective of professional civility, relationships at work exist in the public sphere and are accountable to the organization of which they are a part (Arnett et al., 2009).

Factors Influencing Relationship Development

Several factors influence a relationship's progress toward friendship intimacy, or its stabilization at a work relationship level (for a comprehensive treatment of work relationships and their developmental processes, see Sias, 2009a). These factors may distinguish persons who report that they have work associates who are close friends and those who report that they do not have such friendships. Organizational variables such as structure and norms influence relationship development and maintenance within organizations (Waldron, 2003). The type of work one does can enable or constrain the nature of communicative interaction (Ashcraft, 2000; Fine, 1986; Waldron, 2003), thereby influencing the intimacy of the relationship, since the opportunity to talk to another person is important for relational development (Altman & Taylor, 1973; Marks, 1994). An organization's culture encourages or discourages work relationships and discourse that extend beyond required work involvement (Hebden, 1986; Hess, 1993; Martin, Feldman, Hatch, & Sitkin, 1983). For example, organizational cultures that practice feminist critique of the bureaucratic bifurcation of public and private spheres (Acker, 1995; Mills & Chiaramonte, 1991; Pringle, 1989, cited in Ashcraft, 2000) may promote private discourse that encourages personal intimacy (Ashcraft, 2000). Other organizational cultures may discourage formation of personal relationships in order to prevent preferential treatment based on affectional ties (e.g., Ashcraft, 2000).

Individual level variables such as gender, personality traits, and interaction style also influence work relationship development. Fritz (1997a) found men's and women's information, collegial, and special peer relationships to be characterized by different levels of mutual dependence, honesty, and social support. Women's special peer relationships were reported to be more intense than men's, whereas women's information peer relationships were less intense than men's. Personality traits operate as filters that influence the trajectory of a relationship (Duck, 1977). One's interaction style, when congruent with another's, promotes further relational development (Cappella, 1984).

In addition to organizational and individual level variables that have appeared in the literature, one's personal preference may play a role in whether one develops close relationships at work. People differ in their understanding of the appropriateness and desirability of forming close relationships in the workplace. This issue has been addressed in initial work done on the concept of work relationship orientation (Fritz & Arnett, 1999), which measures the extent to which organizational members expect to locate and nurture, or to avoid and prevent, relational connections in the workplace setting that are close or intimate and transcend public relational constraints governing workplace connections. This construct taps expectations for relationships between persons in work settings that stem from, and reveal, particular understandings of public and private relationships and associated discourse that account for people's tendencies to form or eschew close friendships in organizations.

Work Relationship Orientation

Work relationship orientation identifies a pattern of practices emerging from a reflective or unreflective philosophy of personal affiliation associated with public and private domains of human life (Fritz & Arnett, 1999). For example, some persons avoid developing close relationships at work, because they recognize the challenges that relationships crossing role boundaries present. Bridge and Baxter (1992) made explicit the unique nature of friendships in the workplace, identifying these complex relational forms as blended relationships, defined as "the many kinds of personal relationships that can function simultaneously with both personal and role components" (p. 201). Bridge and Baxter identified several dialectical tensions addressed by friends who were also work associates: autonomy/connection, openness/closedness, judgment/acceptance, and impartiality/favoritism. Their work brings to the surface a number of issues relevant to professional civility, particularly the issue of competing goods within the relationship itself as a private or personal phenomenon interlaced with public workplace role obligations.

Several authors have framed the tension between public and private, from de Tocqueville (2000) and Arendt (1958) to Bellah, Madsen, Sullivan, Swidler, and Tipton (1985), Benhabib (1992), and Taylor (1989), attempting to sort out the appropriate interplay of public and private life. Some scholars, such as Whyte (1956), pointed to the danger of too much emphasis on public roles. On the other hand, Rieff (1966/1987) outlined the danger of a private focus that leads to the "triumph of the therapeutic" in everyday organizational life. The next section addresses issues relevant to an orientation to, or sensitivity to, contexts for close relationships, particularly the costs and benefits associated with sustaining private relationships in the public domain of organizations.

Public and Private Life: Historical Shifts

Varied conceptualizations of the interaction of public and private life have emerged over the last few decades (e.g., Arnett, 2006; Arnett & Arneson, 1999; d'Entrèves & Vogel, 2000; Rawlins, 1998; Sennett, 1974; Thompson, 2011). Several authors note a dichotomy between domestic and public life created by the historical shift of production from the home to industry (e.g., Gurstein, 1996; Marks, 1994; Scollon & Scollon, 1995). The home became a haven of privacy, a place of escape from the impersonality of the public sphere—in Lasch's (1977) terms, a "haven in a heartless world." The ability to get along with others in a civil manner, or sociability, became the hallmark of discourse in locations that demanded interaction with strangers (Gurstein, 1996), such as workplaces and other public spaces. Arnett and Fritz (2003) explored these issues in their work on management in a postmodern moment, highlighting authors who identified changes in cultural practices reflected in expectations for behavior in organizations.

During the decades after World War II, a therapeutic approach to communication, stressing self-disclosure and authenticity, became routine in many non-therapeutic social contexts (Arnett, 1997), emerging as a pervasive ideology of intimacy

(Sennett, 1974). The hallmarks of this approach to interpersonal interaction were an openness and self-disclosure closely connected to a push for equality and democracy in all spheres of life. Gurstein (1996) located the roots of this movement, which she characterized as a "repeal of reticence," in new understandings of literature, the popular press, and appropriate topics of discourse in public settings emerging at the end of the nineteenth century, and traces its gradual spread throughout the social sphere over the subsequent decades of the twentieth century. Diminished concerns for public etiquette and abandonment of formal behavioral prescriptions led to a loss of shared expectations for appropriate interaction in public spaces, resulting in emotivism (MacIntyre, 2007), or individualized standards for behavior based on personal preference.

This ideology of intimacy led to what Arnett (2006) referred to as a blurring of the boundaries between public and private life, in which private discourse was brought to the public arena without a corresponding increase in feelings of intimacy or enduring ties of obligation characteristic of genuine private friendship. Arendt (1958) warned that the blurring of public and private would lead to a loss of both real intimacy and public space (Arnett, 2006), giving rise to a problematic arena that she termed the "social." Most recently, Pitkin (1998) referred to this intertwined sector as "the blob." Arnett (1997) stated that a therapeutic culture characterized by the blurring of public and private was a failed experiment, a moral cul de sac. As Levinas (1969) suggested, differentiation is key to appreciation: "This" is not "that." The public is not the private, and vice versa. Both spheres need affirmation and differentiation that permit distinction and definition for each domain of experience (Arnett, 2006).

This cultural shift in expectations for public interaction has influenced expectations for behavior in organizations, resulting in increased research attention to topics related to the quality of interpersonal interaction in the workplace. Studies of organizational citizenship (Organ, 1988; Organ, Podsakoff, & MacKenzie, 2006); organizational deviance (Robinson & Bennett, 1995) and trust (McAllister, 1995); troublesome/problematic work relationships (Fritz, 1997b, 2002, Fritz, 2006; Fritz & Omdahl, 2006a; Omdahl & Fritz, in press); organizational incivility and rudeness (Andersson & Pearson, 1999; Fritz, 2009, 2012b); and ethical/unethical behavior in the workplace (e.g., Fritz, in press-a; Knouse & Jiacalone, 1992; Schminke, 2010; Treviño, 1986; Treviño & Youngblood, 1990) focus attention on microprocesses of organizational life connected to currents in the social and cultural environment. Studies of workplace ethics highlight the incommensurability of private and public ethical standards (Primeaux, 1992) and the need for publicly articulated codes of ethical conduct to guide behavior in organizations (Fritz, Arnett, & Conkel, 1999; Fritz, O'Neil, Popp, Williams, & Arnett, in press). The point is that although public and private concerns have always been present in organizations, the need to differentiate them is central to this historical moment (Arnett, 2006; Arnett & Fritz, 2003; Arnett et al., 2009).

In contrast to calls for differentiation of public and private domains, there is a body of scholarship suggesting that integration of public and private spheres is appropriate in this historical moment. Marks (1994) argued that the potential for intimacy emerges from the segmented nature of organizational life itself, which fashions the public world into a private space. Marks reconceptualized privacy and its relationship to intimacy and social ecologies, linking private life not to a particular context or social ecology, but to individuals' "constructive inclinations and opportunities" (p. 854). Both the private and the public become individualized or privatized, inviting us to construct and inhabit a private world based on our interests and activities. This private world crosses the boundaries of traditionally discrete and separate contexts or locations such as work, family, and recreation, and self-disclosure becomes the medium through which persons enter each other's private worlds (Petronio, 2002) in the public arena (Marks, 1994).

Private Issues in Public Spaces: For Better or For Worse

Several other studies representing diverse organizational contexts address private concerns that surface in the public arena of work, some resonating with Marks's (1994) call to redraw the boundaries of private life and relationships within the public arena, and others opposing it. For instance, a potential threat to organizational well-being, albeit distally related, stemming from employee health issues may prompt organizational leadership to offer programs to address personal challenges—for example, Employee Assistance Programs to help employees overcome drug or drinking problems (Hollinger, 1988) or to assist employees with weight control (e.g., Colvin, Zopf, & Myers, 1983). Some of these studies, however, reveal the potential danger of intimate spheres in public places, of work sustained by relational ties, and of bonds that create a context for supporting or enabling behavior with damaging corporate and individual consequences (e.g., Hollinger, 1988; Roman, Blum, & Martin, 1992). These studies point to what Palmer (1989) called the tyranny of intimacy, a condition in which close ties in the workplace can be used to keep another person under surveillance. Anyone from a small town can relate to this use of what ordinarily is a constructive social good. Ray (1993) reminded us of similar dangers as supportive communication relationships take on political, informational, codependent, and hegemonic features. The next paragraphs present studies supporting the value of blurring the public and private spheres, studies that highlight the danger of such blurring, and studies that consider both benefits and dangers of blurring public and private domains.

Colvin, Zopf, and Myers (1983) explored the office setting as a weight-control environment, an example of private health concerns intersecting with the public, task-oriented realm. The most interesting result of this study is the authors' comment that the program served as a source of frequent conversation among participants, another illustration of the creation of intimate spaces in the public realm discussed by Marks (1994). In this case, the common personal or private issue of weight loss became a shared, corporate goal of a cohesive workgroup.

DiGiulio (1995) addressed the realm of the private and personal in the public workplace by discussing the role of upper administration, supervisors, and coworkers in helping child social workers deal with personal losses such as the death of a close friend or family member, personal illness or disability, or personal financial or emotional crisis. Participants reported receiving and appreciating assistance in the form of words of encouragement/friendship and willingness to listen to personal concerns. Over 95% of participants believed that employers, supervisors, and coworkers should assist employees with such personal losses. DiGiulio argued that "…personal losses have a strong impact on work performance and…workers expect reassurance and assistance from those in the workplace at the time of a loss" (p. 887), and advocated exploration of informal behavior and formal policies to "create a more functional and humane work environment" (p. 887). This study also demonstrates how the nature of work and the organizational culture, in this case, an apparently person-centered setting (Hebden, 1986), may blend the public and the private in a balanced, organizationally supportive way.

One example of the presence of private issues within the public realm associated with problematic outcomes is alcohol and drug use in the workplace, which affects productivity and jeopardizes investments in employee training and socialization. Hollinger (1988) found that employees who socialized frequently with coworkers were twice as likely as their nonsocializing counterparts to come to work intoxicated. This effect was observed to be constant across age group and gender. Hollinger, citing Manello and Seaman (1979), further noted that employees' inability to differentiate work and nonwork situations may exacerbate this type of behavior.

Such inability to distinguish social boundaries may stem from an informal work culture that encourages friendships that extend beyond the workplace, transcending organizational roles and incorporating extensive socializing outside of work. "…[W]orkers who interact with one another away from the job site will…be more tolerant of any deviance by their peers" (Hollinger, 1988, p. 445). In such cases, the private domain of friendship rather than the public domain of the organization becomes the background for relationships, with friendship norms trumping those of a public work context. These findings are supported by Roman et al.'s (1992) study, which confirmed the influence of workplace interaction on alcoholic employees by pinpointing a "workplace enabling effect of coworker and supervisory support in getting one's job done" (p. 284). This study illustrates the risks involved in moving too far toward the pole of the private.

Ashcraft (2000) offered an intriguing analysis of a feminist organization whose goal was to integrate the public and private spheres through its mission-related policy of "ethical communication," which encouraged open disclosure of private information and refrained from setting policies prohibiting personal relationships in the workplace. Eventually, this organization's leadership recognized that the bonds formed through private, rather than public or professional, relationships threatened the norms of equality and sensitivity to power that constituted the heart of the organization's mission. For the good of the organization, those in administrative positions encouraged an explicit policy discouraging private affectional ties and advocating "professional" behavior and relationships in the workplace (although at the time the article was published, the policy had not achieved written form). This study provides insight into the balance that must be sustained between the public/professional and private/affectional spheres, and it concludes with encouragement to conceptualize "work intimacy" (p. 383) as a means of recognizing the need for a balance between connectedness derived from a shared task and the need to protect autonomy, dual concerns that characterize universal human needs or wants in most contexts of interaction (Brown & Levinson, 1978/1987).

Some studies offer a textured perspective on mixed benefits and dangers of integrating public and private spheres of life. Peters, Witty, and O'Brien (1993) discussed the concept of "work family" as a site for assistance for chemically dependent persons. Peters et al. trace the movement of chemical dependency from its definition as a private issue to one of public concern. Because of the frequency of work-related interpersonal contact, the workgroup may be incorporated into a personal recovery plan. The affected worker "is viewed as a valued member of the work family, and recovery becomes a common work family goal" (p. 5), although some coworkers may believe that this goal of prevention is an intrusion at work. Even though this concern for the individual is directed ultimately toward consequences that benefit the corporation, and hence operates for a "public" outcome, framing the organization as "family" illustrates the unreflective blurring of public and private spheres in practice, risking the resulting danger of cynicism from unmet high expectations (Arnett & Arneson, 1999).

Staley, Kagle, and Hatfield's (1987) study illustrates the struggles that may ensue when the private issue of illness confronts the public place of work and norms for interaction are not clear. Staley et al. argued for the importance of work relationships in a recovering or ill employee's life, suggesting that "coworkers form a significant social milieu and reference group for cancer patients" (p. 102), and that "...day-to-day relationships are critical to a worker's job satisfaction" (p. 102). Previous research, according to Staley et al., indicates that cancer patients returning to work are likely to experience coworkers' changed attitudes toward them and treatment of them. Staley et al.'s study reported that issues related to coworkers involved getting one's work done, coworkers' fear of contagion, and the returning patient's decision to tell or not to tell new coworkers of the patient's cancer history; half of this study's participants indicated that they would not reveal this information to a new employee.

In this study, most of the patients' relationships returned to normal over time; the stability of existing work relationships was an important factor in re-establishing "normalcy." Once normalcy in work relationships was achieved, others were likely to disclose personal information to the cancer patient, such as stories of family members with cancer or information about their own illnesses or diseases. Staley et al. (1987) recognized that discussing personal and painful information is not usual in a task-oriented environment, citing participants' concerns that such disclosure may lead to vulnerability, or changes in work relationships that might be regretted later.

These studies indicate varying degrees of awareness of the consequences for individuals and institutions of integrating or blurring the public and private spheres. In some cases, concern for the consequences of such blurring is articulated explicitly. In other cases, the consequences were incidental to the purpose of the study. These studies also manifest different evaluative stances toward public and private overlap. Some studies explicitly advocate or oppose such blurring; others unreflectively take this blurring for granted. Ashcraft's (2000) study most explicitly addressed this issue, highlighting the organizational and personal confusion that can result from overlapping or blending of public and private domains and calling for a reconsideration of the issue of public and private sphere differentiation.

Implications for Professional Civility

Ashcraft's (2000) concept of work intimacy offers a way to think about work relationships from a constructive, public perspective. Viewed through the lens of professional civility, work intimacy may be characterized tentatively as relational ties characterized by cohesion and appreciation for other persons arising out of a shared task or product focus (e.g., Gersick et al., 2000) within the larger project of an organizational story or narrative. Arnett (1992) articulated this perspective for the context of higher education through his invitation to focus on ideas as the product of institutions of higher education. This shared focus on ideas, which constitutes the task of higher education, provides a context or background for public relationships between persons. Relationships develop as a byproduct of shared task focus.

Ashcraft's (2000) work suggests the importance of the contribution of a common task to the development of organizational relationships. Arnett's (1992) understanding of the value of relationships that are centered on productivity is echoed in one of the premises that Ashcraft (2000) derived from her ethnographic study: empowerment in organizational life is derived from work-centered relationships that transcend the personal or private. This observation is supported by Hogg's (2000) theorizing on the effects of self-perception as a group member, or self-categorizing, which leads to depersonalization (not to be confused with dehumanization).

Depersonalization (e.g., Hess, 2006) seems to capture the sense of inhabiting a role that bestows a sense of public face (Goffman, 1967) or dignity for its inhabitant not on the basis of personal characteristics such as race, gender, or personality, but, from a professional civility standpoint, on the basis of a location in a shared story. Face support, from this perspective, is owed to the role within the story rather than to the individual in the role. Depersonalization in this sense may be helpful in avoiding perceptions of personal face affront leading to incivility spirals (Andersson & Pearson, 1999).

Ashcraft (2000) observed concern on the part of the administration of the organization she studied that when private, personal relational ties become the foreground, power imbalances are perceived to result from assumed favoritism. Hogg (2000) supported this understanding as well, suggesting that strengthening personal relationships or friendships rather than supporting depersonalized, role-based connections may compromise cohesion and adherence to larger group norms by fragmenting the group into cliques based on friendship, which then develop subgroup identities of their own based on dislike for other friendship groups. Ostracism, clique formation, and isolation of group members (Sias, in press, 2009b) are problems for organizations, particularly given the team-based nature of much organizational work today (Larson & LaFasto, 1989; Waldron & Kassing, 2011, pp. 198–199). Personal or group identity-based loyalties may also create conditions for incivility.

Although neither Ashcraft (2000) nor Hogg (2000) used the vocabulary of "common narrative background" in their quite different theoretical orientations— the former from feminist organizational ethnography, the other from quantitative social psychology applied to the organizational context—the processes described in each approach find convergence within the proposed framework of professional civility. McAllister's (1995) work on cognition-based (as opposed to affect-based) trust

offers an important connection to this call for a renewed recognition of the importance of public, role-based relationships as the interpersonal matrix of organizational
life. Cognition-based trust measures the extent to which a fellow employee is reliable and dependable, attributes that are salient to task performance. Likewise, it
seems reasonable that reliability and dependability might be tied to a shared commitment to the organization, the common ground upon which both parties stand
and the narrative background against which the parties enact a relationship.

Cognition-based trust that emerges from a shared narrative forms a foundation
for public work friendships characterized by a primarily task-based work intimacy in
organizational relationships, protecting and promoting persons-in-role and establishing accountability to the larger organization, thereby protecting the place or site of
professional work. A recent study by Davenport Sypher and Gill (in press) revealed
the negative impact of supervisory incivility on both affect-based and cognition-based
trust, with cognition-based trust being damaged slightly more. This effect suggests
that incivility may strain not only the ties between supervisor and employee, but also
a sense of common connection or commitment to a shared project. Such may also
be the case with coworker relationships. Professional civility would tend to reinforce
these bonds, establishing a substantial foundation for work relationships that draw
their strength from shared endeavors. When the focus of attention is on a task rather
than on the relationship itself, the inevitable annoyances and social allergens
(Cunningham, Barbee, & Druen, 1997; Miller & Reznik, 2009) that occur in relationships produce less irritation, and both parties avoid trivialization of crisis in the
workplace (Arnett, 2006; see Chapter 7, this volume).

Guidelines for work relationships based on professional civility should take into
account, following Ashcraft (2000), that the nature of the work in which an organization is engaged may temper the expectations of a local organizational home
(Arnett, 1992) for public and private relationship engagement. Professional civility understood as a reflective orientation to work, organizations, and people
includes a sensitivity to the particularity of organizational culture that may invite
different shades of relational connection. The nature of the place shapes the relationships in it, just as the people make the place (Schneider, 1987).

To create a culture of professional civility, organizations may be able to provide appropriate involvement through work intimacy as a way to support constructive relational ties in the workplace, texturing the natural tendency for interpersonal
bonds to form into cohesion and solidarity with appropriate distance. This relational
"golden mean" between the alienation of an impersonal setting and the potential
tyranny of intimacy in public contexts may help prevent cynicism arising from
unmet high expectations (Arnett & Arneson, 1999) related to intimacy at work.

Such cynicism may stem from close relationships that deteriorate (Sias, 2006) and create disappointment; from the recognition that private relationships generate imbalances of power, violating dearly held principles (e.g., Ashcraft, 2000); or from the incivility that may arise from a climate of informality designed to promote greater personal interaction and harmony (Andersson & Pearson, 1999), but which results in a clashing of private understandings of how interpersonal behavior and relationships in organizations should be enacted. Conflict resulting from different interpersonal workplace relationship preferences or work relationship orientations (Fritz & Arnett, 1999) may be reduced by a professionally civil understanding of work relationships centered on a common task within a public organizational context.

Personal and interpersonal flourishing in work contexts occurs from being invited into a shared community (Arnett, 1986; Lamert & Hopkins, 1995) that protects private lives through public role relationships. The task of the organizational leader becomes one of framing the organizational story (Fairhurst, 2011) in such a way that employees are given opportunity to participate in meaningful ways in organization life. This reconceptualization of public and private life in organizations is akin to Taylor's (1989) notion of "public poetry" (p. 492).

Public poetry is a term used to express the importance of inner meaning stated within a public arena. In organizational terms, public interaction with others in a task setting within a larger, meaningful story takes on private meaning in a life. For professionals, such public poetry is a natural outgrowth of the sense that one's occupation is a calling or a vocation, more than just a job (Cheney, Lair, Ritz, & Kendall, 2010; Sullivan, 2005). Meaning is not found in "me," but in collegial interaction with others through contribution to a project that makes a difference in the world. Taylor is pointing toward a dialectic of public and private, working to maintain public interaction and permitting private meaning appreciation in a particular person's life, a theme echoed in the work of Lutgen-Sandvik, Riforgiate, and Fletcher (2011) on positive emotional experiences at work.

We could call this type of workplace interaction an attempt to write public poetry within workplace relationships. It becomes a meaningful art, not just an instrumental task—a manifestation of communicative design beyond the conventional, propelled by a sense of coordinated effort that transcends the moment, a recognition of participation in Arendt's (1958) significant action in the public sphere. Fairhurst, Jordan, and Neuwirth (1997) pointed to the importance of making organizational missions personally meaningful. Framing the organization as a story offers the potential for such deeply felt public poetry. This reading is consistent with MacIntyre's (2007) exposition of the unity of a single human life emerging from recognition of embeddedness in human traditions, and with the story of the professions as meaningful tradition (Kimball, 1995; Sullivan, 2005). The story of the professions places great value on human persons.

Persons in Institutions: The Power of Roles

Valuing persons within organizations in a professional civility perspective comes from recognition of the dignity afforded to persons in institutional settings tied to the roles they inhabit. The original aims of bureaucracy were to protect persons by depersonalization, such that private ties and connections were no longer the basis of organizational reward (Perrow, 1986). Publicly stated and agreed-upon roles rather than connection to persons in the organization are the basis of evaluation, remuneration, and advancement. In this sense, power, honor, and dignity become invested within a publicly recognized playing field, where "equal" does not mean "the same," and differentiation and hierarchy come from guidelines achievable by anyone in a given position.

Despite differential access to such roles rooted in unequal access to social capital based on sociocultural background, education, and other contingent factors affecting one's possible network of associations (Bourdieu & Wacquant, 1992), roles are designed to protect and promote the dignity of persons within a public organizational system. As flawed human systems, organizations remain sites of inequality and struggle emerging from difference (e.g., Allen, 2011; Ashcraft & Allen, 2003; Collins, Gill, & Mease, in press; Liu & Buzzanell, 2006; Millhous, in press). Roles offer guidelines for public evaluation for role occupants as they navigate challenging organizational terrain.

Professional civility protects and promotes the good of persons through the extension of role protection to public and private boundary management (Petronio, 2002). In a professional civility model, one's private beliefs and practices can be shielded from the scrutiny of others who may not share the convictions that give one's personal life meaning. Professional civility does not prevent persons of similar or different convictions from connecting on a personal level; it simply prevents personal connections from becoming the foundation of work life. Such personal connections as a primary focus of attention put at risk the solidarity possible from a focus on shared tasks. The danger of cliques and associated ostracism (Sias, 2009b, in press) that emerge from unreflective personal enclaves is evident. Work friendships built on task intimacy can provide solidarity built on shared endeavors without the risk of relational or interpersonal quicksand characteristic of a therapeutic orientation moved into the public realm (Arnett, 1997). Close friendships

that develop at work, when managed with professional civility that keeps accountability to the organization as a relational anchor, can provide personal as well as professional support to the relational parties while reassuring others in the workplace
that the particularity of the relationship will not jeopardize productivity, the organization itself, or the interests of others in the workplace.

Understanding limits in relationships points us toward the importance of roles
as a background framework for what one can expect of self and others in the workplace. Roles vary in their specificity, and during the course of work some common
ground of agreement over which tasks each person should do assists coordination
of shared action. Role limits provide guidelines for what is reasonable to ask from
peers, subordinates, and supervisors. Roles offer a sense of stability and focus, permitting attention to move to other elements in the environment, such as providing
assistance to others, a key element of organizational citizenship.

Interpersonal Practices of Professional Civility

The continued challenges of problematic relationships in the workplace (Fritz &
Omdahl, 2006a; Omdahl & Fritz, in press) call for professional civility as communicative virtue, a professional communication ethic within a philosophy of work
life rooted in the history of professions as practice and in civility as communicative virtue. The theoretical coordinates of dialogic civility (Arnett & Arneson,
1999) and organizational citizenship (Organ et al., 2006) offer to professional civility a reminder of limits and the importance of fostering goodwill in work relations
by seeking to assist the organization and others in it to create hope, decrease cynicism, and offer a fitting response to a historical moment of diversity and difference (Arnett et al., 2009). Professional civility protects and promotes persons in
organizations and their well-being in both their work roles and as human beings
as a good of professional practice.

A growing body of scholarly and trade literature relevant to constructive interpersonal communication in the workplace offers additional insights that build
upon, and intersect with, dialogic civility and organizational citizenship, resonate
with the history of professions as practice, and offer extensions of civility as communicative virtue to elaborate an understanding of professional civility as communicative virtue at work. This final section suggests how professional civility as
communicative virtue at work protects and promotes persons with whom one is
engaged in meaningful tasks in an organizational setting. I focus on representative
research and summary material from the communication literature for the first part

of this last section, highlighting the work of Lutgen-Sandvik et al. (2009), Troester and Mester (2007), and Waldron and Kassing (2011).

Just as the original civility literature was designed for popular consumption (such as the works of Erasmus; see Elias, 1978), current popular works keep civility at the forefront of public discussion. As was the case for Lewis, Schmisseur, Stevens, and Weir's (2006) study of popular management literature on the topic of change, themes appear to be generally consistent across segments of scholarly and popular publications regarding interpersonal communication practices relevant to professional civility. I point briefly to the work of Forni (2002, 2008, 2011) as an exemplar of that literature.

Echoes of the Professional Legacy: Positive Emotional Experiences at Work

Lutgen-Sandvik et al.'s (2011) study of positive emotional experiences in the workplace revealed 17 different types of events representing five social discourses. The experiences Lutgen-Sandvik et al. identified in their data took communicative form, were framed as temporal, or taking place over a period of time, and were social in nature—that is, the events took their texture from a matrix of awareness of others' perceptions, thoughts about, and actions toward respondents. These discourses and constituent experiences provide insights into representative communicative practices that embody professional civility and reflect several themes relevant to the history of professions. Although professional civility is not limited to utterances or actions that are positive in nature, these findings offer suggestions for how one may encourage or foster constructive experiences at work for others and for oneself and also highlight the importance of several dimensions of work (such as teamwork, organizational climate, and task meaningfulness) that are jeopardized by incivility and, conversely, can be protected by professional civility.

The social discourse of individuality/uniqueness stressed the worth of the individual and included experiences of appreciation, recognition, and reward, reflecting approbation, or support for competence face needs (Lim & Bowers. 1991), which refers to how one's talents and skills—elements that set one apart—are put to use for the service of the community. This discourse can be understood to manifest the professional's service ethic or sense of call. The belonging/connection discourse stressed social embeddedness—a sense of the richness of personal experience with others as representing best experiences at work, which included experiences of relationships, social support, and teamwork, a reflection of solidarity, or support for fellowship face needs (Lim & Bowers, 1991). This discourse resonates with Sennett's (2008) description of the craft workshop, in which shared labor provides a connection between and among those gathered to engage in the task and who offer support and encouragement in the doing of the work. These two discourses were, respectively, the two most prominent or central discourses represented in the findings. The safety/security discourse, represented by experiences of climate, supervisor, resources, and triumph, emphasized feelings of being safe, comfortable, healthy, and protected from negative events. This discourse also captures a sense of the craft workshop, in which the camaraderie and closeness of a master craftsman, journeymen, and apprentices create an environment of security for accomplishment of the work, which one knows is also contributing to one's own well-being and that of others about whom one cares—Arendt's (1958) labor.

The social discourse of power/empowerment described a feeling of being empowered and/or empowering others in experiences of voice, autonomy, flexibility, and altruistic work. The success/accomplishment social discourse, with experiences of challenge, success, and opportunity, was interpreted as including a sense of meritocracy and creating one's destiny. These two discourses reflect an element of the professional legacy, relatively self-regulated work (Kimball, 1995; Sullivan, 2005), with meaning tied to the act of working itself, and little need for external oversight or management.

Lutgen-Sandvik et al.'s (2011) findings suggest specific elements of discourse that promote positive renderings of others' worth, thus providing concrete communicative practices for engaging coworkers in constructive ways that reflect professional civility. One participant noted, "When my boss told me I was irreplaceable and that she would like to have about 10 of me, that made me feel good." Expressing appreciation to others is one public way to acknowledge others' positive face (Gill & Davenport Sypher, 2009) and connect their contributions to the larger unit (Lim & Bowers, 1991). Another participant in Lutgen-Sandvik et al.'s (2011) study stated, "It made me happy that they felt I knew the job well enough and that I could help teach someone else" (p. 9); yet another related, "It was a wonderful experience to be able to achieve my potential" (p. 10). The sense of mastery and growth made visible in discourse for these employees was retained and remembered as a source of encouragement, a reflection of the good of personal flourishing in the professional civility framework.

The Character of Civility: Principles for Professionals

Troester and Mester (2007), in one of the first book-length applications of communicative practices of civility to the business and professional context, brought scholarly and popular sources to bear on constructive interpersonal communication for the workplace. Troester and Mester offered a contextualized treatment, exploring civility in history; verbal and nonverbal communicative expressions of civility; culture and civility; and civility at the interpersonal, interview, team, and meeting level. Civility issues related to electronic communication, such as cell phones and e-mail, and public speaking contexts rounded out their presentation. A review of the costs of incivility and the benefits of civility provided a concrete rationale for practicing civil discourse in the workplace.

For Troester and Mester (2007), civility is a character trait, an interpersonal style, and a behavioral pattern, and can be summarized in five principles. First, "the best words to choose when caught in an unexpected, emotionally charged situation are no words at all" (p. 78). Reflecting before speaking permits distance between experience and words; this principle reflects the characteristic restraint of professional civility.

Second, "use words respectful of the specific listener to whom they are addressed" (Troester & Mester, 2007, p. 79). Context matters; interpretive competence and role competence govern message competence (Trenholm & Jensen, 2004, p. 11). This principle reflects attention to the particular through the practical wisdom or phronesis of professional civility. Knowing the context—for example, is the setting a formal interview or an office party?—assists in understanding one's formal role and accompanying expectations for discursive behavior.

Third, "respect the reality of the situation by choosing temperate and accurate, not inflammatory, words when describing or commenting on ideas, issues, or persons" (Troester & Mester, 2007, p. 81). This point acknowledges the experience of emotion as an integral part of work experience (Omdahl, in press). Face support for others emerges through descriptive language (Gibb, 1961; Troester & Mester, 2007, p. 82), even when offering necessary evaluation of work. In a reconfigured framework for defensive and supportive communication relevant to productivity prompted by Sennett's (2008) work on the craftsman (see Chapter 6, this volume), evaluation, rather than humiliation, is the goal of supportive, professionally civil discourse.

Fourth, "use objective, nondiscriminatory language that respects the uniqueness of all individuals" (Troester & Mester, 2007, p. 83). Persons in the workplace are a good of professions protected and promoted by professional civility. Troester and Mester (2007) remind us that even in private, when targets of discourse are out of earshot, disrespectful terms promote attitudes that work themselves out in future discourse. Troester and Mester offered the example of lawyers referring to female Medicare recipients whose cases they are working on as "blue hairs" (p. 83); even though these clients never heard the term uttered, its articulation narrowed the focus of these women's identities to a one-dimensional, stereotypical image that denied justice to their being, shaping the lawyers' future attitudes toward these clients.

Fifth, "respect your listeners by using clean language all the time on the job" (Troester & Mester, 2007, p. 84). Troester and Mester recognized a horizon of interpretation for "dirty" and "clean" language, but suggested that a common baseline would be to avoid particular four-letter words and jokes that have sexual connotations—even among members of the same sex. The principle of spillover from words to attitudes to actions holds here. This principle also highlights restraint and self-control as an element of professional civility.

Worth the Risk: Professional Civility in Challenging Contexts

Waldron and Kassing's (2011) treatment of managing risk in workplace communication encounters also offers important applied wisdom from the communication field for professional civility in organizational relationships. Many of their recommendations reflect professional civility. In their treatment of delivering and seeking feedback, for instance, Waldron and Kassing noted that managers "honor" the "expertise" of "those closest to the task" (p. 28) by tapping the insights of salespeople who interact with customers, teachers who engage students on a daily basis, and assembly line workers who know their machines.

Waldron and Kassing (2011) reported the research of Wagoner and Waldron (1999) to offer insights for delivering bad news, such as refusals of requests or information that someone's performance or action needs to be corrected. Waldron and Kassing's summary (pp. 29–31) suggests that professionally civil employees communicate with tact, approbation, and solidarity (Lim & Bowers, 1991). Tact preserves options for response and thereby minimizes imposition on another ("Tell me how you believe you performed this month"; "I can't take your shift, but Lola or George might be able to"). Approbation affirms others' competence ("I so appreciate your efforts. Here is one thing that would push this report to the next level"). Solidarity emphasizes belonging (e.g., "Don't worry—I've made that mistake before"). Each of these approaches protects the face (Brown & Levinson, 1978/1987; Lim & Bowers, 1991) of the other, thereby protecting and promoting persons.

Waldron and Kassing (2011) offered insights related to balancing responsiveness and restraint in peer relationships. As they addressed managing emotions, part of the process of "forging relationships" (p. 46) in the workplace, Waldron and Kassing noted the requirements of competent communication as "learning how and when to disclose personal feelings, recognizing the signs of emotional distress, and providing appropriate kinds of emotional support for distressed peers and subordinates" (p. 46). They noted that such discernment involves "adept management of relational boundaries," recognizing when complete disclosure is called for and when a more circumspect approach is needed.

Of particular relevance is Waldron and Kassing's (2011) treatment of moral emotions, which offers a connection to virtue ethics. Emotions such as indignation (ire at unfairness manifested in a social system or situation), envy (coveting others' qualities, possessions, or recognition), and outrage (fury prompted by others' offensive acts) serve a signaling function (Waldron, 1994), indicating that personal or organizational values have been breached. Admiration at the success of "deserving others" (p. 47) is a positive moral emotion that reflects consistency with public standards. Waldron and Kassing (2011) offered recommendations for dealing with "difficult" team members and resisting bullying and harassment that draw on several strands of research. Their discussion provides multiple communicative options reflecting professional civility for addressing challenging interpersonal interaction in the workplace.

Strategies for engaging problematic or "troublesome others" in the workplace (Fritz, 2002, 2006) can be undertaken within the spirit of professional civility. When negotiating communication with others who present challenges in the workplace, or managing relationships that have taken a turn for the worse (Hess, Omdahl, & Fritz, 2006; Hess & Sneed, in press), strategies that keep the good of the organization at the forefront protect and promote productivity and place as well as persons. For instance, distancing strategies that reduce personal communication (Hess, 2006) offer both parties the space necessary to refocus on work. Repairing relationships is part of the ongoing process of relational maintenance in the workplace (Waldron, 2003); forgiveness plays an important part in restoring the potential for cooperative work when transgressions occur (Waldron & Kloeber, in press). Workplace relationships that take place at a distance (Fay, in press) require particular care in engagement in order to protect and promote persons whose faces are seldom seen, if ever, but whose presence as contributors to the good of workplace productivity and the organization itself is both real and necessary.

By Popular Demand: Marketplace Insights

Several authors offer insights for constructive workplace communication to the general reading public. These accessible works offer advice for personal and professional life consistent with professional civility. Giovinella Gonthier and Kevin Morrisey's (2002) *Rude Awakenings: Overcoming the Civility Crisis in the Workplace,* Margaret Shepherd and Sharon Hogan's *The Art of Civilized Conversation*, and Robert

Sutton's *The No Asshole Rule: Building a Civilized Workplace and Surviving One That Isn't* are three examples of many on the market.

The work of P. M. Forni, founder of the Civility Institute at Johns Hopkins University, is anchored in the humanities and responsive to current findings from research in the sciences and social sciences. Over the last decade, Forni has published three volumes focused on civility in public and private contexts: *Choosing Civility: The Twenty-Five Rules of Considerate Conduct* (2002), *The Civility Solution: What to Do When People Are Rude* (2008), and *The Thinking Life: How to Thrive in the Age of Distraction* (2011). Each of these volumes offers insight for the workplace through exemplars of utterances that express civility toward others and counter incivility in word and deed.

The first two volumes, *Choosing Civility* and *The Civility Solution,* work from background assumptions that form an implicit philosophy of life. The third book brings this background to the foreground, establishing thinking as the foundation for reflective action that situates the human being in the world as an active, responsive creator of meaning with and for self and others. Together, these volumes frame an architecture of authentic action in the world, rising from the intrapersonal to span the interpersonal and public domains of human experience. I focus on the first two volumes here.

Choosing Civility offers an understanding of civility rooted in "respect, restraint, and responsibility" (Forni, 2002, p. 5). The "twenty-five rules" include attentiveness to others, acknowledgment, charitable attributions, listening, accepting and offering praise, respecting others' opinions, time, and space, and apologizing. Forni's reflections extend beyond the human to include kindness to the environment and to animals. Forni's rules highlight action and self-control and include elements of verbal and nonverbal communication; most importantly, these rules are principles rooted in deliberate, thoughtful attention to others, oneself, and one's surroundings.

Particularly relevant to professional civility as communicative virtue "at work" is a section in *The Civility Solution* on "Workplace Woes" (pp. 112–125). Forni offered recommendations for what to say when a boss utters a personal reprimand in public, when a coworker takes over a shared office, when a colleague takes credit for one's work, when a leader lacks relational skills, and when one is a victim of a snide remark, among others. These recommendations are offered not as formulas, but as forms that capture the principles he proposes in encapsulated utterances. As in the first book, civility is not presented as a technique, but as a philosophy of human engagement. The examples provide anchor points for application, priming the reader with principles tied to specific conceptual, attitudinal, and operational communicative manifestations.

Conclusion

Protecting and promoting persons in the workplace is an integral part of professional civility. Relationships are the means by which organizing happens and work gets done; the health and well-being of persons-in-relation in organizations contributes to the goods of productivity and place. An approach to workplace relationships that honors the distinction between public and private spheres is one way to maintain focus on the purpose of shared labor; roles remind us that the dignity of persons in the workplace is reinforced by public acknowledgment of worth in the workplace. Practices of professional civility work to construct, maintain, repair, and restore ties that connect persons to each other, to productivity, and to the organizations that their interaction constitutes.

The concluding chapter returns to the story of the professions and the crisis they face in today's historical moment (Sullivan, 2005). Professional civility offers one way to contribute to renewal of the professional ideal. Through constructive communicative practices in everyday work life, members of the professions can reconstruct their legacy and build outward to a restored civic professionalism.

Conclusion

Protecting and Promoting Professions

Introduction

This chapter offers, by way of conclusion, a discussion of the value of understanding professions as communities of discursive practice (Barge & Little, 2008) that embody and monitor guidelines for professional conduct, inviting discipline and self-correction on the part of professionals, thus defining professional ethics as inherently constitutive of professional identity—and inherently communicative. Professions are integral parts of the marketplace and public sphere (Sullivan, 2005); professionals engage the responsibility of a story of excellence and professional identity through their enactment of profession as practice in word and deed. The focus here will rest on a call for communicative praxis that protects and promotes the good of "profession" by protecting and promoting goods of productivity, place, and persons. By embracing professional civility as a communicative virtue of and for professional practice, professionals can attend to these goods that are historically associated with professions and given particular form in today's historical moment, thereby countering the decline of professions and responding constructively to challenges facing them.

The Ongoing Story of the Professions

As discussed earlier, the term "profession" has historically carried with it expectations for behavior of members of a socially acknowledged set of distinguished occupational categories, beginning with clergy and extending to the other vocations to which "profession" eventually came to refer. The term "professional" in the sense of "occupational" came into common usage in the late eighteenth and early nineteenth centuries (Kimball, 1995, p. 141). Expected behaviors included service to the community through professional work and individual comportment characteristic of respected and dignified members of society. This expectation forms the basis for professional civility as communicative virtue at work.

Continuity and Change

The shift in the meaning of the term "profession" and its cognates marks a turn in the story of the professions (Kimball, 2005). When "profession" referred to a theological vocation, the term was clearly embedded in a narrative framework, with its meaning derived from the symbol system of a Christian worldview. During subsequent rhetorical moments, the story shifted its locale of embeddedness. The work of the professions came to refer to contractual connections between persons (Kimball, 1995). Remuneration for services rendered became part of what was now a contractual obligation between professional and client, reconfiguring the relationship between members of the professions and those they served (Kimball, 1995). Finally, "profession" came to refer to a set of skills and knowledge—practices, in MacIntyre's (2007) terms. Sociologists of the professions noted the functional value of professions to society at large (Larson, 1977; Parsons, 1939), an understanding of the professional ideal that has been diluted or lost over the years, but is now being reclaimed (Sullivan, 2005). The professions' responsiveness to the historical moment has yielded both continuity and change in the self-understanding and enactment of the professional ideal; the shifts just reviewed define elements of change.

What was not lost to the professional ideal—the continuity of professions—was the ethic of selfless service so critical to the theological sense of "profession." Indeed, up until the early twentieth century, the occupational world of business, with its unabashed emphasis on profit-making, was excluded from consideration as a profession (Kimball, 1995). This ethic of service was adopted by the law profession, even as the new meaning of the term "profession" as involving a contractual relation with remuneration began to emerge with the term's connection to law—"a contractual notion of 'service' as the feeable use or benefit to a client" (Kimball, 1995, p. 146). Service itself now had a different rhetorical meaning than "selfless charity" (Kimball, 1995, p. 149). The shift from a religious to a political architectonic influenced this difference in emphasis. Nonetheless, the religious influence associated with the term, connected to service to the larger community, remained in the form of "civil religion" (Bellah, 1967, cited in Kimball, 1995). Professional service would now refer to contractual relations with a client infused with a sense of charitable obligation—that is, service with less concern for remuneration than with serving the client (e.g., Hall & Schneider, 2008).

Each architectonic exemplar of the professions across the history of professions (Kimball, 1995) can be considered to embrace a vision of the good, a background defining what is important in human life, and an end that guides behavior and vocations—a telos. The current understanding of the terms "profession" and "professional" draws from this tradition and shapes general interactive expectations for this broad, diffuse, dynamic group. Challenges to the professions during the last decades of the twentieth century and into the twenty-first suggest the importance of reconnecting professions and professionals to the professional ideal understood as a tradition of practice handed down and invested with an ethic of obligation and service. These challenges were originally addressed in 1995 by Sullivan, who offered an analysis of the crisis and promise of professionalism in the United States, and whose updated volume in 2005 continued what he framed in 1995 as a story of professionalism (Sullivan, 1995, p. xviii). Sullivan (2005) incorporated Kimball's (1995) history as part of that story.

The Crisis and Promise of Professionalism

Sullivan's (1995) work focused on the various ways in which professionalism has been conceptualized and expressed in American culture in the context of shifting forms of professional organization. He noted the value of professionalized forms of work, which "have advanced the welfare of American society . . . and provided important vehicles of upward mobility for once-marginalized immigrants, minorities, and women" (p. xviii). In fact, "[r]eformers of the Progressive Era promoted professionalism precisely as a project for keeping the imperatives of democracy and public service alive within an ever more complex occupational world" (p. xix). However, this vision of professionalism lost traction. The public at large, and academic opinion leaders, ceased to believe that the purpose of the professional was to be of service to the community while making a living by what is earned (Kimball, 1995), and, as Sullivan (1995) noted, professionalism began to be associated with harboring and promoting privilege, a concern that continued and expanded over the next decade. In 2005, Sullivan wrote: "It is now a commonplace that the prestige of the traditional professions is under siege" (p. 42).

Kimball's (1995) history of the professional ideal in the United States from the pre-colonial period to the present day followed the advance and decline of the professional ideal in America, providing a context for Sullivan's (2005) and others' treatment of the contemporary crisis of professionalism as a foundation for profession as practice. Kimball (1995) noted that before the 1950s, scholars praised professionals and encouraged their commitment to professionalism—Flexner (1915/2001) spoke of a "professional spirit" (p. 165), and the Minnesota Occupational Scale of 1931 ranked professionals at the top of a list of seven occupations. In 1954, the chancellor of New York University attributed societal prosperity and happiness to the professions and their "providing for the needs and wants of the people" (Kimball, 1995, p. 311). However, accompanying this perception of the beneficence of professions was an increasingly critical voice from scholars and outside observers, who began to criticize "professionals and professions even as their numbers grew" (Kimball, 1995, p. 311), highlighting a growing concern that the occupational enclave calling itself by the term "profession" was out to advance its own interests and those of its members rather than the interests of society. The decline of the professions happened on several fronts corresponding to what Kimball (1995) and Sullivan (2005) pointed to as the three major identifying features of professions: autonomous association, expertise, and service.

Following medicine's eventual rise to preeminence among the professions and in the eyes of the general public during the twentieth century came a multiplication of occupations claiming professional status, modeling themselves on medicine as the architectonic profession (Kimball, 1995). However, in the 1970s, the medical profession dropped in prestige, with the increase in malpractice suits and the move of physicians to work for large medical establishments (Starr, 1982; Tomes, 2001) rather than independently. As the medical occupation had risen in professional prestige, the "true professional ideal" had also risen; as the medical occupation declined in professional prestige, the professional ideal declined (Kimball, 1995, p. 309).

In the academic community, a shift occurred from a functionalist understanding of professions to one emerging from structuralism and critical theory (Kimball, 1995). This intellectual move from a functionalist to a structuralist and critical view shifted the focus from professionals' contributions to society to how professionals gained authority and control over a social function (Kimball, 1995, p. 313), representing a shift from knowledge to power as the theoretical basis for professional status. The power and prestige granted to professions and professionals was no longer assumed to emerge from expert knowledge applied in service to the community, but from hegemony of expertise and exclusion (Kimball, 1995; Larson, 1977). Such expert knowledge itself came under increasing attack: "Physicians are not only challenged by the proponents of 'alternative medicine,' but face patients armed with all kinds of medical knowledge obtained through the internet. The prevalence of 'emergency' teaching credentials in school classrooms calls into question the value of professional teacher training" (Sullivan, 2005, p. 43).

Finally, professional associations lost their original mission. Professional associations were once assumed to have as one of their goals the protection of the public interest and service to the public, in contrast to labor unions, which were understood to be formed for their members' economic benefit (Kimball, 1995). Professions and professional associations were now also assumed to exist solely for their members' benefit. With this shift in academic and public perception, professions experienced a loss of ethos and a decline in prestige. Sullivan (1995) noted that this downfall in professional image was internal as well as external: "Within as well as without the professions, there is unmistakable skepticism and cynicism about the whole notion of professionalism" (p. 11). Concern continued a decade later as "a suspicion that professionals have broken faith with the public" (Sullivan, 2005, p. 2); much of the blame for the bursting of the U.S. "financial bubble" (p. 3) during the initial years of the twenty-first century was laid at the feet of lawyers and accountants. Such indignation, noted Sullivan, "is premised upon moral expectation" (p. 3), which reflects cynicism from unmet high expectations noted by Arnett and Arneson (1999).

Sullivan's (1995) concern for the compromised story of the professions rested with what he described as the unfulfilled promise of professionalism, a loss of the service ethic that for so long had been the foundation of the professional ethic. According to Sullivan, professionalism lost its direction through excessive focus on technical goals, perhaps due to the shift in the locus of professional work, which is now typically large organizations (see also Larson, 1977, p. xviii). In this context, professionals often experience pressure from economic forces to compete and pursue profit to the exclusion of other concerns when professional standards of excellence come into conflict with economic goals (Sullivan, 1995, p. 6; see also Borden, 2007, for a discussion of journalists' struggle to maintain professional autonomy in reporting while working within news organizations that must be attentive to economic concerns in order to stay in business). Jacobs (1992) addressed this point in her discussion of the difference between the guardian and commercial ethical systems, also highlighted by Borden. Sullivan's original concern was echoed in 2005 with greater urgency as the dynamic conditions of the increased role of technology and continuing globalization confronted an ever-changing world of work in the "new economy" (Sullivan, 2005, p. 6).

A point directly relevant to the issue of professional civility as communicative virtue that emerges from concerns about the meaning and direction of professions is found in Sullivan's (1995) highlighting of Christopher Lasch's discussion and critique of professionalism in *The True and Only Heaven*. Lasch (1991) shared sociologist Alvin Gouldner's concern about a culture of critical discourse embraced by professionals (Gouldner, 1979, cited in Lasch, 1991, p. 527), a disposition tied to modernity's infatuation with progress and technical rationality. This culture of critical discourse is characterized by a habit of criticism from which nothing is immune and to which nothing is sacred (Sullivan, 1995). Lasch identified this orientation as the defining feature of professionalism (Sullivan, 1995). The major concern Lasch expressed is that this culture of critical discourse "is predisposed to degenerate into cynicism and opportunism" (Sullivan, 1995, p. 24) and disdain for persons who are less educated and who engage in manual labor. Lasch (1991) noted: "Both the virtues and the defects of the professional class spring from the habit of criticism, which, unleavened by a sense of its own limits, soon reduced the world to ashes" (p. 528). It is this outlook or phenomenological "turning" toward the world that flies in the face of the tradition of the professions as Kimball (1995) described it and that Sullivan (1995, 2005) and others believe must be reclaimed.

It is not a far step from a critical attitude toward the world in general to incivility toward one's fellows in the workplace; a decade later, Sullivan (2005) turned to another of Lasch's works, *The Revolt of the Elites*, pointing to a "distinctive form of consciousness shared among the symbolic analysts . . . and the creative class" (Sullivan, 2005, p. 216). This habit of mind leads to arrogance and "leads those who master it to . . . see themselves and their lives in strategic terms, often consumed by maneuvering for the better deal in the status competition internal to professional occupations" (Sullivan, 2005, p. 217). Sullivan further noted Lasch's warning that this shared consciousness, if untempered by the development of civic consciousness and broader concerns, would become "the soil of nihilism" (Sullivan, 2005, p. 217), and remarked that professional education is the primary shaper of such consciousness and character.

Sullivan's (2005) discussion opens the way for the connection between micropractices of interpersonal interaction that construct public environments to standpoints or worldviews that engender, support, reinforce, and reproduce such practices. Tannen's (1998) point that we live in an argument culture, a "culture of critique," in which "criticism, attack, or opposition are the predominant if not the only ways of responding to people or ideas" (p. 7) highlights the role that the United States' culture in general plays in reinforcing what is emphasized in specific types of professional education and socialization. Tannen cited the work of Tracy and Baratz (1993) in her discussion of "graduate school as boot camp" (pp. 266–267), a specific instance of professional socialization to the argument culture of academia, in which intellectual "attack" (Infante & Rancer, 1982) is a sign of respect.

It is also instructive to consider Larson's (1977) observation that a significant change for the professions occurred when practitioners of the traditional professions began to gain their legitimacy through specific formal training rather than through a traditional apprenticeship model (p. 4), which took place around the nineteenth century. This shift from a sense of connectedness to a close-knit community of practice (much as Sennett, 2008, described in his discussion of craft) toward an individualized engagement of training surely contributed to an increased focus on the value of technical expertise as well as a modernist epistemology of disembeddedness from standpoint, an inclination to see the self as judging from a vantage point of objectivity, a standing above history (Arnett, Fritz, & Holba, 2007) that makes the self the arbiter of truth. This combination of individualistic focus, a critical standpoint, and a technologized socialization experience is likely to foster a privatized orientation to discourse and subsequent interpersonal style that invites incivility.

In 1995, Sullivan noted a contradiction between the imperatives of the market and the ethical obligation of the professional, identifying a tension between the utilitarian tendency of "efficient deployment of techniques for enhancing individual satisfaction" and "the understanding of society as constituted by ethical ends" (p. 15). A thriving civic culture requires that all be "alive to the concerns of others, tolerant of difference, supportive of others' dignity, and willing to talk and work together across a wide spectrum of vital associations" (pp. xviii–xiv). Sullivan argued in 2005, as he did in 1995, that professional life must let its technical competence be suffused with civic awareness and purpose: "The vital mission of professional work is to infuse economic activity with opportunity for individuals to develop themselves through contributing to public values" (Sullivan, 2005, p. 185). Technical excellence must once again be embedded in civic enterprises that give meaning to expertise. Tempering the technical orientation can expand one's scope of vision and engagement, offering new ways of thinking about interaction with others, the role of the self in relation to others within organizational culture, and the place of a whole life in relation to the larger public sphere, recognizing "linkages among home, work, and public life" (Sullivan, 2005, p. 126).

Economic competition on the societal level is reflected on the personal level within the walls of organizations. The "civic professionalism" called for by Sullivan in both 1995 (p. xix) and 2005 (e.g., pp. 5, 23, 98) finds its microlevel interactive counterpart in the communicative virtue of professional civility. The culture of professionalism in its manifestation with others in organizations, in professional associations, and in the larger civic sphere depends upon the microinteractive processes visible in communication with one another, communicative micropractices that constitute organizational environments and professional identities (e.g., Ashcraft,

Kuhn, & Cooren, 2009). "The ideal of integrity evoked in the ideal of profession-alism" (Sullivan, 1995, p. xvi), the "integrity . . . closely associated with the world of professional life" (Sullivan, 2005, p. 283), includes the communicative integrity manifested in professional civility.

If, as Sullivan (1995) stated, professionalism has become disconnected from its original roots of service to the larger community and "the culture of civic democracy" (p. xviii), a concern that remains to this day (Sullivan, 2005), then it must be recon-nected to those roots. However, it cannot be reconnected externally without an internal overhaul. The internal incivilities of professionals working within organiza-tions whose sole purpose is to colonize each moment of employees' time (Arnett, 2006) reflect a one-sided focus that eclipses the importance of communicative con-cern for others. As organizations increase their attentiveness to corporate social responsibility, not just in terms of the outside world, but also in terms of their inter-nal environments, a new sustainability based on cultivation of a culture of professional civility will connect ideals of service to the "outside" with the reality of care for the "inside." The result can be a renewed organizational system that leaves energy to spare for other pursuits—practices of a renewed civic professionalism (Sullivan, 2005) reflec-tive of the legacy of the "true professional ideal" (Kimball, 1995).

These internal challenges to professional comportment will require both insti-tutional/cultural and individual change. If it is still the case that "an educated, engaged, and well-organized workforce is the basis for the long-term success of any economic entity" (Sullivan, 1995, p. xviii), then professional civility is needed to sustain the engagement and coordination necessary for such a workforce to exist. The evidence from studies of incivility and interpersonal workplace harassment are clear: incivility destroys cultures of productivity (Fritz, 2009; Fritz & Omdahl, 2006b; Pearson & Porath, 2009). Cooperative engagement and interaction with others can be sustained only by particular types of interpersonal organizational arrangements, just as particular types of social and political climates are necessary for social goods to flourish (Sullivan, 1995, p. xviii). As members of the professions reveal themselves as civic professionals within the walls of organizations, they will be more likely to carry that orientation outward to others in the larger community. This vision is one Sullivan (2005) highlighted in his recent work.

Toward a Renewed Professionalism: Professional Civility

Sullivan, in both 2005 and 1995, discussed professionalism as an attribute associ-ated with professional conduct and behavior, as well as an attribute of professions that defines how an occupation organizes its practitioners and relates to its members, its work, and society at large. Professionalism "has emerged as a widely esteemed and sought-after virtue" (Sullivan, 2005, p. 37); "saying someone acts 'professionally' is high praise in any situation, while the most damning epithet hurled at politicians, financiers, and athletes by their enemies is the charge of being "unprofessional" (p. 37). The term secures some agreement in everyday usage, such that "few speak of professional behavior as existing only in the eye of the beholder" (Sullivan, 2005, p. 37).

Professionalism is clearly connected to the ascribed ethic of the professions: "A profession is understood to provide a career, an opportunity for social and economic advancement, while professionalism demands the kind of dedication to purpose characteristic of a vocation or calling" (Sullivan, 1995, p. 6). Professionalism sets the ideal for professional behavior, an implicit, but recognized, set of interactive practices (Sullivan, 1995, 2005) defining a manner of upright and virtuous conduct befitting someone working in the corporate public sphere (e.g., Anderson & Bolt, 2011). The popular image of professionalism remains as a remnant of the legacy of the professions, one of the few remaining "patches" of common sense (Arnett, Fritz, & Bell, 2009, p. 66) still existing in today's marketplace culture.

In the course of his treatment of the crisis of professionalism, Sullivan (2005) identified a number of elements relevant to professions as a practice with a tradition and to professional civility as I develop it here, attributes consistent with, and reflecting, those identified by Kimball (1995), whose discussion Sullivan pointed to. In his earlier work, Sullivan (1995) noted particular elements relevant to the contribution of professions to the good of the human community; professionals need to wield professional skill with a focus on "enhancing the quality of life for all" (p. xv), internally as well as externally. Integrity and trust are critical attributes of professional behavior and practice; integrity is both an aspect of personal responsibility and "a source of human dignity" (p. xv). Integrity is rooted in cooperation, in the conviction that others are trustworthy and that one can engage in common undertakings through cooperative action—in the organizational setting, this collaborative engagement with others is what makes productivity and constructive interpersonal interaction in organizational life possible, a reflection of Sennett's (2008) craft workshop.

From the Inside Out

Sullivan's (2005) continuing project focuses on the external obligations of professionals—obligations to the larger society through service, and contributions to the needs of the civic sphere through civic professionalism. My argument is that in order for professionals to cultivate external service, they must cultivate internal service through professional civility. The communicative virtue of professional civility lays groundwork for a culture of concern for productivity, for the local organizational home, and for others with whom one works. This tripartite concern in turn shapes, maintains, enriches, and supports the telos of the profession(s), including an obligation to the community and larger society. Professional civility as the microlevel counterpart to civic professionalism becomes a communicative practice that can restore the ties that bind professional practitioners to one another and to the institutions of which they are a part.

Professionals are called to enact professions within an organizational "civitas"— to be good corporate citizens, just as professionals throughout history were good community citizens, to carry out the work of dignified occupations in service to their communities. The challenge to professionals today is the issue of professional autonomy in work. Although most professionals now work for corporations rather than independently (Sullivan, 2005), with many more inhabiting nonprofessional, bureaucratic organizations than a professional firm (Wallace, 1995), the sense of autonomy and conflict among cosmopolitans and locals may still exert pressure, although these spheres are not inherently in tension (Wallace, 1993, 1995). The push for profits "puts pressure on professionals to behave competitively with their peers" (Sullivan, 1995, p. 6), a recipe for incivility (Pearson & Porath, 2009). Professional organizations are designed to help combat that tendency and to call professionals to a higher story of integrity; other organizations that employ professionals are also called to a story of integrity as the recognition of all work as dignified and worthy grows stronger. The shifting ground of today's economy affects professionals now more than ever (Sullivan, 2005, pp. 6–11), bringing additional challenges to the integrity of traditions of practice.

The demands of interdependence in the social world (Sullivan, 1995, p. xii), now played out on a global scale (Sullivan, 2005, pp. 170–176), are mirrored in the internal workings of organizations that host the work of professionals. The goal of tapping every person's ability to contribute and make the most of talents and skills with the "hope for financial reward and respected status by contributing to meeting social needs" (Sullivan, 1995, p. xiii) is relevant to the particular organizational setting as well as the national—and global—context. The ideal of human resource theorists of encouraging and fostering workplace creativity, self-directedness, and participation in decision-making at work (e.g., Kramer, 2010, p. 106; Miller, 2011, p. 45) can be realized at the local level in each organizational home when an ethic of professional civility guides workplace interaction.

In organizational settings, professionals are surrounded by a number of other employees who are their peers or who inhabit different, but complementary, roles, and they "either support or undercut these others by their own activities" (Sullivan, 1995, p. xiv). The key to ethical professional conduct is a type of moral recognition, a "responsibility; a disposition to act with regard to the good of self and others within a larger whole, a disposition stemming from an understanding of mutual dependency" (Sullivan, 1995, p. xiv). A "standing disposition to serve" (Sullivan, 2005, p. 22) stems from the recognition that the work of the professions contributes to the good of the "larger social whole" (Sullivan, 2005, p. 22) and is fostered by professionally civil communicative behavior that recognizes and values the contributions of all.

The Price of Incivility

Incivility is unprofessional communicative behavior. Incivility robs the organization and its members of the benefits of cooperative activity and destroys the trust among persons necessary to sustain productive work (Davenport Sypher & Gill, in press). The threat to organizations posed by incivility rests in the disruption of an organizational climate of respect and goodwill that is the byproduct of the disposition to act with integrity within the public space of the institution as a setting for work. Incivility is an indicator of the loss of this moral sense, and the way to its re-establishment is through practices of respect for others manifested in communicative interaction.

It is possible to restore a functionally civil climate pragmatically, through communicative practices. Professional civility, as discussed in earlier chapters, offers the chance to restore and enhance trust and cooperation at the level of shared task involvement, even among those who do not like each other personally or who do different types of work with different orderings of priorities. Herein lies the responsibility of the professional in an organizational setting: to set aside personal liking or disliking, self-preoccupation, an individualistic orientation, unrealistic expectations for the workplace, and disagreements stemming from different work styles (Fritz, 2002, 2006) and embrace a constructive orientation to productivity, the organization, and others in the workplace in order to make the unit better. This approach to organizational life answers Sullivan's (1995) concern that competitive striving brings about a "self-induced narrowness of sympathy" (p. xv). This concern was articulated by Brandeis, as discussed in Chapter 2 of this volume, in his encouragement to identify business as one of the professions, adopting the ideal of service to temper the excesses of self-interest (Kimball, 1995, p. 9).

The key for professional civility, emerging from the work of Kimball (1995) and Sullivan (1995, 2005), is thoughtful concern for others, tolerance of difference, supportiveness of others' dignity, and willingness to talk and work together on a wide variety of organizational tasks spanning both formal endeavors and the less-acknowledged informal, interpersonal undertakings. Technical competence must be suffused with "civic awareness and purpose" (Sullivan, 1995, p. xix); "professionals in their organizational lives must be active citizens, committed to working out a common good as new problems and possibilities arise" (Sullivan, 2005, p. 279). Part of this task of working together requires that professionals learn, or at least recognize the value of, other professionals' specialties, as well as the value of everyone's contributions to the workplace.

Kohn and Schooler (1983) noted the profound influence of communicative activity in reporting relationships on values external to the organization. So will organizational members' internal communicative practices shape practices outside. Sullivan noted that "new understandings of professionalism and forms of professional practice are emerging" (p. xix), a conclusion confirmed by his 2005 work. On the local scale, professionals can reclaim a civic culture in organizations marked by a professional civility that enhances the flourishing of organizations and all who work in them, thus laying the groundwork for renewed contributions beyond the local level.

Professions and Communicative Practices: Enactment and Construction

A New "Rhetoric" of Professions

Kimball found great value in the role of rhetoric, addressing the "rhetoric of professions" (p. 15) in his treatment. He recognized the power of language, emphasizing that the way people thought and talked about professions changed their development, social expectations, and identity throughout the history of professions in the United States. These processes continue to write the ongoing history of professions, defining interactive norms for practitioners and shaping expectations among professionals and between professionals and their various internal and external audiences. As noted in Chapter 5 of this volume, these principles are operative at the micro level of organizational experience. Communicative practices are powerful; they shape climates and cultures, producing and reproducing structures and norms by making particular patterns of behavior more likely than others (Giddens, 1984); in an even more substantive way, communicative practices constitute organizations (Ashcraft et al., 2009).

The meaning of professions and professionals is framed by communicative practices by and about the professions. Language can create and destroy dignity at work (Hodson, 2001); the identity of an occupation and those practicing it springs from the discourse by and about those engaged in the task that is done. Discourse is necessary to generate, secure, and maintain the definition and dignity of a profession in the eyes of its own members, of those with whom professionals work, and of wider audiences. Such processes are rhetorical, or persuasive, in their framing and portrayal of given images and attributes of a particular profession or occupation and expectations for its members.

The idea of a "profession" was and is part of the rhetoric of everyday life—part of the universe of discourse (Mead, 1934, p. 89) within the social imaginary (Taylor, 2007, p. 146) of the culture of the United States. This universe of discourse defines behavioral and communicative expectations accompanying professional identities. The appearance of the terms "professional" and "unprofessional" as descriptions of behavior, typically communicative in nature, in everyday discourse (Sullivan, 1995) suggests that such expectations are part of the way we relay our experiences to each other and interpret others' behaviors; these expectations rest primarily at the implicit level and remain unspoken in most contexts, but when violated, they are made salient.

In the academic realm, the definition of incivility in the workplace has emerged with some precision (Fritz, 2009), following the concept's developing clarity in everyday conversation with the emergence of treatments mentioned earlier (e.g., Forni, 2002, 2008). Such public conversations about communicative expectations for interpersonal interaction suggest a residue of professional expectations, or expectations for professional behavior, that remains associated in public consciousness with practices generally termed as civil, an indicator of the communicative virtue at work that I identify as "professional civility."

Sullivan (2005) stated that professional education and practice are the responsibility of professionals, and the direction these phenomena take will shape the possibilities of professions' contributions to society and, indeed, the future of professionalism. Professional education that includes an orientation to professional civility as the foundation of professional practice orients new members of the profession to constructive engagement of work, the organization, others, and the larger professional "home." If professionalism is "a distinctively modern form of vocational ethos" (Sullivan, 2005, p. xvii), then that ethos must be instilled in members of every profession from the beginning of professional education and practice. As Sullivan (2005) recognized, "Professional renewal has to begin in professional education, or it will have no lasting future" (p. 24).

Summary: Protecting and Promoting the Good(s) of Profession

Sullivan (1995) suggested that "by taking responsibility through one's work for ends of social importance, an individual's skills and aspirations acquire a value for all" (p. xvi). Professional civility's work as communicative virtue in everyday organizational life to protect productivity, place, and persons translates into macrolevel action of professions in the public sphere. As professionals reveal themselves through the words of conversation with others in daily life and work (Arendt, 1958; Oliver, 1961), professions are revealed in the form of contributions to human society. Such contributions become generative as professionals embody a spirit of civic professionalism extending from the "shop floor" to communities and the larger world, where professional identity is revealed anew in the action of great deeds in the public sphere (Arendt, 1958).

Professional civility offers an opportunity for the contemporary workplace to become a location for a renewed sense of professionalism called for by Sullivan (2005). The traditional professions and their kindred occupations that occupy the workspaces of contemporary organizations can make a difference in their own places of employment or local homes (Arnett, 1992), in the civic sphere, and for the future of professions, beginning with communicative practices of civil discourse in day-to-day work life. The constitutive power of communication (Ashcraft et al., 2009) makes a difference for the goods of the professions; practices of professional civility can turn the tide of incivility in the workplace (Davenport Sypher, 2004) and reorient professionals to a renewed sense of integrity and respect for work, institutions, and persons.

The work matters—the tradition of professions places a premium on the work as the craft of professional practice; professional civility protects and promotes productivity. The place matters—where the work is done, whether face to face or in virtual space—and becomes a constructive and healthy environment hosting the labor, work, and action of professionals today through practices of professional civility. Persons matter—the people with whom and for whom professionals work are the human face of the past, present, and future of the tradition of professions; whether members of the same or a different profession or occupation, support staff, clients, external publics, or other audiences, these coparticipants are bound together with professionals in the human condition, and professionals have an obligation to protect and promote their interests through practicing professional civility. There is hope for the professions, and it rests on interactive manifestations of constructive symbolic action undertaken on the "shop floor" (Sennett, 2008)—professional civility, the communicative virtue that will reconstruct the professional legacy from the inside out.

References

Acker, J. (1995). Feminist goals and organizing processes. In M. M. Ferree & P. Y. Martin (Eds.), *Feminist organizations: Harvest of the new women's movement* (pp. 137–144). Philadelphia, PA: Temple University Press.

Albrecht, T. L. (1979). The role of communication in perceptions of organizational climate. In D. Nimmo (Ed.), *Communication yearbook 3* (pp. 343–357). New Brunswick, NJ: Transaction.

Albrecht, T. L. (1984). An over-time analysis of communication patterns and work perceptions among managers. In R. N. Bostrom (Ed.), *Communication yearbook 8* (pp. 538–557). Newbury Park, CA: Sage.

Albrecht, T. L., & Cooley, R. E. (1980). Androgyny and communication strategies for relational dominance: An empirical analysis. In D. Nimmo (Ed.), *Communication yearbook 9* (pp. 699–719). New Brunswick, NJ: Transaction.

Alexander, M. W., Mundrake, G. A., & Brown, B. J. (2009). Pre business college freshman [*sic*] perception of classroom behavior: An analysis among and between genders. *Delta Pi Epsilon Journal, LI*, 99–116.

Alin, P., Taylor, J. E., & Smeds, R. (2011). Cross-boundary analysis. *Project Management Journal, 42*(4), 58–75.

Allen, B. J. (2011). *Difference matters: Communicating social identity* (2nd ed.). Long Grove, IL: Waveland Press.

Altman, I., & Taylor, D. (1973). *Social penetration: The development of interpersonal relationships*. New York, NY: Holt McDougal.

Alvesson, M., & Deetz, S. (1996). Critical theory and postmodernism approaches to organizational studies. In S. R. Clegg, C. Hardy, & W. R. Nord (Eds.), *Handbook of organization studies* (pp. 191–217). Thousand Oaks, CA: Sage.

Alvesson, M., & Willmott, H. (1992). On the idea of emancipation in management and organization studies. *Academy of Management Review, 17,* 432–464.

Anderson, L. E, & Bolt, S. B. (2011). *Professionalism: Skills for workplace success.* Upper Saddle River, NJ: Prentice Hall.

Andersson, L. M., & Pearson, C. M. (1999). Tit for tat? The spiraling effect of incivility in the workplace. *Academy of Management Review, 24,* 452–471.

Ardalan, K. (2006). The philosophical foundation of the lecture-versus-case controversy: Its implications for faculty teaching, research, and service. *International Journal of Social Economics, 33,* 261–281.

Arendt, H. (1958). *The human condition.* Chicago, IL: University of Chicago Press.

Arendt, H. (1976). *The origins of totalitarianism.* New York, NY: Harcourt. (Original work published 1951)

Arendt, H. (1978). *The Jew as pariah: Jewish identity and politics in the modern age* (Ed. R. H. Feldman). New York, NY: Grove Press.

Argyris, C. (1957). *Personality and organization.* New York, NY: Harper.

Aristotle. (1962). *Nicomachean ethics* (M. Ostwald, Trans.). Indianapolis, IN: Bobbs-Merrill.

Arnett, R. C. (1981). Toward a phenomenological dialogue. *Western Journal of Speech Communication, 45,* 201–212.

Arnett, R. C. (1986). *Communication and community: Implications of Martin Buber's dialogue.* Carbondale, IL: Southern Illinois University Press.

Arnett, R. C. (1992). *Dialogic education: Conversation about ideas and between persons.* Carbondale, IL: Southern Illinois University Press.

Arnett, R. C. (1997). Therapeutic communication: A moral cul-de-sac. In S. L. Longenecker (Ed.), *The dilemma of Anabaptist piety: Strengthening or straining the bonds of community?* (pp. 149–159). Camden, ME: Penobscot Press.

Arnett, R. C. (1999). Metaphorical guidance: Administration as building and renovation. *Journal of Educational Administration, 37,* 80–87.

Arnett, R. C. (2001). Dialogic civility as pragmatic ethical praxis: An interpersonal metaphor for the public domain. *Communication Theory, 11,* 315–338.

Arnett, R. C. (2005). Through a glass, darkly. *Journal of Communication and Religion, 29,* 1–17.

Arnett, R. C. (2006). Professional civility. In J. M. H. Fritz & B. L. Omdahl (Eds.), *Problematic relationships in the workplace* (pp. 233–248). New York, NY: Peter Lang.

Arnett, R. C. (2012). Beyond dialogue: Levinas and otherwise than the I–thou. *Language and Dialogue, 2,* 140–155.

Arnett, R. C. (in press-a). The bureaucrat as problematic other: Arendt's warning. In B. L. Omdahl & J. M. H. Fritz (Eds.), *Problematic relationships in the workplace, volume 2.* New York, NY: Peter Lang.

Arnett, R. C. (in press-b). *Communication ethics in dark times: Arendt's rhetoric of warning and hope.* Carbondale, IL: Southern Illinois University Press.

Arnett, R. C., & Arneson, P. (1999). *Dialogic civility in a cynical age: Community, hope, and interpersonal relationships.* Albany, NY: State University of New York Press.

Arnett, R. C., & Fritz, J. M. H. (2001). Communication and professional civility as a basic service course: Dialogic praxis between departments and situated in an academic home. *Basic Communication Course Annual, 13,* 174–206.

Arnett, R. C., & Fritz, J. M. H. (2003). Sustaining institutional ethics and integrity: Management in a postmodern moment. In A. S. Iltis (Ed.), *Institutional integrity in health care* (pp. 41–71). Dordrecht, Netherlands: Kluwer.

Arnett, R. C., Fritz, J. M. H., & Bell, L. M. (2009). *Communication ethics literacy: Dialogue and difference.* Thousand Oaks, CA: Sage.

Arnett, R. C., Fritz, J. H., & Holba, A. (2007). The rhetorical turn to Otherness: Otherwise than humanism. *Cosmos and History: The Journal of Natural and Social Philosophy, 3,* 115–133. Retrieved from http://cosmosandhistory.org/index.php/journal/article/viewFile/57/113

Arnett, R. C., & Holba, A. M. (in press). *An overture to philosophy of communication: The carrier of meaning.* New York, NY: Peter Lang.

Ashcraft, K. L. (2000). Empowering "professional" relationships: Organizational communication meets feminist practice. *Management Communication Quarterly, 13,* 347–392.

Ashcraft, K. L. (2007). Appreciating the "work" of discourse: Occupational identity and difference as organizing mechanisms in the case of commercial airline pilots. *Discourse & Communication, 1,* 9–36.

Ashcraft, K. L., & Allen, B. J. (2003). The racial foundation of organizational communication. *Communication Theory, 13,* 5–38.

Ashcraft, K., Kuhn, T. R., & Cooren, F. (2009). Constitutional amendments: "Materializing" organizational communication. *Academy of Management Annals, 3*(1), 1–64.

Ashforth, B. (1994). Petty tyranny in organizations. *Human Relations, 47,* 755–778.

Baker, S. (2002). The theoretical ground for public relations practice and ethics: A Koehnian analysis. *Journal of Business Ethics, 35,* 191–205.

Baker-Ohler, M., & Holba, A. (2009). *The communicative relationship between dialogue and care.* Amherst, NY: Cambria Press.

Barber, B. (1963). Some problems in the sociology of the professions. *Daedalus, 92,* 669–688.

Barge, J. K., & Little, M. (2008). A discursive approach to skillful activity. *Communication Theory, 18,* 505–534.

Barrett, H. (1991). *Rhetoric and civility: Human development, narcissism, and the good audience.* Albany, NY: State University of New York Press.

Barry, D., & Elmes, M. (1997). Strategy retold: Toward a narrative view of strategic discourse. *Academy of Management Review, 22,* 429–452.

Bateman, T. S., & Organ, D. W. (1983). Job satisfaction and the good soldier: The relationship between affect and employee "citizenship." *Academy of Management Journal, 26,* 587–595.

Bateson, G. (1972). *Steps to an ecology of mind.* New York, NY: Ballantine.

Bauman, I., & Harden, J. (1990, November). *Self-monitoring and politeness.* Paper presented at the meeting of the Speech Communication Association, Chicago, IL.

Baxter, L. A., & Montgomery, B. M. (1996). *Relating: Dialogues and dialectics.* New York, NY: Guilford Press.

Bellah, R. N., Madsen, R., Sullivan, W. M., Swidler, A., & Tipton, S. M. (1991). *The good society.* New York, NY: Alfred A. Knopf.

Benhabib, S. (1992). *Situating the self: Gender, community and postmodernism in contemporary ethics.* New York, NY: Routledge.

Berger, C. R., & Calabrese, R. J. (1975). Some exploration in initial interaction and beyond: Toward a developmental theory of communication. *Human Communication Research, 1,* 99–112.

Berger, P. (1967). *The sacred canopy.* Garden City, NY: Doubleday.

Berger, P., & Luckmann, T. (1967). *The social construction of reality: A treatise in the sociology of knowledge.* Garden City, NY: Anchor.

Bies, R. J. (2001). Interactional (in)justice: The sacred and the profane. In J. Greenberg & R. Cropanzano (Eds.), *Advances in organizational justice* (pp. 189–118). Stanford, CA: Stanford University Press.

Bies, R. J., & Moag, J. S. (1986). Interactional justice: Communication criteria of fairness. In R. J. Lewicki, B. H. Sheppard, & M. H. Bazerman (Eds.) *Research in negotiation in organizations* (Vol. 1, pp. 43–56). Greenwich, CT: JAI Press.

Blackburn, M., & McGhee, P. (2004). Talking virtue: Professionalism in business and virtue ethics. *Global Virtue Ethics Review, 5,* 90–122.

Blau, P. M., & Scott, W. R. (1962). *Formal organizations: A comparative approach.* Chicago, IL: University of Chicago Press.

Blyler, N. R., & Thralls, C. (Eds.) (1993). *Professional communication: The social perspective.* Newbury Park, CA: Sage.

Boje, D. M. (1991). The storytelling organization: A study of story performance in an office-supply firm. *Administrative Science Quarterly, 36,* 106–126.

Boje, D. M. (1995). Stories of the storytelling organization: A postmodern analysis of Disney as "Tamara-Land." *Academy of Management Journal, 38,* 997–1035.

Bok, S. (1995). *Common values.* Columbia, MO: University of Missouri Press.

Bone, J. E., Griffin, C. L., & Scholz, T. M. L. (2008). Beyond traditional conceptions of rhetoric: Invitational rhetoric and a move toward civility. *Western Journal of Communication, 4,* 434–462.

Borden, S. L. (2007). *Journalism as practice: MacIntyre, virtue ethics, and the press.* Burlington, VT: Ashgate.

Bourdieu, P., & Wacquant, L. J. D. (1992). *An invitation to reflexive sociology.* Chicago, IL: University of Chicago Press.

Boyce, M. E. (1995). Collective centering and collective sense-making in the stories and storytelling of one organization. *Organization Studies, 16,* 107–137.

Bretz, R. D., & Judge, T. A. (1994). Person-organization fit and the theory of work adjustment: Implications for satisfaction, tenure, and career success. *Journal of Vocational Behavior, 44,* 32–54.

Brewer, E. W. (2001). Vocational souljourn paradigm: A model of adult development to express spiritual wellness as *meaning, being,* and *doing* in work and life. *Counseling and Values, 45,* 83–93.

Brewer, K. B. (1997). Management as a practice: A response to Alasdair MacIntyre. *Journal of Business Ethics, 16,* 825–833.

Bridge, K., & Baxter, L. A. (1992). Blended relationships: Friends as work associates. *Western Journal of Communication, 56,* 200–225.

Brien, A. (1998). Professional ethics and the culture of trust. *Journal of Business Ethics, 17,* 391–409.

Brown, M. H. (1985). That reminds me of a story: Speech action in organizational socialization. *Western Journal of Speech Communication, 49,* 27–42.

Brown, P., & Levinson, S. (1987). *Politeness: Some universals in language use.* New York, NY: Cambridge University Press. (Original work published 1978)

Brubacher, J. S., & Rudy, W. (1997). *Higher education in transition: A history of American colleges and universities* (4th ed.). New Brunswick, NJ: Transaction.

Buber, M. (1948). *Israel and the world.* New York, NY: Schocken.

Buber, M. (1958). *I and thou* (2nd ed.) (R. G. Smith, Trans.). New York, NY: Scribner.

Burke, K. (1950). *A grammar of motives.* Berkeley: University of California Press.

Buzzanell, P. M., Shenoy, S., Remke, R. V., & Lucas, K. (2009). Responses to destructive organizational contexts: Intersubjectively creating resilience to foster human dignity and hope. In P. Lutgen-Sandvik & B. Davenport Sypher (Eds.), *Destructive organizational communication: Processes, consequences, and constructive ways of organizing* (pp. 293–315). New York, NY: Routledge.

Byrne, D. (1961). Interpersonal attraction and attitude similarity. *Journal of Abnormal Social Psychology, 62,* 713–715.

Caldwell, M. (1999). *A short history of rudeness: Manners, morals, and misbehavior in modern America.* New York, NY: Picador.

Cameron, K. S. (2008). *Positive leadership: Strategies for extraordinary performance.* San Francisco, CA: Berrett-Koehler.

Cappella, J. N. (1984). The relevance of the microstructure of interaction to relationship change. *Journal of Social and Personal Relationships, 1,* 239–264.

Carbaugh, D. (1988). *Talking American: Cultural discourses on* Donahue. Norwood, NJ: Ablex.

Carroll, A. B. (2008). A history of corporate social responsibility: Concepts and practices. In A. McWilliams, D. Matten, J. Moon, & D. S. Siegel (Eds.), *The Oxford handbook of corporate social responsibility* (pp. 19–46). New York, NY: Oxford University Press.

Carter, S. L. (1998). *Civility: Manners, morals, and the etiquette of democracy.* New York, NY: Basic Books.

Chao, G. (1997). Mentoring phases and outcomes. *Journal of Vocational Behavior, 51,* 15–28.

Chao, G. T., Walz, P. M., & Gardner, P. D. (1992). Formal and informal mentorships: A comparison on mentoring functions and contrast with nonmentored counterparts. *Personnel Psychology, 45,* 619–636.

Charlton, B. (1996).Keeping your distance: Manners in the surgery. In D. Anderson (Ed.), *Gentility recalled: "Mere" manners and the making of social order* (pp. 157–166). London, England: The Social Affairs Unit.

Cheney, G., & Ashcraft, K. L. (2007). Considering "The Professional" in communication studies: Implications for theory and research within and beyond the boundaries of organizational communication. *Communication Theory, 17,* 146–175.

Cheney, G., Lair, D. J., Ritz, D., & Kendall, B. E. (2010). *Just a job? Communication, ethics, and professional life.* New York, NY: Oxford University Press.

Christians, C. G., & Traber, M. (Eds.). (1997). *Communication ethics and universal values.* Thousand Oaks, CA: Sage.

Clark, B. R. (1972). The organizational saga in higher education. *Administrative Science Quarterly, 17,* 178–184.

Cohen, A., & Kol, Y. (2004). Professionalism and organizational citizenship behavior: An empirical examination among nurses. *Journal of Managerial Psychology, 18,* 386–405.

Collins, B. L., Gill, R., & Mease, J. (in press). Exploring tensions in workplace relationships: Toward a communicative and situated understanding of tokenism. In B. L. Omdahl & J. M. H. Fritz (Eds.), *Problematic relationships in the workplace, volume 2.* New York, NY: Peter Lang.

Colvin, R. H., Zopf, K. J., & Myers, J. H. (1983). Weight control among coworkers: Effects of monetary contingencies and social milieu. *Behavior Modification, 7,* 64–75.

Comer, D. (1991). Organizational newcomers' acquisition of information from peers. *Management Communication Quarterly, 5,* 64–89.

Cooren, F. (2000). *The organizing property of communication.* Amsterdam, Netherlands: John Benjamins.

Cooren, F. (2004). The communicative achievement of collective minding: Analysis of board meeting excerpts. *Management Communication Quarterly, 17,* 517–551.

Cooren, F. (2006). Arguments for the in-depth study of organizational interactions: A rejoinder to McPhee, Myers, and Trethewey. *Management Communication Quarterly, 19,* 327–340.

Cooren, F., & Fairhurst, G. T. (2003). The leader as a practical narrator: Leadership as the art of translating. In D. Holman & R. Thorpe (Eds.), *Management and language* (pp. 85–103). London, England: Sage.

Cooren, F., Thompson, F., Canestraro, D., & Bodor, T. (2006). From agency to structure: Analysis of an episode in a facilitation process. *Human Relations, 59,* 533–565.

Corman, S. R., & Poole, M. S. (2000*). Perspectives on organizational communication: Finding common ground.* New York, NY: Guilford Press.

Cortina, L., Magley, V., Williams, J., & Langhout, R. (2001). Incivility in the workplace: Incidence and impact. *Journal of Occupational Health Psychology, 6,* 64–80.

Coupland, J. (2003). Small talk: Social functions. *Research on Language and Social Interaction, 36,* 1–6.

Crawford, M. (2009). *Shop class as soulcraft: An inquiry into the value of work.* New York, NY: The Penguin Press.

Crozier, M. (1964). *The bureaucratic phenomenon.* Chicago, IL: University of Chicago Press.

Crozier, M., & Friedberg, E. (1980). *Actors and systems* (A. Goldhammer, Trans.). Chicago, IL: University of Chicago Press.

Csikszentmihalyi, M. (1990). *Flow: The psychology of optimal experience.* New York, NY: Harper & Row.

Cunningham, M. R., Barbee, A. P., & Druen, P. B. (1997). Social allergens and the reactions they produce: Escalation of annoyance and disgust in love and work. In R. M. Kowalski (Ed.), *Aversive interpersonal behaviors* (pp. 189–214). New York, NY: Plenum Press.

Dansereau, F., Graen, G., & Haga, W. J. (1975). A vertical dyad linkage approach to leadership within formal organizations: A longitudinal investigation of the role making process. *Organizational Behavior and Human Performance, 13,* 46–78.

Davenport Sypher, B. (2004). Reclaiming civil discourse in the workplace. *Southern Communication Journal, 69,* 257–269.

Davenport Sypher, B., & Gill, M. (in press). The relative predictability of workplace incivility on interpersonal and organizational trust. In B. L. Omdahl & J. M. H. Fritz (Eds.), *Problematic relationships in the workplace, volume 2.* New York, NY: Peter Lang.

Davetian, B. (2009). *Civility: A cultural history.* Toronto, Canada: University of Toronto Press.

de Tocqueville, A. (2000). *Democracy in America* (H. C. Mansfield & D. Winthrop, Trans. & Eds.). Chicago, IL: University of Chicago Press. (Original work published 1835)

Deetz, S. A. (1992). *Democracy in an age of corporate colonization.* Albany, NY: State University of New York Press.

Deetz, S. A. (2005). Critical theory. In S. May & D. K. Mumby (Eds.), *Engaging organizational communication theory and research: Multiple perspectives.* (pp. 85–112). Thousand Oaks, CA: Sage.

D'Entrèves, M. P., & Vogel, U. (2000) (Eds.). *Public and private: Legal, political and philosophical perspectives.* London, England: Routledge.

DeTurk, S. (2011). Allies in action: The communicative experiences of people who challenge social injustice on behalf of others. *Communication Quarterly, 59,* 569–590.

DeWine, S., Nicotera, A. M., & Parry, D. (1991). Argumentativeness and aggressiveness: The flip side of gentle persuasion. *Management Communication Quarterly, 4,* 386–411.

DiGiulio, J. F. (1995). A more humane workplace: Responding to child welfare workers' personal losses. *Child Welfare, 74,* 877–888.

Dillard, J. P. (1990). A goal-driven model of interpersonal influence. In J. P. Dillard (Ed.), *Seeking compliance: The production of interpersonal influence messages* (pp. 41–56). Scottsdale, AZ: Gorsuch Scarisbrick.

Dillard, J. P., Segrin, C., & Harden, J. M. (1989). Primary and secondary goals in the production of interpersonal influence messages. *Communication Monographs, 56,* 19–38.

Dillard, J. P., & Witteman, H. (1985). Romantic relationships at work: Organizational and personal influence. *Human Communication Research, 12,* 99–116.

Dubinskas, F. A. (1992). Culture and conflict: The cultural roots of discord. In D. M. Kolb & J. M. Bartunek (Eds.), *Hidden conflict in organizations* (pp. 187–208). Newbury Park, CA: Sage.

Duck, S. (1977). *The study of acquaintance.* Farnborough, England: Gower.

Duck, S., Foley, M. K., & Kirkpatrick, D. C. (2006). Uncovering the complex roles behind the "difficult" coworker. In J. M. H. Fritz & B. L. Omdahl (Eds.), *Problematic relationships in the workplace* (pp. 3–19). New York, NY: Peter Lang.

Eakins, B., & Eakins, G. (1976). Verbal turn-taking and exchanges in faculty dialogue. In B. DuBois & I. Crouch (Eds.), *The sociology of the languages of American women* (pp. 53–62). San Antonio, TX: Trinity University Press.

Elias, N. (1978). *The history of manners.* New York, NY: Urizen Books.

Elias, N. (1982). *Power and civility.* New York, NY: Pantheon Books.

Englehardt, T. (2000). *The foundations of Christian bioethics.* Lisse, Netherlands: Swets & Zeitlinger.

Fairhurst, G. T. (1993). The leader-member exchange patterns of women leaders in industry: A discourse analysis. *Communication Monographs, 60,* 321–351.

Fairhurst, G. T. (2004). Textuality and agency in interaction analysis. *Organization, 11,* 335–353.

Fairhurst, G. T. (2011). *The power of framing: Creating the language of leadership.* San Francisco, CA: Jossey-Bass.

Fairhurst, G. T., & Chandler, T. A. (1989). Social structure in leader-member interaction. *Communication Monographs, 56,* 215–239.

Fairhurst, G. T., Green, S. G., & Snavely, B. K. (1984). Face support in controlling poor performance. *Human Communication Research, 11,* 272–295.

Fairhurst, G. T., Jordan, J. M., & Neuwirth, K. (1997). Why are we here? Managing the meaning of an organizational mission statement. *Journal of Applied Communication Research, 25,* 243–263.

Fairhurst, G. T., Rogers, L. E., & Sarr, R. A. (1987). Manager-subordinate control patterns and judgments about the relationship. In M. McLaughlin (Ed.), *Communication yearbook 10* (pp. 395–415). Newbury Park, CA: Sage.

Fay, M. J. (in press). Out of sight, out of . . . the loop? Relationship challenges for teleworkers and their co-located peers, managers, and organizations. In B. L. Omdahl & J. M. H. Fritz (Eds.), *Problematic relationships in the workplace, volume 2.* New York, NY: Peter Lang.

Fay, M. J., & Kline, S. L. (2011). Coworker relationships in high-intensity telecommuting. *Journal of Applied Communication Research, 39,* 144–163.

Fay, M. J., & Kline, S. L. (2012). The influence of informal communication on organizational identification and commitment in the context of high-intensity telecommuting. *Southern
Communication Journal, 77,* 61–76.

Ferguson, A. (2004). *An essay on the history of civil society.* Kila, MT: Kessinger. (Original work published 1767)

Fine, G. A. (1986). Friendships in the workplace. In V. J. Derlega & B. A. Winstead (Eds.), *Friendship
and social interaction* (pp. 185–206). New York, NY: Springer-Verlag.

Fisher, W. R. (1987). *Human communication as narration: Toward a philosophy of reason, value, and
action.* Columbia, SC: University of South Carolina Press.

Flexner, A. (2001). Is social work a profession? *Research on Social Work Practice, 11,* 152–165.
(Reprinted from *Proceedings of the National Conference of Charities and Corrections, 1915.*
Chicago, IL: National Conference of Charities and Corrections)

Follett, M. P. (1941). *Dynamic administration: The collected papers of Mary Parker Follett* (Ed. H.
Metcalf & L. Urwick). London, England: Pitman.

Ford, J. D., & Ford, L. W. (2003). Conversations and the authoring of change. In D. Holman & R.
Thorpe (Eds.), *Management and language* (pp. 141–156). Thousand Oaks, CA: Sage.

Forni, P. M. (2002). *Choosing civility: The twenty-five rules of considerate conduct.* New York, NY: St.
Martin's Press.

Forni, P. M. (2008). *The civility solution: What to do when people are rude.* New York, NY: St. Martin's
Press.

Forni, P. M. (2011a). The case for formality. *Spectra, 47*(3), 8–10.

Forni, P. M. (2011b). *The thinking life.* New York, NY: St. Martin's Press.

Fredrickson, B. L., & Dutton, J. E. (2008). Unpacking positive organizing: Organizations as sites of
individual and group flourishing. *Journal of Positive Psychology, 3,* 1–3.

Friedson, E. (1991). Nourishing professionalism. In E. D. Pellgrino, R. M. Veatch, & J. P. Langan
(Eds.), *Ethics, trust, and the professions: Philosophical and cultural aspects* (pp. 193–220).
Washington, DC: Georgetown University Press.

Fritz, J. H. (1997a). Men's and women's organizational peer relationships: A comparison. *Journal of
Business Communication, 34,* 27–46.

Fritz, J. H. (1997b). Responses to unpleasant work relationships. *Communication Research Reports,
14,* 302–311.

Fritz, J. M. H. (2002). How do I dislike thee? Let me count the ways: Constructing impressions of
troublesome others at work. *Management Communication Quarterly, 15,* 410–438.

Fritz, J. M. H. (2006). Typology of troublesome others at work: A follow-up investigation. In J. M.
H. Fritz & B. L. Omdahl (Eds.), *Problematic relationships in the workplace* (pp. 21–46). New
York, NY: Peter Lang.

Fritz, J. M. H. (2009). Rudeness and incivility in the workplace. In Wright, S., & Morrison, R. (Eds.),
Friends and enemies in organizations: A work psychology perspective (pp. 168–194). Hampshire,
England: Palgrave Macmillan.

Fritz, J. M. H. (2010). Christian approaches to communication scholarship and pedagogy. In D. Cali
(Ed.), *Faith and the media: Reflections by Christian communicators* (pp. 77–95). Mahwah, NJ:
Paulist Press.

Fritz, J. M. H. (2011). Civility in the workplace. *Spectra, 47*(3), 11–14.

Fritz, J. M. H. (2012a). Crisis communication in the workplace: Professional civility as ethical response to problematic interactions. In S. A. Groom & J. M. H. Fritz (Eds.), *Communication ethics and crisis: Negotiating differences in public and private spheres* (pp. 67–86). Madison, NJ: Fairleigh Dickinson University Press.

Fritz, J. M. H. (2012b). Women's communicative leadership in higher education. In E. Ruminski & A. Holba (Eds.), *Communicative understandings of women's leadership development: From ceilings of glass to labyrinth paths* (pp. 3–25). Lanham, MD: Lexington Books.

Fritz, J. M. H. (in press-a). Ethics matters: Why ethical communication makes a difference in today's workplace. In J. Wrench (Ed.), *Workplace communication for the 21st century: Tools and strategies that impact the bottom line.* Westport, CT: Praeger.

Fritz, J. M. H. (in press-b). Organizational misbehavior. In L. Crothers & J. Lipinski (Eds.), *Bullying in the workplace: Symptoms, causes and remedies.* New York, NY: Routledge.

Fritz, J. M. H. (in press-c). Protecting and promoting workplace relationships: Professional civility. In B. L. Omdahl & J. M. H. Fritz (Eds.), *Problematic relationships in the workplace, volume 2.* New York, NY: Peter Lang.

Fritz, J. M. H. (in press-d). A review of concepts relevant to problematic relationships in the workplace. In B. L. Omdahl & J. M. H. Fritz (Eds.), *Problematic relationships in the workplace, volume 2.* New York, NY: Peter Lang.

Fritz, J. M. H., & Arnett, R. C. (1999, November). *Toward a new construct influencing communication at work: Work friendship orientation within the narrative organization.* Paper presented at the meeting of the National Communication Association Annual Convention, Chicago, IL.

Fritz, J. M. H., & Arnett, R. C. (2007, November). *Professional civility as communicative and rhetorical practice in organizations: Social style grounded in substance.* Paper presented at the meeting of the National Communication Association, Chicago, IL.

Fritz, J. M. H., Arnett, R. C., & Conkel, M. (1999). Organizational ethical standards and organizational commitment. *Journal of Business Ethics, 20,* 289–299.

Fritz, J. M. H., & Omdahl, B. L. (Eds.) (2006a). *Problematic relationships in the workplace.* New York, NY: Peter Lang.

Fritz, J. M. H., & Omdahl, B. L. (2006b). Reduced job satisfaction, diminished commitment, and workplace cynicism as outcomes of negative work relationships. In J. M. H. Fritz & B. L. Omdahl (Eds.), *Problematic relationships in the workplace* (pp. 131–151). New York, NY: Peter Lang.

Fritz, J. M. H., O'Neil, N. B., Popp, A. M., Williams, C. D., & Arnett, R. C. (in press). The influence of supervisory behavioral integrity on intent to comply with organizational ethical standards and commitment. *Journal of Business Ethics.*

Fritz, J. M. H., & Sawicki, J. (2006). A framework for a Spiritan university. *Spiritan Horizons, 1,* 53–68.

Gadamer, H. G. (1986). *Truth and method.* New York, NY: Crossroad.

Galanti, S. P. (1986, March 3). More firms quiz customers for clues about competition. *Wall Street Journal,* p. 1.

Gannon, M. J. (2008). *Paradoxes of culture and globalization.* Thousand Oaks, CA: Sage.

Gardner, D. G., Dunham, R. B., Cummings, L. L., & Pierce, J. L. (1987). Focus of attention at work and leader-follower relationships. *Journal of Occupational Behavior, 8,* 277–294.

Gardner, H. G. (Ed.) (2007). *Responsibility at work: How leading professionals act (or don't act) responsibly.* San Francisco, CA: Jossey-Bass.

Gardner, H., Csikszentmihalyi, M., & Damon, W. (2001). *Good work: When excellence and ethics meet.* New York, NY: Basic Books.

Garner, J. T. (2009b). When things go wrong at work: Organizational dissent messages and audience. *Communication Studies, 60,* 197–218.

Gecas, V. (1981). Contexts of socialization. In M. Rosenberg & R. Turner (Eds.), *Social psychology: Sociological perspectives* (pp. 165–199). New York, NY: Basic Books.

Geddes, D., & Baron, R. (1997). Workplace aggression as a consequence of negative performance feedback. *Management Communication Quarterly, 10,* 433–454.

Gersick, C. J. G., Bartunek, J. M., & Dutton, J. E. (2000). Learning from academia: The importance of relationships in professional life. *Academy of Management Journal, 43,* 1026–1054.

Gibb, J. R. (1961). Defensive communication. *Journal of Communication, 11,* 141–149.

Giddens, A. (1984). *The constitution of society: Outline of the theory of structuration.* Berkeley, CA: University of California Press.

Giles, H., & Powesland, P. (1975). *Speech style and social evaluation.* New York, NY: Academic Press.

Giles, H., & Smith, P. (1979). Accommodation theory: Optimal levels of convergence. In H. Giles & H. St. Clair (Eds.), *Language and social psychology* (pp. 45–65). Oxford, England: Blackwell.

Gill, M. J., & Davenport Sypher, B. (2009). Workplace incivility and organizational trust. In P. Lutgen-Sandvik & B. Davenport Sypher (Eds.), *Destructive organizational communication: Processes, consequences, and constructive ways of organizing* (pp. 53–73). New York, NY: Routledge.

Ginsberg, B. (2011). *The fall of the faculty: The rise of the all-administrative university.* New York, NY: Oxford University Press.

Goffman, E. (1959). *The presentation of self in everyday life.* New York, NY: Doubleday Anchor.

Goffman, E. (1967). *Interaction ritual: Essays on face-to-face behavior.* Garden City, NY: Anchor Books.

Gonthier, G., & Morrissey, K. (2002). *Rude awakenings: Overcoming the civility crisis in the workplace.* Chicago, IL: Dearborn Trade.

Gordon, T. (1970). *PET: Parent effectiveness training.* New York, NY: Wyden.

Gottman, J. (1994). *Why marriages succeed or fail . . . and how you can make yours last.* New York, NY: Simon & Schuster.

Gouldner, A. (1957). Cosmopolitans and locals: Toward an analysis of latent social roles-I. *Administrative Science Quarterly, 2,* 281–305.

Gouldner, A. (1958). Cosmopolitans and locals: Toward an analysis of latent social roles-II. *Administrative Science Quarterly, 2,* 444–480.

Graen, G. (1976). Role-making processes in complex organizations. In R. Dubin, (Ed.), *Handbook of work, organization, and society* (pp. 1201–1246). Chicago, IL: Rand McNally.

Graen, G., Dansereau, F., & Minami, T. (1972). Dysfunctional leadership styles. *Organizational Behavior and Human Performance, 7,* 216–236.

Graen, G., Orris, J. B., & Johnson, T. W. (1973). Role assimilation processes in a complex organization. *Journal of Vocational Behavior, 3,* 395–420.

Graen, G. B., & Uhl-Bien, M. (1995). Relationship-based approach to leadership: Development of a leader-member exchange (LMX) theory of leadership over 25 years—Applying a multi-level multi-domain perspective. *Leadership Quarterly, 6,* 219–247.

Graham, J. W. (1986, August). *Organizational citizenship informed by political theory.* Paper presented at the meeting of the Academy of Management, Chicago, IL.

Graham, J. W. (1991). An essay on organizational citizenship behavior. *Employee Responsibilities and*

Rights Journal, 4, 249–270.

Grant, A. M. (2007). Relational job design and the motivation to make a prosocial difference. *Academy of Management Review, 32,* 393–417.

Grice, H. P. (1975). Logic and conversation. In A. P. Martinich (Ed.), *Philosophy of language* (pp. 165–175). New York, NY: Oxford University Press.

Groom, S. A., Fritz, J. M. H., & Arnett, R. C. (2007, June). *Examining organizational reputation from the inside out.* Paper presented at the International Conference on Reputation, Brand, Identity and Competitiveness, Oslo, Norway.

Gurstein, R. (1996). *The repeal of reticence.* New York, NY: Hill & Wang.

Guzley, R. M. (1992). Organizational climate and communication climate: Predicators of commitment to the organization. *Management Communication Quarterly, 5,* 379–402.

Habermas, J. (1984). *The theory of communicative action: Vol. 1. Reason and the rationalization of society* (T. McCarthy, Trans.). Boston, MA: Beacon Press.

Habermas, J. (1987). *The theory of communicative action: Vol. 2. Lifeworld and system: A critique of functionalist reason* (T. McCarthy, Trans.). Boston, MA: Beacon Press.

Hall, A., & Berardino, L. (2006). Teaching professional behaviors: Differences in the perceptions of faculty, students, and employers. *Journal of Business Ethics, 63,* 407–415.

Hall, M. A., & Schneider, C. E. (2008). Learning from the legal history of billing for medical fees. *Journal of General Internal Medicine, 23,* 1257–1260.

Hammoud, A., & Buzzanell, P. (in press). "The most vulnerable . . . [and] most resilient people": Communicatively constituting Palestinian refugees' resilience. In B. L. Omdahl & J. M. H. Fritz (Eds.), *Problematic relationships in the workplace, volume 2.* New York, NY: Peter Lang.

Harden, J. M. (1984). *Rhetorical example as narrative: A case study of selected television commercials* (Unpublished master's thesis). University of Georgia, Athens, GA.

Harden, J. M. (1993). *Organizational socialization states, communication in peer relationships, and a model of the organizational socialization process* (Unpublished doctoral dissertation). University of Wisconsin, Madison, WI.

Harrison, R. (1972). Understanding your organization's character. *Harvard Business Review, May/June,* 119–128.

Harrison, W. H. (2004). Loving the creation, loving the creator: Dorothy L. Sayers's theology of work. *Anglican Theological Review, 86,* 239–257.

Hatch, N. O. (Ed.) (1988). *The professions in American history.* Notre Dame, IN: University of Notre Dame Press.

Hebden, J. (1986). Adopting an organization's culture: The socialization of graduate trainees. *Organizational Dynamics, 15,* 54–72.

Hegstrom, T. G. (1995). Focus on organizational dissent: A functionalist response to criticism. In J. Lehtonen (Ed.), *Critical responses to communication research and pedagogy* (pp. 83–94). St. Ingbert, Germany: Röhrig Universitätsverlag.

Hess, J. (1993). Assimilating newcomers into an organization: A cultural perspective. *Journal of Applied Communication Research, 21,* 189–210.

Hess, J. A. (2006). Distancing from problematic coworkers. In J. M. H. Fritz & B. L. Omdahl (Eds.), *Problematic relationships in the workplace* (pp. 205–232). New York, NY: Peter Lang.

Hess, J., Omdahl, B. L., & Fritz, J. M. H. (2006). Turning points in relationships with disliked coworkers. In J. M. H. Fritz & B. L. Omdahl (Eds.), *Problematic relationships in the workplace* (pp.

89–106).

Hess, J. A., & Sneed, K. A. (in press). Communication strategies to restore working relations: Comparing relationships that improved with ones that remained problematic. In B. L. Omdahl & J. M. H. Fritz (Eds.), *Problematic relationships in the workplace, volume 2.* New York, NY: Peter Lang.

Hickson, M., & Roebuck, J. B. (2009). *Deviance and crime in colleges and universities: What goes on in the halls of ivy.* Springfield, IL: Charles C. Thomas.

Hirokawa, R. Y., & Pace, R. (1983). A descriptive investigation of the possible communication-based reasons for effective and ineffective group decision making. *Communication Monographs, 50,* 363–379.

Hirokawa, R. Y., & Scheerhorn, D. R. (1986). Communication in faulty group decision making. In R. Y. Hirokawa & M. S. Poole (Eds.), *Communication and group decision making* (pp. 63–80). Beverly Hills, CA: Sage.

Hoban, G. (2002). *Teacher learning for educational change.* Buckingham, England: Open University Press.

Hodge, R., & Kress, G. (1988). *Social semiotics.* New York, NY: Cornell University Press.

Hodson, R. (2001). *Dignity at work.* Cambridge, England: Cambridge University Press.

Hoel, H., Sheehan, M. J., Cooper, C. L., & Einarsen, S. (2011). Organizational effects of workplace bullying. In S. Einarsen, H. Hoel, D. Zapf, & C. L. Cooper (Eds.), *Bullying and harassment in the workplace: Developments in theory, research, and practice* (2nd ed., pp. 129–147). Boca Raton, FL: CRC Press/Taylor & Francis.

Hofstede, G. (2001). *Culture's consequences: Comparing values, behaviors, institutions, and organizations across nations* (2nd ed.). Thousand Oaks, CA: Sage.

Hogg, M. (2000). Social identity and self-categorization processes in organizational contexts. *Academy of Management Review, 25,* 121–140.

Hogh, A., Mikkelsen, E. G., & Hansen, Å. M. (2011). Individual consequences of workplace bullying/mobbing. In S. Einarsen, H. Hoel, D. Zapf, & C. L. Cooper (Eds.), *Bullying and harassment in the workplace: Developments in theory, research, and practice* (2nd ed., pp. 107–128). Boca Raton, FL: CRC Press/Taylor & Francis.

Holba, A. (2007). *Philosophical leisure: Recuperative praxis for human communication.* Milwaukee, WI: Marquette University Press.

Holba, A. (2008). Revisiting Martin Buber's I-it: A rhetorical strategy. *Human Communication, 11,* 495–510. Retrieved from http://www.paca4u.com/journal%20alabama%20page.htm

Holba, A. M. (2011). Listening through leisure: Meeting the Other in the spirit of civility. *Listening: Journal of Communication Ethics, Religion, and Culture, 46,* 51–62.

Hollinger, R. C. (1988). Working under the influence (WUI): Correlates of employees' use of alcohol and other drugs. *Journal of Applied Behavioral Science, 24,* 439–454.

Holmes, J., & Stubbe, M. (2003). *Power and politeness in the workplace: A sociolinguistic analysis of talk at work.* London, England: Pearson.

Horan, S. M., & Chory, R. M. (2009). When work and love mix: Perceptions of peers in workplace romances. *Western Journal of Communication, 73,* 349–369.

Hosman, L. A. (1989). The evaluative consequences of hedges, hesitations, and intensifiers: Powerful and powerless speech styles. *Human Communication Research, 15,* 383–406.

Hullman, G. A. (2004). Interpersonal communication motives and message design logic: Exploring their interaction on perceptions of competence. *Communication Monographs, 71*, 208–225.

Humphrey, R. (1984). *Attributional processes in work settings* (Unpublished doctoral dissertation). University of Michigan, Ann Arbor, MI.

Hunter, F. T. (1984). Socializing procedures in parent-child and friendship relations during adolescence. *Developmental Psychology, 20*, 1092–1099.

Hutton, J. (1999). The definition, dimensions, and domain of public relations. *Public Relations Review, 25*, 199–214.

Infante, D. A. (1987). Aggressiveness. In J. C. McCroskey & J. A. Daly (Eds.), *Personality and interpersonal communication* (pp. 157–191). Newbury Park, CA: Sage.

Infante, D. A., & Rancer, A. S. (1982). A conceptualization and measure of argumentativeness. *Journal of Personality Assessment, 46*, 72–80.

Infante, D. A., & Rancer, A. S. (1996). Argumentativeness and verbal aggressiveness: A review of recent theory and research. In B. R. Burleson (Ed.), *Communication yearbook 19* (pp. 319–351). Thousand Oaks, CA: Sage.

Jablin, F. (1984). Assimilating new members into organizations. In R. N. Bostrom (Ed.), *Communication yearbook 8* (pp. 594–626). Newbury Park, CA: Sage.

Jacobs, J. (1994). *Systems of survival: A dialogue on the moral foundations of commerce and politics*. New York, NY: Vintage. (Original work published 1992)

Johannesen, R. L., Valde, K. W., & Whedbee, K. E. (2008). *Ethics in human communication* (6th ed.). Long Grove, IL: Waveland Press.

Johnson, D. (2012). Swearing by peers in the work setting: Expectancy violation valence, perceptions of message, and perceptions of speaker. *Communication Studies, 63*, 136–151.

Johnson, P. R., & Indvik, J. (2001a). Rudeness at work: Impulse over restraint. *Public Personnel Management, 30*, 457–465.

Johnson, P. R., & Indvik, J. (2001b). Slings and arrows of rudeness: Incivility in the workplace. *Journal of Management Development, 20*, 705–713.

Judge, T. A., & Ferris, G. R. (1992). The elusive criterion of fit in human resource staffing decisions. *Human Resource Planning, 154*, 47–67.

Kaptein, M., & Schwartz, M. S. (2008). The effectiveness of business codes: A critical examination of existing studies and the development of an integrated research model. *Journal of Business Ethics, 77*, 111–127.

Kassing, J. (1998). Development and validation of the organizational dissent scale. *Management Communication Quarterly, 12*, 183–229.

Kassing, J. W. (2001). From the look of things: Assessing perceptions of organizational dissenters. *Communication Research, 21*, 553–574.

Kasson, J. F. (1990). *Rudeness & civility: Manners in nineteenth-century America*. New York, NY: Hill & Wang.

Katz, R. (1980). Time and work: Toward an integrative perspective. In B. M. Staw & L. L. Cummings (Eds.), *Research in organizational behavior* (Vol. 2, pp. 81–128). Greenwich, CT: JAI Press.

Keashly, L. (in press). Hostile work relationships. In B. L. Omdahl & J. M. H. Fritz (Eds.), *Problematic relationships in the workplace, volume 2*. New York, NY: Peter Lang.

Keashly, L., & Jagatic, K. (2011). North American perspectives on hostile behaviors and bullying at work. In S. Einarsen, H. Hoel, D. Zapf, & C. L. Cooper (Eds.), *Bullying and harassment in the workplace: Developments in theory, research, and practice* (2nd ed., pp. 41–71). Boca Raton, FL:

CRC Press/Taylor & Francis.

Kervin, L. K., & Turbill, J. (2003). Teaching as craft: Making links between pre-service training and professional practice. *English Teaching: Practice and Critique, 2*(3), 22–34.

Kiggundu, M. N. (1983). Task interdependence and job design: Test of a theory. *Organizational Behavior and Human Performance, 31,* 145–172.

Kimball, B. A. (1986). *Orators and philosophers: A history of the idea of liberal education.* New York, NY: Teachers College Press.

Kimball, B. A. (1995). *The "true professional ideal" in America: A history.* Lanham, MD: Rowman & Littlefield.

Kingwell, M. (1995). *A civil tongue: Justice, dialogue, and the politics of pluralism.* University Park: Pennsylvania State University Press.

Kingwell, M. (2000). *The world we want: Virtue, vice, and the good citizen.* New York, NY: Penguin.

Kirby, E. L., & Krone, K. J. (2002). "The policy exists but you can't really use it": Communication and the structuration of work-family policies. *Journal of Applied Communication Research, 30,* 50–77.

Kinney, T. A. (in press). Workplace bullying as interpersonal violence? A reconceptualization in progress. In B. L. Omdahl & J. M. H. Fritz (Eds.), *Problematic relationships in the workplace, volume 2.* New York, NY: Peter Lang.

Kisselburgh, L. G., & Dutta, M. J. (2009). The construction of civility in multicultural organizations. In P. Lutgen-Sandvik & B. Davenport Sypher (Eds.), *Destructive organizational communication: Processes, consequences, and constructive ways of organizing* (pp. 121–142). New York, NY: Routledge.

Knouse, S. B., & Giacalone, R. A. (1992). Ethical decision-making in business: Behavioral issues and concerns. *Journal of Business Ethics, 11,* 369–377.

Kohn, M. L. (1977). *Class and conformity: A study in values* (2nd ed.). Chicago, IL: University of Chicago Press.

Kohn, M. L., Naoi, A., Schoenbach, L., Schooler, C., & Slomczynski, K. (1990). Position in the class structure and psychological functioning in the United States, Japan, and Poland. *American Journal of Sociology, 95,* 964–1008.

Kohn, M. L., & Schooler, C. (1983). *Work and personality: An inquiry into the impact of social stratification.* Norwood, NJ: Ablex.

Kolb, D. M., & Bartunek, J. M. (1992). *Hidden conflict in organizations: Discovering behind-the-scenes disputes.* Newbury Park, CA: Sage.

Konovsky, M. A., & Organ, D. W. (1996). Dispositional and contextual determinants of organizational citizenship behavior. *Journal of Organizational Behavior, 17,* 253–266.

Kram, K. (1983). Phases of the mentor relationship. *Academy of Management Journal, 26,* 608–625.

Kram, K. E. (1985). *Mentoring at work: Developmental relationships in organizational life.* Glenview, IL: Scott, Foresman.

Kram, K., & Isabella, L. (1985). Mentoring alternatives: The role of peer relationships in career development. *Academy of Management Journal, 28,* 110–132.

Kramer, M. (2010). *Organizational socialization: Joining and leaving organizations.* Malden, MA: Polity.

Krause, E. A. (1996). *Death of the guilds: Professions, states, and the advance of capitalism, 1930 to the present.* New Haven, CT: Yale University Press.

Kristof, A. L. (1996). Person-organization fit: An integrative review of its conceptualizations, measurement, and implications. *Personnel Psychology, 49,* 1–49.

Kultgen, J. (1988). *Ethics and professionalism.* Philadelphia, PA: University of Pennsylvania Press.

Kurth, S. (1970). Friendships and friendly relations. In G. McCall, M. McCall, N. Denzin, G. Suttles, & S. Kurth (Eds.), *Social relationships* (pp. 136–170). Chicago, IL: Aldine Press.

Lakoff, R., & Johnson, M. (1980). *Metaphors we live by.* Chicago, IL: University of Chicago Press.

Lamert, S. J., & Hopkins, K. (1995). Occupational conditions and workers' sense of community: Variations by gender and race. *American Journal of Community Psychology, 23,* 151–179.

Langer, E., & Newman, H. (1979). The role of mindlessness in a typical social psychological experiment. *Personality and Social Psychology Bulletin, 5,* 295–298.

Larson, M. S. (1977). *The rise of professionalism: A sociological analysis.* Berkeley, CA: University of California Press.

Larson, C. E., & LaFasto, F. M. J. (1989). *Teamwork: What must go right/What can go wrong.* Newbury Park, CA: Sage.

Lasch, C. (1977). *Haven in a heartless world: The family besieged.* New York, NY: W. W. Norton & Co.

Lasch, C. (1991). *The true and only heaven: Progress and its critics.* New York, NY: W. W. Norton & Co.

Laverty, M. (2009) Civility, tact, and the joy of communication. In D. Kerdeman (Ed.), *Philosophy of education yearbook 2009* (pp. 228–37). Urbana, IL: Philosophy of Education Society.

Lee, Y., & Wilkins, V. M. (2011). More similarities or more differences? Comparing public and nonprofit managers' job motivations. *Public Administration Review, 71,* 45–56.

Leeds-Hurwitz, W. (Ed.) (1995). *Social approaches to communication.* New York, NY: Guilford.

Leitko, T. A., Greil, A. L., & Peterson, S. A. (1985). Lessons at the bottom: Worker nonparticipation in labor management committees as situational adjustment. *Work and Occupations, 12,* 285–306.

Leoussi, A. S. (1996). Keeping up appearances. In D. Anderson (Ed.), *Gentility recalled: 'Mere' manners and the making of social order* (pp. 95–106). London, England: The Social Affairs Unit.

Levinas, E. (1969). *Totality and infinity: An essay in exteriority* (A. Lingis, Trans.). Pittsburgh, PA: Duquesne University Press.

Lewis, L. K. (2006). Employee perspectives on implementation communication as predictors of perceptions of success and resistance. *Western Journal of Communication, 70,* 23–46.

Lewis, L. K., Schmisseur, A. M., Stephens, K. K., & Weir, K. E. (2006). Advice on communicating during organizational change: The content of popular press books. *Journal of Business Communication, 43,* 113–137.

Liden, R. C., & Graen, G. (1980). Generalizability of the vertical dyad linkage model of leadership. *Academy of Management Journal, 23,* 451–465.

Lim, S., & Cortina, L. M. (2005). Interpersonal mistreatment in the workplace: The interface and impact of general incivility and sexual harassment. *Journal of Applied Psychology, 90,* 483–496.

Lim, T.-S., & Bowers, J. W. (1991). Facework: Solidarity, approbation, and tact. *Human Communication Research, 17,* 415–450.

Liu, M., & Buzzanell, P. M. (2006). When workplace pregnancy highlights difference: Openings for detrimental gender and supervisory relations. In. J. M. H. Fritz & B. L. Omdahl (Eds.), *Problematic relationships in the workplace* (pp. 47–67). New York, NY: Peter Lang.

Louis, M. R. (1980). Surprise and sense-making: What newcomers experience in entering unfamiliar organizational settings. *Administrative Science Quarterly, 25,* 226–251.

Lozano-Reich, N. M., & Cloud, D. (2009). The uncivil tongue: Invitational rhetoric and the problem of inequality. *Western Journal of Communication, 2,* 220–226.

Lutgen-Sandvik, P., & Davenport Sypher, B. (Eds.) (2009). *Destructive organizational communication: Processes, consequences, and constructive ways of organizing.* New York: Routledge.

Lutgen-Sandvik, P., Namie, G., & Namie, R. (2009). Workplace bullying: Causes, consequences, and corrections. In P. Lutgen-Sandvik & B. Davenport Sypher (Eds.), *Destructive organizational communication: Processes, consequences, & constructive ways of organizing* (pp. 27–52). New York, NY: Routledge.

Lutgen-Sandvik, P., Riforgiate, S., & Fletcher, C. (2011). Work as a source of positive emotional experiences and the discourses informing positive assessment. *Western Journal of Communication, 75,* 2–27.

Lutz, C. S. (2009). *Tradition in the ethics of Alasdair MacIntyre: Relativism, Thomism, and philosophy.* Lanham, MD: Lexington Books. (Original work published 2004)

Lyotard, J. F. (1984). *The postmodern condition: A report on knowledge* (Trans. G. Bennington & B. Massumi). Minneapolis, MN: University of Minnesota Press.

MacIntyre, A. (1994). A partial response to my critics. In J. Horton & S. Mendus (Eds.), *After MacIntyre: Critical perspectives on the work of Alasdair MacIntyre* (pp. 284–286). Notre Dame, IN: University of Notre Dame Press.

MacIntyre, A. (2007). *After virtue* (3rd ed.). Notre Dame, IN: University of Notre Dame Press.

Madlock, P. E., & Kennedy-Lightsey, C. (2010). The effects of supervisors' verbal aggressiveness and mentoring on their subordinates. *Journal of Business Communication, 47,* 42–62.

Maister, D. H. (1997). *True professionalism: The courage to care about your people, your clients, and your career.* New York, NY: The Free Press.

Malinowski, B. (1972). Phatic communion. In J. Laver & S. Hutcheson (Eds.), *Communication in face-to-face interaction* (pp.146–152). Harmondsworth, England: Penguin. (Original work published 1923)

Malone, P., & Hayes, J. (2012). Backstabbing in organization: Employees' perceptions of incidents, motives, and communicative responses. *Communication Studies, 63,* 194–219.

Mancl, A. C., & Penington, B. (2011). Tall poppies in the workplace: Communication strategies used by envious others in response to successful women. *Qualitative Research Reports in Communication, 12,* 79–86.

Manning, S. (1997). The social worker as moral citizen: Ethics in action. *Social Work, 42,* 223–230.

Markell, P. (2011). Arendt's work: On the architecture of *The Human Condition. College Literature, 38,* 15–44.

Marks, S. L. (1994). Intimacy in the public realm: The case of coworkers. *Social Forces, 72,* 843–858.

Martin, J., Feldman, M. S., Hatch, M. J., & Sitkin, S. B. (1983). The uniqueness paradox in organizational stories. *Administrative Science Quarterly, 28,* 438–453.

May, L. (1996). *The socially responsive self: Social theory and professional ethics.* Chicago. IL: University of Chicago Press.

May, S., & Mumby, D. K. (Eds.) (2005). *Engaging organizational communication theory and research: Multiple perspectives.* Thousand Oaks, CA: Sage.

May, W. F. (2001). *Beleaguered rulers: The public obligation of the professional.* Louisville, KY: Westminster John Knox Press.

Mayfield, J., Mayfield, M., & Kopf, J. (1995). Motivating language: Exploring theory with scale development. *Journal of Business Communication, 34,* 329–344.

Mayo, C. (2002). Civility and its discontents: Sexuality, race, and the lure of beautiful manners. In S. Rice (Ed.), *Philosophy of education yearbook 2001* (pp. 78–87). Urbana, IL: Philosophy of Education Society.

McAllister, D. J. (1995). Affect- and cognition-based trust as foundations for interpersonal cooperation in organizations. *Academy of Management Journal, 38,* 24–59.

McCall, G. J., & Simmons, J. L. (1978). *Identities and interactions.* New York, NY: The Free Press.

McCarther, S. M. (2010). A black who wore white—a look back: Reflections of a segregated nursing education program at General Hospital No. 2 in Kansas City, Missouri. *American Educational History Journal, 37,* 291–311.

McGlone, M. S., & Batchelor, J. A. (2003). Looking out for number one: Euphemism and face. *Journal of Communication, 53,* 251–265.

McLeod, J. M., & Chaffee, S. H. (1972). The construction of social reality. In J. Tedeschi (Ed.), *The social influence process* (pp. 50–59). Chicago, IL: Aldine-Atherton.

McPhee, R. D. (1989). Organizational communication: A structurational exemplar. In B. Dervin, L. Grossberg, B. J. O'Keefe, & E. Wartella (Eds), *Rethinking communication* (pp. 199–212). Newbury Park, CA: Sage.

McPhee, R. D. (2004). Text, agency and organization in the light of structuration theory. *Organization, 11,* 355–371.

Mead, G. H. (1934). *Mind, self, and society.* Chicago, IL: University of Chicago Press.

Meglich, P. (2007). Establish a respectful workplace to counteract interpersonal workplace harassment. *Journal of Applied Business and Economics, 7*(3), 13–26.

Meglich, P. (2008). Gender effects of interpersonal workplace harassment. *Journal of Applied Business and Economics, 8*(4), 9–23.

Metts, S., Cupach, W. R., & Lippert, L. (2006). Forgiveness in the workplace. In B. L. Omdahl & J. M. H. Fritz (Eds.), *Problematic relationships in the workplace* (pp. 249–278). New York, NY: Peter Lang.

Miller, C., & Reznik, R. (2009, November). *Social allergens in the workplace: Exploring the impact of emotion, perception of the allergen, and repair work on confrontation frequency and relational well-being.* Paper presented at the meeting of the National Communication Association, Chicago, IL.

Miller, K. (2006). Communication as constructive. In G. J. Shepherd, J. St. John, & T. Striphas (Eds.), *Communication as . . . perspectives on theory* (pp. 31–37). Thousand Oaks, CA: Sage.

Miller, K. (2011). *Organizational communication: Approaches and processes.* Boston, MA: Wadsworth.

Miller, K. I. (2000). Common ground from the post-positivist perspective: From "straw person" argument to collaborative coexistence. In S. R. Corman & M. S. Poole (Eds.), *Perspectives on organizational communication: Finding common ground* (pp. 46–67). New York, NY: Guilford Press.

Millhous, L. M. (in press). Contemplating an upward spiral: When cultural diversity emerges in problematic workplace relationships. In B. L. Omdahl & J. M. H. Fritz (Eds.), *Problematic relationships in the workplace, volume 2.* New York, NY: Peter Lang.

Mills, A., & Chiaramonte, P. (1991). Organization as gendered communication act. *Canadian Journal of Communication, 16,* 381–398.

Moch, M. K., & Fields, W. C. (1985). Developing a content analysis for interpreting language use in organizations. In S. B. Bacharach (Ed.), *Research in the sociology of organizations* (4th ed., pp. 81–126). Greenwich, CT: JAI Press.

Moore, G. (2002). On the implications of the practice-institution distinction: MacIntyre and the application of modern virtue ethics to business. *Business Ethics Quarterly, 12,* 19–22.

Moore, W. E. (1970). *The professions: Roles and rules.* New York, NY: Russell Sage Foundation.

Morgan, G. (1986). *Images of organization.* Beverly Hills, CA: Sage.

Mumby, D. (2000). Common ground from the critical perspective: Overcoming binary oppositions. In S. R. Corman & M. S. Poole (Eds.), *Perspectives on organizational communication: Finding common ground* (pp. 68–86). New York, NY: Guilford Press.

Myers, K. K. (2010). Workplace relationships and membership negotiation. In S. W. Smith & S. R. Wilson (Eds.), *New directions in interpersonal communication research* (pp. 135–156). Thousand Oaks, CA: Sage.

Nakamura, J. (2007). Practicing responsibility. In H. Gardner (Ed.), *Responsibility at work: How leading professionals act (or don't act) responsibly* (pp. 285–310). San Francisco, CA: Jossey-Bass.

Naughton, M., & Laczniak, G. R. (1993). A theological context of work from the Catholic social encyclical tradition. *Journal of Business Ethics, 12,* 981–994.

Noordegraaf, M. (2007). From "pure" to "hybrid" professionalism: Present-day professionalism in ambiguous public domains. *Administration and Society, 39,* 761–785.

Nunnally, J. C. (1978). *Psychometric theory* (3rd ed.). New York, NY: McGraw-Hill.

Nussbaum, M. C. (2000). *Women and human development.* Cambridge, MA: Cambridge University Press.

Oakley, J., & Cocking, D. (2001). *Virtue ethics and professional roles.* New York, NY: Cambridge University Press.

O'Barr, W. M. (1982). *Linguistic evidence: Language, power, and strategy in the courtroom.* New York, NY: Academic Press.

Ohman, R. (2003). *Politics of knowledge: The commercialization of the university, and professions, and print culture.* Middletown, CT: Wesleyan University Press.

O'Keefe, B. J. (1988). The logic of message design: Individual differences in reasoning about communication. *Communication Monographs, 55,* 80–103.

O'Keefe, B. J. (1991). Message design logic and the management of multiple goals. In K. Tracy (Ed.), *Understanding face-to-face interaction: Issues linking goals and discourse* (pp. 101–117). Hillsdale, NJ: Lawrence Erlbaum.

O'Keefe, B. J. & McCornack, S. A. (1987). Message design logic and message goal structure: Effects on perceptions of message quality in regulative communication situations. *Human Communication Research, 14,* 68–92.

O'Keefe, B. J. & Shepherd, G. J. (1987). The pursuit of multiple objectives in face-to-face persuasive interactions: Effects of construct differentiation on message organization. *Communication Monographs, 54,* 396–419.

Oliver, R. T. (1961). *Conversation: The development and expression of personality.* Springfield, IL: Charles C. Thomas.

Omdahl, B. L. (2006). Towards effective work relationships. In J. M. H. Fritz & B. L. Omdahl (Eds.), *Problematic relationships in the workplace* (pp. 279–294). New York, NY: Peter Lang.

Omdahl, B. L. (in press). Resilience, civility, positive communication, and forgiveness in the academy. In B. L. Omdahl & J. M. H. Fritz (Eds.), *Problematic relationships in the workplace, vol-*

ume 2. New York, NY: Peter Lang.

Omdahl, B. L., & Fritz, J. M. H. (2006). Stress, burnout, and impaired mental health: Consequences of problematic work relationships. In J. M. H. Fritz & B. L. Omdahl (Eds.), *Problematic relationships in the workplace* (pp. 109–128). New York, NY: Peter Lang.

Omdahl, B. L., & Fritz, J. M. H. (Eds.) (in press). *Problematic relationships in the workplace, volume 2*. New York, NY: Peter Lang.

O'Reilly, C. A., Chatman, J. A., & Caldwell, D. F. (1991). People and organizational culture: A profile comparison approach to assessing person-organization fit. *Academy of Management Journal, 34*, 487–516.

Organ, D. W. (1988). *Organizational citizenship: The good soldier syndrome*. Lexington, MA: Lexington Books.

Organ, D. W. (1990). The motivational basis of organizational citizenship behavior. In B. M. Staw & L. L. Cummings (Eds.), *Research in organizational behavior* (vol. 12, pp. 43–72). Greenwich, CT: JAI Press.

Organ, D. W., Podsakoff, P. M., & MacKenzie, S. B. (2006). *Organizational citizenship behavior: Its nature, antecedents, and consequences*. Thousand Oaks, CA: Sage.

Packard, V. (1957). *The hidden persuaders*. London, England: Longmans, Green.

Palmer, P. J. (1989). *The company of strangers*. New York, NY: Crossroad.

Parsons, T. (1939). The professions and social structure. *Social Forces, 17*, 457–467.

Patton, T. O. (2004). In the guise of civility: The complicitous maintenance of inferential forms of sexism and racism in higher education. *Women's Studies in Communication, 27*, 60–87.

Pearce, W. B. (1994). *Interpersonal communication: Making social worlds*. New York, NY: HarperCollins College Publishers.

Pearce, W. B. (2007). *Making social worlds: A communication perspective*. Malden, MA: Blackwell.

Pearce, W. B., & Pearce, K. A. (2004). Taking a communication perspective on dialogue. In R. Anderson, L. A. Baxter, & K. N. Cissna (Eds.), *Dialogue: Theorizing difference in communication studies* (pp. 39–56). Thousand Oaks, CA: Sage.

Pearson, C., Andersson, L., & Porath, C. (2000). Assessing and attacking workplace incivility. *Organizational Dynamics, 29*, 123–137.

Pearson, C., & Porath, C. (2009). *The cost of bad behavior: How incivility is damaging your business and what to do about it*. New York, NY: Portfolio.

Peck, M. S. (1994). *A world waiting to be born: Civility rediscovered*. New York, NY: Bantam.

Pellegrino, E. D. (1995). Toward a virtue-based normative ethics for the health professions. *Kennedy Institute of Ethics Journal, 5*, 253–277.

Pellegrino, E. D., & McElhinney, T. (1982). *Teaching ethics, the humanities, and human values in medical schools*. Washington, DC: Society for Health and Human Values.

Pellegrino, E. D., Veatch, R. M., & Langan, J. P. (Eds.) (1991). *Ethics, trust, and the professions: Philosophical and cultural aspects*. Washington, DC: Georgetown University Press.

Perrow, C. (1986). *Complex organizations: A critical essay*. New York, NY: McGraw-Hill.

Peters, R. H., Witty, T. E., & O'Brien, J. K. (1993). The importance of the work family with structured work and relapse prevention. *Journal of Applied Rehabilitation Counseling, 24*, 3–5.

Petronio, S. (2002). *The boundaries of privacy: Dialectics of disclosure*. New York, NY: State University of New York Press.

Pierce, C. A., Byrne, D., & Aguinis, H. (1996). Attraction in organizations: A model of workplace romance. *Journal of Organizational Behavior, 17,* 5–32.

Pitkin, H. F. (1998). *The attack of the blob.* Chicago, IL: University of Chicago Press.

Placencia, M. E. (2004). Rapport-building activities in corner shop interaction. *Journal of Sociolinguistics, 8,* 215–245.

Podsakoff, P. M., MacKenzie, S. B., Moorman, R. H., & Fetter, R. (1990). Transformational leader behaviors and their effects on followers' trust in leader, satisfaction, and organizational citizenship behaviors. *Leadership Quarterly, 1,* 107–142.

Porath, C. L., & Erez, A. (2009). Overlooked but not untouched: How rudeness reduces onlookers' performance on routine and creative tasks. *Organizational Behavior and Human Decision Processes, 109,* 29–44.

Porath, C. L., & Erez, A. (2007). Does rudeness really matter? The effects of rudeness on task performance and helpfulness. *Academy of Management Journal, 50,* 1181–1197.

Primeaux, P. (1992). Experiential ethics: A blueprint for personal and corporate ethics. *Journal of Business Ethics, 11,* 779–788.

Pritchard, M. S. (2006). *Professional integrity: Thinking ethically.* Lawrence, KS: University Press of Kansas.

Putnam, R. (2000). *Bowling alone: The collapse and revival of American community.* New York, NY: Simon & Schuster.

Quinn, R. E. (1977). Coping with cupid: The formation, impact, and management of romantic relationships in organizations. *Administrative Science Quarterly, 22,* 30–45.

Rafaeli, A., & Sutton, R. I. (1991). Emotional contrast strategies as means of social influence: Lessons from criminal interrogators and bill collectors. *Academy of Management Journal, 34,* 749–775.

Rawlins, W. K. (1981). *Friendship as a communicative achievement: A theory and an interpretive analysis of verbal reports* (Unpublished doctoral dissertation). Temple University, Philadelphia, PA.

Rawlins, W. K. (1985). Stalking interpersonal communication effectiveness: Social, individual or situational integration? In T. W. Benson (Ed.), *Speech communication in the twentieth century* (pp. 109–129). Carbondale, IL: Southern Illinois University Press.

Rawlins, W. K. (1992). *Friendship matters: Communication, dialectics, and the life course.* Hawthorne, NY: Aldine de Gruyter.

Rawlins, W. K. (1998). Theorizing public and private domains and practices of communication: Introductory concerns. *Communication Theory, 8,* 369–380.

Ray, E. B. (1993). When the links become chains: Considering dysfunctions of supportive communication in the workplace. *Communication Monographs, 60,* 106–111.

Richmond, V. P., & McCroskey, J. C. (1992). *Communication: Apprehension, avoidance, and effectiveness.* Scottsdale, AZ: Gorsuch Scarisbrick.

Rieff, P. (1987). *The triumph of the therapeutic: Uses of faith after Freud.* Chicago, IL: University of Chicago Press. (Original work published 1966)

Ritchie, D. (1987). *Power, coorientation, and the flow of information.* Paper presented at the meeting of the International Communication Association, Toronto, Canada.

Robinson, S. L., & Bennett, R. J. (1995). A typology of deviant workplace behaviors: A multidimensional scaling study. *Academy of Management Journal, 38,* 555–572.

Rogers, L. E., & Farace, R. V. (1975). Analysis of relational communication in dyads: New measurement procedures. *Human Communication Research, 1,* 222–239.

Roman, P. M., Blum, T. C., & Martin, J. K. (1992). "Enabling" of male problem drinkers in work groups. *British Journal of Addictions, 87,* 275–289.

Ruminski, E. L., & Holba, A. H. (Eds.) (2012). *Communicative understandings of women's leadership development: From ceilings of glass to labyrinth paths.* Lanham, MD: Lexington Books.

Sakurai, K., & Jex, S. M. (2012). Coworker incivility and incivility targets' work effort and counterproductive work behaviors: The moderating role of supervisor social support. *Journal of Occupational Health Psychology, 17,* 150–161.

Sanchez-Burke, J., Lee, F., Chao, I., Zhao, S., Nisbett, R., & Coo, J. (2003). Conversing across cultures: East-West communication styles in work and nonwork contexts. *Journal of Personality and Social Psychology, 85,* 363–371.

Schaufeli, W. B., Leiter, M. P., & Maslach, C. (2008). Burnout: 35 years of research and practice. *Career Development International, 14,* 204–220.

Schein, E. H. (1968). Organizational socialization and the profession of management. *Industrial Management Review, 9,* 1–16.

Schein, E. H. (1971). The individual, the organization, and the career: A conceptual scheme. *Journal of Applied Behavioral Science, 7,* 401–426.

Schminke, M. (Ed.) (2010). *Managerial ethics: Managing the psychology of morality.* New York, NY: Routledge.

Schneider, B. (1987). The people make the place. *Personnel Psychology, 40,* 437–453.

Schöen, D. (1983). *The reflective practitioner: How professionals think in action.* New York, NY: Basic Books.

Schrag, C. (1986). *Communicative praxis and the space of subjectivity.* Bloomington, IN: Indiana University Press.

Scollon, R., & Scollon, S. W. (1995). *Intercultural communication: A discourse approach.* Cambridge, MA: Blackwell.

Scott, C. R., Corman, S. R., & Cheney, G. (1998). Development of a structurational model of identification in the organization. *Communication Theory, 8,* 298–336.

Searle, J. R. (2000). What is a speech act? In R. J. Stainton (Ed.), *Perspectives in the philosophy of language: A concise anthology* (Vol. 2, pp. 253–268). Peterborough, Canada: Broadview Press.

Seeger, M. W. (1997). *Ethics and organizational communication.* Cresskill, NJ: Hampton.

Seibold, D. R., & Myers, K. K. (2006). Communication as structuring. In G. J. Shepherd, J. St. John, & T. Striphas (Eds.), *Communication as…Perspectives on theory* (pp. 143–152). Thousand Oaks, CA: Sage.

Sellars, M. (2004). Ideals of public discourse. In C. T. Sistare (Ed.), *Civility and its discontents: Civic virtue, toleration, and cultural fragmentation* (pp. 15–24). Lawrence, KS: University Press of Kansas.

Selznick, P. (1994). *The moral commonwealth: Social theory and the promise of community.* Berkeley, CA: University of California Press. (Original work published 1992)

Sen, A. K. (1985). *Commodities and capabilities.* Oxford, England: Elsevier Science Publishers.

Sen, A. K. (1993). Capability and well-being. In M. C. Nussbaum & A. K. Sen (Eds.), *The quality of life* (pp. 30–53). Oxford, England: Clarendon Press.

Sen, A. (1999). *Development as freedom.* New York, NY: Random House.

Sennett, R. (1974). *The fall of public man: On the social psychology of capitalism.* New York, NY: Vintage.

Sennett, R. (2008). *The craftsman.* New Haven, CT: Yale University Press.

Sherblom, J. C., Keranen, L., & Withers, L. A. (2002). Tradition, tension, and transformation: A structuration analysis of a game warden service in transition. *Journal of Applied Communication Research, 30,* 143–162.

Shils, E. (1997). *The virtue of civility: Selected essays on liberalism, tradition, and civil society* (S. Grosby, Ed.). Indianapolis, IN: Liberty Fund.

Shotter, J., & Cunliffe, A. L. (2003). Managers as practical authors: Everyday conversations for action. In D. Holman & R. Thorpe (Eds.), *Management and language* (pp. 15–37). London, England: Sage.

Sias, P. M. (1996). Constructing perceptions of differential treatment: An analysis of coworker discourse. *Communication Monographs, 63,* 171–187.

Sias, P. M. (2009a). *Organizing relationships: Traditional and emerging perspectives on workplace relationships.* Thousand Oaks, CA: Sage.

Sias, P. M. (2009b). Ostracism, cliques, and outcasts. In P. Lutgen-Sandvik & B. Davenport Sypher (Eds.), *Destructive organizational communication: Processes, consequences, and constructive ways of organizing* (pp. 145–163). New York, NY: Routledge.

Sias, P. M. (in press). Exclusive or exclusory: Workplace relationships, ostracism, and isolation. In B. L. Omdahl & J. M. H. Fritz (Eds.), *Problematic relationships in the workplace, volume 2.* New York, NY: Peter Lang.

Sias, P. M., Gallagher, E. B., Kopeneva, I., & Pederson, H. (2012). Maintaining workplace friendships: Perceived politeness and predictors of maintenance tactic choice. *Communication Research 39,* 239–268.

Sias, P. M., Heath, R. G., Perry, T., Silva, D., & Fix, B. (2004). Narratives of workplace friendship deterioration. *Journal of Social and Personal Relationships, 21,* 321–340.

Simons, T. (2002) Behavioral integrity: The perceived alignment between managers' words and deeds as a research focus. *Organization Science, 13,* 18–35.

Smith, C. A., Organ, D. W., & Near, J. P. (1983). Organizational citizenship behavior: Its nature and antecedents. *Journal of Applied Psychology, 68,* 653–663.

Sokolowski, R. (1991). The fiduciary relationships and the nature of professions. In E. D. Pellgrino, R. M. Veatch, & J. P. Langan (Eds.), *Ethics, trust, and the professions: Philosophical and cultural aspects* (pp. 23–43). Washington, DC: Georgetown University Press.

Sokolowski, R. (2000). *Introduction to phenomenology.* New York, NY: Cambridge University Press.

Sonnenfeld, J. A. (1985). Shedding light on the Hawthorne studies. *Journal of Occupational Behavior, 6,* 111–130.

Squires, G. (2005). Art, science and the professions. *Studies in Higher Education, 30,* 127–136.

Staley, J. C., Kagle, J. D., & Hatfield, A. K. (1987). Cancer patients and their co-workers: A study. *Social Work in Health Care, 13,* 101–112.

Starr, P. (1982). *The social transformation of American medicine.* New York, NY: Basic Books.

Stech, E. L. (1975). Sequential structure in human social communication. *Human Communication Research, 1,* 168–179.

Stohl, C. (1986). The role of memorable messages in the process of organizational socialization. *Communication Quarterly, 34,* 231–249.

Sullivan, J. (1988). Three roles of language in motivation theory. *Academy of Management Review, 1,* 104–115.

Sullivan, W. M. (1995). *Work and integrity: The crisis and promise of professionalism in America.* New York, NY: HarperCollins.

Sullivan, W. M. (2005). *Work and integrity: The crisis and promise of professionalism in America* (2nd ed.). San Francisco, CA: Jossey-Bass.

Sutton, R. I. (1991). Maintaining norms about expressed emotions: The case of bill collectors. *Administrative Science Quarterly, 36,* 245–268.

Sutton, R. I. (2007). *The no asshole rule: Building a civilized workplace and surviving one that isn't.* New York, NY: Business Plus.

Sypnowich, C. (2000). The civility of law: Between public and private. In M. P. D'Entrèves & U. Vogel (Eds.), *Public and private: Legal, political and philosophical perspectives* (pp. 93–116). London, England: Routledge.

Taggar, S., & Haines, V. Y. (2006). I need you, you need me: A model of initiated task interdependence. *Journal of Managerial Psychology, 21,* 211–230.

Tannen, D. (1991). *You just don't understand: Men and women in conversation.* New York, NY: Ballantine.

Tannen, D. (1998). *The argument culture: Moving from debate to dialogue.* New York, NY: Random House.

Tannen, D. (2002). Agonism in academic discourse. *Journal of Pragmatics, 34,* 1651–1669.

Taylor, C. (1989). *Sources of the self: The making of the modern identity.* Cambridge, MA: Harvard University Press.

Taylor, C. (2004). *Modern social imaginaries.* Durham, NC: Duke University Press.

Taylor, C. (2007). *A secular age.* Cambridge, MA: Belknap Press.

Taylor, J. R., & Van Every, E. J. (2000). *The emergent organization: Communication as site and surface.* Mahwah, NJ: Lawrence Erlbaum.

Thompson, J. B. (2011). Shifting boundaries of public and private life. *Theory, Culture and Society, 28,* 49–70.

Tims, A. R. (1986). Family political communication and social values. *Communication Research, 13,* 5–17.

Tomes, N. (2001). Merchants of health: Medicine and consumer culture in the United States, 1900–1940. *Journal of American History, 88,* 519–547.

Tracy, K. (1997). *Colloquium: Dilemmas of academic discourse.* Norwood, NJ: Ablex.

Tracy, K. (2008). "Reasonable hostility": Situation-appropriate face-attack. *Journal of Politeness Research, 4,* 169–191.

Tracy, K., & Baratz, S. (1993). Intellectual discussion in the academy as situated discourse. *Communication Monographs, 60,* 300–320.

Tracy, K., & Tracy, S. J. (1998). Rudeness at 911: Re-conceptualizing face and face attack. *Human Communication Research, 25,* 225–251.

Trenholm, S., & Jensen, A. (2004). *Interpersonal communication* (5th ed.). New York, NY: Oxford University Press.

Treviño, L. K. (1986). Ethical decision making in organizations: A person-situation interactionist model. *Academy of Management Review, 11,* 601–617.

Treviño, L. K., & Youngblood, S. A. (1990). Bad apples in bad barrels: A causal analysis of ethical decision-making behavior. *Journal of Applied Psychology, 75,* 378–385.

Troester, R. L., & Mester, C. S. (2007). *Civility in business and professional communication.* New York, NY: Peter Lang.

Troup, C. L., & Fulmer, L. (2007, November). *Domestic courtesy: Restraint as an expression of love at home*. Paper presented at the meeting of the National Communication Association, Chicago, IL.

Twale, D. J., & De Luca, B. M. (2008). *Faculty incivility: The rise of the academic bully culture and what to do about it*. San Francisco, CA: Jossey-Bass.

Van Maanen, J. (1975). Breaking in: Socialization to work. In R. Dubin (Ed.), *Handbook of work, organization, and society* (pp. 67–120). Chicago, IL: Rand McNally.

Van Maanen, J., & Schein, E. G. (1979). Toward a theory of organizational socialization. In B. M. Staw (Ed.), *Research in organizational behavior* (pp. 209–264). Greenwich, CT: JAI Press.

Van Vianen, A. E. M. (2000). Person-organization fit: The match between newcomers' and recruiters' preferences for organizational culture. *Personnel Psychology, 53*, 113–149.

Volf, M. (1991). *Work in the spirit: Toward a theology of work*. New York, NY: Oxford University Press.

Wagoner, R., & Waldron, V. R. (1999). How supervisors convey routine bad news: Facework at UPS. *Southern Communication Journal 64*, 193–210.

Waldron, V. R. (1994). Once more, with feeling: Reconsidering the role of emotion in work. In S. Deetz (Ed.), *Communication yearbook 17* (pp. 388–416).

Waldron, V. R. (2003). Relational maintenance in organizational settings. In D. J. Canary & M. Dainton (Eds.), *Maintaining relationships through communication: Relational, contextual, and cultural variations* (pp. 163–184). Mahwah, NJ: Lawrence Erlbaum.

Waldron, V. R., & Kassing, J. W. (2011). *Managing risk in communication encounters: Strategies for the workplace*. Thousand Oaks, CA: Sage.

Waldron, V. R., & Kelley, D. (2008). *Communicating forgiveness*. Thousand Oaks, CA: Sage.

Waldron, V. R., & Kloeber, D. N. (in press). Communicating forgiveness in work relationships. In B. L. Omdahl & J. M. H. Fritz (Eds.), *Problematic relationships in the workplace, volume 2*. New York, NY: Peter Lang.

Wallace, J. E. (1993). Professional and organizational commitment: Compatible or incompatible? *Journal of Vocational Behavior, 42*, 333–349.

Wallace, J. E. (1995). Organizational and professional commitment in professional and nonprofessional organizations. *Administrative Science Quarterly, 40*, 228–255.

Wanous, J. P. (1992). *Organizational entry: Recruitment, selection and socialization of newcomers* (2nd ed.). Reading, MA: Addison-Wesley.

Ward, L. (1968). *Some effects of the structure of relationships on interpersonal behavior in the dyad* (Unpublished PhD dissertation). University of Wisconsin, Madison, WI.

Watson, K. M. (1982). An analysis of communication patterns: A method of discriminating leader and subordinate roles. *Academy of Management Journal, 25*, 107–120.

Watts, R. J. (2003). *Politeness*. New York, NY: Cambridge University Press.

Watzlawick, P., & Beavin, J. (1967). Some formal aspects of communication. *American Behavioral Scientist, 10*(8), 4–8.

Watzlawick, P., Beavin, J., & Jackson, D. D. (1967). *Pragmatics of human communication*. New York, NY: Norton.

Weick, K. (1976). Educational organizations as loosely coupled systems. *Administrative Science Quarterly, 21*, 1–19.

Weick, K. E. (1995). *Sensemaking in organizations*. Thousand Oaks, CA: Sage.

Whyte, W. (1956). *The organization man*. New York, NY: Simon & Schuster.

Wieland, S. M. B., Bauer, J. C., & Deetz, S. (2009). Excessive careerism and destructive life stresses: The role of entrepreneurialism in colonizing identities. In P. Lutgen-Sandvik & B. Davenport

Sypher (Eds.), *Destructive organizational communication: Processes, consequences, and constructive ways of organizing*. New York, NY: Routledge.

Willihnganz, S., Hart, J. L., & Willard, C. A. (2003). The logic of message design in organisational argument. In D. Holman & R. Thorpe (Eds.), *Management and language* (pp. 104–120). London, England: Sage.

Woods, R. H., Badzinski, D. M., Fritz, J. M. H., & Yeates, S. E. (2012). The "ideal professor" and gender effects in higher education. *Christian Higher Education, 11,* 158–176.

Woolley, A. (2008). Does civility matter? *Osgoode Hall Law Journal, 46*(1), 175–188.

Zemke, R., Raines, C., & Filipczak, B. (2000). *Generations at work: Managing the clash of veterans, boomers, xers and nexters in your workplace*. New York, NY: AMACOM.

Author Index

Acker, J., 176, 209
Aguinis, H., 174, 227
Albrecht, T. L., 113, 117, 120, 209
Alexander, M.W., 9, 209
Alin, P., 126, 209
Allen, B.J., 2, 49, 186, 209, 211
Altman, I., 175, 209
Alvesson, M., 108, 161, 209, 210
Anderson, L.E., 54, 55, 103, 131, 203, 210, 213, 223, 227
Andersson, L.M., x, 2, 10, 12, 71, 72, 93, 129, 130, 141, 178, 183, 185, 210, 227
Ardalan, K., 137, 210
Arendt, H., 8, 10, 11, 17, 29, 31, 40, 43, 45, 46, 57, 58, 64, 92, 94, 134, 135, 136, 138, 151, 160, 161, 177, 178, 185, 189, 208, 210, 224
Argyris, C., 143, 210
Aristotle, 13, 23, 25, 26, 34, 35, 36, 40, 44, 75, 210
Arnett, R.C., ix, x, xi, xiv, 2, 3, 7, 9, 10, 11, 12, 13, 14, 15, 17, 18, 20, 23, 27, 28,

31, 39, 40, 41, 43, 45, 46, 47, 48, 59, 63, 64, 69, 70, 71, 84, 89, 91, 92, 93, 94, 96, 97, 98, 99, 100, 102, 103, 104, 105, 106, 107, 108, 109, 115, 117, 119, 120, 123, 124, 127, 130, 131, 132, 136, 138, 139, 140, 142, 143, 144, 146, 149, 152, 154, 155, 156, 157, 158, 159, 160, 161, 162, 163, 164, 165, 166, 167, 168, 169, 170, 173, 174, 175, 176, 177, 178, 179, 181, 182, 183, 184, 185, 186, 187, 199, 201, 202, 203, 208, 210, 211, 217, 219
Ashcraft, K.L., 2, 13, 17, 49, 110, 112, 113, 116, 117, 175, 176, 181, 182, 183, 184, 185, 186, 201, 206, 208, 211, 213
Ashforth, B., 147, 211

Badzinski, D.M., 158, 233
Baker, S., 25, 211
Baker-Ohler, M., 156, 211
Baratz, S., 85, 200, 231

Barbee, A.P., 186, 214
Barber, B., 4, 25, 49, 50, 56, 211
Barge, J.K., 17, 35, 46, 54, 91, 93, 119, 140, 195, 211
Baron, R., 73, 218
Barrett, H., 74, 75, 76, 156, 164, 211
Barry, D., 161, 211
Bartunek, J.M., 126, 152, 174, 215, 218, 222
Batchelor, J.A., 80, 225
Bateman, T.S., 99, 105, 211
Bateson, G., 113, 211
Bauer, J.C., 99, 232
Bauman, I., 114, 211
Baxter, L.A., 13, 19, 83, 109, 116, 121, 140, 174, 175, 176, 177, 211, 212, 227
Beavin, J., 77, 113, 232
Bell, L.M., xiii, 2, 23, 46, 64, 93, 115, 139, 155, 168, 173, 203, 211
Bellah, R.N., 7, 161, 177, 197, 211
Benhabib, S., 177, 211
Bennett, R.J., 178, 228
Berardino, L., 7, 219
Berger, C.R., 115, 211, 212
Berger, P., 115, 127, 212
Bies, R.J., 94, 212
Blackburn, M., 5, 24, 212
Blau, P.M., 157, 212
Blum, T.C., 179, 229
Blyler, N.R., 120, 212
Boje, D.M., 161, 162, 212
Bok, S., 3, 14, 212
Bolt, S.B., 54, 55, 131, 203, 210
Bone, J.E., 2, 212
Borden, S.L., ix, 5, 9, 11, 15, 16, 23, 24, 27, 34, 35, 39, 46, 47, 48, 71, 91, 199, 212
Bourdieu, P., 186, 212
Bowers, J.W., 79, 80, 98, 107, 108, 109, 150, 188, 189, 191, 223
Boyce, M.E., 161, 212
Brandeis, P., 56, 205
Bretz, R.D., 162, 212
Brewer, E.W., 168, 212
Brewer, K.B., 24, 212
Bridge, K., 19, 140, 174, 175, 176, 177, 212
Brien, A., 4, 5, 212

Brown, B.J., 9, 209
Brown, M.H., 126, 151, 212
Brown, P., 22, 65, 75, 76, 78, 79, 80, 83, 106, 108, 126, 181, 191, 212
Brubacher, J.S., 79, 212
Buber, M., 18, 102, 134, 210, 213, 220
Burke, K., 127, 213
Buzzanell, P., 96, 98, 153, 213, 219
Buzzanell, P.M., 186, 213, 223
Byrne, D., 163, 174, 213, 227

Calabrese, R.J., 115, 211
Caldwell, D.F., 162, 227
Caldwell, M., 69, 72, 213
Cameron, K.S., 130, 213
Cappella, J.N., 113, 176, 213
Carbaugh, D., 68, 213
Carroll, A.B., 6, 213
Carter, S. L., 2, 3, 10, 63, 65, 69, 111, 143, 147, 213
Chaffee, S.H., 113, 225
Chao, G., 174, 213
Chao, G.T., 163, 213
Chao, I., 229
Chandler, T.A., 175, 215
Charlton, B., 213
Chatman, J.A., 162, 227
Cheney, G., 2, 7, 9, 13, 41, 62, 122, 185, 213, 229
Chiaramonte, P., 176, 225
Christians, C.G., 22, 34, 54, 213
Clark, B.R., 161, 213
Cloud, D., 3, 65, 224
Cocking, D., 5, 7, 9, 15, 23, 24, 26, 27, 28, 29, 30, 31, 36, 226
Cohen, A., 100, 213
Collins, B.L., 113, 186, 213
Colvin, R.H., 179, 180, 213
Coo, J., 21, 229
Cooley, R.E., 113, 209
Cooper, C.L., 130, 220, 221
Cooren, F., 13, 79, 110, 112, 113, 114, 115, 118, 122, 127, 149, 202, 211, 214
Corman, S.R., 117, 121, 214, 225, 226, 229
Cortina, L.M., 118, 129, 214, 223
Coupland, J., 84, 214

Crawford, M., 136, 214
Crozier, M., 117, 120, 214
Csikszentmihalyi, M., 5, 47, 133, 151, 155, 214, 218
Cummings, L.L., 151, 168, 217, 221, 227
Cunliffe, A.L., 148, 149, 230
Cunningham, M.R., 184, 214
Cupach, W.R., 141, 225

Damon, W., 5, 47, 133, 155, 218
Dansereau, F., 148, 175, 214, 218
Davenport, S. B., 1, 2, 3, 7, 73, 74, 79, 80, 118, 128, 130, 184, 189, 205, 208, 213, 214, 218, 222, 224, 230, 232, 233
Davetian, B., 3, 16, 22, 63, 64, 65, 66, 67, 74, 214
Deetz, S., 6, 118, 209, 232
Deetz, S.A., 99, 117, 214
D'Entrèves, M.P., 204
De Luca, B.M., 2, 5, 88, 157, 232
DeTurk, S., 81, 215
DeWine, S., 85, 215
DiGiulio, J.F., 180, 215
Dillard, J.P., 77, 174, 215
Druen, P.B., 184, 214
Dubinskas, F.A., 126, 215
Duck, S., 114, 121, 126, 176, 215
Dunham, R.B., 151, 168, 217
Dutta, M.J., 2, 68, 222
Dutton, J.E., 4, 130, 152, 174, 216, 218

Eakins, B., 121, 215
Eakins, G., 121, 215
Einarsen, S., 130, 220, 221
Elias, N., 3, 16, 57, 64, 65, 69, 70, 74, 188, 215
Englehardt, T., 24, 215
Erez, A., 78, 108, 111, 129, 228

Fairhurst, G.T., 22, 83, 109, 113, 114, 115, 116, 117, 120, 121, 148, 149, 150, 155, 159, 165, 171, 175, 185, 214, 215
Farace, R.V., 113, 228
Fay, M.J., 116, 192, 215, 216
Feldman, M.S., 176, 210, 224

Ferguson, A., 39, 64, 216
Ferris, G.R., 162, 221
Fetter, R., 228
Fields, W.C., 121, 122, 123, 125, 126, 130, 157, 159, 225
Filipczak, B., 2, 233
Fine, G.A., 174, 175, 216
Fisher, W.R., 41, 216
Fix, B., 140, 230
Fletcher, C., 4, 94, 130, 151, 185, 224
Flexner, A., 56, 57, 137, 147, 198
Follet, M.P., 52, 216
Foley, M.K., 114, 215
Ford, J.D., 140, 148, 216
Ford, L.W., 140, 148, 216
Forni, P.M., 2, 3, 10, 17, 22, 27, 63, 69, 70, 72, 74, 79, 83, 103, 111, 131, 188, 193, 207, 216
Fredrickson, B.L., 4, 130, 216
Friedberg, E., 117, 214
Friedson, E., 4, 54, 216
Fritz, J.M.H., xiv, 1, 2, 3, 6, 7, 8, 9, 10, 13, 15, 18, 19, 21, 23, 31, 46, 64, 65, 71, 72, 73, 74, 82, 91, 92, 93, 94, 97, 100, 103, 108, 111, 115, 116, 117, 118, 129, 130, 139, 140, 141, 155, 156, 157, 158, 159, 160, 161, 162, 163, 164, 168, 173, 174, 176, 177, 178, 179, 185, 187, 192, 201, 202, 203, 205, 207, 210, 211, 213, 214, 215, 216, 217, 219, 220, 221, 222, 223, 225, 226, 227, 230, 232, 233
Fulmer, L., 41, 231

Gadamer, H.G., 68, 106, 217
Galanti, S.P., 58, 217
Gallagher, E.B., 108, 174, 230
Gannon, M.J., 21, 217
Gardner, D.G., 151, 168, 217
Gardner, H.G., 5, 6, 16, 47, 58, 59, 61, 62, 133, 136, 155, 217, 218, 226
Gardner, P.D., 163, 213
Garner, J.T., 167, 218
Gecas, V., 27, 218
Geddes, D., 73, 218
Gersick, C.J.G., 152, 174, 182, 218

Giacalone, R.A., 222
Gibb, J.R., 18, 80, 81, 142, 143, 144, 145,
    146, 147, 165, 169, 190, 218
Giddens, A., 78, 112, 115, 116, 121, 206, 218
Giles, H., 70, 125, 218
Gill, M., 80, 128, 184, 205, 214
Gill, M.J., 2, 80, 118, 184, 189, 218
Gill, R. 113, 186, 213
Ginsberg, B., 137, 139, 145, 218
Goffman, E., 78, 79, 143, 183, 218
Gonthier, G., 5, 63, 131, 192, 218
Gordon, T., 82, 103, 218
Gottman, J., 113, 218
Gouldner, A., 12, 157, 200, 218
Graen, G.B., 148, 175, 214, 218, 223
Graham, J.W., 17, 18, 91, 92, 101, 102, 103,
    106, 158, 159, 164, 218
Grant, A.M., 13, 219
Green, S.G., 120, 150, 171, 215
Greil, A.L., 113, 223
Grice, H.P., 76, 219
Griffin, C.L., 2, 212
Groom, S.A., 9, 217, 219
Gurstein, R., 177, 178, 219
Guzley, R.M., 108, 118, 219

Habermas, J., 64, 74, 219
Haga, W.J., 175, 214
Haines, V.Y., 108, 231
Hall, A., 7, 219
Hall, M.A., 135, 107, 219
Hammoud, A., 96, 98, 153, 219
Hansen, A.M., 130, 220
Harden, J., xiv, 114, 211
Harden, J.M., 77, 127, 215, 219
Harrison, R., 125, 157, 219
Harrison, W.H., 61, 219
Hart, J.L., 141, 233
Hatch, M.J., 176, 224
Hatch, N.O., 5, 6, 8, 49, 219
Hatfield, A.K., 181, 230
Hayes, J., 1, 224
Heath, R.G., 140, 230
Hebden, J., 125, 176, 180, 219
Hegstrom, T.G., 156, 166, 219
Hess, J., 83, 134, 168, 176, 183, 192, 219,

220
Hickson, M., 2, 88, 220
Hirokawa, R.Y., 171, 220
Hoban, G., 137, 220
Hodge, R., 123, 124, 159, 220
Hodson, R., 60, 136, 137, 207, 220
Hoel, H., 130, 220, 221
Hofstede, G., 21, 220
Hogg, M., 183, 220
Hogh, A., 130, 220
Holba, A., xiii, 13, 41, 47, 84, 89, 156, 201,
    211, 217, 220
Holba, A.H., 156, 229
Holba, A.M., 9, 20, 45, 211, 220
Hollinger, R.C., 179, 180, 220
Holmes, J., 60, 113, 116, 126, 151, 220
Hopkins, K., 185, 193, 223
Horan, S.M., 174, 220
Hosman, L.A., 171, 220
Hullman, G.A., 82, 220
Humphrey, R., 121, 221
Hunter, F.T., 113, 221
Hutton, J., 25, 221

Indvik, J., 2, 221
Infante, D.A., 85, 200, 221
Isabella, L., 125, 150, 156, 163, 174, 175, 222

Jablin, F., 113, 221
Jackson, D.D., 77, 113, 232
Jacobs, J., 145, 199, 221
Jagatic, K., 118, 221
Jensen, A., 77, 190, 231
Jex, S.M., 229
Johannesen, R.L., 172, 221
Johnson, D., 1, 115, 221
Johnson, M., 159, 223
Johnson, P.R., 2, 221
Johnson, T.W., 148, 218
Jordan, J.M., 155, 185, 215
Judge, T.A., 162, 212, 221

Kagle, J.D., 181, 230
Kaptein, M., 10, 221
Kassing, J.W., 18, 103, 106, 141, 148, 156,
    166, 183, 188, 191, 192, 221, 232

Kasson, J.F., 69, 72, 221

Katz, R., 113, 221

Keashly, L., 1, 118, 221

Kelley, D., 232

Kendall, B.E., 7, 41, 62, 185, 213

Kennedy-Lightsey, C., 130, 224

Keranen, L., 122, 229

Kervin, L.K., 137, 222

Kiggundu, M.N., 108, 222

Kimball, B.A., ix, x, 3, 4, 5, 6, 8, 9, 12, 13, 15, 26, 29, 30, 33, 38, 39, 43, 45, 46, 47, 48, 49, 50, 51, 52, 53, 55, 56, 57, 59, 88, 90, 91, 94, 95, 99, 100, 101, 102, 112, 133, 134, 135, 137, 138, 173, 186, 189, 196, 197, 198, 199, 200, 202, 203, 205, 206, 222

Kingwell, M., 2, 3, 16, 38, 63, 64, 65, 66, 67, 68, 69, 70, 74, 76, 77, 78, 80, 84, 94, 106, 111, 167, 222

Kinney, T.A., 118, 130, 222

Kirby, E.L., 121, 222

Kirkpatrick, D.C., 114, 215

Kisselburgh, L.G., 2, 68, 222

Kline, S.L., 116, 215, 216

Kloeber, D.N., 141,192, 232

Knouse, S.B., 178, 222

Kohn, M.L., 117, 206, 222

Kol, Y., 100, 213

Kolb, D.M., 126, 215, 222

Konovsky, M.A., 166, 222

Kopeneva, I., 108, 174, 230

Kopf, J., 126, 225

Kram, K.E., 125, 150, 156, 163, 174, 175, 222

Kramer, M., 18, 112, 115, 119, 124, 163, 204, 222

Krause, E.A., 12, 56, 157, 222

Kress, G., 123, 124, 159, 220

Kristof, A.L., 162, 222

Krone, K.J., 121, 222

Kuhn, T.R., 13, 110, 112, 202, 211

Kultgen, J., 4, 6, 8, 16, 54, 55, 56, 58, 223

Kurth, S., 175, 223

Laczniak, G.R., 61, 226

LaFasto, F.M.J., 61, 183, 223

Lakoff, R., 159, 223

Lair, D.J., 7, 41, 62, 185, 213, 218

Lamert, S.J., 185, 223

Langan, J.P., 6, 216, 227, 230

Langer, E., 115, 223

Langhout, R., 129, 214

Larson, C.E., 61, 183, 198, 223

Larson, M.S., 4, 6, 29, 47, 49, 50, 53, 90, 196, 199, 201, 223

Lasch, C., 85, 177, 200, 223

Laverty, M., 3, 74, 75, 76, 79, 223

Lee, F., 21, 229

Lee, Y., 162, 223

Leeds-Hurwitz, W., 112, 223

Leiter, M.P., 139, 229

Leitko, T.A., 113, 117, 223

Leoussi, A.S., 55, 223

Levinas, E., 178, 210, 223

Levinson, S., 22, 65, 75, 76, 78, 79, 80, 83, 106, 108, 126, 181, 191, 212

Lewis, L.K., 138, 165, 188, 223

Liden, R.C., 175, 223

Lim, S., 118, 223

Lim, T.S., 79, 80, 98, 107, 108, 109, 150, 188, 189, 191, 223

Lippert, L., 141, 225

Little, M., 17, 35, 46, 54, 91, 93, 119, 140, 195, 211

Liu, M., 186, 223

Louis, M.R., 120, 223, 224

Lozano-Reich, N.M., 2, 65, 224

Lucas, K., 98, 213

Luckmann, T., 115, 212

Lutgen-Sandvik, P., 4, 12, 94, 130, 131, 151, 153, 185, 188, 189, 218, 222, 224, 230, 232

Lutz, C.S., 30, 224

Lyotard, J.F., 30, 64, 161, 224

MacKenzie, S.B., 7, 99, 100, 105, 167, 178, 227, 228

MacIntyre, A., v, ix, x, 6, 7, 8, 9, 11, 14, 15, 16, 23, 24, 25, 26, 27, 28, 29, 30, 31, 32, 33, 34, 35, 36, 37, 38, 39, 40, 41, 42, 43, 46, 47, 48, 50, 78, 88, 90, 91, 93, 105, 107, 109, 140, 142, 143, 144,

158, 161, 178, 185, 196, 212, 224, 226
Madlock, P.E., 130, 224
Madsen, R., 7, 161, 177, 211
Magley, V., 129, 214
Maister, D.H., 7, 54, 88, 131, 149, 224
Malinowski, B., 84, 224
Malone, P., 1, 224
Mancl, A.C., 152, 189, 224
Manning, S., 138, 224
Markell, P., 136, 224
Marks, S.L., 175, 177, 179, 180, 224
Martin, J., 176, 224
Martin, J.K., 179, 229
Maslach, C., 139, 229
May, L., 47, 224
May, S., 117, 224
May, W.F., 47, 48, 101, 135, 224
Mayfield, J., 126, 225
Mayfield, M., 126, 225
Mayo, C., 3, 79, 225
McAllister, D.J., 178, 183, 225
McCall, G.J., 112, 223, 225
McCarther, S.M., 147, 225
McCornak, S.A., 82, 226
McCroskey, J.C., 74, 221, 228
McElhinney, T., 24, 227
McGhee, P., 5, 24, 212
McGlone, M.S., 80, 225
McLeod, J.M., 113, 225
McPhee, R.D., 121, 214, 225
Mead, G.H., 112, 207, 225
Mease, J., 113, 186, 213
Meglich, P., 118, 225
Mester, C.S., 2, 3, 12, 22, 63, 70, 73, 188, 189, 190, 191, 231
Metts, S., 141, 225
Mikkelsen, E.G., 130, 220
Miller, C., 184, 225
Miller, K.I., 113, 117, 143, 204, 225
Millhous, L.M., 186, 225
Mills, A., 176, 225
Minami, T., 148, 218
Moag, J.S., 94, 212
Moch, M.K., 121, 122, 123, 125, 126, 130,

159, 225
Moore, G., 24, 90, 226
Moore, W.E., 4, 226
Moorman, R.H., 228
Morgan, G., 159, 226
Morrissey, K., 5, 131, 218
Mumby, D., 117, 128, 214, 224, 226
Mundrake, G.A., 9, 209
Myers, J.H., 179, 180, 213, 214
Myers, K.K., 113, 156, 214, 226, 229

Nakamura, J., 60, 226
Namie, G., 118, 130, 224
Namie, R., 118, 130, 224
Naoi, A., 117, 222
Naughton, M., 61, 226
Near, J.P., 99, 230
Neuwirth, K., 155, 185, 215
Newman, H., 115, 223
Nicotera, A.M., 85, 215
Nisbett, R., 21, 229
Noordegraaf, M., 4, 12, 18, 46, 53, 54, 57, 58, 59, 60, 88, 96, 97, 99, 138, 157, 226
Nunnally, J.C., 127, 226
Nussbaum, M.C., 30, 226, 229

Oakley, J., 5, 7, 9, 15, 23, 24, 26, 27, 28, 29, 30, 31, 36, 226
O'Barr, W.M., 226
O'Brien, J.K., 181, 227
Ohman, R., 6, 226
O'Keefe, B.J., 82, 225, 226
Oliver, R.T., 8, 78, 208, 226
Omdahl, B.L., x, xi, xiii, 1, 2, 3, 21, 31, 73, 117, 118, 129, 150, 168, 170, 178, 187, 190, 192, 202, 210, 213, 214, 215, 216, 217, 219, 220, 221, 222, 223, 225, 226, 227, 230, 232
O'Reilly, C.A., 162, 227
Organ, D.W., 7, 15, 17, 18, 91, 92, 99, 100, 101, 102, 103, 104, 105, 140, 159, 166, 167, 178, 187, 211, 222, 227, 230
Orris, J.B., 148, 218

Pace, R., 171, 220
Packard, V., 143, 227
Palmer, P.J., 179, 227
Parry, D., 85, 215
Parsons, T., 56, 196, 227
Patton, T.O., 3, 227
Pearce, K.A., 113, 114, 151, 227
Pearce, W.B., 112, 113, 114, 161, 227
Pearson, C.M., x, 1, 2, 3, 10, 12, 14, 71, 72,
    93, 111, 112, 118, 128, 129, 130, 131,
    141, 178, 183, 185, 202, 204, 210,
    227
Peck, M.S., 2, 63, 65, 70, 111, 227
Pederson, H., 108, 174, 230
Pellegrino, E.D., 6, 23, 24, 25, 31, 32, 48, 227
Penington, B., 152, 169, 224
Perrow, C., 186, 227
Perry, T., 140, 230
Peters, R.H., 181, 227
Peterson, S.A., 113, 223
Petronio, S., 84, 179, 186, 227
Pierce, C.A., 174, 227
Pierce, J.L., 168, 217
Pitkin, H.F., 178, 228
Placencia, M.E., 84, 228
Podsakoff, P.M., 7, 91, 99, 100, 102, 105,
    167, 178, 227, 228
Porath, C., 1, 2, 3, 14, 72, 93, 111, 112, 118,
    128, 129, 131, 202, 204, 227
Porath, C.L., 78, 108, 129, 228
Powesland, P., 70, 125, 218
Primeaux, P., 9, 10, 161, 178, 228
Pritchard, M.S., 5, 228
Putnam, R., 2, 228

Quinn, R.E., 33, 174, 228

Rafaeli, A., 88, 228
Raines, C., 2, 233
Rancer, A.S., 85, 200, 221
Rawlins, W.K., 11, 114, 175, 177, 228
Ray, E.B., 179, 228
Remke, R.V., 98, 213
Richmond, V.P., 74, 228

Rieff, P., 177, 228
Riforgiate, S., 4, 94, 130, 151, 185, 224
Ritchie, D., 115, 228
Ritz, D., 7, 41, 62, 185, 213
Robinson, S.L., 178, 228
Roebuck, J.B., 2, 88, 220
Rogers, L.E., 113, 114, 215, 228
Roman, P.M., 179, 181, 229
Rudy, W., 59, 212
Ruminski, E.L., xiii, 156, 217, 229

Sakurai, K., 129, 229
Sanchez-Burks, J., 21, 229
Sarr, R.A., 114, 215
Schaufeli, W.B., 139, 229
Scheerhorn, D.R., 171, 220
Schein, E.G., 119, 232
Schein, E.H., 5, 127, 229
Schminke, M., 178, 229
Schmisseur, A.M., 165, 188, 223
Schneider, C.E., 135, 197, 219
Schoenbach, L., 107, 212
Scholz, T.M.L., 2, 212
Schooler, C., 107, 196, 212
Schrag, C., 14, 96, 97, 151, 229
Schwartz, M.S., 10, 221
Scollon, R., 76, 177, 229
Scollon, S., 76, 177, 229
Scott, C.R., 121, 229
Scott, W.R. 157, 212
Searle, J.R., 113, 126, 229
Seeger, M.W., 172, 229
Segrin, C., 77, 215
Seibold, D.R., 113, 115, 156, 229
Sellars, M., 3, 66, 229
Selznick, P., 3, 47, 166, 167, 229
Sen, A.K., 30, 229
Sennet, R., 18, 48, 61, 69, 95, 104, 108, 135,
    136, 137, 142, 144, 145, 146, 147,
    148, 151, 169, 170, 173, 177, 178,
    189, 190, 201, 203, 208, 229
Sheehan, M.J., 130, 220
Shenoy, S., 98, 213
Shepherd, G.J., 82, 225, 226, 229
Sherblom, J.C., 122, 229

Shils, E., 8, 63, 66, 230
Shotter, J., 148, 149, 230
Sias, P.M., 19, 60, 108, 114, 117, 118, 125, 140, 142, 152, 169, 174, 175, 183, 185, 196, 230
Silva, D., 140, 230
Simmons, J.L., 112, 225,
Simons, T., 130, 150, 162, 230
Sitkin, S.B., 176, 224
Slomczynski, K., 127, 222
Smeds, R., 126, 209
Smith, C.A., 99, 100, 101, 104, 218
Smith, P., 70, 125, 230
Snavely, B.K., 120, 150, 171, 215
Sneed, K.A., 192, 220
Sokolowski, R., 12, 106, 230
Sonnenfeld, J.A., 143, 230
Squires, G., 5, 28, 30, 41, 137, 151, 230
Staley, J.C., 181, 182, 230
Starr, P., 198, 230
Stech, E.L., 113, 230
Stephens, K.K. 165, 223
Stohl, C., 126, 127, 151, 230
Stubbe, M., 60, 113, 116, 126, 151, 220
Sullivan, J., 126, 230
Sullivan, W.M., 4, 5, 6, 7, 8, 9, 10, 12, 15, 19, 29, 38, 43, 45, 46, 47, 48, 49, 53, 54, 55, 56, 59, 62, 88, 90, 94, 95, 101, 104, 133, 134, 135, 137, 138, 139, 142, 147, 150, 154, 157, 161, 173, 177, 185, 186, 189, 191, 195, 196, 197, 198, 199, 200, 201, 202, 203, 204, 205, 206, 207, 208, 211, 230, 231
Sutton, R.I., 5, 72, 88, 128, 131, 193, 231
Swidler, A., 7, 161, 177, 211
Sypnowich, C., 3, 231

Taggar, S., 231
Tannen, D., 84, 85, 88, 200, 231
Taylor, C., 9, 51, 78, 137, 144, 161, 177, 185, 231
Taylor, D., 175, 209
Taylor, J.E., 126, 209
Taylor, J.R., 113, 231

Thompson, F., 114, 214
Thompson, J.B., 177, 231
Thralls, C., 120, 212
Tims, A.R., 113, 231
Tipton, S.M., 7, 161, 177, 211
Tomes, N., 198, 231
Traber, M., 22, 34, 54, 213
Tracy, K., 65, 69, 78, 85, 88, 200, 226
Tracy, S.J., 69, 78, 226
Trenholm, S., 77, 190, 231
Treviño, L.K., 178, 231
Troester, R.L., 2, 3, 12, 22, 63, 70, 73, 188, 189, 190, 191, 231
Troup, C.L., 41, 231
Turbill, J., 137, 222
Twale, D.J., 2, 5, 88, 157, 232

Uhl-Bien, M., 148, 175, 218

Valde, K.W., 172, 221
Van Maanen, J., 119, 232
Van Vianen, A.E.M., 162, 232
Veatch, R.M., 6, 216, 227, 230
Vogel, U., 177, 214, 231
Volf, M., 61, 232

Wacquant, L.J.D., 186, 212
Wagoner, R., 150, 191, 232
Waldron, V.R., 141, 148, 150, 166, 175, 183, 188, 191, 192, 232
Wallace, J.E., 4, 12, 158, 204, 232
Wanous, J.P., 163, 232
Ward, L., 113, 115, 232
Watson, K.M., 113, 232
Watts, R.J., 79, 232
Watzlawick, P., 77, 113, 232
Weick, K.E., 116, 120, 169, 232
Weir, K.E., 165, 188, 223
Whedbee, K.E., 172, 221
Whyte, W., 177, 232
Wieland, S.M.B., 99, 232
Wilkins, V.M., 162, 223
Willard, C.A., 141, 233
Williams, C.D., 10, 97, 117, 130, 155, 178, 217

Williams, J., 103, 129, 214
Willihnganz, S., 141, 149, 233
Willmott, H., 118, 161, 210
Withers, L.A., 122, 229
Witteman, H., 174, 215
Witty, T.E., 181, 227
Woods, R.H., 158, 233
Woolley, A., 85, 233

Yeates, S.E., 158, 233
Youngblood, S.A., 178, 231

Zemke, R., 2, 233
Zhao, S., 21, 80, 229
Zopf, K.J., 179, 180, 213

Subject Index

Abuse. *See* Verbal abuse
Academic context. *See* Higher education;
    Institution(s)
Accountability
    as attribute of professionals, 6, 35, 55, 62
    based on role, 34
    institutional, to the community, 162
    of managers to an organization, 162
    provided by background narrative of orga-
        nization, 162
    in public work friendships, to organization,
        184, 187
Acknowledgment, 98, 194
    as element of civility, 75, 103
Action
    Arendtian, 8, 10, 11, 12, 15, 17, 30, 31,
        42, 45, 46, 57, 61, 64, 128, 133,
        134–136, 140, 153, 185, 208
    as basis for ethics in Homeric society, 33
    communicative. *See* Communicative action
    constructive, 11, 168, 172
    cooperative, 66, 68, 105, 108, 203
    coordinated, 3, 4, 14, 27, 35, 74, 107, 129

corrective, 67, 103
as distinct from labor and/or work, 12, 57,
    134, 135, 136
as element of professional life, 12
ethical, 27
meaningful, 13, 45, 99, 103
professional, 43, 46, 73, 94
as professional distinctiveness, 135
rhetorical, 64
strategic. *See* Personal strategic action
virtuous, 14, 24, 42
See also Public sphere
Addams, Jane, 138
Administrative density, 139
Administrative guardians, 145
Administrative roles, 137
Affect. *See* Positive affect
Affective atmosphere, 169, 170
Agent, embedded. *See* Embedded agent
Altruism. *See* Organizational citizenship
All-administrative university, 145
Apology, 141
Apprentice, 145, 146, 147, 189

Apprenticeship, 49, 201

Anger, 67, 68

Architectonic occupation(s), 8, 9, 55, 57, 90, 137 *See also* Craftwork; Profession; Professions

Arête, 13, 24

Argument(s), 85, 88, 98, 102, 144

    assertive, 88

Argument culture, 85, 200

    of academia, 200

Argumentativeness, 16, 85, 95

Aristotle. *See* Virtue ethics

Aristotelian ethics, 24, 25, 26, 29, 31, 32, 33, 34, 35, 36, 40, 75, 90

    See also Virtue ethics

Arrogance, 73, 148, 200

Art, 50, 138

    vs. craft, 137

    and public poetry, 185

    vs. science, 137

Assertiveness, 85

    as element of civility, 74

Attentiveness, 108

    to corporate social responsibility, 202

    to face needs of coworkers, 109

    to goals of self and others, 109

    to goods, 97, 162

    lack of, as incivility, 71

    to limits, 96

    to local norms/to the local and particular, 28, 157

    to mission, 163

    to the other/others, 75, 77, 99, 193

    to the "positive face" of an organization, 106

    thoughtful, 2

Attribution(s), 128

    charitable. *See* Charitable attributions

Attribution biases, 121

Authentic self, 11

Author manager, 148

Authority, 38, 67, 73, 144

    attributes of speech lacking, 171

    community, 47

    in craftwork framework of defensiveness/supportiveness, rather than control, 145

    evaluative, 37

    of the expert, 145

    of moral frameworks, 144

    of practice, 144

    pseudo-, 145

    role-based, 123

    over social functions, of professionals, 198

    of a tradition, 11

Autonomy

    as characteristic of professions/professionals, 4, 5, 18, 49, 56, 60

    as element of concern in politeness, 76, 79, 80, 84, 107, 108

    as element of integration/separation dialectic, 84, 109

    personal, 86

Autonomy face. *See* Face

Background framework

    professional civility as, 9, 131

    roles as, 187

    of shared understanding of the good, 143

    tradition of professions and civility as communicative virtue, for professional civility, 105

Backstabbing, 1, 73

Balance

    between connection and autonomy, 181

    between hope and cynicism, 156

    between internal and external goods, 90

    between multiple spheres of life, 7, 40, 96, 181

    between professional autonomy and organizational demands, for professionals, 18

Behavioral integrity, 130, 162

Behavioral modeling. *See* Modeling

Bioethics, 24

Blended relationships, 19, 177

Boundaries

    blurring of, public and private, 178

    in contexts of assertive argument, 88

    of coworkers, respecting, 98

    of norms, 124

    organizational, narrowing, 169

    professional, 19, 60

of professions, expanded, 147
public and private, 84, 172, 178, 179, 180
relational, 192
role, 28, 98, 176
Broken covenant, 161
Bullying, 1, 55, 73, 118, 130, 192
Bullying relationships, 130
negative effects of, 130
Bureaucrat, 27
Bureaucratic organizations, as location for professional work, x, 97, 204
Bureaucratization, 157
of the academy, 139
See also Higher education
Burnham, Daniel, 138
Business
differentiated from professions, 55, 56, 134, 135, 196
excluded from professions, 56, 196
included in professions, 56, 57, 205
"managed professional," 60
as practice, 24, 90
as a profession, 29, 56, 57, 61, 205

Calling. *See* Professional work; Vocation
Canon of professions. *See* Professions
Capabilities perspective, 30
Care
contextual, 108
disinterested, as Levinasian, 158
for the inside (of organizations, on part of professionals), 202
for institutions. *See* Care for institutions
for local home, 12, 154, 155, 156–160
about one's work, as a defining feature of professions, 88
Care for institutions, xiii, xiv, 10, 15, 19, 92, 100, 153, 155, 156, 158, 162
Certainty
as civil/virtuous communicative response, 81
in craftwork framework of defensiveness/supportiveness, connected with expertise/public standards, 147
as element of defensive climate, 81, 147

provided by formal ritual(s), 70, 109
Change. *See* Organizational change
Character, 35
and civility, 65, 74
of an institution, 166
moral, 77, 94
of an organization, 157
professional, 37, 51, 200
shaped by professional civility, 13
virtues of, 35
virtuous, 26, 30
See also Virtue ethics
Character-based ethics. *See* Virtue ethics
Character traits. *See* Virtue ethics
Charitable attributions, 193
Charitable responses, 155
Choosing Civility; The 25 Rules of Considerate Conduct, 193
Christian colleges and universities, 158
Christian worldview, 196
Citizenship, 84, 101, 102
as (rhetorical) action in the public sphere, 64
dialogic, 68
moral, 138
organizational. *See* Organizational citizenship
Civic engagement/participation
as professional obligation, 203
and professionals, 42, 45
Civic professionalism, x, 194, 201, 202, 203, 204, 208
Civic responsibility/service, 7, 46
Civic virtue
civility as, 8, 16, 20, 62
civility as communicative manifestation of, ix, 16
and organizational citizenship. *See* Organizational citizenship
See also Civility
Civil behavior. *See* Civility
Civil dialogue, 66
Civil discourse, 68, 88
in the organization/workplace, 7, 8, 118, 190, 208
professionally. *See* Professionally civil dis-

course
Civilité, 65
Civility
  as aesthetic-ethical good, 74
  and argumentativeness/verbal aggression,
    85
  assertiveness as element of, 74
  attributes/examples of/nature of, 5, 65, 69,
    73, 74–78; 78–85, 190–191
  and Cicero, 67
  as civic virtue, 8, 16, 20, 62, 66–69, 102,
    106
  and civil society, 39
  and civilization, 64–66
  and communication theory, 16, 78–85
  as communicative construct, 73
  communicative/discursive initiative as ele-
    ment of, 71, 74
  as communicative manifestation of civic
    virtue, ix, 16, 74, 92, 93, 103, 110
  as communicative virtue, 3, 4, 8, 16, 17,
    19, 20, 62, 64, 73, 74–78, 78–85, 86,
    89, 90, 91, 92, 94, 95, 105, 107, 116,
    142, 187
  contrasted with incivility, 71, 94
  and conversation, 66, 67, 71, 76, 78, 79,
    83, 84, 93
  as conversational virtue, 66, 67
  cultural expressions of, variations in/culture
    specific nature of, 22, 64, 65, 66, 67
  and defensive/supportive communication,
    80–82
  dialogic. *See* Dialogic civility
  as distinct from conflict-avoidance/nice-
    ness, 65
  effects of, 73
  Erasmus's work on. *See* Erasmus
  ethic of, 3, 7, 8, 10
  and euphemistic expressions. *See*
    Communication
  four cardinal virtues required for, 75
  and group distinctiveness, 70
  as hegemony, 2, 3, 68
  historical background of, 64–66
  as interpersonal ritual, 69–71
  and/as just talking, 2, 64, 66, 78, 106

  and message design logic, 82–83
  operating on/at content and relational
    dimensions/levels, 77, 79
  in organizational life/the workplace, 4, 9,
    10, 95, 131, 132, 164, 189–190
  and others' comfort, 69
  and phatic communication, 84
  and politeness theory/face, 79–80
  popular work on, 63, 64, 188, 193
  and power. *See* Power
  and professionalism/the professions, x, 3,
    4–8
  in public life, 2, 3, 16, 64, 65, 66, 67, 69,
    72, 73
  and the public sphere. *See* Public sphere
  and relational dialectics, 83–84
  responsiveness as element of, 74
  and rhetorical process, 74
  scholarly work on, 63, 64
  as substitute for political critique, 3
  as virtue, 44
  See also Civic virtue; Public sphere
Civility Institute, the, 193
Civilizing process, 65, 74
Climate. *See* Organizational climate
Cliques, 183, 186
Collectivism, 21
Colonization
  by corporations. *See* Corporate colonization
  as imposition of authority beyond one's
    expertise, 145
Commitment. *See* Organizational commit-
    ment
Committed conversations. *See* Conversation(s)
Common center, 10, 11, 14, 18, 99, 103, 153,
    155, 156, 162, 169
  and diversity, 161
  provided by professional civility, 14
Common good. *See* Good(s)
Common ground, 70
  of the good, 3, 11
  minimal, 3, 13, 158, 160
  among organizational scholars, 117
  and roles, 187
  shared commitment to an organization as,
    184

Common sense, x
  civility, no longer, 2
  professional civility as, 99
  professionalism as, 203
  public, 10, 99
  shared practices as, 157
  shared, professional civility as road map for, 93
  tied to a particular place, 163
  and unreflective practices, 115
Common task, 84, 105, 150
  distal, 101
  and organizational relationships, 183, 185
  proximal, 101
Communication
  background principles of, 76
  as a carrier of meaning, 20
  as constitutive, 110, 112–117
  content/information(al) dimension of, 20, 77, 79, 82, 113, 149
  direct (style), 68
  and "direct indirectness," 109
  effect on employee values, 117–127
  ethical implications of, 116, 118
  euphemistic, 80
  high-context, 21, 78
  influence of, on managers, 120
  influence of, on subordinates, 120, 121
  informational clarity of, 76
  indirect, 21, 80
  low-context, 68
  and organizational values, 122–127
  patterning, as social structure, 115
  phatic. *See* Phatic communication
  public relational, 84
  relational, 18, 162
  relational/relationship dimension of, 77, 79, 149
  ritualized, 78, 108
  shaping influence/power of, 110, 111, 112, 114, 115, 117, 119, 121, 126, 128, 163, 164, 191, 206
  supportive. *See* Supportive communication
  of values in organization, framework for examining, 124
  See also Ritual(s)

Communication climate, 108
  defensive/supportive, 81
Communication competence, 13, 191–192
Communication ethic(s), xi, 20
  organizational, 29
  professional civility, as a, 13
  professional civility, as organizational, 119
  professional civility, as professional, 87, 112, 132, 187
  professional civility, as virtue-based approach to, 20
  See also Professional civility
Communication privacy management theory, 84
Communication rules, 2
Communicative action, 3, 17, 19, 20, 41, 42, 93, 94, 95, 102, 108, 122, 132
  and organizational citizenship, 102
  and productivity, 139–148
  constructive, 13, 91
  ethical, 3
  virtuous, 42, 81
Communicative competence, 28, 76, 77
  goal competence as element of, 77
  interpretive competence as element of, 77, 190
  message competence as element of, 77, 190
  metaprofessional, professional civility as. *See* Professional civility
  role competence, as element of, 77, 190
Communicative courage, 38, 41
Communicative dialectics, 16, 83–84, 95
Communicative discernment. *See* Discernment
Communicative good, 35, 71
Communicative habits, 157
  of the heart, 7
  virtuous , 35
Communicative honesty, 3, 38
Communicative interaction, 13, 22, 24, 82, 112, 114, 117, 118, 124, 156, 174, 205
  and civility, 69, 70, 77, 78
  as element of professional practice, 19
  enabled or constrained by type of work, 175
  professional, 17

and professional civility, 54, 111
routine, 156
See also Routine(s)
Communicative justice, 38
Communicative phronesis. *See* Phronesis
Communicative pragmatics, 38
Communicative praxis, 14, 93, 156, 195
Communicative ritual. *See* Ritual
Communicative routines. *See* Routine(s)
*Communicative Understandings of Women's
    Leadership Development: From Ceilings
    of Glass to Labyrinth Paths,* xiii
Communicative vice. *See* Incivility
Communicative virtue
    at work. *See* Professional civility
    civility as. *See* Civility
Communicative virtues, 75, 94. *See also*
    Virtues
Communicative work, 65
Communities
    of discourse, 195
    of memory, 43
    organizational, 60, 90, 119
    of practice, 37–40, 45
    and practices, 34
Community
    external, 89
    of memory, 18, 94, 120, 123, 127, 154,
        156
    organizational, 32, 101, 126, 156
    of practice, 14, 27, 46, 47, 201
Competence. *See* Communicative competence
Competence face. *See* Face
Complaining/complaint(s), 34, 102, 104, 141,
        166, 167
    about coworker(s), 34
    difference from constructive dissent, 165
    habitual, 18, 165, 167
    about work, 151
Compliance. *See* Conscientiousness
Conceptual kaleidoscope, 105
Conscientiousness. *See* Organizational citizen-
    ship
Consequentialist ethics, 14, 28, 119
Constitutive approach. *See* Communication
Contractual commitment. *See* Profession

Control
    becoming authority in craftwork framework
        of defensiveness/supportiveness, 145
    as element of defensive communication cli-
        mate, 81, 145, 165
Conventional design logic, 82, 83, 84, 108,
        109, 149, 166, 185
Conversation(s)
    casual, 140, 168
    civility as grounded in, 93
    committed, 140
    as defining feature of human condition, 78,
        139
    as element of public sphere, 66, 67
    idle, 104
    with oneself, 168
    private, 169
    and professional civility. *See* Professional
        civility
    public, 109, 207
    tied to action in public sphere, 140, 208
    around work routines, 174
    See also Civility; Professional civility
Conversational ritual. *See* Ritual
Conversational routines. *See* Routine(s)
Cooperation, 141, 205
    and organizational citizenship, 101
    and practices, 38
    and professions, 46
    as rooted in integrity, 203
Coordinated action, 3, 4, 14, 27, 35, 74, 107,
        129
Corporate colonization, 6
Corporate social responsibility, 6, 156, 202
Corrective action, 67, 103
Corrective feedback, 114, 156
Cosmopolitan(s), 12, 157, 204
    orientation, 158
Covenantal orientation. *See* Organizational cit-
    izenship
Courage, 33, 35, 38, 41, 75
    communicative. *See* Communicative
        courage
Courtesy
    as category of organizational citizenship,
        102, 103, 141

connected to civility, 5, 43, 69
domestic, 41
See also Organizational citizenship
Coworker(s)
  difficult, 114
  disliked , 108
  as inescapable part of work, 134
  and issues of public/private domain,
    180–182
  as persons in professional civility frame-
    work, 60, 119
Craft, 41, 48, 104, 133, 201
  vs. art
  love of the, 138
  professions/professions as, 50, 133, 134,
    135, 136–138
Craftwork, 18, 144
  as architectonic vocation, 136
  and defensive/supportive communication,
    145, 146, 147, 169
  model, 142, 169
Crisis. *See* Trivialization of crisis
Crisis of incivility, x, 1, 6, 9, 13, 110
  related to crisis of professionalism, 110
  See also Incivility
Crisis of professionalism, x, 15, 53, 110, 198,
    203
  related to crisis of incivility, 110
  See also Professionalism
Critical theorists/theory, 118, 159, 161, 198
Criticism, 67, 75, 167
  constructive, 75, 150, 167, 170
  as element of culture of critical discourse,
    200
Critique of professions. *See* Professions
Cultural diversity. *See* Diversity
Culture
  and civility. *See* Civility
  dimensions of, 21
Cynicism
  appropriate, 18, 106, 159
  and managerial/supervisory behavioral
    modeling, 97, 130
  routine, 18, 102, 106, 152, 155, 156, 167,
    168
  from unmet high expectations, 59, 98, 171,

181, 184, 199
  See also Disappointment

Democracy, 74, 178
  liberal, as tradition, 26
  and professions, 6, 197, 202
Defensive communication, 80–81, 95, 142,
    144, 145, 190
  in craftwork framework of
    defensiveness/supportiveness, 142–148
Defensive communication climate(s), 81
Deference, 126
Description, as element of supportive commu-
    nication climate, 81, 145
Design logic. *See* Message design logic
Dialectic(s). *See* Relational dialectics
Dialogic citizen, 66
Dialogic civility, x, 62, 87, 92, 93, 95
  connections to organizational citizenship,
    102, 105–107
  as a philosophy of communication, 17, 91,
    96–99
Dialogic justice. *See* Justice
Dignity
  human. *See* Human dignity
  and professions. *See* Professions
  and roles, 183, 186
  vocational, as attribute of professions. *See*
    Vocational dignity
  at work, 60, 137, 206–207
Dimensions of culture. *See* Culture
Direct communication. *See* Communication
Disappointment, 96
  and cynicism, 139, 165
  and dissent, 165, 167
Discernment
  and civility, 67
  communicative, 35
  and competent communication, 191–192
  and dissent, 168
  and a fitting response, 96
  and group decision-making, 171
  and the hiring process, 163
  and organizational citizenship, 140
Discourse
  civil. *See* Civil discourse

courteous, 89
deliberative, 106
equity, 152, 169
professionally civil. *See* Civil discourse
professionally skillful. *See* Professional discourse
public. *See* Public discourse
virtuous. *See* Virtuous discourse
Discourses of positive assessment, 95, 130, 131
Disinterest
in craftwork framework of defensiveness/supportiveness, 146–147
Disinterested care. *See* Care
Disliked coworkers/others, 83, 108
Disposition(s), 31, 34
and ethical professional conduct, 205
and manners, 75
and vocations/professions, 154, 200
natural, 35
to serve, 205
vicious, 71
See also Virtue; Virtues
Dissent
constructive, 106, 156, 165, 171
organizational. *See* Organizational dissent
Distance
and civility, 71, 73, 79, 83, 84
and disliked others, 83
and formality, 27, 70, 83
interspaces of, 99
and politeness theory, 107, 108
professional, 108
and professional civility, 99, 107, 108, 160, 174, 184, 190
in relationships, 70, 108, 192
and tact, 68, 77
See also Formality
Diversity
cultural, 2
and difference, 64, 96, 160, 197
generational, 2
within organizations, 156, 161
Domestic courtesy. *See* Courtesy
Dwelling place(s), organizations as, 2, 18, 94, 156

Education
as architectonic profession, 52
higher. *See* Higher education
as one of the four great traditional/original learned professions, 4, 50
as a profession, 4
and professionals. *See* Professions
and professions. *See* Professions
Educational institution(s), 9
different types of, 157–158
with faith-grounded mission, 162–163
Embarrassment, 67
Embedded agent, 14
Embedded practice. *See* Practice(s)
Emotion(s)
and expressive design logic, 82
as integral part of work experience, 190
managing, 191
moral, 192
positive, 131
as result of bullying/hostile relationships, 130
strong, 68
See also Positive emotional experience(s)
Emotivism, x, 14, 178
Empathy, as element of supportive communication climate 81, 146
Employee satisfaction. *See* Job satisfaction
Environment
communication/communicative, 118, 127
external, 18
internal, 155, 202, 208
metaphorical, 160
organizational. *See* Organizational environment
as produced by Arendtian work, 135
public, 72, 77, 169, 200
social system, 116
symbolic , 117, 120, 169
work , 4, 5, 7, 14, 72, 89, 96, 112, 117–119, 121, 139, 148, 180
Envy, 152, 169, 192
Equality, 178, 181
among professions/professionals. *See* Professions
and task mastery, 170

as element of supportive communication
climate, 81, 147
of secular and religious occupations, 51
Erasmus, 65, 69, 188
Ethic of service
as characteristic of professions. *See*
Professions
Ethical norms. *See* Professions
Ethics
communication. *See* Communication ethics
consequentialist. *See* Consequentialist ethics
history and tradition as foundation for, 30
organizational communication, 118
professional. *See* Professional ethics
and the professions. *See* Professions
role-based. *See* Role-based ethics
tied to socially local and particular, 43
virtue. *See* Virtue ethics
workplace, 178
Etiquette
and civility, 63, 70
and logonomic systems, 123
and professionalism, 54, 55
public, 178
Eudamonia, 30
See also Well-being
Euphemistic communication. *See*
Communication
Evaluation, 118
in craftwork framework of
defensiveness/supportiveness, 144–145,
190
as element of defensive communication climate, 81, 142, 143, 144
function of a professional ethic, 32
by public standards, 76
roles as basis for, 186
Exchange orientation. *See* Organizational citizenship
Exclusion, in craftwork framework of defen-
siveness/supportiveness, 146, 147
Expert
antisocial, 145
closed to ideas, 148
and craft, 145–148
and sociable expertise, 170

Expertise, 145
antisocial, 144, 169
and craftwork, 145–147
and inequality, 170
language of, 147
managerial, relative to those supervised,
149, 150
and professions. *See* Professions
sociable, 144, 147, 169–170
technical, 54, 201
of those closest to the task, 191
Expression
of authentic self, 11
constructive, of concern, 166
individual, 68
Expressive design logic, 82, 83, 141, 165
External goods. *See* Good(s)
External standards. *See* Virtue ethics

Face
autonomy, 79, 80, 107, 108
competence, 79, 80, 107, 109, 188
fellowship, 79, 80, 107, 188
negative, 75, 76, 79, 80, 109, 126
positive, 76, 79, 80, 83, 106, 150, 189
Face needs. *See* Face
Face-saving, 76, 170
Face support, 19, 81, 183, 190
Family
problematic metaphor for organization, 98,
159, 181
work, 181
Feedback, 150, 170, 191
corrective, 114, 156, 166
from task, 27
Fellowship face. *See* Face
Fitting response
less-than-, 71, 96, 97, 151, 187
Focus of attention
common project as, 101
craft as, in genuine professional work, 133
directed toward constructive action, 168
as directing words, 169
and dissent, 168
as distinguishing between mastery/hege-
mony and disinterest/exclusion, 147

and incivility, 129
and phenomenology, 106
and trivialization of crisis, 98, 104
personal connections as primary, 184
resulting from particular types of discourse, 141, 151, 152, 153
task as, 146, 184
unprofessional, 73, 141
at work, 168
on work, 153
Forgiveness, 32, 141, 192
Formal distance. *See* Distance; Formality
Formal ritual(s). *See* Ritual(s)
Formality, 70, 83, 109
    as conventional style (of message design logic), 83
    as element of civility, 74
Flourishing. *See* Human flourishing
Framing
    and leadership, 116, 155, 159, 185
    to oneself, as conversational partner, 168
Freire, Paulo, 138
Friendship(s)
    and/in civic life, 28, 36
    cliques based on, 183
    close, 113, 175, 176, 186
    extending beyond the workplace, 180
    as a good, 26, 28
    indicated by language use in organizational contexts, 125
    private, 178, 180
    public. *See* Public friendship
    based on task intimacy, 186
    at work, 140, 152, 174, 175, 176, 180, 184, 186
Functionalist approach/perspective, 56, 117, 118
    shift from understanding of professions from, to ones emerging from structuralism and critical theory, 198

Generational diversity. *See* Diversity
Gestalt virtue. *See* Professional civility
Goal(s)
    and communicative pragmatics, 68
    and discourse, 82, 109, 141, 170, 190

as element of communication competence, 77
    guiding influence strategies, 77
    of self and other, 82
    as telos, 25, 32, 35, 39
Goal enactment, 111
Good(s)
    common, 3, 28, 53, 55, 59, 60, 66, 73, 98, 101, 102, 156, 206
    emergent, 92
    external, 14, 31, 35, 37, 39, 40, 90
    four, of professions, 16, 48, 89
    internal/internal to practice(s), 14, 25, 31, 37, 40, 48, 59, 71, 89, 90
    intrinsic, 14, 26, 30
    substantive, 29, 101
    See also Virtues
Good life, a/the, 9, 26, 27, 31, 34, 42, 45, 48, 66, 90, 133. *See also* Virtues
Good professional. *See* Professional
Good work, 6, 62, 133, 134, 136, 153, 155, 169, 174
Gossip/gossiping, 34, 72, 73, 152
Grice's maxims, 76
Group distinctiveness. *See* Civility
Guest (metaphor of), 59, 155, 156–160, 171

Harassment, 70, 73, 129, 192,
    interpersonal. *See* Interpersonal harassment
    workplace, 202
Harm(s)
    from incivility, 3, 14
    See also Incivility
Health care professions/professionals, 53, 57, 149
    See also Medicine
Hegemony, 128
    and civility. *See* Civility
    in craftwork framework of defensiveness/supportiveness, 147
    professional, 198
    of uncivil organizational culture, 128
Heroic society, 27, 33
Hesed, 100
High-context communication. *See* Communication

Higher education, 49, 88, 137, 139, 183. *See also* Educational institutions; Incivility
Historical moment, 12, 14
  and civility/rudeness, 72,
  of diversity and difference/virtue contention, 97, 158, 160, 187
  as element of dialogic civility, x, 96
  of Gibb's work on defensive and supportive communication climates, 143
  postmodern, 9, 24, 177
  and practices, 39
  and professions, 8, 11, 16, 19, 24, 25, 26, 29, 39, 50, 62, 87, 90, 91, 92, 95, 96, 98, 107, 110, 133, 136, 137, 138, 153, 154, 171, 173, 194, 195
  and public/private concerns in organizations, 179
  responsiveness to, 92, 96, 196
  and rhetorical interruptions, 139
  and virtue ethics, 32
  See also Responsiveness
History
  of civility. *See* Civility
  of organizational theory, 131
  of professions, 9, 10, 12, 15, 16, 17, 25, 28, 30, 33, 38, 42, 43, 45, 48, 50, 55–56, 58, 87, 88, 90, 91, 92, 94, 101, 109, 147, 158, 173, 187, 188, 197, 206
  of term "profession," 46, 50
  of (true) professional ideal in America, 4, 8, 15, 26, 39, 43, 45, 50, 133, 138, 198
  of virtue ethics, 32
Home. *See* Local home
Homeric ethic(s)/virtues, 29, 32, 33, 90
See also Role-based ethics
Homeric society. *See* Heroic society
Homeric virtues. *See* Homeric ethic(s)/virtues
Honesty, 3, 35, 38, 176
  communicative. *See* Communicative honesty
Hope
  and cynicism, 18, 156, 187
  discourse of, 153
  as element of dialogic civility, x, 96–99
  and professions, 9, 133, 208

  realistic, 98, 102, 132
  result of managerial behavior, 97, 148–150
Hostile work relationships. *See* Problematic workplace relationships
Human capabilities. *See* Capabilities perspective
Human condition
  and civility, 65, 74
  conversation as defining element of, 78, 93
  and labor, work, and action, 10, 31, 45, 92, 133, 134–136
  limits of, 133
  and narrative, 41
  and phatic communication, 84
  and professionals, 208
  variations in ability as part of, 147
  and work, 134–139
Human dignity, 14, 203
Human flourishing, 11, 14
  and care for institutions, 156
  as characterizing good human life, 24
  and civility, 65, 71, 74, 81, 94
  and professional civility, 11
  and professions/professional practice, 7, 9, 11, 23, 25, 46, 53, 59, 61, 134
  See also Virtue ethics; Virtues
Human relations
  movement, 143
  pseudo, 143
  and pseudo-participation, 143
Human resources approach/human resource theorists, 204
Humiliation, in craftwork framework of defensiveness/supportiveness, 145, 170, 190
Humor, 67
Hybridized professionalism. *See* Professionalism
Hypervirtue. *See* Professional civility

Ideal(s). *See* Regulative ideals
Ideological complexes, 123
Ideology/ideologies
  and belief systems, 55
  in craftwork framework of defensiveness/supportiveness, 146
  of equality of secular and religious occupa-

tions, 51
of intimacy, 177–178
managerial, 161
vs. narrative or story, 161
of participation among equals, 47
and social semiotics, 123
totalizing, 161
Imagination
vs. fantasy, 168
Kantian, 103
Implicit communication rules. *See*
    Communication rules
Incivility
apparent, as civility, 65
as characteristic of professionals' behavior, 5
as communicative vice, 14, 16, 71–74, 78,
    81, 94, 128
compared to running a red light, 69
contrasted with professional behavior, 55
costs associated with, 1, 112, 129, 130, 190
as crisis. *See* Crisis of incivility
definition of, 71
effects of, 3, 14, 17, 31, 71, 72–73, 78, 90,
    128–131
effects of witnessing, 72, 78, 108, 129
examples of, 72, 73
in higher education/the academy, 2, 88
as inverse of professionalism, x
professional, 73
shaped by historical moment, 72
verbal aggression as, 85
workplace, 73
See also Harm(s); Rudeness
Indirect communication. *See* Communication
Individual integration, 11
Individualism, 2, 21
Indweller, 155, 157, 159, 160
Influence strategies. *See* Strategies
Informality
in public interaction, 70
in the workplace, as explanation for incivil-
    ity, 2, 10, 185
In-group relationship(s), 148, 175
Initiative. *See* Civility
Injustice, 81, 106, 164
organizational, 152

Institution(s)
academic . *See* Educational institutions
care for. *See* Care for institutions
challenges to, as element of historical
    moment of Gibb's work on defensive
    and supportive communication cli-
    mates, 143
of civil society/the public sphere, 64, 65,
    66, 67, 70, 71, 72, 74, 77, 85
consequences for, as result of blurring pub-
    lic and private spheres, 182
constructive approach to, 93
as context for professional practice/work, 7,
    12, 39, 57, 58, 60, 96, 158, 204
different types protecting and promoting
    different goods, 157
educational. *See* Educational institutions
effects of communication on, 111
as flawed, 164
leaders' responsibility to protect and pro-
    mote, 116
one of three aspects of verbal interaction,
    122
privileged, 68
professional, 158
relationship to practices, 39
respect for, 208
and roles, 186–187
social, as imperfect, 67
as vulnerable, 166
See also Professions, Professional(s)
Insult(s), 67–68, 70, 72, 125
Integrity, 35
behavioral. *See* Behavioral integrity
communicative, 8, 202
as element of professional behavior and
    practice, 203
of a human life, 20, 40, 41
institutional/of an institution's aims and
    goals, 165, 167, 171–172
of practices, 39, 204
of professions. *See* Professions
Interactional justice. *See* Justice
Interactive norms, 88, 132, 206
Interactive routines, 12, 19, 70, 88
Intercultural communication, 21

Internal goods. *See* Goods
Interpersonal communication
  and conversation, 8, 139
  philosophy of, 15, 91
  and popular press publications, 188, 190
  in the professional civility framework, 142
  study of, shifts over time, 10–11
  in the workplace, 187
Interpersonal harassment, 1
Interpersonal quicksand, 186
See also Therapeutic orientation
Interpersonal ritual. *See* Ritual
Interrupt/ing/ions, 121
  cooperative, 80
  as part of typology of uncivil behavior, 73
  rhetorical. *See* Rhetorical interruption
Interspaces, 71, 84, 99
  conversational, from personalized language, 171
  in the workday, 151
Intimacy
  feigned , 84
  ideology of, 177, 178
  and language/discourse, 125, 176
  and organizational life, 179
  and relationships, 175
  tyranny of. *See* Tyranny of intimacy
  work/task, 181, 182, 184, 186
Intrinsic goods. *See* Good(s)
Invidious comparison, 170

Jealousy, 152, 169
Job satisfaction, 105
  and incivility, 129, 130
  and verbal aggressiveness, 130
  and work relationships, 182
Job types. *See* Professions
Jokes, 191
Journalism, ix
  and internal and external goods, 35
  as practice, 11
  profession of, 11, 15, 24, 35, 49
Journalism as Practice: MacIntyre, Virtue
    Ethics, and the Press, ix
Judgment
  argumentative parameters for, 160

and blended relationships, 177
in craftwork framework of defensiveness/
    supportiveness 142, 145, 147
as element of defensive communication cli-
    mate, 142, 143, 144, 145
ethical, 14
exercising, as opposed to following rules,
    32, 77
of others' attributes, 114, 121, 152
practical, 77
professional background for, 164
professional ethic as resource for, 32
tied to the particular, 35
"Just talking "
  as civic virtue, 76
  as conversational virtue of civility/civil dia-
      logue, 66
  and democratic society/public sphere, 2,
      64, 66, 70, 76
  as dissent, 167
  as element of professional civility, 107
  in organizational context, 106, 107
Justice, 35, 38, 159, 191
  and certainty, 81
  and civility, 2, 66, 75
  communicative. *See* Communicative justice
  dialogic, models/theories of, 66, 67
  interactional, 94
  principles of, 66, 67
  procedural, 59

Kaleidoscope. *See* Conceptual kaleidoscope
  as resource for invention, 16

Labor, 8, 10, 11, 15, 17, 30, 31, 42, 45, 46,
    55, 92, 100, 104, 128, 133, 134, 135,
    136, 153, 189, 208
  as distinct from work and action, 8, 12, 57,
      134
  intellectual, 57
  manual, 57, 134, 200
  professional, 94, 135, 136
  shared, 189, 194
  structures of, 117
  trace of, 136
  worthwhile, 118

Language
  clean, 191
  and communication style, 82
  content and relationship dimensions of, 77
  descriptive, 190
  of expertise, 147
  framing. *See* Framing
  foul, 55
  influence of, 13, 119, 112, 114, 119, 160,
      206
  nondiscriminatory, 190
  nonpersonalized, 171
  in the organizational socialization context,
      119–127
  and organizational space, 168, 170, 171
  personalized, 171
  as producer of reality, 113, 125
  and professions, 13, 47, 50, 206
  shaping power of, 112, 119
  and values in the organizational context,
      121–127
  See also Communication, Framing,
      Organizational socialization
Language functions in organizations
  indicating friendship, 125
  maintaining power relations, 126
  organizing relationships, 125
  social identity, 125
Law
  as architectonic profession, 52
  as one of the four great traditional/original
      learned professions, 4, 50
  profession, 4, 49, 50, 59, 196
  rule of, as tradition, 26
Leadership
  communicative, 156
  ethic of care approach, 156
  and framing, 116
  organizational, 159, 179
  See also Professional civility
Learned professions. *See* Professions
Legacy of professions, 88, 95, 136, 188, 189,
      194, 202, 203, 208
  civility as, 4–10
  as resource for invention, 16
Legal profession, 51, 52

Leisure, 41, 89
  philosophical, 47
  recuperative, 13, 41
Liberal democracy. *See* Democracy
Liberal professions. *See* Professions
Life, unity of a. *See* Unity of a life
Limits, 131
  and caring for a local home, 154
  of civil discourse, 88
  of change, 166
  of communities, 161
  dialogic, of relationships, 108
  as element of dialogic civility, x, 96–99,
      102
  and freedom, 164
  hedges and qualifiers as, 171
  of the human condition, 133
  in relationships, 187
  of ritualized communication, 108
  mission, 103, 106, 107, 149, 161, 166
  organizational, 97, 98, 99, 106, 124, 140,
      153, 155
  professional, 200
  role, 187
Listening
  active, 82, 103, 141
  and civility, 73, 80, 82, 193
  poor/unresponsive or "bad" listening, 82
  and professional civility, 163
Local home, 35, 43, 94
  academic, 157
  care/caring for, 154, 155, 159, 160
  as emergent good of professional practice,
      92
  institutional, 18, 48, 94
  and the metaphor of "guest," 59, 156–160
  and organizational socialization, 163
  organizations as, for professions, x, 89, 97,
      103, 105, 120, 153, 154, 156, 171
  tension with profession, 157, 159
Local norms. *See* Norms
Locals, 12, 204
Logonomic systems, 123, 128
"Lone wolf" syndrome, 105
Low-context communication. *See*
      Communication

Macrolevel action/practices, 12, 208
Managed professional business, 60
Manager(s), 148–156
   and professional civility, 148–156
   author. *See* Author manager
   See also Organizational mission
Manners,
   and civility, 63, 65, 75
   as interpersonal ritual, 69–71
   as minor morals, 75
Manual labor. *See* Labor
Mastery
   in craftwork framework of defensiveness/
      supportiveness, rather than superiority,
      147
   and positive emotional experiences at work,
      189
   task-, 170
Meaning
   and action, 135
   background structure of, 101
   and communicative interaction, 112, 113,
      121
   and context, 123
   and expertise, 201
   and framing, 116
   of/in human life, 2, 3, 21, 41, 43, 96, 128,
      144, 165, 186, 193
   -making significance of narrative, 41
   and metaphor, 159
   and moral frameworks, 144
   and narrative, 97
   and philosophy of communication, 20, 21
   and positive assessments, 95, 131
   of a practice, 42, 42
   of "profession." *See* Profession
   of/in professional life, 12, 135, 167
   and professional socialization, 151
   of/in professional work, 45, 135, 138
   and public poetry, 185
   in relationships, 114, 122, 149
   of service, 196
   shared, for behaviors, 70
   shared, in high context communication, 78
   of the task/the work, 151, 189
   of virtues, 31

   of work/work life/organizational life, 20,
      21, 43, 54, 98, 107, 151, 122, 124,
      127, 139, 151, 165, 167, 185
   See also Professional civility
Mechanic professions. *See* Professions
Medicine
   alternative, 199
   as architectonic profession, 52, 198
   as an institution, 143
   as one of the four great traditional/original
      learned professions, 4, 50
   as a profession, 4, 26, 49, 50, 53, 137, 199
   See also Health care professions/profession-
      als
Memorable messages, 126, 127, 151
Mentor(s), 105, 114, 164
   peer , 150
Mentoring, 146, 156
   and craftwork, 147
   and expertise, 170
   formal vs. informal, 163–164
   forms of, 163
   lack of, for underrepresented groups,
      163–164
   and mission, 155
   as one of the four great traditional/original
      learned professions, 4, 50
   and productivity, 148
   professional. *See* Professional mentoring
   the professional, challenges of, 164
   and protection of institutional/local home,
      18
   in the socialization process, 163
   supervisory. *See* Supervisor(s')/Supervisory
      behavior
Message design logic, 16, 82, 95, 109, 149
   See also Expressive design logic,
      Conventional design logic, Rhetorical
      design logic
Metanarrative crisis, x
Metanarratives, 161
Metaphor(s). *See* Meaning
Metapractice. *See* Professions
Metaprofession. *See* Professions
Micro-affirmations, 80
Micro level

of interaction, 12,
of organizational experience, 206
Micropractices, 12
communicative, 201
Microprocesses, 20, 178
of communicative action/interaction and
language, 19, 20, 112, 201
Minimal common ground. *See* Common
ground
Mission. *See* Organizational mission
Modeling
behavioral, 97
and expertise, 170
managerial/supervisory, 97, 130
Moral framework, 54
and defensive/supportive communication,
144
and meaning, 144
Moral tradition. *See* Tradition
Morality, 12, 43
and civility, 63
Mumford, Lewis, 138

Narrative(s)
agreed-upon, 32
as linguistic form, 127
and meaning, 97
metaprofessional, 149
occupational, 157
order/unity, of a human life, 31, 33, 40, 41,
42, 136
organization's/organizational, 43, 97, 106,
107, 155, 156, 160, 182
petite, 30
and practice, 25
and productivity, 136
professional, 10
of/and the professions, 7, 25, 30, 32, 33,
50, 53, 95, 101
public, organization as, 18, 160–164, 171
shared, 184
and tradition, 25, 42
and virtues, 32
Negative face. *See* Face
Negative politeness. *See* Politeness
Neutrality

in craftwork framework of
defensiveness/supportiveness, as disinterest, 146
as element of defensive communication climate, 81, 146
Nicomachean Ethics, 75
Nonverbal behavior/messages
and civility, 74, 190, 193
and incivility, 71, 72
and professional civility, 28
and "tall poppy" phenomenon, 152
Norms, 67, 124
communicative, 22
of (proper) conduct/interaction, 66, 69, 85,
88, 89, 93
of a cooperative system, 104
of discourse, 88
freedom from, 11
friendship, 181
group, 183
implicit, 78
interactive, 88, 132, 182, 206
internalized, 104
lack of agreement on, 10
local, 28
organizational, 175, 181
as patterns of behavior, 115, 206
of politeness, 89
professional. *See* Professions
and professions. *See* Professions
societal, changing, as contributing factor to
increased incivility, 2

Occupational culture, 22, 88
Occupations
architectonic. *See* Architectonic occupations
conflict between and among, 126
considered to be professions. *See* Professions
dignified, professions as. *See* Professions
honorific, 53
professionalizing, 99
On Civility in Children, 65
Organization(s)
as local home for professional work. *See*
Local home
as public narrative(s). *See* Narrative

Organization society, 6
Organizational change, 165
Organizational citizenship, x, 7, 15, 17, 18,
    19, 87, 91, 92, 93, 95, 99–105
  altruism as dimension/element of, 102,
    103, 104
  civic virtue as dimension/element of , 18,
    92, 101, 102, 103, 105
  communicative elements/items in, 102, 104
  compliance, generalized, as element of, 104
  conceptualizations of, 100–104
  connections to dialogic civility, 102,
    105–107
  conscientiousness as dimension/element of,
    102, 104
  courtesy as a dimension/element of, 102,
    103
  covenantal vs. exchange orientation, 101,
    158, 159
  definition of, 99
  dimensions of, 102–104, 106
  reflective, 156
  sportsmanship. *See* Sportsmanship
Organizational climate
  and courtesy, 103
  damaged by incivility, 14, 72, 188
  inviting productivity and constructive rela-
    tionships, 120
  and professional civility, 120
  of respect and goodwill, 205
  supportive, 95
  See also Communication climate
Organizational commitment, 97
  and incivility, 129
  and managerial/supervisory behavioral
    modeling, 97, 130
Organizational culture, 201
  feminist, 176
  influenced by communicative practices, 88,
    112, 113, 117
  mentoring and the unsaid of, 123
  and professional civility, 17
  and public/private distinction, 176, 180
  uncivil, 128
  values of, 124
  variations in, 19, 176, 180, 184

Organizational culture scheme, 125
Organizational dissent, 18, 103, 105, 106,
    166, 167
Organizational environment(s), x, 5, 7, 13
  and ambiguity, 98
  and civility, 7
  and collective becoming, 99
  conducive to productivity, 119
  "corporate social responsibility for," 156
  effects of communication/language on,
    116, 122, 127, 157, 201
  effects of incivility on, 129
  and enlarged space, 155
  and envy and jealousy, 152
  internal, 7
  and professional civility, x, 111, 116, 169
Organizational misbehavior, 1
Organizational mission. 18, 185
  managers as standard bearers of, 10
  See also Attentiveness; Limits; Mentoring
Organizational professional, 138
Organizational relationships, 19, 108
  based on task/work intimacy, 184, 186
  and a common task, 183
  constructive, 120
  multiple forms of, 175
  professional civility in, 191
  See also Professional civility
Organizational socialization, 117
  and care for institutions, 158
  communication in, 110, 119
  as context for effects of communication on
    organizational members, 119–127,
    128, 129
  defined, 119
  and the good of organizations, 18
  and implicit/tacit knowledge, 168
  and the local home, 163
  mission-sensitive, 155, 162
  and professional civility, 110, 112
  role of organizational members in, 155
Organizational space, 155, 160
  enlarged, 168–171
  and learning, 170
  threats to, 169
Organizational stories, 126, 127, 151, 161

competing/counter, 162
  as organizational narrative, 161, 162
  See also Narrative
Ostracism, 118, 183, 186
Out-group relationship(s), 75
Out-groups, 70

Parvenu, 160
Peer relationships, 19, 163
  collegial, 175
  information, 176
  responsiveness and restraint in, 191
  special, 125, 174, 175, 176
Peers
  and attribution(s), 128
  communication/interaction with, 117, 128,
    168
  competitive behavior with, by professionals,
    204
  and constructive work experience, 150
  conversation with/among, 19
  as coworkers, 204
  deviance by, 180
  distressed, 191
  and feedback, 170
  as "good audience," 156
  as information providers, 164
  as mentors, 150
  and professional civility, 18
  professionally civil, 150–153
  and role limits, 187
  troublesome, 73, 141
People. *See* Persons
Personal strategic action, 11
Persons
  and civility, 64, 65, 66, 69, 74, 75, 77, 81,
    84, 85, 94
  in context of practices and traditions,
    42–43
  and incivility, 71, 72, 78
  as "good" of profession(s), x, 8, 10, 12, 17,
    19, 21, 22, 32, 33, 48, 58, 60–61, 87,
    89, 90, 92, 94, 95, 96, 97, 98, 101,
    128, 129, 130, 132, 136, 141, 172,
    190, 208
  as "good" protected and promoted by pro-
    fessional civility, x, 8, 12, 13, 17, 19,
    21, 22, 32, 33, 48, 58, 60–61, 87, 89,
    90, 92, 94, 95, 101, 102, 103, 104,
    108, 119, 129, 130, 141, 152, 153,
    173–194
Petite narrative. *See* Narrative
Phatic communication
  and civility, 16, 84
  and professional civility, 95, 109
  as public relational communication, 84
Phenomenological encounter, 106
Phenomenological turning, 41
  toward goods, 132
  toward place of work, 171
  toward work, 89
  toward the world, 200
Phenomenology, 41
  communicative, 45
  existential, of public conduct, 65
  of the professions, 30
  of work, 45
Philosophy of communication, xi, 17, 21
  and culture, 21
  dialogic civility as, 91, 96–99
  and meaning, 20
  professional civility as, 20, 87, 89
Philosophy of life, 21, 192
  and professionalism, 54
Philosophy of work life, 12, 20, 21, 87, 187
Phronesis, 27
  communicative, 13
  and communicative discernment, 35
  and defensive/supportive communication,
    81
  and dialogic justice, 66
  and the expert, 148
  as intellectual virtue, 35
  of professional civility, 190
  as regulative ideal, 27
  tact as, 68
Place,
  and civility, 64
  as "good" of profession, 8, 12, 17, 18, 19,
    21, 22, 33, 43, 48, 58, 59–60, 87, 89,
    90, 92, 95, 96, 97, 98, 101, 132, 133,
    136, 141, 153, 154–172, 173, 184,

192, 194, 195, 208
as "good" protected and promoted by professional civility, 8, 12, 13, 17, 18, 19,
20, 21, 22, 33, 43, 48, 58, 61, 87, 89,
90, 92, 95, 97, 102, 103, 104, 105,
119, 128, 132, 141, 152, 153,
154–172, 184, 192, 194, 195, 208
and incivility, 72, 128
and problematic behaviors in the workplace, 130
Politeness, 80, 89, 108, 114, 126
conventions, 123
language of, in the workplace, and power,
126
negative, 108
as part of background principles of conversation, 76
positive, 107
Politeness theory
assumptions of, 79–80
and civility, 16, 75, 79–80, 83, 84
in communication scholarship, 80
connection to relational dialectics, 83, 84
and Goffman, 78
and professional civility, 95
Positive affect, 131
Positive assessment. *See* Discourses of positive
assessment; Positive emotional experi-
ence(s)
Positive emotional experience(s), 131, 151,
185, 188–189
Positive face. *See* Face
Positive organizing, 4, 130
Positive politeness. *See* Politeness
Postmodern historical moment. *See* Historical
moment
Post-positivistic perspective, 117
Power, 120, 121, 123, 124
attributes of speech lacking, 171
and a background narrative, 162
and civility, 2, 68, 147
of communication, 13, 17, 110, 112, 113,
114, 116, 117, 118, 121, 132, 163,
206, 208
corrupting, of institutions, 39
of envy and jealousy, 169

and ideology, 123
imbalances, 183, 185
judgments of, 114
and knowledge, 147
of language, 119, 128, 206
language of, in the workplace, and politeness, 126
lording, over others, 73
of metaphor, 159
of professional civility, 111, 119
and professions, 5, 9, 53, 54, 198
of a real problem, affected by trivialization
of crisis, 165
of roles, 115, 186–187
supervisory, 125
as theoretical basis for professional power,
198
See also Communication; Language
Power distance, 21
Power relations. *See* Language functions in
organizations
Practical wisdom. *See* Phronesis
Practice(s)
Borden's additional elements added to
MacIntyre's conceptualization, 48
embedded, 11, 89, 131
examples of, according to MacIntyre, 36
interactive, 2, 8, 74, 203
profession(s) as, 12, 30, 31, 38, 44, 45–62,
87, 90, 91, 92, 95, 116, 133, 142, 195,
198
tradition(s) of, ix, 10, 30, 33, 42, 49, 56,
91, 92, 105, 110, 133, 146, 158, 197,
204
unreflective, 115, 152
virtues sustaining goods of. *See* Virtues
Practitioner(s)
quasi-managerial, 60
reflective, 97
Pragmatics. *See* Communicative pragmatics
Praxis, 116
communicative. *See* Communicative praxis
professional, 19
rhetorical, 126
Privacy, 60, 177
Private life, 3, 13, 47

and coworker boundaries, 98
as part of being a professional, 7, 47, 55
and public life, as bifurcated, 7
in relation to professional civility, 13, 41,
    89
in relation to public life, 47, 177, 177–182,
    185
and virtuous practices, 41
See also Public life
Private relationship(s), 19, 175, 176, 177
    as distinct from public relationships, 174
    and the local home, 184
    and power imbalances, 185
    in public context of work, 19, 175, 176,
        177
Private sphere, 47
    in balance with public sphere, 96, 98
    blurring of public sphere and, 181, 182
    differentiation of/distinction, from public
        sphere, 92, 99, 173, 182, 194
    integration with public sphere, 179, 181
    separate from public sphere, 176
    unity of public sphere and, by idea of call-
        ing, 40
    See also Public sphere
Privilege
    as attribute of professions, 5, 6, 197
    social, 81
Pro bono public work done by professionals, 55
Problematic (interpersonal) behaviors in the
        workplace. *See* Problematic workplace
        behaviors
Problematic Relationships in the Workplace, x
Problematic Relationships in the Workplace,
        Volume 2, xi
Problematic relationships in the workplace, 1,
        21, 187
Problematic workplace behaviors, 1
effects of, 129
Productivity, 2, 15, 18, 19, 20, 22, 60, 156,
        162, 203
    and alcohol and drug use in the workplace,
        180
    climate of, 169
    and communicative action, 139–148
    as concern of professionalism, 55

as craft of good work, 134
damaged/decreased/lowered, as result of
    incivility in the workplace, 1, 14, 72,
    118, 128, 129, 130, 202
and defensive/supportive communication,
    142–148, 190
as distinct from cooperation, 101
effects of bullying on, 130
and forgiveness, 141
as foundation for professional good in the
    world, 136
as generativity of professional practice, 93
as "good" of profession, x, 8, 12, 17, 21,
    31, 33, 43, 48, 58–59, 61, 72, 87, 89,
    90, 92, 94, 95, 96, 97, 98, 132,
    133–153, 195, 208
as "good" protected and promoted by pro-
    fessional civility, 8, 12, 13, 17, 43, 48,
    58, 72, 87, 89, 90, 92, 95, 99, 102,
    103, 104, 108, 118, 119, 133–153,
    174, 194, 195, 204, 208
increased, as result of civility in the work-
    place, 3
and labor, work, and action, 57
as manifestation of human fecundity, 136
non-work-related talk as protecting and
    promoting, 151
and organizational citizenship, 101, 102,
    103, 104, 105, 140
and organizational climate, 120
and personal relationships, 187
and problematic behaviors in the work-
    place, 130
and problematic others in the workplace,
    192
and problematic supervisors, 139
and professional identity, 136
as protected and promoted by managers,
    148–150
as protected and promoted by peers,
    150–153
relationships centered on, 183, 187
as responsibility of professionals, 205
and satisfaction, 105
valuing the work itself as foundation for,
    139

and work relationships taking place at a distance, 192

Profession

as architectonic occupation, 8, 9, 55, 57, 90, 137

as contractual commitment/obligation to client, 52, 196, 197

as dignified occupation, 13, 46, 47, 51, 58, 94, 204

as practice, 12, 31, 44, 45–62, 87, 90, 92, 95, 116, 133, 142, 195, 198

definition of (or lack thereof), 47, 49

practice of, as moral metacommunity, 94

rhetoric of, as term. *See* Professions

See also Professions

Professional(s)

challenges of managing, 149–150

and civility, 5

expected behavior of, 4, 5, 6, 7, 12, 14, 30, 47, 55, 59, 198

good, a/the, 5

and incivility, 202

occupational, 60

organizational. *See* Organizational professional

in professional civility framework, 89, 93, 96, 97, 102, 108, 135, 136, 137, 139, 140, 142, 153, 154. 155, 156, 158, 162, 164, 168, 171, 172, 173, 185, 189–191, 195, 202, 203, 204, 206, 207, 208

program, 60

situated, 60

socialization. *See* Professional socialization

Professional associations, 52, 89, 199, 201

Professional behavior, 7, 181, 203

agreement on meaning in everyday usage, 203

contrasted with incivility, 55

and professional civility, 207

professional civility as architectonic formation of, 47

professionalism as ideal for, 203

Professional boundaries, 19, 60

Professional civility

as architectonic discourse structure, 119

as architectonic of professional behavior, 47

as communication ethic for the professional workplace, 16

as communicative enactment of professional ideal, 48

as communicative ethic, 3, 8, 21, 23, 89

as communicative praxis, 156, 195

as communicative virtue, 43

as communicative virtue of/for professional practice, 195

as communicative virtue at work, x, 11–15, 24–30, 48, 62, 86, 87–110, 126, 142, 162, 187, 196, 207

conceptual coordinates of, 96–107

and conversation(s), 13, 18, 19, 22, 93, 104, 107, 108, 109, 139, 140, 141, 148, 150, 152, 168, 169, 170, 171, 174, 180, 208

culture of, 87–88, 120, 131, 184, 202

development of the idea, ix–x

gestalt nature of, 28, 41, 91,100

as gestalt virtue, 91

as hypervirtue, 91

as interactive communicative virtue, 90

and leaders/leadership, 97, 98, 101, 109, 116, 128, 141, 149, 154, 155, 156, 159, 165, 185

as metaprofessional communicative competence, 28

not a therapeutic approach to discourse, 142

as organizational communication ethic, 119

as philosophy of communication, 20

as philosophy of work life, 21

practices of, 17, 62, 107–109, 119, 163, 164, 168–171, 187–194, 208

as professional communication ethic, 13, 20, 87, 112, 132, 187

as professional communicative practice, 124

as professional communicative virtue, 35, shaping influence of, 13

theoretical coordinates of, 91–95, 187

theoretical framework of, summary of, 91–92

as virtue-based approach to communication ethics, 20

See also Restraint(s)
Professional communication, 13
Professional communication ethic, 13, 20
  professional civility as, 87, 112, 132, 187
Professional competence, 28
Professional discourse
  practices of, 119
  skilled, 107
Professional ethics, 53
  codes of, 9
  as constitutive of professional identity, 95
  from virtue ethics perspective, 9, 23, 25,
    26–30, 32
Professional ethos, 134, 157, 173
  deconstruction of, 6
  See also Crisis of professionalism
Professional ideal, ix, xiii, 3, 30, 36, 56, 90,
    196, 197
  attributes/elements of, 49, 55
  continuity and change in, 196
  history/development of, 4, 26, 39, 43, 45,
    46, 55, 133, 138, 198
  professional civility as communicative
    enactment of, 48
  renewal of, 194
  as tradition of practice, 197
  true, the. *See* True professional ideal
  See also Crisis of professionalism
Professional identity, 33, 86, 126, 142, 150
  and action, 135, 208
  and civility, 5, 7
  elements of, 45
  and hybridized professionalism, 97
  and negative politeness, 108
  and productivity, 136
  and professional civility, 14, 95, 126
  professional ethics as inherently constitutive
    of, 195
  and professionalism, 54–58
  professionalism as element of, x
  and roles, 34
  work as central element of, 59
Professional/local home tension, 12, 157, 158,
    204
  and metaphor of "guest," 159
Professional mentoring, 27

Professional occupations, 60, 200. *See also*
    Professions
Professional organizations, 71, 204
Professional relationships(s), 28, 38,181
  friendship as, for professional civility, 36
Professional role identity, 27
Professional roles
  moral significance of, 29
  and professional civility, 90, 93
  and virtue ethics, 23, 26, 27, 29
Professional socialization, 7
  and academics, 157
  to argument culture of academia, 200
  and love of the work/craft, 138
  as not technique-driven, 28
  and professional civility, 112, 132
  as source of occupational meaning, 157
  and virtue ethics, 27
Professional spirit, 56, 198
Professional status, 39
  occupations claiming, 5, 198
  occupations seeking, 54
  and social obligation, 54
  as sought-after achievement, 53, 97, 198
  theoretical basis for, 198
  See also Status
Professional work
  calling, professional work as, x, 5, 7, 8, 9,
    40, 41, 46, 50, 51, 53, 54, 55, 100,
    134, 139, 142, 185, 203
  collegial organization of, 47, 154
  as vocation, 40, 46, 50, 51, 52, 55, 134,
    138, 185, 203, 207
Professionalism
  civic. *See* Civic professionalism
  and civility, x
  crisis of. *See* Crisis of professionalism
  crisis and promise of, x, 4, 6, 45, 197–202
  critiques of, 200
  culture of, 201
  expanded idea of, 60
  expert, 60
  hybridized, 97, 99
  as implicit virtue, 45
  negative attributes of/cynicism about, 197,
    199, 200

and organizational citizenship, 100, 101, 104
positive attributes of, x, 44, 53–54, 54–58, 60, 88, 104, 202
and professional civility, 202–208
and the public sphere, 203
pure, 97
renewed, 202–208
scale, 100
situated, 96, 107
story of, 197
traditional/elite, 60
values of traditional, 54
virtue of, 49, 104
volumes dedicated to, 131
Professionalization, 53
of baseball, 56
of everyone, 99
of social work, 56
Professionally civil communication (behavior, comments, messages, discourse, etc.), 22, 28, 93, 124, 131, 146, 150, 153, 156, 160, 169, 172, 190, 205
characteristics of, 141, 151, 152–153, 165, 166, 169, 191
See also Professional civility
Professions
as architectonic occupations, 8, 9, 57, 90, 137
broadening scope of, 16, 58, 137
canon of, 16
characteristics/attributes of, 4, 5, 45–62, 137
critique of, 147
as distinct from business and trades, 55, 56, 134, 196
emerging/marginal, 56
and ethic of service, 4, 6, 41, 42, 47, 51, 52, 188, 196, 199
four great traditional/original learned, 4, 50
history of. *See* History
and the idea of craft, 136
as ideological formations, 49
learned, 4, 51, 52, 53, 56
liberal, 51, 56
mechanic, 56

new "rhetoric" of, 206–207
occupations aspiring to be, 54
occupations considered to be, 29, 53, 54, 56, 88, 139
as practice. *See* Practice(s)
as relevant to professional civility, 88–89
rhetoric of, ix, 51, 206
rhetorical moments in history of, 5, 50–54
as similar to skilled crafts, 136
teleological structure of, 24
as tradition(s) of practice, 49, 92, 110
Protection and promotion of goods, 17, 19, 60, 62, 64, 65, 73, 89, 102, 104, 142
Protonorms, 22, 34, 54
Provisionalism, 165
in craftwork framework of defensiveness/supportiveness, 147
as element of supportive communication climate, 81
Prudence. *See* Restraint
Public discourse, 3, 66, 70, 106
Public friendship, 28, 36, 151
Public life, 10, 103
civility in, 2, 16, 70, 94
and coworker boundaries, 98
dichotomy between domestic life and, 177
and shared understanding of the good, 143
See also Private life
Public narrative, organizations as. *See* Organization(s)
Public Relations Society of America, 25
Public relationship(s), 174, 175, 183
Public service, 6, 54, 56, 197
Public sphere
and action, 64, 135, 136, 140, 185, 208
in balance with private sphere, 98
blurring of private sphere and, 181, 182
and civility, 2, 63, 64, 65, 69, 70, 73–74, 77, 80, 85
differentiation of/distinction, from private sphere, 92, 99, 173, 182, 194
home as escape from impersonality of, 177
and incivility, 71, 78
integration with private sphere, 179, 181
and professional civility, 89, 109, 128, 175
and professions, 5, 12, 19, 51, 57, 59, 89,

195, 201, 203, 208
separate from private sphere, 176
unity of private sphere and, by idea of calling, 40
See also Private sphere
Publics, 55, 208
Pure professionalism. *See* Professionalism

Quality of work life, 1

Rapport talk. *See* Phatic communication
Recuperative leisure. *See* Leisure
Reflective practitioner(s). *See* Practitioner(s)
Regional Planning Association of America,
138
Regulative ideals, 27
Relational architecture of job design, 13
Relational dialectics
and civility, 83–84
and workplace relationships, 174, 177
See also Communicative dialectics
Relationship(s)
blended. *See* Blended relationships
communication, 128, 179
organizational. *See* Organizational relationships
peer. *See* Peer relationships
practice-situated, 38
private. *See* Private relationships
problematic. *See* Problematic relationships
in the workplace
professional. *See* Professional relationship(s)
public. *See* Public relationship(s)
role/role-based, 113, 126, 127, 184, 185
troublesome, 178
work/workplace. *See* Workplace relationships
See also Troublesome others
Resilience, 96, 98, 153
Respect
and civility, 2, 3, 70, 73, 77, 81, 83, 190,
191, 193, 205
and clean language, 191
and distance, 73, 77, 83
and formality, 83
intellectual "attack" as sign of, in argument

culture of academia, 200
and interactional justice, 94
organizational climate of, 205
for others' contributions, 107
for professional boundaries, 19
and professional civility, 107
for professional work, 149
for professionals, declining, 5
for professions, 19
and rudeness, 72
for standards, as a virtue, 38
for work, institutions, and persons, 208
Responsibility
civic. *See* Civic responsibility/service
and civility, 193
corporate social. *See* Corporate social
responsibility
guidelines for, established by background
narrative, 162
and integrity, 203
and organizational citizenship, 102
of organizational leaders, 116
for a place, 154
professional, 89
and professional civility, 131
and the professions/professionals, 1–11, 19,
134, 154, 156, 195, 205, 207, 208
and role-based authority, 123
social. *See* Social responsibility
at work, 6
of work, 31
Responsiveness
as element of civility, 74
as element of professional civility, 91, 92,
96
to the historical moment, x, 92, 96, 196
lack of, in ideology, 146
to a reflective/ongoing tradition, 107, 164
and restraint, in peer relationships, 191
to "rhetorical interruptions," 109
Restraint(s)
and civility, 2, 41, 68, 75, 77, 84, 193
as an element of civility, 68, 74, 77
as an element of professional civility, 41,
191
external/physical, 74

internal, 74
lack of, characterizing incivility, 71
in peer relationships, 191
and professional civility, 165, 169, 190,
    191
as prudence, 41
self -, 67, 74, 76
and self-disclosure, 84
Rhetoric of profession.
    moments in history of . *See* Professions
Rhetoric of professions. *See* Professions
Rhetorical design logic, 82, 83, 109, 141, 166,
    170
Rhetorical interruption(s), 109, 139, 168, 170
Rhetorical moments in history of professions.
    See Professions
Ritual(s)
    communicative, 70, 109
    conversational, 109
    formal, 70
    interaction, 78, 84
    interpersonal, 69–71
    private, 70
    public, 70
    work, 137
    See also Communication
Role-based/driven ethics, 27
    See also Homeric ethic(s)/virtues;
        Professional ethics
Role identity. *See* Professional role identity
Role structure, 43
Roles
    professional. *See* Professional roles
    social, 34
    work, 114, 142, 187
Routine(s)
    of a collegial model of professional work,
        154
    and common sense, 163
    conversational, 19
    communicative, 70, 84
    communicative interaction, 156
    of discourse, 155
    interactive, 12, 19, 70, 88
    moments of respite and, 109
    organizational, 170

of organizational behavior, professional
    civility as part of,
    provincial/stylized, 70
    work, 174
    and work practices, 151
Rudeness, 69, 108, 111, 178
    definition of, 72
    focused, 72
    and incivility, 71, 72, 73
    opposite of civility, manners, politeness,
        and courtesy, 69
    and task performance, 129
    unfocused, 72
    as violation of interaction ritual, 78
    See also Incivility

Satisfaction. *See* Job satisfaction
Self-control, 191, 193
Self-disclosure
    and civility, 84
    excessive, 35
    limited, 35
    patterns of, defining friendship, 113
    and professional civility, 35
    and public/private domains, 179
    and a therapeutic approach to communica-
        tion, 177–178
Self-restraint. *See* Restraint
Service
    civic. *See* Civic service
    ethic. *See* Professions
    orientation, as characteristic of professions,
        5, 51
Shame, 150 ,170
Shop Class as Soulcraft, 136
Situated professionalism. *See* Professionalism.
Small talk. *See* Phatic communication
Soap opera star, 103, 141
Social constructionist perspective, 114, 117
Social harmony, 77, 78
Social imaginary, 78, 207
Social imagination, collective, 63
Social institutions. *See* Institution(s)
Social integration, 11
Social responsibility, 6
    corporate. *See* Corporate social responsibil-

ity
of professionals, 53, 60
Social role. *See* Roles
Social undermining, 1
Social work
as a profession, 5, 138
professionalization of, 56
Socialization
organizational. *See* Organizational socialization
professional. *See* Professional socialization
Speech acts, 93, 122, 126
See also Organizational stories; Memorable messages
Spontaneity
in craftwork framework of defensiveness/supportiveness, 146
as element of supportive communication climate, 81
Sportsmanship, 18, 102
communicative elements of, 102, 166
conceptualizations of, 102, 166–167
and dialogic civility, 106
Standard bearer(s)
managers as, of organizational mission, 10
professionals as, of occupational ideal, x
professions as, of occupations/vocations, 8, 137
Status
of business-related occupations, 56
competition, 200
differences, 115
guidelines for, established by background narrative, 162
judgments of others,' 114
professional, 5, 53, 54, 97, 198
of professionals/professions, 8, 9, 13, 15, 46, 56, 58, 88, 139
Stranger(s)
and civility, 71, 177
and guests, 159
and ritual, 70
Strategic action. *See* Personal strategic action
Strategies
as applications of politeness theory, 80
communicative, 152

conversational, 76
distancing, 192
for engaging problematic or "troublesome" others, 192
for improvement, offered by managers, 150
influence, 77
in relation to goals, 77
Strategy
in craftwork framework of defensiveness/supportiveness, as supportive orientation, 146
as element of defensive communication climate, 81, 146, 165
Steward(s)/stewardship
and ethic of care approach to leadership, 156
and guest, 59–60
and managers, 149
of an organizational dwelling, 154
professionals as, 156
and professions, 62
Stress
as cause of incivility in the workplace, 2
as result of incivility in the workplace, 1
ritual, as decreasing/helpful in moments of, 70, 109
Structuration, 79, 121
Structuration theory, 78
Superior-subordinate communication, 117
Superior-subordinate interaction, 120
Superior/subordinate relationships, 119
Superiority
in craftwork framework of defensiveness/supportiveness, as mastery, 147
as element of defensive communication climate, 81, 147
Supervisor(s')/supervisory behavior, 125
Supervisor(s')/supervisory behavioral integrity, 130
Supervisor(s')/supervisory communication, 130
negative, 130
positive, 130
Supervisor(s')/supervisory incivility, 130, 184
Supervisor(s')/supervisory mentoring, 130

Supervisor(s')/supervisory modeling, 130, 163
Supervisor(s')/supervisory perceived social support, 129
Supervisor(s')/supervisory support, 181
Supportive communication, 16, 18, 80, 95, 142, 144, 145, 165, 190
Supportive communication climate, 81
Supportive communication relationships, 179
Swearing in the workplace, 1

Tact
    and civility, 5, 75, 84
    and criticism, 67
    Gadamerian, 68
    as communicative virtue of tastefulness, 75
    as phronesis, 68
    and professional civility, 38, 108, 191
Tall poppy phenomenon, 152, 169
Teamwork
    as element of professionalism, 55
    examples of, 61
    and professional civility, 188
Technology
    and professionalism, 199
    proliferation of, as contributing to incivility, 2
Technique(s)
    application of virtues as beyond, 34
    civility as philosophy of human engagement rather than, 193
    communicative, 22
    contradiction between ethical obligation of professional and, 201
    implementation by managers, as pseudo human relations, 143
Telos
    of human life, 30
    of profession(s), 8, 15, 47
    of virtue ethics. *See* Virtue ethics
The Civility Solution: What to Do When People Are Rude, 193
The Hidden Persuaders, 143
The Thinking Life: How to Thrive in the Age of Distraction, 193
Theology
    as architectonic profession, 51

as one of the four great traditional/original learned professions, 4, 50
    as a profession, 4, 50, 51, 52, 59
Theories-in-use, 121, 128
Theory-generated principles of justice, 66
Therapeutic approach to communication, 177
Therapeutic communication style, 15
    critique of, imported into public domain, 15
Therapeutic culture, 178
Therapeutic discourse
    pitfalls of importing into public domain, 142
Therapeutic orientation moved into public realm, 186
    See also Interpersonal quicksand
Tolerance
    as element of civility, 75
    and professional civility, 166, 205
Totality
    in craftwork framework of defensiveness/supportiveness, 147, 148
Trades
    as distinct from professions, 53, 55, 56, 134
    necessity to the human community, 136
    as similar to professions, 56
Tradition of practice. *See* Narrative; Practice(s); Professional ideal
Traditions, 42–43. *See also* Narrative; Practice(s)
Trivialization of crisis, 98, 102, 104, 165, 167, 184. *See also* Complaint; Constructive dissent
Troublesome behavior(s) in the workplace, x
Troublesome others in the workplace, 73, 192. *See also* Soap opera star
True professional ideal, xiii, 8, 15, 33, 46–58, 88, 135, 137, 198, 202. *See also* Professional ideal
Trust, 178
    affect-based, 183, 184
    cognition-based, 183, 184
    destroyed by incivility, 205
    generated by mission-consistent, 205
    and in-group relationships, 175
    and out-group relationships, 175

and patterns of messages, 113
and positive emotional experiences, 131
and productivity, 149
and professional civility, 100, 169
and professions, 55
and value schemata, 122
as element of professional behavior and
    practice, 203
managerial practices, 97
Turning. *See* Phenomenological turning
Turnover/turnover intentions
    employee, increased, due to of incivility in
        the workplace, 1, 129
    as result of unmet high expectations, 163
Tyranny of intimacy, 108, 179, 184

Uncertainty avoidance, 21
Uncivil behavior(s), 72, 73, 76, 78
    typology of, 73
    in the workplace, 73, 152
    See also Incivility
Uncivil communication. *See* Incivility
Uncivil interaction in the workplace, 13
Uncivil organizational culture, 128
Unethical behavior
    of professionals, 6
    in the workplace, 178
Unity of a life, 33, 40
    and professional civility, 107
Unprofessional behavior, 55, 205, 207
Utilitarian discourse system, 76
Utilitarian ethics/perspective, 14, 17, 71, 90
    and professional civility, 90, 119

Values
    employee, 111, 117
    See also Communication
    organizational, 121–127, 192
    supervisory modeling of, 130
    types of, in an organization, 127
Variable analytic perspective, 117
Verbal abuse, 73, 129
Verbal aggressiveness/aggression, 16, 130
    and civility, 85
    and professional civility, 95
Vice, communicative. *See* Communicative

vice; Incivility
Violence, 68, 73
    workplace, 73
Virtue
    communicative. *See* Civility
    communicative, at work. *See* Professional
        civility
    frameworks for. *See* Virtue frameworks
    gestalt. *See* Gestalt virtue
    hyper. *See* Hypervirtue
    implicit, professionalism as. *See*
        Professionalism
Virtue contention/disagreement,
    (historical) moment of, 10–11, 97, 144,
    162
Virtue ethics, 14, 16, 17, 71, 144
    Aristotelian, 33
    and character traits, 24, 31
    and civility, 3, 74
    and consequentialist ethics, 14
    and craftwork, 144
    and external standards, 144
    and human flourishing, 11, 14
    and incivility, 71
    MacIntyre's, ix, 11, 30–43
    and moral emotions, 192
    and professional civility, 15, 22, 91, 92,
        119
    and the professions, 23–44, 134
    tradition)s) of, 32, 33–34
    See also Character; Human flourishing;
        Virtues
Virtues
    of character, 35
    as character traits, 24
    and civility, 45, 69–70, 75
    communicative, 38, 75, 94
    and communities, 33, 37–40
    examples of, 41
    and the good for human being(s), 30, 32
    and human flourishing, 26, 40, 74
    and institutions, 39
    intellectual, 35
    of journalists, 35
    of process, 101
    and practices, 26, 32, 36–37, 38, 39, 40,

42–43, 48
professional, 23
and professional civility, 38–39, 43, 89–95
and professions, 46, 48, 200
and a single human life, 40
sustaining goods of practices, 48
and the unity of a life, 40–42
Virtuous discourse, 94
Vita activa, 134
Vocation
    profession(s) as, 25, 40, 46, 50, 51, 185, 196, 203
    work as. *See* Work
    See also Professional work
Vow, 50, 51, 137

Well-being, 30
    and civility, 3, 69
    and the craft workshop, 189
    harmed by bullying relationships, 130
    of an organization/organizational, 165, 179
    of others, 3, 69
    of persons, 187
    of persons-in-relation, 194
    and productivity, 133
    See also Eudamonia
Work, 10, 11, 15, 17, 30, 42, 45, 46, 92, 94, 128, 133, 134–136, 153, 208
    from Christian perspective, 61
    communicative. *See* Communicative work
    of communicative practices, 9
    conversational, 8
    as distinct from labor and action, 57, 134, 135
    good. *See* Good work
    and the human condition, 134–139

intimacy. *See* Intimacy
meaning of, 20, 107
professional. *See* Professional work
and professionalism, 59
as vocation, 134, 138
friendship(s). *See* Friendship(s)
Work relationship orientation, 176–177, 185
Work relationships. *See* Workplace relationships
Workplace civility. *See* Civility
Workplace incivility. *See* Incivility
Workplace relationship(s), ix–xi, 174–177, 182
    as accountable to institutions/organizations, 172, 173
    close, 176
    communicative constitution of, 114
    constructive, 99
    factors influencing development of, 175, 176
    and issues of public/private spheres, 179–182, 194
    hostile, 130
    and negative turning points, 168
    and organizational culture, 175
    personal, 181
    preferences, 185
    professional. *See* Professional relationships
    from a professional civility perspective, 182–186, 187–193, 194
    Sias's treatment of/volume on, 19, 114
    taking place at a distance, 192
Workplace violence. *See* Violence
World-building, 8, 57
World view, 21
    Christian. *See* Christian worldview